BALZAC
and
THE NINETEENTH CENTURY

Herbert J. Hunt

BALZAC
and
THE NINETEENTH CENTURY

Studies in French literature presented to
HERBERT J. HUNT
by pupils, colleagues and friends

Edited by
D. G. Charlton, J. Gaudon and Anthony R. Pugh

LEICESTER UNIVERSITY PRESS
1972

First published in 1972 by Leicester University Press
Distributed in North America by Humanities Press Inc., New York

Copyright © Leicester University Press, 1972

Designed by Arthur Lockwood

Set in Monotype Walbaum 374

Printed in Great Britain by
T. and A. Constable Ltd, Hopetoun Street, Edinburgh

ISBN 0 7185 1106 9

Contents

Part I   BALZAC

CONTENTS

CONTENTS

Part II FROM CONSTANT TO ZOLA

CONTENTS

List of plates

Editorial note

Unless otherwise stated, references to Balzac's *Comédie humaine* are to the Pléiade edition in 11 volumes (Gallimard, Paris, 1935–59), edited by Marcel Bouteron, thus: II, 400 refers to page 400 of volume II. The contents of the Pléiade edition are reproduced on pp. 391–5.

For Balzac's writings which fall outside the *Comédie humaine*, the following abbreviations have been used:

Corr.	*Correspondance*, ed. R. Pierrot (Garnier, Paris, 1960–9), 5 vols.
L.H.	*Lettres à Madame Hanska*, ed. R. Pierrot (Éditions du Delta, Paris, 1967–71), 4 vols.
O.D.	*Œuvres diverses*, ed. M. Bouteron and H. Longnon (Conard, Paris, 1935–40), 3 vols.

In addition, the following abbreviations of periodical publications have been used:

Année balz.	*L'Année balzacienne*
F.Q.	*French Quarterly*
F.R.	*French Review*
F.S.	*French Studies*
M.F.	*Mercure de France*
M.L.	*Modern Languages*
M.L.R.	*Modern Language Review*
O.M.	*Oxford Magazine*
R.H.L.F.	*Revue d'Histoire Littéraire de la France*
R.L.C.	*Revue de Littérature Comparée*
R.R.	*Romanic Review*

In accord with the Press practice places of publication are given only for books published outside the United Kingdom.

The Editors wish to express their gratitude to Professor F. W. J. Hemmings and to the Secretary and officers of the Leicester University Press for their invaluable help in the publication of this volume.

D. G. C.
J. G.
A. R. P.

Herbert J. Hunt:
career and influence

J. N. D. KELLY

ALL the other essays in this volume have been prepared by scholars expert in those studies in which the man we seek to honour has himself worked and made his distinguished mark. This introductory note is by one who has read Professor Hunt's chief works with admiration and profit, but whose own research has been done in quite different fields. Any title he has to contribute to this symposium must rest on the close knowledge he has had of Professor Hunt for most of his professional career and the special opportunities he has had for observing his impact on others. What follows is therefore written from a largely personal angle, and is intended to convey some impression of the man himself. There is perhaps a certain fittingness in this, for one of the professor's characteristic, and also most attractive, traits is his embarrassed reluctance to be classified as a *savant* and his preference for being assessed, if assessed he must be, by wider criteria.

It was over 35 years ago, in October 1935, that my acquaintance with Herbert Hunt began. He had been Tutor in French (in 1938, when the statutes were reformed, he became Fellow) at St Edmund Hall, Oxford, since 1927, and I joined him as a younger colleague. Very soon we became firm friends, and that friendship has continued to the present day. From the very start until 1944, when he left Oxford to become Professor of French Literature at London, I was a regular and frequent visitor to his house in St Margaret's Road, almost next door to the church he attended. Among my most vivid memories are the warm welcome he and his family extended to myself and many others, the generosity and rare quality of his hospitality, his wonderful joy in family life and his pride in his garden, and the atmosphere of liveliness and relaxed affection which pervaded his home. A friend calling on him at Tredington today is likely to come away with much the same impressions, and it is pleasant to think that, although so many years have slipped by, Herbert Hunt himself seems to have changed very little in appearance or anything else.

From time to time Hunt has reminisced about his earlier life: about his childhood and upbringing at Lichfield, where he was born in 1899 and sang in the cathedral choir, about his experience of service in the First World War and then as an undergraduate at Magdalen, about his spells as a schoolmaster at Imperial Service College and later at Durham School. At Oxford, where in addition to his position at St Edmund Hall he was Lecturer in French at Jesus College, he was certainly one of the most remarkable teachers of his time. That was a very different epoch from the present, with no agreed limitation of a man's teaching load, and Hunt's timetable of classes, lectures and tutorials not infrequently reached 35 hours a week; yet those years saw the preparation and production of two substantial works based on painstaking research. As a tutor he was exacting, frank and even forthright in criticism and sparing of praise, and his first-year pupils tended to regard him as a slave-driver; but they soon learned that along with a gruff exterior he possessed the kindliest of hearts, and where necessary inexhaustible patience. Little wonder that, as the result of the rigorous standards he set them, they often found themselves achieving successes which surprised them.

His departure from Oxford was a severe blow to his college and the University, but with the scholarly reputation which his writings had won him his promotion to a professorship was natural and indeed inevitable. The chair at the Royal Holloway College had just been established, and the College was fortunate in having a man of such an energetic, capable and warm-hearted personality appointed as its first holder. He at once threw himself into the responsibilities of his new position, quickly making contacts with the University and with his colleagues in other colleges, and as a result of the confidence he inspired he was in due course made Chairman of the Board of Studies in Romance Languages. Soon, too, he was forming valuable contacts with the Institut Français, and thanks to him members of its staff used to visit the College from time to time, and their lectures became a regular and stimulating feature of the life of the department. A further, and very characteristic, initiative which he took was to put out feelers to French universities, and as soon as post-war conditions made it practicable he arranged a scheme for annual exchanges of students between Royal Holloway College and the University of Poitiers. He took endless trouble over these, and there must be scores of women in France and elsewhere who recall with gratitude not only the introduction he gave them to British student life and academic habits, but the visits he planned for them, and personally supervised with gay informality, to Oxford and other places of interest.

These and similar activities are proof that Hunt, being the benevolent and sociable man he has always been, gave an unusually wide and refreshing interpretation to his functions as a professor. As head of his department he was, as all who know him would expect, very considerate to colleagues and students, genial in personal relations, quick to appreciate difficulties, and ready to respond sympathetically in any situation where help was needed. A host of illustrations could be given of this, and as a single homely example one may be permitted to recall the Principal's startled surprise when, in a period of fuel shortage, the professor once presented himself in her study bearing a sack of coal for herself and a colleague. The famous hospitality of St Margaret's Road was recreated at Egham, if anything on a more generous scale, with open house for staff and students – not to mention visitors from Oxford. Yet kindlinesses like these illustrate only one side of his nature. On the College Council, on which he served 1953–4, 1955–7 and 1964–6, his firm grasp of business was apparent, and his constructive interventions contributed much to the wise government of the College. Moreover he has always been outspoken about his strong likes and dislikes in various directions, and while invariably courteous towards people who differ from him he has never had any compunction about declaring his views. There are elements of toughness, independence, and down-to-earth common sense in his make-up which remind one that as a boy at Lichfield he had breathed the air once breathed by Dr Johnson.

So much for the personal side; his qualities as a man go far to explain the far-reaching influence Professor Hunt has exercised both as a teacher of students and as a senior member of the colleges and universities he has served. Through the wisdom of the University

of Warwick, which appointed him Senior Fellow for 1966–70, he
was enabled to continue the good work after relinquishing his chair
at London. His contributions to scholarly knowledge of French
literature, as every reader of this volume is aware, have been widely
ranging and of the highest distinction; they have also been marked
by his impatience with the shoddy, the superficial, the impression-
istic. His first book, on *Le Socialisme et le Romantisme en France*
(1935), represented a major advance in our appreciation of the social
and political interests of the French Romantics and of Romantic
elements in early nineteenth-century French socialistic thinkers.
His second work, *The Epic in 19th century France* (1941), was equally
original in its probing of a previously neglected poetic tradition and
equally illustrative of Hunt's extremely thorough historical scholar-
ship and his gift for lucid exposition – based, moreover, on detailed
study of a range of primary sources that would have daunted less
devoted and meticulous scholars. Both books remain standard authorities, as do his later books on Balzac, *Honoré de Balzac: a biography*
(1957) and *Balzac's 'Comédie Humaine'* (1959), and the high esteem
in which his studies of this novelist are held is amply illustrated by
the section in this volume devoted to essays by an international
group of *Balzaciens*. Hugo has been another of his preferred authors;
in particular, his edition of *La Légende des Siècles* continues to be
widely used.

These are the works on which his reputation mainly rests, but
the bibliography of his publications which Dr West has included in
this volume displays the range of his many articles, covering both
the subjects already mentioned and other areas such as the French
theatre of the twentieth century. Inevitably a scholar like Hunt,
who has preferred to investigate his chosen themes in depth and with
conscientious attention to detail, has felt obliged to limit his explora-
tions; but although he is always modest about his excursions in other
fields, even a brief conversation (when he is prepared to be drawn
out) reveals the width of his learning and his acute critical penetra-
tion. Nor has he kept these things to himself; many a research
student, as well as his undergraduates, remains indebted to his
informed understanding of authors on whom he has not touched
in his writings, while his work on the editorial board of *French
Studies* has been a further signal example of his readiness to place

his knowledge at the disposal of the world of scholars. It is true of him, as of fine teachers generally, that his influence is to be measured not only by his books, but by the vision, encouragement, and practical assistance he has given to others; and in Herbert Hunt's case this generosity is itself the reflection of a singularly generous and large-hearted nature.

Select bibliography of the works of Herbert J. Hunt

† CONSTANCE B. WEST

1932

'Ouvriers-poètes de l'époque romantique', *F.Q.*, XIV (September), 85-112.

'Ouvriers-poètes du romantisme. Un fabuliste, Pierre Lachambeaudie', *F.Q.*, XIV (December), 162-72.

1933

'L'impulsion socialiste dans la pensée politique de Victor Hugo', *R.H.L.F.*, XL (April), 209-23.

'Une querelle de journalistes sous Louis-Philippe. Alexandre Dumas père contre Buloz', *M.F.*, CCXLV (1 July), 72-110.

1934

'Alfred de Musset et la Révolution de Juillet. La leçon politique de *Lorenzaccio*', *M.F.*, CCLI (1 April), 70-88.

1935

Le Socialisme et le Romantisme en France: étude de la presse socialiste de 1830 à 1848 (Oxford, Clarendon Press), x + 399 pp.

1936

Review

R. A. Lochore, *History of the Idea of Civilisation in France, 1830–1870* (Bonn, 1935). *M.L.R.*, XXXI (April), 263.

1937

'Edgar Quinet and Nineteenth-Century Democracy', *M.L.*, XIX (October), 9-20.

Reviews

M. L. Johnson, *Beaumarchais and his Opponents. New Documents on his Lawsuits* (New York, 1936). *M.L.R.*, xxxii (July), 491.

Norah E. Hudson, *Ultra-Royalism and the French Restoration* (1936). *M.L.R.*, xxxii (October), 633-4.

Mabel Silver, *Jules Sandeau, l'homme et la vie* (Paris, 1937). *M.L.R.*, xxxii (October), 635-6.

F. C. Green (ed.), *Diderot's Writings on the Theatre* (1936). *M.L.R.*, xxxii (October), 665.

1938

'Logic and Linguistics. Diderot as "Grammairien-Philosophe" ', *M.L.R.*, xxxiii (April), 215-33.

1940

Review

K. N. McKee, *The Role of the Priest on the Parisian Stage during the French Revolution* (Baltimore and London, 1939). *M.L.R.*, xxxv (October), 565-6.

1941

The Epic in Nineteenth-Century France. A Study in Heroic and Humanitarian Poetry from 'Les Martyrs' to 'Les Siècles morts' (Oxford, Basil Blackwell & Mott), xiv + 446 pp.

1945

Victor Hugo, *La Légende des Siècles*. Selected and edited by H. J. Hunt. (Blackwell's French Texts: Oxford, Basil Blackwell & Mott), xxvi + 239 pp.

'The Œdipus theme in French drama', *M.L.*, xxvi (July), 32-7.

1946

Reviews

H. F. Stewart (ed.), *The Heart of Pascal, being his Meditations and Prayers, Notes for his Anti-Jesuit Campaign, Remarks on Language and Style, etc.* (1945). *O.M.*, lxiv (31 January), 153-4.

E. M. Grant, *The Career of Victor Hugo* (Cambridge, Mass., and London, 1945). *M.L.R.*, xli (April), 214-15.

A. J. George, *Pierre-Simon Ballanche, Precursor of Romanticism* (Syracuse, New York, 1945). *R.R.*, XXXVII (December), 363-7.

1947

'Saint Joan of Arc in some recent French dramas', *F.S.*, I (October), 302-33.

Reviews

M. Glotz and M. Maire, *Salons du XVIIIe siècle* (Paris, 1945). *F.S.*, I (April), 170.

N. Edelman, *Attitudes of Seventeenth-Century France towards the Middle Ages* (New York, 1946). *O.M.*, LXV (19 June), 450-1.

Ph. Erlanger, *Louis XIII* (Paris, 1946); Mme Saint-René Taillandier *La Jeunesse du Grand Roi. Louis XIV et Anne d'Autriche* (Paris, 1945); P. Gaxotte, *La France de Louis XIV* (Paris, 1946). *F.S.*, I (July), 263-6.

Margaret H. Gamble, *L'Amérique dans l'œuvre de Victor Hugo* (Philadelphia, 1946). *M.L.R.*, XLII (October), 544.

1948

Reviews

G. Duveau, *La Vie ouvrière en France sous le Second Empire* (Paris, 1946). *F.S.*, II (April), 177-81.

Enid Starkie, *Arthur Rimbaud* (1948). *O.M.*, LXVI (17 June), 550.

1949

'A Contemporary Dramatist: René Bruyez', pp. 77-106 in *Studies in French Language, Literature and History presented to R. L. Graeme Ritchie* (Cambridge, Cambridge University Press).

'Célimène: *coquette* or *coquine*?', *F.S.*, III (October), 324-34.

Reviews

W. D. Pendell, *Victor Hugo's Acted Dramas and the Contemporary Press* (Baltimore and London, 1947). *M.L.R.*, XLIV (January), 125.

D. O. Evans, *Le Socialisme romantique. Pierre Leroux et ses contemporains* (Paris, 1948). *F.S.*, III (April), 171-4.

M. Nadaud, *Mémoires de Léonard, ancien garçon maçon* (Paris, 1948). *F.S.*, III (July), 280-1.

1950

Reviews

J.-B. Barrère, *La Fantaisie de Victor Hugo, 1802–1851* (Paris, 1949); P. Souchon, *Victor Hugo, l'homme et l'œuvre* (Paris, 1949); P. Souchon (ed.), *Pages d'amour de Victor Hugo* (Paris, 1949). *F.S.*, IV (January), 81-4.

L. W. Wylie, *Saint-Marc Girardin, bourgeois* (Syracuse, New York, 1947). *M.L.R.*, XLV (January), 92-3.

W. G. Moore, *Molière, a new criticism* (1949). *O.M.*, LXVIII (8 June), 534-6.

G. Atkinson, *Les Idées de Balzac d'après 'la Comédie humaine'* (5 vols.) (Geneva and Lille, 1949). *M.L.R.*, XLV (October), 557-8.

G. V. Dobie, *Alphonse Daudet* (1949). *O.M.*, LXIX (19 October), 43-4.

Studies in French Language, Literature and History presented to R. L. Graeme Ritchie (1949). *O.M.*, LXIX (26 October), 74-6.

H. F. Stewart, *Pascal's Pensées* (1950). *O.M.*, LXIX (30 November), 183-4.

1951

Reviews

D. Mornet, *Rousseau, l'homme et l'œuvre* (Paris, 1950). *F.S.*, V (April), 174-6.

A. Craig Bell, *Alexandre Dumas. A Biography and a Study* (1950). *F.S.*, V (April), 179-81.

Sister Mary U. Clark, *The Cult of Enthusiasm in French Romanticism* (Washington, 1950). *M.L.R.*, XLVI (July and October), 522-4.

C. Beaumont Wicks, *The Parisian Stage, Alphabetical Indexes of Plays and Authors, Part I (1800–1815)* (Alabama, 1950). *M.L.R.* XLVI (July and October), 550-1.

T. R. Palfrey, *'Le Panorama littéraire de l'Europe' (1833–1834): une revue légitimiste sous la Monarchie de Juillet* (Evanston, Ill., 1950). *M.L.R.*, XLVI (July and October), 551.

Edith Melcher, *The Life and Times of Henri Monnier, 1799–1877* (Cambridge, Mass., 1950). *F.S.*, V (October), 366-8.

1952

'The "Human Comedy": first English reactions', pp. 273-90 in *The French Mind. Studies in Honour of Gustave Rudler* (Oxford, Clarendon Press).

'A Contemporary Dramatist: Marcelle Maurette', *F.S.*, VI (October), 373-5.

Reviews

J.-B. Barrère, *La Fantaisie de Victor Hugo, thèmes et motifs* (Paris, 1950). *F.S.*, VI (January), 81-3.

R. L. Graeme Ritchie, *France, a Companion to French Studies* (1951). *M.L.R.*, XLVII (April), 277.

J. G. Marash, *Henri Monnier, Chronicler of the Bourgeoisie* (1951). *F.S.*, VI (July), 259-60.

D. O. Evans, *Social Romanticism in France, 1830–1848* (1952). *F.S.*, VI (October), 373-5.

The French Mind. Studies in Honour of Gustave Rudler (1952). *O.M.*, LXXI (16 October), 16-18.

1953

Reviews

J. Tild, *Théophile Gautier et ses amis* (Paris, 1951). *F.S.*, VII (January), 76-7.

W. Staaks, *The Theatre of Louis-Benoît Picard* (Los Angeles and Cambridge, 1952). *M.L.R.*, XLVIII (July), 348-9.

J.-B. Barrère, *Hugo, l'homme et l'œuvre* (Paris, 1952). *F.S.*, VII (October), 365-7.

R. A. Sayce, *Style in French Prose. A Method of Analysis* (1953). *O.M.*, LXXII (22 October), 39-40.

May Daniels, *The French Drama of the Unspoken* (1953). *O.M.*, LXXII (5 November), 72.

1954

'Balzac and the English Tongue', *M.L.R.*, XLIX (October), 434-41.

Reviews

C. Beaumont Wicks, *The Parisian Stage, Alphabetical Indexes of Plays and Authors, Part II (1816–1830)* (Alabama, 1953). *M.L.R.*, XLIX (April), 244-5.

Henri de Saint-Simon, *Selected Writings*, ed. and trans. F. M. H. Markham (1953); M. E. Elbow, *French Corporative Theory, 1798–1948. A Chapter in the History of Ideas* (New York and London, 1953). *F.S.*, VIII (April), 171-4.

A. Parménie and C. Bonnier de la Chapelle, *Histoire d'un éditeur et de ses auteurs: P.-J. Hetzel (Stahl)* (Paris, 1953). *F.S.*, VIII (July), 274-7.

E. Gautier, *Le Génie satirique de Louis Veuillot* (Lyons and Paris, 1953). *M.L.R.*, XLIX (October), 515-17.

Odette de Mourgues, *Metaphysical, Baroque and Précieux Poetry* (1953). *O.M.*, LXXIII (21 October), 38-9.

Grace Franks, *The French Medieval Drama* (1954). *O.M.*, LXXIII (2 December), 142.

1955

Reviews

P. Spencer, *Politics of Belief in Nineteenth-Century France: Lacordaire, Michon, Veuillot* (1954). *M.L.R.*, L (April), 217-19.

L. Cellier, *L'Épopée romantique* (Paris, 1954). *F.S.*, IX (July), 273-5.

A. R. Vidler, *Prophecy and Papacy. A Study of Lamennais, the Church and the Revolution* (1954). *M.L.R.*, L (July), 344-5.

J. C. Alciatore, *Stendhal et Maine de Biran* (Geneva and Lille, 1954); V. Brombert, *Stendhal et la voie oblique. L'auteur devant son monde romanesque* (Paris, 1954). *M.L.R.*, L (October), 542-3.

I. Putter, *The Pessimism of Leconte de Lisle: Sources and Evolution* (1954). *R.R.*, XLVI (October), 236-7.

1956

Reviews

R. A. Sayce, *The French Biblical Epic in the Seventeenth Century* (1954). *O.M.*, LXXIV (2 February), 244.

F. C. Green, *Jean-Jacques Rousseau. A Critical Study of his Life and Writings* (1955). *F.S.*, X (April), 174-6.

M. Levaillant, *La Crise mystique de Victor Hugo (1843–1856) d'après des documents inédits* (Paris, 1954). *F.S.*, X (July), 270-1.

M. D. R. Leys, *Between Two Empires. A History of French Politicians and People between 1814 and 1848. F.S.*, X (October), 361-2.

A. J. George, *The Development of French Romanticism. The Impact of the Industrial Revolution on Literature* (New York, 1955). *M.L.R.*, LI (October), 602-5.

1957

Honoré de Balzac. A Biography (London, Athlone Press), xii+ 198 pp.
'Balzac's Pressmen', *F.S.*, XI (July), 230-45.

Reviews

J. Gaudon, *Victor Hugo dramaturge* (Paris, 1955). *F.S.*, XI (January), 68-9.
J.-B. Barrère, *Le Regard d'Orphée ou De Fantômes et de poésie* (1956). *F.S.*, XI (January), 85-6.
M. Lecuyer, *Balzac et Rabelais* (Paris, 1956). *M.L.R.*, LII (October), 609-11.

1958

' "Portraits" in *La Comédie humaine*', *R.R.*, XLIX (April), 112-24.
'Balzac and Lady Ellenborough', *F.S.*, XII (July), 247-59.

Reviews

F. G. Healey, *Rousseau et Napoléon* (Geneva and Paris, 1957). *M.L.R.*, LIII (January), 121-2.
R. Mortier, *Les 'Archives littéraires de l'Europe' (1804–1808) et le cosmopolitisme littéraire sous le Premier Empire* (Brussels, 1957). *M.L.R.*, LIII (January), 122.
A. Glauser, *Hugo et la poésie pure* (Geneva and Paris, 1957). *F.S.*, XII (January), 80-1.
M. Regard, *L'Adversaire des romantiques, Gustave Planche, 1808–1857*, 2 vols. (Paris, 1955). *F.S.*, XII (April), 167-9.
A. Levin, *The Legacy of Philarète Chasles. Vol. I. Selected Essays in Nineteenth-Century Literature* (North Carolina, 1957). *M.L.R.*, LIII (April), 268.
P. Savey-Casard, *Le Crime et la peine dans l'œuvre de Victor Hugo* (Paris, 1956); Hugo, *Claude Gueux*, ed. P. Savey-Casard (Paris, 1956). *F.S.*, XII (July), 274-5.

V. Hugo, *Choix de poèmes*, ed. J. Gaudon (1957); *idem, Quatre-vingt-treize*, ed. J. Boudout (Paris, 1957). *F.S.*, XII (October), 379-80.

1959

Balzac's 'Comédie humaine' (London, Athlone Press), xv+ 506 pp.

Reviews

H. de Balzac, *La Vieille Fille*, ed. P.-G. Castex (Paris, 1957). *F.S.*, XIII (January), 72-3.

D. Vouga, *Balzac malgré lui* (Paris, 1957). *F.S.*, XIII (January), 73-5.

J. Pommier, *L'Invention et l'écriture dans 'la Torpille' de Honoré de Balzac* (Geneva and Paris, 1957). *M.L.R.*, LIV (January), 117-19.

H. de Balzac, *Splendeurs et misères des courtisanes*, ed. A. Adam (Paris, 1958). *F.S.*, XIII (April), 174-6.

The Oxford Companion to French Literature, ed. Sir Paul Harvey and J. E. Haseltine (1959). *F.S.*, XIII (July), 257-9.

V. Hugo, *Les Misérables*, ed. M.-F. Guyard, 2 vols. (Paris, 1957). *F.S.*, XIII (July), 271-3.

S. Mellon, *The Political Uses of History. A Study of Historians in the French Restoration* (1958). *F.S.*, XIII (October), 362-4.

H. de Balzac, *Le Cabinet des Antiques*, ed. P.-G. Castex (Paris, 1958). *F.S.*, XIII (October), 365-6.

1960

Reviews

R. Journet and G. Robert, *Autour des 'Contemplations'* (Paris, 1955); *idem, Le Manuscrit des 'Contemplations'* (Paris, 1956); *idem, Notes sur 'les Contemplations'* (Paris, 1958); *idem, Des 'Feuilles d'automne' aux 'Rayons et les Ombres'* (Paris, 1957). *F.S.*, XIV (January), 74-7.

V. Hugo, *Notre-Dame de Paris*, ed. M.-F. Guyard (Paris, 1959). *F.S.*, XIV (April), 177.

H. Krains, *Les Meilleures Pages*, ed. J. Dechamps (Brussels, 1959). *F.S.*, XIV (April), 179-80.

J. Borel, *Personnages et destins balzaciens. La création littéraire et ses sources anecdotiques* (Paris, 1959). *F.S.*, XIV (July), 264-7.

H. de Balzac, *L'Envers de l'histoire contemporaine*, ed. M. Regard (Paris, 1959). *F.S.*, xiv (July), 267-8.

1961

'Lamartine vu par ses contemporains britanniques', pp. 99-111 in *Premières journées européennes d'études lamartiniennes* (Macon).

Reviews

M. Le Yaouanc, *Nosographie de l'humanité balzacienne* (Paris, 1959). *F.R.*, xxxiv (January), 307-9.

H. de Balzac, *Illusions perdues: le manuscrit de la collection Spoelberch de Lovenjoul*, ed. Suzanne Bérard (Paris, 1959). *F.S.*, xv (April), 174-5.

H. de Balzac, *Le Père Goriot*, ed. P.-G. Castex (Paris, 1960). *F.S.*, xv (July), 271-2.

1962

'Le Sens épique des *Misérables*', *Bulletin de la Faculté des Lettres de Strasbourg*, xl (February), 303-14.

Reviews

H. de Balzac, *Les Petits Bourgeois*, ed. R. Picard (Paris, 1960). *F.S.*, xvi (January), 73-4.

J.-B. Barrère, *La Fantaisie de Victor Hugo, 1852–1885*, t. ii (Paris, 1960). *F.S.*, xvi (January), 74-7.

H. de Balzac, *Correspondance*, ed. R. Pierrot, t. i (1809–juin 1832), (Paris, 1961). *F.S.*, xvi (April), 189-90.

H. de Balzac, *Le Colonel Chabert*, ed. P. Citron (Paris, 1961). *F.S.*, xvi (October), 381-2.

1963

Reviews

H. de Balzac, *Béatrix*, ed. M. Regard (Paris, 1962). *F.S.*, xvii (January), 74-5.

G. Delattre, *Les Opinions littéraires de Balzac* (Paris, 1961). *R.R.*, liv (April), 137-41.

H. de Balzac, *Correspondance*, ed. R. Pierrot, t. ii (Juin 1832–1835), (Paris, 1962). *F.S.*, xvii (October), 376-7.

A. Dumas, *Vingt ans après*, ed. C. Samaran (Paris, 1962). *F.S.*, xvii (October), 377.

1964

Balzac's 'Comédie humaine' (London, Athlone Press), xv + 508 pp.; second edition with supplementary bibliography.

'L'Amour platonique chez Balzac', *Bulletin de la Société Honoré de Balzac de Touraine*, ix, 8-15.

Reviews

R. Simaika, *L'Inspiration épique dans les romans de Victor Hugo* (Geneva and Paris, 1962). *F.S.*, xviii (January), 69-70.

V. Hugo, *Le Rhin*, extracts chosen and presented by J. Gaudon (1962). *F.S.*, xviii (April), 181.

J. Mallion, *Victor Hugo et l'art architectural* (Paris, 1962). *F.S.*, xviii (July), 280-1.

O. W. Russell, *Étude historique et critique des 'Burgraves' de Victor Hugo* (Paris, 1962). *F.S.*, xviii (July), 281-2.

F. Lotte (ed.), *Armorial de la Comédie humaine* (Paris, 1963). *F.S.*, xviii (July), 282.

P. Reboul, *Le Mythe anglais dans la littérature française sous la Restauration* (Lille, 1962). *F.S.*, xviii (October), 391-3.

1965

Reviews

D. G. Charlton, *Secular Religions in France, 1815–1870* (1963). *F.S.*, xix (January), 72-4.

A. Py, *Les Mythes grecs dans la poésie de Victor Hugo* (Geneva and Paris, 1963). *F.S.*, xix (January), 75-7.

P. Bertault, *Balzac and the Human Comedy*, trans. R. Monges (1963). *F.S.*, xix (April), 191-2.

H. de Balzac, *Une ténébreuse affaire*, ed. Suzanne Bérard (Paris, 1963). *F.S.*, xix (April), 192.

H. de Balzac, *La Maison du chat-qui-Pelote, Le Bal de Sceaux, La Vendetta*, ed. P.-G. Castex (Paris, 1963). *F.S.*, xix (April), 192-3.

J. Gaudon (ed.), *Ce que disent les tables parlantes. Victor Hugo à Jersey* (Paris, 1963). *F.S.*, xix (April), 193-4.

V. Hugo, *Les Contemplations*, ed. J. Seebacher, 2 vols. (Paris, 1964). *F.S.*, xix (July), 303-4.

H. de Balzac, *Correspondance*, ed. R. Pierrot, t. III (1836–1839), (Paris, 1964). *F.S.*, XIX (July), 304-5.

H. de Balzac, *Les Paysans*, ed. J.-H. Donnard (Paris, 1964). *F.S.*, XIX (July), 305-6.

H. de Balzac, *Histoire de la grandeur et de la décadence de César Birotteau*, ed. P. Laubriet (Paris, 1964). *F.S.*, XIX (October), 417-18.

1966

Reviews

H. de Balzac, *Eugénie Grandet*, ed. P.-G. Castex (Paris, 1965). *F.S.*, XX (January), 81-2.

V. Hugo, *Un carnet des 'Misérables', octobre-décembre 1860*, ed. J.-B. Barrère (Paris, 1965). *F.S.*, XX (July), 306.

J.-B. Barrère, *Victor Hugo* (Bruges, 1965). *F.S.*, XX (July), 307.

P. Nykrog, *La Pensée de Balzac dans 'la Comédie humaine', esquisse de quelques concepts-clé* (Copenhagen, 1965). *F.S.*, XX (October), 416-18.

1967

H. de Balzac, *Eugénie Grandet*, edited with introduction and notes by H. J. Hunt (London, Oxford University Press), 273 pp.

Reviews

O. Välikangas, *Les Termes d'appellation et d'interpellation dans 'la Comédie humaine' d'Honoré de Balzac* (Helsinki, 1965). *F.S.*, XXI (January), 68-9.

A. Maurois, *Victor Hugo and his World*, trans. O. Bernard (1966). *F.S.*, XXI (January), 72.

A. J. Mount, *The Physical Setting in Balzac's 'Comédie humaine'* (1966). *F.S.*, XXI (October), 360.

D. Adamson, *The Genesis of 'Le Cousin Pons'* (1966). *F.S.*, XXI (October), 361-2.

1968

H. de Balzac, *Cousin Pons: part two of Poor Relations*. Translated and introduced by Herbert J. Hunt (Harmondsworth, Penguin Classics), 334 pp.

Reviews

C. Affron, *Patterns of Failure in 'La Comédie humaine'* (New Haven and London, 1966). *F.S.*, XXII (January), 78-80.

H. de Balzac, *Correspondance*, ed. R. Pierrot, t. IV (1840–avril 1845), (Paris, 1966). *F.S.*, XXII (January), 80-1.

H. de Balzac, *Le Curé de village*, ed. P. Citron (Paris, 1967). *F.S.*, XXII (April), 166.

P. W. Lock, *Balzac: 'Le Père Goriot'* (1967). *F.S.*, XXII (July), 257-8.

1969

Reviews

F. W. J. Hemmings, *Balzac. An Interpretation of 'La Comédie humaine'* (New York, 1967); H. de Balzac, *Lettres à Madame Hanska*, ed. R. Pierrot, t. I, 1832–40 (Paris, 1967). *F.S.*, XXIII (January), 81–4.

H. de Balzac, *Le Père Goriot*, ed. C. Gould (1967). *F.S.*, XXIII (April), 188-9.

J. Borel, *'Séraphîta' et le mysticisme balzacien* (Paris, 1967). *F.S.*, XXIII (October), 412-14.

Madeleine Fargeaud, *Balzac et 'la Recherche de l'Absolu'* (Paris, 1968). *F.S.*, XXIII (October), 414-16.

H. de Balzac, *Le Curé de Tours, La Grenadière, L'Illustre Gaudissart*, ed. Suzanne Bérard (Paris, 1968). *F.S.*, XXIII (October), 416-17.

1970

Reviews

B. N. Schilling, *The Hero as Failure, Balzac and the Rubempré Cycle* (1968). *F.S.*, XXIV (January), 70-2.

A. de Musset, *La Confession d'un enfant du siècle*, ed. M. Allem (Paris, 1968). *F.S.*, XXIV (January), 73-4.

H. de Balzac, *Lettres à Madame Hanska*, ed. R. Pierrot, t. II (1841–juin 1845); t. III (août 1845–mars 1847), (Paris, 1968): *idem, Correspondance*, ed. R. Pierrot, t. V (mai 1845–août 1850), (Paris, 1969). *F.S.*, XXIV (July), 300-2.

V. Hugo, *Cromwell*, ed. A. Ubersfeld (1969). *F.S.*, XXIV (October), 406-7.

Part I

BALZAC

Balzac and the modern reader

SYLVIA RAPHAEL

In certain quarters Balzac is not popular. Few will deny that he has faults. He is sometimes diffuse, vulgar, crudely sentimental, even boring. These, however, are not the faults which some modern critics[1] stress when they wish to suggest that Balzac has no appeal to the modern reader. Balzac is obviously not a modern writer; techniques and modes of novel writing have greatly developed and changed since the first half of the nineteenth century. But these changes should not blind us to the fact that there is much in Balzac's vast output which has a great deal in common with some of the features claimed to be typical of modern novels, and that much of the fashionable denigration of Balzac is unjust.

One of the complaints made against Balzac is that he presents us with a static, closed society described in tedious detail, often selected with a view to pointing a moral or proving a theory. Such writing lacks the element of discovery of 'reader participation' which is claimed to be a feature of Stendhal and of some modern novelists and to be more in tune with modern sensibility. As R. Albérès puts it, "Au XXᵉ siècle le roman exige donc d'exprimer une expérience qui ne sera pas *racontée*, qui ne passera pas par le laminoir du *récit*. Car, dans le '*récit*', *tout est expliqué d'avance*: il présuppose un 'conteur' qui connaît la fin de l'histoire, qui a son avis sur elle, qui la narre en fonction même de tout ce qu'il sait."[2] And Albérès gives as an example the figure of Rastignac. He suggests that Balzac studies Rastignac's scruples knowing that Rastignac will become a cynic; consequently "le conteur fausse l'expérience parce qu'il sait déjà à quoi elle aboutira. Il arrange et explique les événements en fonction d'un résultat *déjà connu*, qu'ils produiront." Albérès adds, "on ne veut plus maintenant que le roman soit faussé par le souci de

[1] e.g. R. Albérès, *Histoire du roman moderne* (Paris, 1962); D. Vouga, *Balzac malgré lui* (Paris, 1957); N. Sarraute, *L'Ère du soupçon* (Paris, 1956).
[2] Albérès, *op. cit.*, p. 130.

C

raconter, et de construire une histoire". Yet, even in a modern
novel the writer must select and arrange his material with a certain
conclusion in mind, and it is surely very naïve to suggest that the
twentieth-century novelist writes without having any idea of what
he is aiming at. If the portrayal of Rastignac is 'faussé' because
Balzac knew what would happen to him, then the hero of *La
Modification* is 'faussé' because the whole book is designed to show
how and why he returns in the end to his wife and family. Since
Sartre clearly knew to what philosophical conclusions Roquentin's
experience would lead him, the hero of *La Nausée* must be 'faussé'
too. And Mathias must be 'faussé' to fit in to the overall pattern of
Le Voyeur. The angle of vision is different, the manner of telling
is different, but modern novelists might not be flattered by Albérès'
remark about the twentieth-century novel that "le conteur ne
comprend pas entièrement, et ne domine pas entièrement, ce qu'il
raconte".[1] Techniques can be misleading; Butor, Sartre and Robbe-
Grillet know what they want to say as much as Balzac does, only
they say it differently.

Daniel Vouga in his *Balzac malgré lui* makes substantially the
same attack from a slightly different angle. He maintains that
Balzac's work is static. "La réalité est pour lui comme projetée sur
un écran qu'il regarde; et la conscience ne la ressent ni ne la recrée."[2]
Vouga, like Albérès, suggests that Balzac's work is falsified "puisque
les objets qu'il se donne ne sont plus des réalités vivantes, puisqu'ils
sont des images telles qu'il veut qu'elles soient." Balzac is thus
accused of constructing a closed world, falsified by preconceived
notions of what he thinks the world is or should be. Consequently
in reading Balzac, we do not get the feeling of an experiencing
consciousness, of a world in which anything is unexplained or
unexpected, in which the surprising or accidental has any place.
"C'est un monde qui doit être stable et cohérent pour que le
déterminisme puisse jouer" and "une fois les caractères posés dans
un certain milieu, il n'y a plus qu'a laisser fonctionner l'engrenage".[3]
This is contrasted unfavourably with Stendhal whose heroes "restent
maîtres d'agir et de sentir, dans leur indétermination, comme
Stendhal lui-même, selon le moment et les circonstances."[4]

[1] Alberes, *op. cit.*, p. 130.   [2] Vouga, *op. cit.*, p. 104.   [3] *ibid.*, p. 111.
[4] *ibid.*, p. 91.

To some extent Balzac himself is responsible for the prevalence of this point of view. The grouping of his work into *Études* and *Scènes*, into the all-embracing whole of the *Comédie humaine*, naturally makes people aware that he conceives of an overall scheme of things of which he is describing certain facets. The 'Avant-Propos' to the *Comédie humaine*, in which Balzac describes himself as the secretary of society and likens his novels to scientific studies of human beings comparable to zoological studies of animal species, contributes to the illusion that his books are descriptions of static types (the miser, the over-devoted father), or concrete proofs of theories (like *La Maison du chat-qui-pelote* which claims to be a proof that artist and bourgeois can never marry happily). Some are misled too by the long descriptions which may superficially give the impression that all Balzac does is to make a careful inventory of what he sees about him. But exact observation no more turns a writer into a novelist than do scientific theories; the authors of the green Michelin guides or the compères of fashion shows can be just as detailed and accurate.

For all his protestations, however, Balzac is not a scientist, a philosopher, or even a historian. His fame has not been achieved because of his pre-eminence in any of these fields, but as a novelist, and it is as such that he merits our consideration. It is significant that he began to write novels before he had any idea of systematizing his work, although admittedly once the idea of classification took hold, it was bound to affect the way he conceived of his novels and provided the impetus for much of his writing. Balzac is a great novelist, not because he claims to classify human phenomena according to preconceived notions, or describes accurately individual types or typical individuals, but because in his work he expresses the living experience of people in whose lives he and the reader become involved.

There are other ways of looking at le Père Goriot and M. Grandet than as characters not susceptible of development, whose predetermined characteristics permit of no doubt as to the final outcome of their activities. Yet even if this point of view were the only possible one, conclusions about these two celebrated Balzacian figures tell us nothing about the 2,500 other characters whom Balzac created. They are, however, often cited as sufficient evidence for dismissing Balzac as an author devoid of interest for the modern sensibility.

Le Père Goriot and M. Grandet are old men. Not unnaturally the Balzacian character who is more akin to the developing hero of some modern novels is a young man, just as Julien Sorel and Fabrice del Dongo are young. But Lucien de Rubempré or Eugène de Rastignac (to mention only two of the best known) are either ignored or misinterpreted by those who find Balzac lacking in interest because, they say, he presents static personalities in a closed world.

We first meet Eugène and Lucien as very young men with their way to make in the world; they are still malleable, they have their choices to make and they make them as much as any 'existentialist' hero, freely choosing in the light of circumstances, sometimes with good fortune and sometimes with bad. If we are interested in the experiences which lead men to adopt certain attitudes to life and in sharing imaginatively in these experiences, we can do this with Rastignac and Rubempré as much as with Meursault and Roquentin. Only we must not be misled by technique. Albérès complains that "Balzac nous disait ce que ressentait Rastignac, mais c'était Balzac qui parlait".[1] Of course it is. Balzac wrote the novel, just as Camus and Sartre wrote their novels and no amount of present tense or first-person pronoun can do away with this fact. Balzac too can make effective use of the first-person technique[2] when he wants to, whether it be in a whole novel as in Le Lys dans la vallée or in parts of novels such as Raphaël de Valentin's account of his early life in La Peau de chagrin. Jean Rousset has suggested that the particular form of first-person technique used in the roman par lettres is closely linked to the twentieth-century novel which "a ce trait commun avec la forme épistolaire, qu'il immerge personnages et lecteurs dans un présent en train de se faire et refuse à l'auteur le point de vue panoramique du témoin omniscient."[3] Balzac's use of the roman par lettres technique is not confined to Les Mémoires de deux jeunes mariées; he also uses it in portions of other novels, as

---

[1] Albérès, op. cit., p. 92.
[2] A. Robbe-Grillet clearly oversimplifies when he limits the technique of the traditional novel to the "emploi systématique... de la troisième personne" (Pour un nouveau roman, Collection Idées, Paris, 1963, p. 37).
[3] J. Rousset, Forme et signification (Paris, 1962), p. 71.

in *Béatrix* where in Sabine du Guénic's letters we learn of her early married life and become aware of her emotions and reactions as she experiences them.[1]

But despite the so-called old-fashioned "se dit-il" and similar expressions which abound in *Le Père Goriot*, Eugène de Rastignac is an experiencing personality, observed and felt from the inside just as much as is Félix de Vandenesse or Antoine Roquentin. "Paris est donc un bourbier." (II, 886) is a remark which enables the reader to share with Rastignac the gradual realization of the true nature of Paris. We are inside his experience when after his visit to Madame de Restaud he says (II, 899) "je suis venu faire une gaucherie dont j'ignore la cause et la portée, je gâterai par-dessus le marché mon habit et mon chapeau..." We feel with him his discomfiture when the supercilious coachman obviously knows more than he does about the branches of the De Beauséant family, and the irritated "Tout le monde aujourd'hui se moque donc de moi" (II, 900) comes straight from the lived experience of the personality. If, as Madame Magny claims,[2] the characteristic modern hero has not made up his mind about anything in advance and "il se laisse modeler par ses expériences" (she gives as an example Sartre's Roquentin), Rastignac is as modern as anybody. Sartre shows us directly the experiences which motivate Roquentin's conclusions about the world; Balzac does the same for Rastignac. At the beginning of *Le Père Goriot* he knows nothing of Parisian society; the visits to Madame de Restaud, to Madame de Beauséant, the discovery of Père Goriot's secrets, the conversations with Vautrin who happens to live in the same pension, all these go to mould the cynicism and 'arrivisme' which gradually supersede the young man's innocence and sense of duty. It is not in fact till the final "A nous deux maintenant" (he has, after all, just been engaged in the generous and disinterested action of attending Père Goriot's funeral) and the laconic "Rastignac alla dîner chez Madame de Nucingen" that the reader is fully aware that cynicism has won the day. Moreover we do not know from *Le Père Goriot* whether or not Rastignac will be successful. Far from being 'closed', as far as he is concerned the

---

[1] Despite the letter framework, it would probably be inaccurate to describe *Le Lys dans la vallée* as a genuine *roman par lettres*.

[2] C. E. Magny, *Les Sandales d'Empédocle* (Neuchâtel, 1945), p. 144.

novel ends on an opening note. We have lived with Eugène the experiences which turn him from the path of honesty and duty to that of cynical 'arrivisme', and we leave him ready to start on a ruthless career. With what result *Le Père Goriot* does not tell us and although we can learn this from other works of Balzac, that is, for this novel, no more important than the success or failure of Roquentin's finished work is important for *La Nausée*.[1]

But of all Balzacian personalities, there is none more 'open', less determined in advance, more at the mercy of chance, than Lucien de Rubempré, the hero or anti-hero of *Illusions perdues*. This has been well seen by Gaëtan Picon who says that "nous reprenons chaque fois l'histoire de Lucien avec le cœur de quelqu'un qui n'a pas fini de vivre, quelqu'un qui a encore des illusions à perdre et que la route, chaque matin, retrouve plein d'espoir".[2] Here is no hero whose character is predetermined, who has been invented to prove a point or a preconceived theory. In Picon's words he is a "projectile prêt à partir"[3] and we go with him on his journey, sharing his experiences and impressions and filled with "angoisse" at the moments of his choice. We experience with Lucien his discomfiture in the salon of Madame de Bargeton, the "coup de poignard" of De Marsay's mocking smile at the opera. We go with him on his walk through the Tuileries gardens in which he becomes aware of his badly-cut clothes, of his awkward provincial appearance in contrast to that of the smart young men of Parisian society. His "Voilà le monde que je dois dompter" (IV, 622) is the equivalent of Rastignac's famous "A nous deux maintenant!", but this time the challenge comes at the beginning and not at the end of the story and we experience with Lucien the ups and downs of his chequered career. It is through his experience that we come to know the life of the poor intellectual in Paris, living in a garret and eating cheap meals chez Flicoteaux, as well as that of the successful journalist and society man. Through his disappointments and disillusionment we

---

[1] The ending of *Le Père Goriot* is so 'open' that it can in fact (wilfully or otherwise) be misunderstood. Cf. Malcolm Jones's reference, *R.L.C.*, XXIV (1950), 226 n.2, to the first American translator who surmised that Rastignac married Victorine and returned to live in the provinces; also E. C. Hobart, *Notes and Queries*, CCII (September 1957), 293-4.

[2] G. Picon, *L'Usage de la lecture* (Paris, 1961–2), vol. II, p. 97.

[3] *ibid.*, p. 94.

become aware of the cynicism of publishers and the venality of the press. Much has been made of *Illusions perdues* as a study of Paris versus the Provinces, or as an attack on the press of Restoration Paris. To Georg Lukacs, for instance, the theme of the novel is the transformation of literature into goods.[1] But *Illusions perdues* is not a monograph on the economy of publishing or of the press; it is a novel of an individual destiny in which both writer and reader are deeply involved.

To use the terminology of Suzanne Bérard, the novelist is a "romancier des âmes" as well as a "peintre de mœurs".[2] The interest aroused by the latter largely depends on the success of the former. So much stress has been laid on Balzac as "le peintre de mœurs" that there is a tendency to forget that he is also and perhaps more importantly a "romancier des âmes". That Balzac like other great novelists found the stuff of his novels in his own experience and sensibility has been abundantly demonstrated and the more we know about his life the more we find him in his works. The living sensibility of the author is there in the experiences of Rubempré, as of Rastignac, and Balzac has the art of communicating this to the reader. As we read *Illusions perdues* we want to know what will happen to Lucien, how will he turn out, will he make the grade or not? It is only with Lucien's suicide in the course of *Splendeurs et misères des courtisanes* that we know his failure and degradation are complete. *Illusions perdues* remains the recorded experience of his success and failure but even so ends on a question mark, with a new beginning as Lucien rides off to Paris with Carlos Herrera: "Je recommence une existence terrible" (IV, 1048.) Balzac would probably have agreed with Sartre that we cannot know what a man is until he is dead. The studies of the life of Angoulême, or of the Parisian press or theatre, are successful because we see them through a lived experience. This surely is the difference between a Balzac novel and, say, Sebastien Mercier's *Tableau de Paris*.

Balzac is able not only to portray the feelings and experiences of young men which could reasonably, in some measure, be his own. He has an imaginative quality which enables him to enter so deeply into the feelings of others that he can express them as a living

[1] *Balzac et le réalisme français* (Paris, 1967), p. 50.
[2] *La Genèse d'un roman de Balzac: Illusions perdues 1837* (Paris, 1961), vol. II, p. 255.

experience even although by the nature of things they cannot be
his. In the often-quoted passage from *Facino Cane*[1] Balzac has himself described the powerful imaginative gift which enabled him to
feel and identify himself with others. When Balzac depicts the
frustrations of Madame de Bargeton, or Madame de la Baudraye,
or the disappointments of Madame de Mortsauf or Julie d'Aiglemont
he is not expressing his own experience in disguise, but the lived
experience of others which he was able imaginatively to share. He
knew from his sister Laure, from his friend Madame Carraud, what
it meant to be an intelligent, gifted woman without outlet for her
tastes, her talents or her emotions, condemned to the narrow life of
provincial France during the Restoration. He could feel imaginatively
with them and if Balzac is justly celebrated as a "peintre de mœurs"
who depicts the corruption and excitement of French life in Restoration Paris, as well as the dullness of life in the provinces, it is
because his novels are filled with people who *live* these "mœurs",
not with abstractions based on scientific or philosophical theories.
Whatever Balzac's theories may be, however many general statements he may make, however irritated we may become by his
claims to point a moral or prove a theory, the essential part of his
novels is the portrayal of the lived experience of human beings in
which the perceptive reader shares.

It is this powerful imagination which is Balzac's great quality.
By using that imagination about the reality of which he is such a
painstaking and acute observer, Balzac is able to give us a new vision
of the world which, while it may distort and exaggerate, may, like
the works of Ionesco or Lewis Carroll, stimulate the reader's imagination and enlarge his understanding. *Splendeurs et misères des
courtisanes* is a case in point. Here is a novel based on the carefully
observed, 'realistic' elements of Paris society with which Balzac has
made us familiar; the corruption, the pursuit of pleasure, of money,
of rank, as well as loyalty and love. Most of the characters in the
book are personalities we have met elsewhere in the *Comédie
humaine*. The imagination of Balzac has combined all these elements
to form a fantasy which is as incredible but as illuminating as *Alice*

---

[1] "En entendant ces gens, je pouvais épouser leur vie, je me sentais leur guenilles
sur le dos, je marchais les pieds dans leurs souliers percés; leurs désirs, leurs
besoins, tout passait dans mon âme, ou mon âme passait dans la leur" (vi, 67).

in Wonderland. Naturally, when people try to judge this work as if it were a piece of 'reportage' or a sociological document, they find it sadly wanting. When R. Albérès says in his *Histoire du roman moderne* (p. 422) that "Balzac utilise les aventures rocambolesques des Vautrin et des Rastignac pour faire de la sociologie" he is mistaking a possible by-product for the essence. It would be a strange kind of sociology, anyway, which is based on "aventures rocambolesques" although the latter can and do very properly form the basis of certain works of imagination.

A further complaint made against Balzac is that he constructs monolithic characters devoid of subtlety and hence of interest to the modern reader. For Nathalie Sarraute, "l'avarice *était* le père Grandet, elle en constituait toute la substance... La vie... a abandonné ces formes autrefois si pleines de promesses, et s'est transportee ailleurs."[1] She implies that Balzac produced only what she calls "types littéraires", whereas "ce qui maintenant importe c'est... de montrer la coexistence de sentiments contradictoires et de rendre dans la mesure du possible, la richesse et la complexité de la vie psychologique".[2] Yet, if the "coexistence de sentiments contradictoires" is to be the criterion of the modern writer, then Balzac is as 'modern' as anyone. Through much of his work there is a tension and an irony which have their roots precisely in the "coexistence de sentiments contradictoires".

Eugène de Rastignac and Lucien de Rubempré immediately spring to mind as characters who are a prey to conflicting feelings; in both the conflict is between personal integrity and family loyalty on the one hand and worldly ambition on the other. A less obvious case is that of Agathe Bridau in *La Rabouilleuse*, sometimes looked on as an embodiment of maternal affection and as the femine counterpart of le Père Goriot. That too-indulgent mother does violence to her own maternal feelings when, realizing the unworthiness of her son, she casts him out. "Êtes-vous digne d'être aimé?... pensez à chercher un appartement, vous ne demeurerez plus avec nous" (III, 916). Agathe's tragedy lies in the conflict between her maternal feelings and her awareness of her son's evil-doing. When she sees him in

---

[1] Sarraute, *op. cit.*, p. 62. [2] *ibid.*, p. 69.

the street some months later, a horrible destitute figure, she gives
him her purse but "se sauva comme si elle venait de commettre un
crime." (III, 930.) She is so much affected by her conflict of feelings
that "Elle resta deux jours sans pouvoir rien prendre." (III, 930.)

Félix de Vandenesse is a character quite obviously torn by two
contradictory feelings which are given external expression in the
figures of Madame de Mortsauf and Lady Dudley. But the contradictory feelings within Madame de Mortsauf herself are all the more
striking because they are not fully revealed till the end of *Le Lys
dans la vallée*. The character who is often regarded as being an
unshakeable devotee of domestic virtue and conventional morality
is revealed on her death-bed to have been beset by doubts and
desires which have made her life an agony: "Les accents de cette
voix magnifique peignaient les combats de toute une vie" and she
exclaims "Tout a été mensonge dans ma vie" (VIII, 1005). Even
César Birotteau, hero of "la probité commerciale", is a prey to
contradictory feelings, his love for his daughter conflicting with his
desire to owe nothing to his future son-in-law. It is not without a
struggle that César gives in – "durant la nuit, le digne homme se
querellerait avec lui-même sur ce point" (V, 582) – and that fatherly
affection triumphs over his very strict interpretation of commercial
duty.

Not only does Balzac create characters who have to cope with
"sentiments contradictoires"; he is full of them himself. His contradictory attitude in the field of politics is so well known that there
is no need to dwell on it here. This self-confessed right-wing sup-
porter of Church and State was so great a favourite with Karl Marx
that his French son-in-law, Lafargue, said of him, "He admired
Balzac so much that he wished to write a review of his great work,
La Comédie humaine, as soon as he had finished his work on
economics."[1] Distinguished left-wing critics (e.g. Lukacs, Wurmser)
find in Balzac rich support for their political attitudes and he has
even been referred to with approval by followers of Mao Tse-tung.[2]

Balzac's social attitudes are equally contradictory. Madame de
Mortsauf's letter to Félix de Vandenesse is cited by André Wurmser[3]

---

[1] quoted in a letter to *The Times* by R. W. Bullard, 24 April 1966.
[2] see *Times Saturday Review*, 26 October 1968.
[3] *La Comédie inhumaine* (Paris, 1964), pp. 168-70.

as proof of Balzac's calculating and callous 'arrivisme'. Yet in that same letter there is revealed an appreciation of human worth that almost reminds us of Robert Burns. "Quand notre pauvre homme de la Rhétorière vient se coucher fatigué de ses labours, croyez-vous qu'il n'ait pas rempli des devoirs? il a certes mieux accompli les siens que beaucoup de gens haut placés." (VIII, 888.) That "rank is but the guinea-stamp" appears too to be the sentiment behind her remark that "la politesse exquise, les belles façons viennent du cœur et d'un grand sentiment de dignité personnelle; voilà pourquoi, malgré leur éducation, quelques nobles ont mauvais ton, tandis que certaines personnes d'extraction bourgeoise ont naturellement bon goût." (VIII, 889.) We can contrast this with the snobbish attitude to the bourgeoisie which comes out very clearly in the description of the ball in *César Birotteau* where the aristocratic ladies present "se dessinaient sur toute la bourgeoisie par leurs grâces molles, par le goût exquis de leurs toilettes et par leur jeu, comme trois premiers sujets de l'Opéra se détachant sur la lourde cavalerie des comparses." (V, 459.) Clearly Balzac is able to see both sides of the question.

Balzac's attitude to many of his characters is ambivalent just because of the "coexistence de sentiments contradictoires" in those characters and in himself. Rastignac's skill in rising to the top, despite his initial gaucherie and poverty, arouses his creator's admiration as well as blame for the methods he adopts. Although Lucien de Rubempré's weakness is fully portrayed and contrasted with the strength of D'Arthez and the Cénacle, Balzac obviously enjoys the triumph of the handsome young hero and admires him in his success; "le salon retentissait d'applaudissements, les actrices embrassaient le néophyte, les trois négociants le serraient à l'étouffer, Du Bruel lui prenait la main et avait une larme a l'œil, enfin, le directeur l'invitait a dîner." (IV, 733.) Here is a situation after Balzac's own heart. Even such a scoundrel as Du Tillet arouses in Balzac a certain admiration for his taste in furnishings, if for nothing else, as the description of his flat in *César Birotteau* suggests (V, 499-500).

On the other hand, the virtuous César Birotteau is made a figure of fun, directly comparable to Molière's 'Bourgeois Gentilhomme' as he paces up and down "enveloppé dans sa robe de chambre

d'indienne verte, à pois couleur chocolat", with his "air... exorbitam-
ment niais" (v, 327). His equally virtuous future son-in-law is also
mocked when in Vauquelin's study he is "hébété de ne rien voir
d'extraordinaire dans le cabinet où il croyait trouver des monstruo-
sités, de giganteques machines, des métaux volants, des substances
animées." (v, 410.) Balzac admires and ridicules these characters at
one and the same time.   Similarly, his contempt for the shallow
egoism of the Baron du Châtelet who is treated with almost savage
irony (IV, 500-1) does not preclude a certain admiration for the
baron's worldly skill and for his handling of Madame de Bargeton
which enable him to triumph over Lucien in the end. Madame de
Bargeton herself, with whose intelligence and gifts Balzac so clearly
sympathizes at the beginning of *Illusions perdues*, becomes vain,
petty and vindictive under the influence of life in Paris. Madame
de La Baudraye develops in the opposite direction; to start with she
is a petty provincial snob (despite her gifts) "qui, dès l'âge de dix-
sept ans, se convertissait uniquement par ambition" (IV, 54), but
she rises to a certain moral grandeur during her life in Paris with
Lousteau, only to compromise with society in the end, when she discovers the worthlessness of her lover. The most ambivalent of all
Balzac's characters is surely Vautrin, the ex-convict who will stop
at nothing to gain his ends, yet who is capable of sincere affection,
self-sacrifice, loyalty and devotion and who ends by becoming chief
of police. He is perhaps the most extreme of a whole host of characters
in whom good and evil are inextricably mixed and of whom Balzac
both approves and disapproves.

   Far from telling us what to think, as he is sometimes accused of
doing,[1] Balzac presents us with contradictions which cannot be
resolved and it is here that much of his richness and originality lies.
Perhaps we can apply to Balzac himself Emile Blondet's remarks to
Lucien de Rubempré: "en littérature chaque idée a son envers et
son endroit; personne ne peut prendre sur lui d'affirmer quel est
l'envers. Tout est bilatéral dans le domaine de la pensée. Les idées
sont binaires. Janus est le mythe de la critique et le symbole du
génie... Ce qui met Molière et Corneille hors ligne, n'est-ce pas la
faculté de faire dire *oui* à Alceste et *non* à Philinte, à Octave et à

---

[1] cf. J. Fletcher in *Flaubert: Trois Contes* (1968), p. 23.

Cinna. Rousseau dans *la Nouvelle Héloise,* a écrit une lettre pour et une lettre contre le duel, oserais-tu prendre sur toi sa véritable opinion? Qui de nous pourrait prononcer entre Clarisse et Lovelace, entre Hector et Achille? Quel est le héros d'Homère? quelle fut l'intention de Richardson? La critique doit contempler les œuvres sous tous leures aspects.'' (IV, 789.) It is because Balzac sees and feels the life around him in so many 'aspects' that he is able to present the human comedy with its strengths and its weaknesses for the reader to judge or not as he thinks fit. Critics who accuse Balzac of presenting a static world of monolithic characters should take to heart the last sentence of Blondet's advice. They have failed to consider *La Comédie humaine* in all its aspects, and so they have not seen how much it has to offer to the modern reader.

Melmoth et les romans du
jeune Balzac[1]

MOÏSE LE YAOUANC

Il faut un peu de hardiesse pour présenter aujourd'hui une étude sur les rapports du *Melmoth* de Charles Maturin avec les premières œuvres de Balzac. N'y a-t-il pas eu les pages d'Alice M. Killen,[2] de Baldensperger,[3] de Paulo Ronai,[4] d'Albert Prioult,[5] puis celles de Maurice Bardèche[6] et de S. R. B. Smith,[7] et récemment celles de Max Milner,[8] de Roland Chollet[9] et de Pierre Barbéris?[10] Seraient-elles mauvaises, foncièrement erronées? Aucunement. Mais tout n'ayant pas été dit – le contraire serait étonnant – je voudrais apporter des observations complémentaires, des précisions, voire quelques rectifications, de manière à établir un tableau d'ensemble, au moins provisoire.

Balzac, comme on sait, a connu *Melmoth* très tôt. On peut même dire qu'il l'a lu dès l'année de sa traduction en français. Publié en Angleterre en 1820, le roman fut mis à la portée des lecteurs français l'année suivante, grâce à deux traductions données presque en même temps, celle de Mme Bégin, annoncée par la *Bibliographie de la France* le 9 mars 1821,[11] et celle de Jean Cohen[12] annoncée le 6 avril.

---

[1] Cet article est le premier volet d'une étude dont le second est présenté par *l'Année balzacienne* (1970) sous le titre: '*Melmoth* et Balzac au temps de *la Comédie humaine*'.

[2] *Le Roman terrifiant ou 'roman noir' de Walpole à Anne Radcliffe et son influence sur la littérature française jusqu'en 1840* (Paris, 1925).

[3] *Orientations étrangères chez H. de Balzac* (Paris, 1927).

[4] *Une page de Maturin copiée par Balzac, R.L.C., juillet–septembre* 1931.

[5] *Balzac avant la Comédie humaine* (Paris, 1930).

[6] *Balzac romancier*, thèse (Paris, 1940).

[7] *Balzac et l'Angleterre* (1953).

[8] *Le Diable dans la littérature française* (Paris, 1960), t. I.

[9] Balzac, *Romans de jeunesse* (Cercle du Bibliophile, 1962).

[10] *Aux sources de Balzac. Les Romans de jeunesse* (Paris, 1963).

[11] *L'Homme du mystère, ou Histoire de Melmoth le voyageur, par l'auteur de Bertram,* traduit [...] par Madame E.F.B. (Librairie nationale et étrangère, 1821), 3 vols.

[12] *Melmoth, ou l'Homme errant, par M. Mathurin auteur de Bertram, etc. traduit* [...] *par Jean Cohen* (Hubert, 1821), 6 vols.

Balzac cite *Melmoth*, en épigraphe, au début d'un chapitre de
l'Héritière de Birague dont le nom paraît le 26 janvier 1822 dans la
même *Bibliographie*. Compte tenu des délais d'impression, on doit
donc faire remonter à 1821 sa rencontre avec le livre de Maturin.

La distance entre la traduction de Mme Bégin et celle de Jean
Cohen n'est pas infinie. Cependant les différences sont assez impor-
tantes dans le détail, et surtout la traduction de Cohen est plus
complète. Aussi a-t-on eu raison de chercher à connaître la version
que Balzac a utilisée.

Avec plus ou moins d'assurance, on a opté pour celle de Cohen,
en invoquant deux faits. En 1828 Balzac a voulu donner une
réimpression de *Melmoth*, et c'est avec Hubert, l'éditeur de Cohen,
qu'il s'est mis en rapport; d'autre part, en 1835, dans une note
placée à la fin de *Melmoth réconcilié*, il s'est référé à "*Melmoth ou
l'Homme errant*, traduit par M. Cohen". Mais ces données, pré-
cieuses pour l'époque de *la Comédie humaine*, n'apportent guère de
garanties, on l'avouera, pour les années 1821–7. D'autres recherches
s'imposent.

Outre l'épigraphe, déjà évoquée, de *l'Héritière de Birague*, il s'en
trouve deux dans *Jean-Louis*. Malheureusement celles-ci,[1] au lieu
d'être de véritables extraits, représentent l'interprétation libre de
deux passages du Récit de l'Espagnol, c'est-à-dire de Monçada. Dans
l'épigraphe de *l'Héritière*: "Fussé-je à l'autel... ma main fût-elle
unie à la sienne... il empêcherait bien ce mariage. Une idée d'espoir
surnaturel errait dans son esprit... (Mathurins *Melmoth*, xiv ch.)",
si le numéro du chapitre est fantaisiste, le drame évoqué est celui
d'Isidora se refusant à épouser le fiancé qu'on lui impose: "Quand
ma main et celle de Montillo seraient déjà unies", écrit Cohen,
"Melmoth saurait bien m'arracher à lui. La persuasion vague du
pouvoir surnaturel dont il était doué remplissait son esprit".[2] La
ressemblance est évidente. Et pourtant les textes diffèrent assez
sensiblement. Or la traduction Bégin, elle, donne: "Fussé-je à l'autel,

[1] L'une (I, 138) présente de façon très elliptique le passage qui montre le frère
lai avec qui Monçada s'est enfui, en train de rêver et de se féliciter d'avoir, en
tuant son père, gagné plus que Judas (*Melmoth*, 1821, t. II, ch. xv et *l'Homme du
mystère*, t. II, ch. ix). L'autre (II, 66) n'est pas expressément présentée comme
venant de *Melmoth*. Mais elle évoque, semble-t-il, le moment où Monçada et le
frère lai aperçoivent le jour après une terrible marche dans les souterrains
(*Melmoth*, 1821, t. II, ch. xiv, et *l'Homme du mystère*, t. II, ch. ix).
[2] voir *l'Heritière*, III, 177, et Cohen, t. VI, ch. xl, p. 255.

ma main fût-elle unie à celle de Montilla, Melmoth empêcherait ce mariage. Une idée de pouvoir surnaturel errait dans son esprit".[1] Peu importe que Balzac mette "espoir" au lieu de "pouvoir", c'est, à n'en pas douter, la traduction Bégin qu'il utilise en 1821 et tout au début de 1822.

Mais ensuite? Nous ne sommes pas démunis pour répondre. Comme on le sait, au cours de 1822, Balzac a pris pour modèle – en allant jusqu'au plagiat[2] – l'une des grandes scènes amoureuses entre l'Homme Errant et Isidora, d'abord quand il a voulu expliquer à Mme de Berny ce qu'est le véritable amour, puis quand, dans le Centenaire, il a fait donner par Tullius Béringheld la même explication à Marianine. Or un examen attentif des textes permet de dire que la lettre à Mme de Berny et le duo de Béringheld et de Marianine présentent des concordances un peu plus nettes avec la version de Cohen qu'avec celle de Mme Bégin;[3] et surtout qu'un ou deux traits caractérisant, selon Balzac, le parfait amour se trouvent chez Cohen, mais non chez Mme Bégin.[4] En définitive, l'ensemble de cette enquête conduit à une solution complexe. Balzac, apparemment, a commencé par se procurer la traduction parue la première, celle de Mme Bégin, et l'a utilisée pendant quelque temps; mais bientôt il a voulu disposer de l'ouvrage le plus complet, celui de Cohen, et il a dû l'acquérir vers le printemps de 1822.

A en juger seulement par les textes où le jeune Balzac s'est expressément référé à Melmoth, il semble avoir été surtout frappé par deux épisodes: la fuite de Monçada dans les souterrains, rapportée dans le Récit de l'Espagnol, et l'histoire des amours d'Immalie-Isidora et de Melmoth.[5] Mais arrive-t-on à une conclusion semblable lorsque l'on considère l'influence du livre de Maturin sur l'imagination créatrice du romancier?

André Lebreton a supposé qu'en composant la preface de l'Héritière de Birague Balzac s'était souvenu du début de Melmoth.[6]

---

[1] III, ch. xxxiv, pp. 174–5.
[2] voir P. Ronai, art. cit., et Prioult, op. cit., pp. 173–5.
[3] voir Bégin, op. cit., t. III, p. 11, et Cohen, op. cit., t. V, pp. 107–9.
[4] Preuve décisive: l'idée que l'abaissement à l'égard de l'être aimé est une preuve d'amour est donnée par Cohen (t. V, p. 107), négligée par Mme Bégin (t. III, p. 11), retenue par Balzac (Corr., t. I, p. 170).
[5] voir aussi Corr., t. I, pp. 263–4 (1825): "les Isidora (permettez-moi de prendre ce touchant emblème de la grâce et de la soumission)".
[6] Balzac, l'homme et l'œuvre (Paris, 1905), pp. 63–4.

D

Cette idée, qui ne heurte pas les données de la chronologie,[1] n'est
nullement à négliger. Les deux jeunes gens, A. de Viellerglé et
R'hoone, qui viennent de Paris pour recueillir la succession d'un
oncle provincial, qui sont reçus par Mme Scrupule, la gouvernante,
et qui, dans un coffret, découvrent un manuscrit contenant l'histoire
même de *l'Héritière de Birague*, rappellent assez bien le jeune
Melmoth qui, arrivé de Dublin, assiste aux derniers moments d'un
oncle soigné par une vieille gouvernante, recueille l'héritage et
trouve dans un cabinet jusque là soigneusement fermé un manuscrit
racontant quelques épisodes de la vie de Melmoth. N'aperçoit-on
pas là la première influence exercée par *Melmoth* sur la création
balzacienne?[2]

   L'auteur du *Centenaire*, tout le monde l'accorde, doit beaucoup à
Melmoth. Et l'on a eu raison de montrer qu'il s'était inspiré de
Maturin pour la peinture du personnage central,[3] pour l'invention
de quelques épisodes ou de circonstances secondaires,[4] et même pour
la technique, puisque dans *le Centenaire* comme dans *Melmoth* on

---

[1] Au cours de cet article je suivrai pour la chronologie des œuvres celle qu'a
établie P. Barbéris dans *Aux sources de Balzac*.
[2] Cette préface a été écrite vraisemblablement vers la fin de 1821. Une action un
peu plus ancienne sur l'imagination de Balzac n'est pas à exclure. A la fin du ch.
viii de *Falthurne* (éd. Castex, p. 102), la fuite d'Angélina, ses frayeurs, ses re-
mords, l'horreur du lieu, de la chapelle où elle est unie au terrible Arnolpho,
font songer à la fuite d'Isidora et à son mariage avec Melmoth dans un monastère
en ruines (*Melmoth*, tr. Cohen, ch. xx). Que Balzac se soit inspiré de Maturin
n'est nullement impossible, s'il est vrai que les derniers chapitres de *Falthurne*
ont été écrits, non pendant l'été de 1820 mais, comme l'indique Pierre Barbéris,
presque un an après.
[3] Sur les côtés à la fois fantastiques et 'melmothiens' du Centenaire (regards,
éclats de rire, manteau immobile dans la tempête, longévité, pouvoir de se
transporter au loin, de franchir les portes les mieux fermées, d'apporter la
délivrance, les richesses, la santé) voir Bardèche, *op. cit.*, p. 126, et Milner, *op.
cit.*, t. I, p. 327.
[4] On a bien vu que les embrassements fantastiques d'où Tullius Béringheld est
né ont pour source l'union d'Isidora et de Melmoth, que le sacrifice de Marianine
vient de l'Histoire de Guzman et de sa famille, que ses frayeurs rappellent
celles d'Isidora fuyant avec Melmoth, que le repaire du Centenaire ressemble à
l'appartement souterrain du Juif Adonias, l'hôte de Monçada. Dans ce dernier
cas, il faut le souligner, l'imitation est presque aussi étroite que pour le duo
amoureux de Marianine et Béringheld. La tapisserie, la table couverte de tissus,
la lampe, les sphères, les parchemins, les squelettes, les instruments d'acier
(*le Centenaire*, IV, 171–2), tout vient de *Melmoth* (t. IV, pp. 158–9). On remarquera,
d'ailleurs, qu'avant de décrire l'appartement d'Adonias, Maturin compare le
souterrain y conduisant à ceux "des Pyramides ou des Catacombes". Or le
Centenaire, qui s'est établi dans les Catacombes, a, quelques années plus tôt,
pénétré dans les Pyramides.

trouve un emploi systématique du retour en arrière et des tiroirs, des histoires incluses.

Cependant, une fois reconnu très positif le bilan des travaux antérieurs, quelques observations critiques s'imposent. Et pour commencer il convient de dénoncer certains rapprochements injustifiés entre les deux romans. Une relecture ne confirme nullement que l'on doive établir un rapport entre la conduite du directeur de conscience de la famille Monçada à l'égard d'Alonzo, et l'éducation donnée au jeune Béringheld par le Père de Lunada. Mais surtout on a exagéré les ressemblances physiques du Centenaire et de Melmoth. Celui-ci, contrairement à ce que l'on a dit, a une taille simplement au-dessus de la moyenne.[1] On a affirmé encore que Béringheld-le-Centenaire devait à Melmoth son air extrêmement vieux, sa ressemblance avec un squelette "pétrifié". Or Maturin répète que son héros, à part l'éclat des yeux, n'a rien de très remarquable, et qu'il paraît un homme d'âge moyen.[2]

Inversement, des ressemblances entre *Melmoth* et *le Centenaire* ont été négligées. Et d'abord l'on doit noter que pour la conception fondamentale du personnage principal Balzac s'est moins éloigné qu'on ne l'a dit de Maturin. Il a lié le pouvoir de Béringheld à sa science occulte, à la découverte du secret d'un grand maître des rose-croix; mais il avait lu chez Maturin, dans l'Histoire des amants, qu'à l'origine Melmoth avait été un jeune homme passionné par l'étude, très savant, que sa curiosité avait entraîné vers les recherches les plus difficiles et les plus occultes.[3]

Pour les épisodes, les personnages secondaires, bien des rapports restent à signaler. Si le Père de Lunada rappelle le directeur de la famille Monçada, c'est par son désir de dominer cette maison en s'emparant de ses secrets.[4] Au reste il a été essentiellement conçu à l'image d'un autre ecclésiastique de *Melmoth*, le Père José, confesseur d'Isidora et de sa mère: sans être vraiment malveillant, ce prêtre est curieux et autoritaire, et surtout, comme Lunada, il aime le confort et la bonne chère.[5] L'histoire de Butmel, elle aussi, a subi l'influence de celle d'Isidora: quand Balzac a imaginé que l'ami de

[1] voir notamment *Melmoth*, t. I, ch. iv, pp. 124–5.
[2] voir *ibid.*, t. VI, ch. xxxiv, pp. 18–20.
[3] *Melmoth*, t. VI, p. 198.
[4] *Le Centenaire*, II, ch. viii.
[5] *Melmoth*, t. V., ch. xxvii, et *le Centenaire*, I, 244–5.

Lagradna était conduit par le Centenaire dans une montagne de
l'Inde, et qu'il n'avait de relations, pendant de longues années,
qu'avec quelques êtres humains, il se rappelait l'enfance indienne
d'Immalie-Isidora. D'autre part, la peinture de la démence d'Inès,
une victime du Centenaire, est le développement d'un bref passage
du manuscrit de Stanton. L'Espagnole d'Horace de Saint-Aubin,
rendue folle par le meurtre de son amant, reste silencieuse tout le
jour, sauf à onze heures du soir où elle jette un faible cri et dit:
"Grégorio, ne le tue pas, grâce..." de même que chez Maturin un
Espagnol, devenu fou à la suite de la mort tragique de sa jeune
épouse, une autre Inès, garde le silence "dans le cours de la journée",
et s'écrie vers minuit: "Ils viennent! Ils viennent!"[1] Mais surtout il
faut remarquer combien le récit des circonstances qui ont entouré la
conception quasi-miraculeuse de Tullius Béringheld se rapproche du
début de *Melmoth*. Certes Balzac a transposé. Mais, à n'en pas
douter, le tournebride de Béringheld, tout au moins par ses hôtes,
rappelle la cuisine de l'oncle Melmoth. De même que Maturin avait
groupé autour d'un feu de tourbe bien nourri la gouvernante,
"deux ou trois" *suivants* et Biddy Brannigan, "médecin femelle"
du village et "sibylle ridée", sachant dire "la bonne aventure",
Horace de Saint-Aubin place autour d'un brillant feu de bois de
sapin le concierge du château et sa femme, quelques villageois,
trois ou quatre commères, dont "la sage-femme du village, vieille
sorcière qui cumulait avec ses fonctions *obstétriques* le droit de dire
la bonne aventure, de jeter des sorts".[2] S'il fait faire par cette sibylle
des révélations sur le Centenaire, Maturin avait imaginé que le
jeune Melmoth s'était renseigné sur le Voyageur en interrogeant
successivement la gouvernante et Biddy Brannigan.[3] Et si la décré-
pitude mentale du comte Béringheld, père de Tullius devant la loi,
a pour origine son saisissement en apercevant l'autre Béringheld, la
maladie de l'oncle Melmoth a été causée par la peur qu'il a
éprouvée en se trouvant en présence de l'autre Melmoth.[4]

La comparaison du début de *Melmoth* avec les chapitres du *Centenaire* racontant les événements de la nuit où la comtesse Béringheld

[1] *Le Centenaire*, III, 100–2, et *Melmoth*, t. I, pp. 103–4.
[2] *Melmoth*, t. I, ch. I, et *Le Centenaire*, I, ch. VI.
[3] *Le Centenaire*, I, ch. VII, et *Melmoth*, t. I, ch. II.
  Le Centenaire, II, ch. II, et *Melmoth*, t. I, ch. I.

est devenue mère montre bien l'importance et la complexité de la dette de Balzac envers Maturin.[1] Le jeune romancier n'a pas seulement utilisé *Melmoth* pour inventer une histoire, il a demandé à son devancier des leçons de réalisme. Et l'on en aperçoit d'autres preuves ici et là. Quand, vers le début du *Centenaire*, il montre l'ouvrier involontairement responsable de la mort de Fanny Lamanel foudroyé par le désespoir et mettant "la main sur son cœur, comme pour indiquer que c'était là le siège de son mal", il se rappelle une mimique saisissante de Biddy Brannigan.[2] Et vers la fin, quand, rapportant les propos de Lagloire, il lui fait répéter "pour lors", il lui prête un tic de langage qu'il avait remarqué chez la vieille Espagnole qui, dans le roman de Maturin, raconte les malheurs d'Inès de Cardoza.[3] *Melmoth* a fourni à l'auteur du *Centenaire* bien plus que des figures ou des situations romanesques, que des recettes de technique.

Il reste maintenant à voir si l'imitation du livre de Maturin reste sensible dans les œuvres rédigées après *le Centenaire*. Pour *le Vicaire des Ardennes*, datant aussi de 1822, on a peine à suivre M. Bardèche quand il établit un rapport de filiation entre l'histoire d'Immalie-Isidora et l'intrigue centrale du *Vicaire*: l'amour de Joseph et de Mélanie. Par contre, au début, les bavardages des habitants d'Aulnay sur la place de l'église rappellent la scène du tournebride dans *le Centenaire*, et par conséquent celle de la cuisine de l'oncle Melmoth. De même le manuscrit contenant l'histoire de Joseph est à rapprocher des Mémoires de Tullius Béringheld et des manuscrits de *Melmoth*. Surtout, lorsque Joseph, persuadé que Mélanie est sa sœur, perd l'espoir de pouvoir l'épouser, il se trouve dans la même situation que John Sandal renonçant à son mariage avec Eléonore Mortimer. Une influence de l'Histoire des amants sur *le Vicaire* paraît d'autant plus vraisemblable que, par ailleurs, la jeunesse contrainte de Mme de Rosann chez sa tante, la janséniste demoiselle Ursule de Karadeuc, présente d'incontestables analogies

---

[1] Signalons encore une concordance de détail entre le début de *Melmoth* et la scène du tournebride. Chez Maturin, quand Biddy Brannigan se rassied après avoir porté son diagnostic sur l'oncle Melmoth, la sonnette de celui-ci retentit. Parallèlement, chez Balzac, dès que Lagradna a fini son intervention inspirée et s'assied, la cloche du tournebride se fait entendre (*Melmoth*, t. I, p. 14, et *le Centenaire*, I, 232).

[2] *Le Centenaire*, I, 115, et *Melmoth*, t. I, p. 14.

[3] *Le Centenaire*, IV, 133–40, et *Melmoth*, t. I, ch. ii.

avec la vie d'Eléonore Mortimer, réfugiée chez sa tante, une bigote puritaine.[1]

Oeuvre publiée en 1825, mais dont la composition remonte, comme l'a montré Pierre Barbéris, à 1823 pour l'essentiel, *Wann-Chlore* doit sans doute plus à *Melmoth* que *le Vicaire des Ardennes*. Balzac, qui admirait fort le personnage d'Isidora et voyait en lui un type de l'amour féminin,[2] s'en est apparemment quelque peu inspiré lorsqu'il a dessiné le caractère d'Eugénie d'Arneuse. Comme Isidora, Eugénie a une mère égoïste, sèche, soucieuse de respecter les conventions sociales, et elle souffre auprès d'elle de devoir constamment réprimer sa sensibilité.[3] Comme chez Isidora, l'amour chez elle est un don total de soi-même.[4] Si Isidora mourante répond au prêtre qui lui promet le paradis: "Le paradis [...] L'y trouverai-je?", Balzac écrit à propos des femmes aimant à la manière d'Eugénie: "partout où va cet être [objet de leur passion], elles vont: la fange, l'échafaud, les prisons, un palais, tout leur est une douce patrie pourvu qu'*il* y soit".[5] Mais il est probable qu'en peignant l'amour d'Eugénie, il s'est souvenu aussi de l'Histoire des amants. La ressemblance est grande entre la jeune fille rêvant à Landon parti subitement, évoquant l'image de l'absent, voulant cacher ses sentiments, mais dépérissant, menant une existence de visionnaire, et Eléonore Mortimer attendant le retour de son cousin John Sandal, se retranchant dans ses pensées, vivant dans une sorte de rêve et côtoyant la folie.[6] Bref, pour décrire la passion amoureuse chez Eugénie, Balzac, semble-t-il, a mis à profit plusieurs notations psychologiques trouvées dans *Melmoth*.

Mais parmi les œuvres rédigées après *le Centenaire*, une de celles dont les emprunts à *Melmoth* sont les moins contestables est *la Dernière Fée*. L'édition de 1823 en contient déjà un. Lorsqu'Abel et Catherine entreprennent de définir l'amour, et spécialement lorsqu'Abel dit à propos de la Fée: "Elle serait ma mère, mon père, ma sœur tout à la fois... tout pour moi. Tout me viendrait d'elle: lumière, bonheur, joie.[...] Enfin je vivrais en elle, elle serait mon

[1] *Le Vicaire*, I, 135–7, et *Melmoth*, pp. 150–1.
[2] cf. ci-dessus, p. 37, note 5.
[3] *Melmoth*, t. v, ch. xxv, et *Wann-Chlore*, I, 197–200 et II, 21, 33 *et passim*.
[4] *Melmoth*, t. v, ch. xxvi, pp. 98–100, et *Wann-Chlore*, I, 199.
[5] *Melmoth*, t. vi, ch. xli (fin), et *Wann-Chlore*, I, 200.
[6] *Wann-Chlore*, II, 61–7, et *Melmoth*, t. vi, ch. xxxvi, p. 86.

matin, mon jour, mon soleil, plus que toute la nature..."[1] l'on entend l'echo du duo du *Centenaire*: une nouvelle fois Balzac s'est inspiré de l'entretien amoureux d'Isidora et de Melmoth. Plus importante est l'autre imitation du roman de Maturin que l'on découvre dans la seconde version de *la Dernière Fée*,[2] tout à la fin. Trahi par sa duchesse anglaise, Abel a perdu la raison, mais Catherine, toujours éprise, prend soin de lui. Elle l'a conduit dans un village d'Écosse, épiant en vain une trace de raison chez celui qui ne la reconnaît plus, passant une partie du jour à le promener dans la campagne en "s'assurant qu'aucun objet proscrit n'offenserait la vue du malheureux auquel elle s'est dévouée". Enfin, un jour, Abel donne à la jeune fille une joie longtemps attendue: "Tout à coup, le malheureux retire doucement sa tête; une idée semble naître en lui, il regarde fixement Catherine, la contemple attentivement[...] enfin, son œil revint à la raison, et il s'écria: 'C'est Catherine!' "

Quelle est la source principale de ce chapitre final? Assurément l'Histoire des amants.[3] Quand John Sandal, désespéré, est devenu subitement fou, Eléonore s'est consacrée entièrement à lui et elle l'a emmené dans sa chaumière du Yorkshire. "Tous les jours elle le conduit à la promenade et cherche les sentiers les plus écartés" afin d'éviter des rencontres "fatigantes pour son ami". Un jour un coup de théâtre se produit. "Il lève lentement la tête et fixe les yeux sur elle[...] son regard est celui d'un être raisonnable[...]" Il veut parler, ne réussit point, et rend presque aussitôt le dernier soupir. Eléonore meurt à son tour le lendemain en disant: "Je meurs heureuse, il m'a reconnue". Balzac, manifestement, s'est inspiré de ce récit, en remplaçant le dénouement, apaisé, mais tragique, de Maturin par un dénouement heureux.[4]

Peut-être faut-il aussi reconnaître une influence de *Melmoth* dans le deuxième *Falthurne*, œuvre inachevée et datant de 1823 comme *la Dernière Fée*. Certes l'être mystérieux qui apparaît dans la vallée

---

[1] *La Dernière Fée*, 1823, I, ch. iv, 105-6.
[2] Publiée en 1824, elle a été mise au point, comme l'a montré P. Barbéris, peu après la sortie de la première édition.
[3] voir *Melmoth*, t. VI, ch. xxxviii, pp. 196–7 et 218.
[4] L'imitation de *Melmoth* n'est point douteuse. Quand Balzac évoque la promenade d'Abel avec Catherine: "Ils marchaient ensemble en faisant retentir les feuilles séchées qui tombaients des arbres", il se souvient de la page qui chez Maturin raconte la dernière sortie de John Sandal: "les feuilles desséchées résonnent sous leurs pas" (*Melmoth*, t. VI, p. 218).

alpestre semble être, non une créature du démon, mais un ange.
Pourtant il fait par instants songer à Melmoth. Lui aussi se fait voir
à ceux qui sont dans le malheur et arrive on ne sait d'où, lui aussi
parle les langages les plus divers et des sons mélodieux accompagnent
sa venue. Bref, Falthurne semble être une sorte d'anti-Melmoth
possédant certains traits ou attributs de Melmoth.[1] Et d'autre part
le ton, l'atmosphère générale ne sont pas sans analogie avec ceux de
l'Histoire des Indiens, c'est-à-dire du début de l'histoire d'Immalie-
Isidora.

On peut être tenté de voir dans *Annette et le Criminel*, ouvrage
de 1823-4, la reprise transposée de cette histoire d'Isidora; comme
l'Espagnole, Annette est une très pure jeune fille qui s'éprend d'un
être terrible, au passé inavouable. En fait d'autres lectures, en
particulier celle de *Jean Sbogar*, ont dû agir plus fortement sur
l'imagination de Balzac. Cependant çà et là on aperçoit des souvenirs
de *Melmoth*. Avec sa religion, sa ferveur mystique, sa passion dans
l'amour, Annette ressemble à Isidora.[2] D'autre part, la scène de
l'arrivée chez Mlle Sophy, près d'une porte du château de Durantal,
et aussi la conversation tenue chez une voisine, "au coin de son feu,
dans son arrière-boutique, entourée de sept ou huit habitants",
doivent être regardées comme de nouvelles variantes, après celles
du *Centenaire* et du *Vicaire*, du tableau de la veillée chez l'oncle
Melmoth. Une reconnaissance de dette est même presque signée
par Balzac quand il appelle Mlle Sophy la "sibylle du lieu".[3]

En laissant de côté les imitations que l'on ne peut regarder comme
certaines, et d'autre part les œuvres dont l'attribution à Balzac peut
être contestée,[4] l'on est en mesure, au terme de cette enquête, de
formuler quelques conclusions sur les rapports de *Melmoth* avec la
production juvénile de Balzac.

Premier point: dans son utilisation du roman de Maturin, Balzac
n'a laissé entièrement de côté aucun des grande épisodes. Il s'est
surtout inspiré des deux premiers chapitres, de l'Histoire de Guzman,

---

[1] voir *Falthurne*, éd. Castex, pp. 163-6 et 183.

[2] voir, par exemple, *Annette*, II, 107, et *Melmoth*, t. v, ch. xxvi.

[3] *Annette*, III, ch. xvi.

[4] Notons simplement ceci: l'influence de *Melmoth* est visible dans le portrait du
narrateur du *Pacte* (1822; vi, 158-61 et 178), dans la peinture du chimiste de
l'Anonyme, assis devant une table chargée d'ossements humains (1823; III, 172),
dans les raisonnements destructeurs d'Edouard, le héros du *Corrupteur* (1827;
I, 101 et 107-8).

de l'Histoire des amants. L'histoire d'Immalie-Isidora lui a fourni quelques scènes, et bien des traits; mais de cette aventure qui semble l'avoir particulièrement intéressé, si l'on en juge par sa correspondance et par une épigraphe, il n'a pas repris pleinement le thème fondamental. Quant à l'histoire de Monçada, source de deux épigraphes, il en a relativement peu tiré parti: en particulier il n'a rien retenu de ce qui était peinture satirique de la vie dans les couvents et de l'Inquisition.

Autre point important: quand on se préoccupe de définir l'influence de *Melmoth* sur le jeune Balzac, *le Centenaire* ne doit pas être seul un objet d'attention; d'autres œuvres (presque toutes) portent la marque de cette influence.

Mais celle-ci apparaît bien différente suivant que l'on considère *le Centenaire* ou les autres romans. Dans le premier cas elle résulte d'une imitation volontaire, systématique, présente un peu partout, même si elle est déguisée par des transpositions, même si, finalement, l'œuvre balzacienne diffère profondément de celle de Maturin par sa ligne générale et si, dans le détail, l'on ne peut parler que très rarement de plagiat. Au contraire, pour les autres romans il s'agit plutôt de réminiscences, d'emprunts à demi volontaires, d'étendue limitée, explicables par la forte impression que tel ou tel passage de Maturin avait fait sur l'esprit de Balzac.

Enfin, de la lecture attentive de *Melmoth* le jeune romancier a tiré des enseignements multiples et durablement féconds. Il a enrichi sa technique, il a appris à créer une atmosphère fantastique autour d'un personnage étrange, il a retenu, pour en exploiter la valeur pathétique, certaines situations romanesques (par exemple celle du fiancé devenu fou, soigné fidèlement par son amie), il a pris des leçons touchant la psychologie amoureuse et le langage de la passion. Et, ce qui est plus important encore peut-être, il a trouvé chez Maturin le modèle de scènes saisissantes par la vigueur du trait, par leur précision réaliste.

Interpretation of the *contes philosophiques*

ANTHONY R. PUGH

W<small>HILE</small> there is still room for argument about the correct interpretation of Balzac's major works, the 'meaning' of the *contes philosophiques* was settled once and for all, it would seem, by Balzac's own spokesman, Félix Davin, on the occasion of the launching of the *Études philosophiques* in 1835. According to Davin, the *contes* all illustrate the central thesis of *La Peau de chagrin*. Commentators have invariably taken their cue from Davin. It is the purpose of this paper to challenge the traditional interpretation, particularly as far as the original stories of 1831 are concerned. On two counts, it seems to me, the traditional labels can be discounted. On the one hand, recent research into the origins of the stories shows that they were often to begin with quite independent of the philosophical 'system' they were later said to illustrate. On the other hand, an unbiased attempt to interpret the various tales as autonomous works, in which every detail may be expected to contribute to the total meaning, often produces results at variance with the orthodox Davin line.[1]

Four years before Davin, the foundations of the systematic interpretation had been laid by Philarète Chasles, who supplied a preface for the second edition of *La Peau de chagrin*, published in September 1831. This is what he had to say about the general theme:

> Le désordre et le ravage portés par l'intelligence dans l'homme, considéré comme individu et comme être social... cette idée... M. de Balzac l'a jetée dans ses contes... Un homme de pensée et de philosophie, qui s'attache à peindre la désorganisation produite par la pensée, tel est M. de Balzac. *Voilà sur quelles bases sont*

---

[1] Davin's *Introduction aux Études philosophiques* is reprinted in XI, 203–22, see particularly pp. 216-17. Chasles's preface is in the same volume, pp. 180–8, see particulaly pp. 181–2. The *Études philosophiques* discussed in this paper are all in vol. IX of the Pléiade edition.

appuyés ces contes de nuances diverses, de formes variées, que M.
de Balzac a osé lancer.

In this context, Chasles mentions only one of the *contes* specifically:
El Verdugo. "Cette pensée première", writes Chasles, "s'élève
jusqu'aux proportions de la tragédie dans *El Verdugo*, où le parricide
est sublime, parricide ordonné par une famille et au nom d'une
chimère sociale, le parricide pour sauver un titre. Ainsi, partout
l'égoïsme: égoïsme de la famille, égoïsme physique, personnalités
féroces qui naissent d'une civilisation sensuelle et raffinée."

El Verdugo is set in occupied Spain. The precarious happiness of
a young French officer, attracted by the daughter of the local
marquis ("le vieillard le plus entiché de sa grandesse qui fût en
Europe") is shattered when, with the connivance of the local inhabitants, English soldiers arrive off-shore. The officer reports to his
general. As a reprisal, 200 local citizens are shot. The family of the
aristocrat is threatened with immediate hanging, but the marquis
pleads successfully to have the sentence commuted to beheading,
and asks that his son be spared. "Je devine l'importance de sa dernière
demande," says the French general, "je fais grâce à celui de ses fils
qui remplira l'office de bourreau." This fearful message is delivered,
and in a scene of great power, the members of the family plead in
turn with the eldest son not to flinch. In a sombre final paragraph
we are told that the executioner was given the nickname of 'el
verdugo', and he is not expected to live long after the birth of a
second son has ensured the succession.

This story was originally published, not in the volume of *contes*,
but in a journal called *La Mode*, on 29 January 1830. The date is
an important clue to the preoccupations which really inspired it. It
was exactly contemporary with the apocryphal *Mémoires de Sanson*,
and one paragraph in that work gives the source of the story quite
clearly and the context shows the meaning Balzac attached to it:

En Espagne, en Italie, en Allemagne et quelquefois même en
France, lorsque plusieurs coupables étaient condamnés au dernier
supplice, souvent il n'y avait moyen de faire accomplir l'arrêt
qu'en accordant la vie à celui qui voulait bien exécuter les autres...
Dès que la justice est reduit à cette déshonorante extrêmité, de
permettre le parricide pour qu'un moindre attentât soit puni, c'est

que la mort infligée comme punition est antipathique avec les
mœurs...[1]

The story was therefore first conceived as an illustration of the
inhumanity of capital punishment.

Readers of *La Mode* would probably not have suspected this. But
nor would they have singled out as the important thing the "désordre parté par l'intelligence... le parricide ordonné au nom d'une
chimère sociale". To them it would have been the notion of reprisal
which would have seemed so appalling (indeed, without the "chimère
sociale" the whole family would have perished). The title Balzac
gave the story in *La Mode* indicates how he interpreted it in 1850:
'Souvenirs soldatesques, El Verdugo, Guerre d'Espagne (1809)'. One
significant exchange, which we omitted from our brief summary,
points clearly to the impact the story must have had on those first
unindoctrinated readers; it comes just before the last paragraphs:

> – Mon général, dit un officier à moitié ivre, Marchand vient de
> me raconter quelque chose de cette exécution... Je parie que vous
> ne l'avez pas ordonnée...

> – Oubliez-vous, Messieurs, s'écria le général G..t..r, que, dans
> un mois, cinq cents familles françaises seront en larmes, et que
> nous sommes en Espagne? Voulez-vous laisser nos os ici?

These lines must have appeared very telling to a reader of *La Mode*:
to him *El Verdugo* was a 'scène de la vie militaire' the horror of
which was offset and in a subtle way intensified by an appeal to his
patriotism.

Yet in 1851, this military tale gets transferred to a new category,
of 'contes philosophiques'. One suspects that there was really something fortuitous in the creation of this new category. The unexpected
success of *La Peau de chagrin* led Balzac to make hasty plans for
exploiting it, publishing a new edition, to be embellished by the
inclusion of several stories of not too dissimilar inspiration. The first
hint of this project is probably the note (undated) in Balzac's Album:
"La 2e édition de la *Peau de chagrin* pourrait prendre le titre de

---

[1] O.D., t. I, p. 253. On *El Verdugo*, see J. W. Conner, 'The genesis of Balzac's
El Verdugo', *Leuvense Bijdragen*, XLIV (1957), 135–9.

Contes et romans philosophiques",[1] and he lists half a dozen, which do not include *El Verdugo*. On 22 August 1831, barely three weeks after the publication of *La Peau*, Balzac signed the contract with Gosselin for the second edition, with "eight or ten" satellites, defined as "romans ou contes philosophiques". In the event, there were 12. Some are at best 'contes fantastiques', and one is an allegory. If we were to try to find something which they might be said to have in common, it would probably be that they depend on inner strain rather than external force (at least for the dénouements), but that is not to say that the primary inspiration is a theory about the nature of man's inner drives, or the destructive nature of thought. And in fact, Philarète Chasles does not insist too loudly on any unifying factor in his preface. Most of it is given over to an attempt to make people take very seriously the author of *La Peau de chagrin*. He says simply that the basic *attitude*, the "fonds misanthropique", can be found in four other stories, attaining tragic proportions in *El Verdugo*.

Chasles's suggestions very soon hardened into a theory, and by the end of 1834, when Davin wrote an *Introduction aux Études philosophiques* for a new and comprehensive edition of the 'philosophical' works to be published by Werdet, the facts of history are sacrificed in the cause of systematic exposition: "*Après avoir poétiquement formulé*, dans la *Peau de chagrin*, le système de l'homme, considéré comme organisation... l'auteur... montre *l'idée* exagérant *l'instinct*, arrivant à la passion, et qui, incessamment placée sous le coup des influences sociales, devient désorganisatrice." He then defines the theme of the various stories, and of *El Verdugo*, he says that it is "l'idée de dynastie mettant une hache dans la main d'un fils, lui faisant commettre tous les crimes en un seul". Yet these formulas – those of Chasles and of Davin – ignore the surer instinct of the creative writer who, when he is actually composing his story, finds it organizing itself along different lines. Had Balzac consciously reminded himself that he was illustrating any such notion, it is unlikely that the military occupation would have loomed so large. To us the military setting is in no sense mere padding, but an integral part of the whole.

El Verdugo is a particularly clear case of the way in which a story, conceived quite independently of the *contes philosophiques*, has been

[1] A. 182, f. 9, ed. Bardèche (Paris, 1963), t. xxviii, p. 669; *Corr.*, no. 334.

assimilated to the theory created, *a posteriori*, for the *contes philo-sophiques*, and its origins quietly forgotten. The same process has undoubtedly affected other works in the same collection. *Le Réquisi-tionnaire*, for example, first appeared on 23 February 1831 in *La Revue de Paris*, before the 'system' had been formulated, and again we should ask what those first readers would have made of it. There is, admittedly, something of a puzzle about *Le Réquisitionnaire*. The last paragraph reads as follows, with half a dozen words deliberately omitted:

> La mort de la comtesse fut causée… sans doute par quelque vision terrible. A l'heure précise ou madame de Dey mourait à Carentan, son fils était fusillé dans le Morbihan. Nous pouvons joindre ce fait tragique à toutes les observations sur les sympathies qui mécon-naissent les lois de l'espace; documents que rassemblent avec une savante curiosité quelques hommes de solitude, et qui serviront un jour à asseoir les bases d'une science nouvelle à laquelle il a manqué jusqu'à ce jour un homme de génie.

Undoubtedly Balzac took such matters very seriously, and in 1832, he delved more deeply into them, in *Louis Lambert*. Early on in *Le Réquisitionnaire*, he says of Mme de Dey that "par un bonheur qui ne couronne pas les efforts de toutes les mères, elle était adorée de son fils, leurs âmes s'entendaient par de fraternelles sympathies" and he tries to explain the psychological conditions that would render possible the mother's death by telepathy. However, as with *El Verdugo*, that theme could hardly make for a satisfactory and dramatic *nouvelle*. And indeed, the interest of the story lies else-where. It is one of Balzac's cleverest short stories, depending for its effect on suspense and uncertainty. From the outset we are invited to share the concern of the worthies of Carentan, to whom Mme de Dey's behaviour is extremely mysterious. This lady, who has been taking great care not to offend the different factions in post-Revolu-tionary Normandy, has suddenly closed her salon. Why? And why might her act produce "de funestes résultats?" Balzac deliberately misleads us, suggests various false trails. She is obviously expecting a visitor whom she wants nobody to meet. Like the habitués of her salon, we speculate: is it her son who has fled the country? a Chouan leader? an aristocrat from Paris? a lover? In fact, it is her son, who has written to tell her that he is back in France, but in prison. "Ne doutant pas de ses moyens d'evasion" (another misleading hint), he intends to come to see her within the next three days. The tension mounts. The three days pass. "Encore quelques moments, et il sera là, pourtant! car il vit encore, j'en suis certaine. Mon cœur me le dit. N'entendez-vous rien, Brigitte? Oh! je donnerais le reste de ma vie pour savoir s'il est en prison ou s'il marche à travers la campagne!"

Balzac completes his exposition with a sentence of real virtuosity "Telle était la situation des choses et des esprits dans la maison de madame de Dey pendant que, sur le chemin de Paris à Cherbourg, un jeune homme vêtu d'une carmagnole brune,... se dirigeait vers Carentan." For a moment we imagine this is the son in disguise, though we soon realize it is in fact someone quite different: it is a 'réquisitionnaire', who is to be billeted at the *château*. Balzac nevertheless preserves the ambiguity. This 'réquisitionnaire' is in advance of his fellows, he has a noble appearance, the mayor is obviously sceptical. The boy arrives, and is shown by Brigitte into the room prepared for the son. "La comtesse... monta rapidement l'escalier, ayant à peine la force de se soutenir; puis, elle ouvrit la porte de sa chambre, *vit son fils*, se précipita dans ses bras, mourante: – Oh mon enfant, mon enfant! s'écria-t-elle en sanglotant et le couvrant de baisers empreints d'une sorte de frénésie. – Madame, dit l'inconnu." By saying "vit son fils" and not "crut voir son fils", Balzac maintains the ambiguous tone of the narration. The countess gives the soldier her son's room. The night is full of anxiety, hope gradually dies. And in the morning, Brigitte finds her mistress lifeless. Brigitte gives a straightforward explanation of her death "Elle aura probablement entendu ce réquisitionnaire qui achève de s'habiller et qui marche dans la chambre de monsieur Auguste en chantant leur damnée Marseillaise, comme s'il était dans une écurie. Ça l'aura tuée!" We would probably prefer to explain it in terms of intense disappointment and fear following an evening of violent emotions. But Balzac, in his last paragraph, already quoted, offers a third explanation: "La mort de la comtesse fut causée par un sentiment plus grave, et sans doute par quelque vision terrible, etc."

It would be impossible, it seems to me, to present the parapsychological case more tactfully. All three explanations of the countess's death are plausible, and beyond a suggestion in the last lines that superior minds will prefer the more unusual hypothesis, we are left to choose. And ambiguity – the possibility of more than one explanation – is a fundamental part of the texture of the entire story. To say that *Le Réquisitionnaire* is a study of telepathic sympathy between mother and son[1] is really a denial of what makes the story so powerful and so fascinating, and it renders a large part of it irrelevant. Yet, led by Balzac, that is the position even the most enlightened commentators adopt. In 1834 – after he had written *Louis Lambert*, and explored the phenomenon of second sight further – Balzac added an epigraph from that novel, explicitly drawing our attention to the theme of abolishing time and space by "un phénomène de vision". Beyond praising its "simplicity", Chasles did not mention *Le Réquisitionnaire*, but Davin says dogmatically that it illustrates the main thesis by showing "une mère tuée par la violence du sentiment maternel".

Two *contes* of 1831 were substantially modified and expanded in the Werdet edition, and it is striking that in both cases Davin's description fits the later version – proof that Davin's assertions tell us nothing about the original inspiration of the stories. One of these is *L'Enfant maudit*, which, like *El Verdugo* has a long pre-history which takes it out of the category of 'philosophical' story altogether. The other is *Le Chef d'œuvre inconnu*, written in August 1831.[2] By this time Balzac had almost certainly worked out his formula, and so we might expect a more blatantly 'demonstrative' *nouvelle*. The first thing that strikes us when we read the first version is that the central character is not Frenhofer, but Poussin, who is torn between the claims of his vocation and his love for Gillette. In the end, the claim of art is stronger, and the story ends with Gillette sobbing. If this illustrates any thesis, it is surely that 'thought' (here the artistic vocation) destroys love. But if Poussin once loses Gillette's love, it may be that his art will suffer. This is the significance of Frenhofer in the original scheme. Cut yourself off from life, and your art suffers. Art becomes a substitute for life, instead of a manifestation of life involving healthy conflict with other aspects, and

---

[1] H. J. H., I'm afraid (*Balzac's 'Comédie humaine'*, p. 36).
[2] For details of *L'Enfant maudit*, see the edition by F. Germain (Paris, 1965); for *Le Chef d'œuvre*, the study by P. Laubriet, *Un catéchisme esthétique, Le Chef d'œuvre inconnu de Balzac* (Paris, 1961).

E

the creator usurps the place of God, and is destroyed; the perfection
of Frenhofer's Catherine is entirely in his imagination, it is not
transposed on to the canvas at all. The connection of this with
Poussin's problem is underscored by the use of sexual imagery to
describe Frenhofer's love for his art: his devotion to painting has
canalized all his energies, including the sexual. Gillette's fears are
justified. Because of this interplay between the different themes of
the story, we do not have any sense that the story is crudely illustrating a thesis, though the basic scheme is a simple one.

When Davin came to put a label on *Le Chef d'œuvre inconnu* he
said it showed us "l'art tuant l'œuvre", a description which hardly
even applies to Frenhofer in the 1831 version, never mind to
Poussin. Probably Balzac had already ideas for amplifying the
character of Frenhofer. Since 1831, the theme of the madness which
can accompany creative gifts had been explored openly in *Louis
Lambert*, undoutedly a key stage in the emergence of an explicit
'philosophy'. Some months before Davin's Introduction (in which,
significantly, *Le Chef d'œuvre* is called a "première initiation à la
tragédie de Louis Lambert"), the idea of an excessive preoccupation
with art inhibiting the creative impulse is mentioned in *Séraphîta*,
as M. Laubriet has astutely observed. Already in the Gosselin
edition, Balzac had allowed Frenhofer a moment of lucidity, though,
like Goriot, he soon fell back into illusion. In 1837 this theme of
doubt is stressed. He doubts because he thinks too much, and because
he doubts, he cannot create. Now he cannot take refuge in illusion.
When he realizes that his visitors can find no masterpiece, and that
they, not he, are right, he locks away his painting, and "le lendemain, Porbus, inquiet, revint voir Frenhofer, et apprit qu'il était
mort dans la nuit, après avoir brûlé ses toiles". Frenhofer dies, like
Mme de Dey, because the source of his vitality has been taken from
him.

The new emphasis on Frenhofer and painting (there are many
added passages on the nature of imitation in art) quite changes the
design of the story, and paradoxically the effect is to make it appear
even less 'demonstrative' or schematic. We lose the sense of there
being a central figure, with two forces clamouring for his allegiance.
Now everything is a function of everything else; there are a series
of conflicts which together illuminate in considerable depth the

artist's dilemma, and from which there emerge suggestive parallels. Davin's formula is once again inadequate. One might formulate the difference by saying that whereas the 1831 version dealt with the artist's uncomfortable relation with life, as a man, the revised version treats primarily his problems as an artist.

I have argued that the orthodox interpretation of the *contes philosophiques* of 1831 was a case of being wise after the event, and that it would be a pity if the finest of these stories were for ever imprisoned in Davin's neat pigeon-holes. But what of the *études* written after Balzac had become conscious of the unifying formula? Here we can hardly deny that the formulas did suggest the matter of new stories to Balzac. A couple of years before Davin's Introduction, Balzac noted in his Album: "Dans *El Verdugo* un fils tue son père pour une idée, et dans *le Roi*, le père tuant son fils."[1] By 1834 *Le Roi* (which may be linked with an episode recounted in the *Mémoires de Sanson*) had been replaced by *Un Drame au bord de la mer*. In the appointed sequence, after three stories of 1831 (*Le Réquisitionnaire*, *El Verdugo*, and *L'Elixir de longue vie*, in which says Davin, "l'idée Hérédite devient meurtrière à son tour"), *Un Drame au bord de la mer* shows how "la paternité, à son tour, est devenue tueuse". That description clearly applies to the basic layer of the story, the killing of the criminal youth by his outraged father (although the idea which prompts the killing is honour rather than paternity). But the completed work is much more complex, filtered through two narrators: a fisherman who, in contrast to the boy of the 'drama', is a model son, and Louis Lambert himself who passes the story on to his uncle, and whose reaction shows another aspect of the paralysing power of ideas. Davin's formula may have been the starting point, but it does not adequately define the work which finds it organizational centre in a highly complex experience probably not fully grasped by the writer before he set to work.

The same point could be made of those curious twins of 1837, *Gambara* and *Massimilla Doni*, ostensibly variations of the so-called theme of *Le Chef d'œuvre* that "l'art tue l'œuvre". Once again all kinds of cross-currents and parallels come into play, which make the

---

[1] A. 182, f. 13, *ed. cit.*, p. 672. Cf. *Mémoires de Sanson*, *O.D.*, t. I, pp. 309–14; on *Un Drame*, see M. Le Yaouanc, 'Introduction a *Un Drame au bord de la mer*', *Année balz.* (1966), 127–56.

'meaning' far too involved to be enshrined in a simple phrase. And that, probably, is the lesson to be drawn from this examination of just a few of Balzac's *contes philosophiques*. Simple statements of the significance of even the simplest works can rarely be trusted, because even where historical research permits us to say that the statements do correspond to the first idea in the author's mind – and this is by no means always the case – they cannot do justice to the complex aesthetic experience we have when we read the work, and it is only through our aesthetic experience that we can arrive at some real understanding of the vision the author wishes to communicate.

Point of view in Balzac's short stories

PETER W. LOCK

In the preface to the first edition of *Le Lys dans la vallée* Balzac referred briefly to the problem of narrative perspective during a discussion of the distinction to be made between first person narrator and the person of the author:

> Dans plusieurs fragments de son œuvre, l'auteur a produit un personnage qui raconte en son nom. Pour arriver au vrai, les écrivains emploient celui des artifices littéraires qui leur semble propre à prêter le plus de vie à leurs figures. Ainsi, le désir d'animer leurs créations a jeté les hommes les plus illustres du siècle dernier dans la prolixité du roman par lettres, seul système qui puisse rendre vraisemblable une histoire fictive. Le *je* sonde le cœur humain aussi profondément que le style épistolaire et n'en a pas les longueurs. A chaque œuvre sa forme. (XI, 276.)

Balzac's purpose in this preface was to deny that the novel in question was directly autobiographical, and to warn his readers against attributing to the author direct complicity in the emotions expressed by the narrator. The choice of point of view, he maintained, depended not upon the author's personal feelings and attitudes but rather upon the exigencies of the work of art itself. Such pronouncements are comparatively rare in Balzac's writings since in common with his contemporaries he devoted little time to theoretical discussions of the problems connected with the writing of fiction. He insisted, notably in his article on *La Chartreuse de Parme*, that the novel should obey certain principles and contain unity of composition, but he seldom entered into a detailed examination of the technical aspects of his craft. And his fictions themselves, viewed as a whole, often seem to contain little experimentation or scope for examination of narrative technique; the overall structures are so visible, the rhythms so predictable and the rhetoric so insistent that the works seem to be immediately accessible in their massively simple outlines, and to invite discussion on thematic rather than technical grounds.

A similarly broad view usually obtains with respect to the role of the narrator in the *Comédie humaine*. Balzac himself was ready to grant the story-teller unlimited powers: "Le narrateur est tout. Il est historien; il a son théâtre; sa dialectique profonde qui meut ses personnages; sa palette de peintre et sa loupe d'observateur" (XI, 180). And in many of his most famous works Balzac stands resolutely between reader and fictional world, occupying a position of limitless privilege, controlling the lives of his characters, commenting on their conduct, summarizing their past and predicting their future. Particular actions and emotions are raised to the level of universal experience or else deduced from 'laws' which the narrator posits as having general application. Apophthegms, maxims and epigrams confer a dogmatic tone on a narrative commentary which apparently leaves little to the reader's imagination. The narrator's words, like those of "L'illustre" Gaudissart, contain "à la fois du vitriol et de la glu" (IV, 14), and his voice is loud and assertive, garrulous and discursive. The reader is frequently addressed directly and urged to join the narrator in his assessment of character and to share in his triumphant demonstrations, discoveries, and dénouements.

It is also often maintained that Balzac's omniscience and his evident involvement in his fictional world are accompanied by uncritical admiration for the success of his characters in a world whose degraded values they share. Lucien Goldmann, for example, defining the nineteenth-century novel as essentially "critique et oppositionnelle" and as representing specifically "une forme de résistance à la société bourgeoise en train de se développer" considers that Balzac's work may well constitute an exception to this general tendency:

Mais le problème se pose de savoir si, parallèlement à cette forme littéraire, ne se sont pas développées d'autres formes qui correspondraient aux valeurs conscientes et aux aspirations effectives de la bourgeoisie; et, sur ce point, nous nous permettons de mentionner, à titre de suggestion tout à fait générale et hypothétique, l'eventualité que l'œuvre de Balzac... constitue la seule grande expression littéraire de l'univers structuré par les valeurs conscientes de la bourgeoisie: individualisme, soif de puissance, argent, érotisme qui triomphent des anciennes valeurs féodales de l'altruisme, de la charité et de l'amour.[1]

And André Wurmser, whose *La Comédie inhumaine* is a lengthy, stimulating, vehemently critical assessment of Balzac's world in terms of the values it embodies, consistently emphasizes the ignoble drive for wealth, position and power which not only possesses the majority of the characters in the *Comédie humaine* but also receives the approbation of their creator. Balzac himself, as man and as artist, represents the epitome of the ambitious, ruthless *arriviste*, and his views and comments reveal unwavering admiration for the successful members of the bourgeoisie whose existence was governed by a single categorical imperative: 'enrichissez-vous'.[2]

A very different stance is adopted by Per Nykrog in his rigorous reconstruction of the unity of Balzac's system of thought.[3] Working from the rarefied atmosphere of the *Études analytiques* and the *Études philosophiques*, thence descending into the arena of the *Études de mœurs*, Nykrog examines the *Comédie humaine* as a vast interplay of dynamic forces with cosmic as well as social significance. For Nykrog, Balzac approaches his highly individualized society with a set of laboriously established abstract conceptions whose general application is tested out in recurring situations, each one of which may reveal a different face of the same truth and indirectly point to a fundamental unity discovered beyond apparent diversity. Nykrog calls Balzac's approach an experimental approach which "se révèle comme extrêmement fécond pour la reproduction littéraire des phenomènes de la vie, puisqu'il permet, et même suggère, de construire des jeux d'ensemble, où des univers différents et des attitudes différentes sont confrontés, opposés, sans que le romancier n'ait à se prononcer en faveur de l'une ou de l'autre des attitudes fondamentales mais contradictoires".[4]

Among the most experimental of Balzac's works are his *contes* and *nouvelles*. It should be remembered that after publishing *Les*

[1] Lucien Goldmann, 'Introduction aux problèmes d'une sociologie du roman', in *Revue de l'Institut de Sociologie* (1963), p. 240.
[2] André Wurmser, *La Comédie inhumaine* (Paris, 1964).
[3] Per Nykrog, *La Pensée de Balzac* (Copenhagen, 1965).
[4] *ibid.*, p. 321.

Chouans in 1829, Balzac immediately turned to short fiction and produced the *Scènes de la vie privée* (1830) and the group of philosophical stories which were published just after *La Peau de chagrin* under the heading of *Romans et contes philosophiques* in 1831. In retrospect these series can be seen as laying the groundwork for two of the three major divisions of the *Comédie humaine* (the third division, *Les Études analytiques*, had already been prepared with the publication of the anecdotal *Physiologie du mariage* in 1829). The six *Scènes de la vie privée* demonstrate a new concern with the dramatic representation of everyday reality and reveal considerable diversity in narrative technique – from the basically 'scenic' presentation of *La Vendetta* and *La Paix du ménage* to the 'pictorial' handling of *La Maison du chat-qui-pelote* and *Une Double Famille*. Balzac continued to experiment with short fiction until the end of his life, and although his greatest output was from 1830 to 1832 and coincided with the vogue of the short story in France, he nonetheless produced some 20 of his 50[1] short works between 1832 and 1845, among them such divergent masterpieces as *Melmoth réconcilié* (1835), *Les Secrets de la Princesse de Cadignan* (1839) and *Honorine* (1843).

A study of point of view in these 50 short works permits an assessment of the function of the narrator in the *Comédie humaine*, and leads to important conclusions concerning Balzac's attitude towards his characters and their values. In only 29 of the stories is a conventional third-person narrator used throughout; in five other works the third-person narrator predominates, but information, evaluation and judgment are yielded by means of such devices as letters (*La Femme abandonnée*) or summary by a character (as, for example, in *Les Marana*). In four other stories the function of the third-person narrator is reduced to providing situation or setting; the main events are related by a character who has been present as observer or as active participant (Nathan in *Un Prince de la Bohème*, Derville in *Gobseck*, Desplein in *La Messe de l'athée*, the Consul-

---

[1] In his introduction to a collection of Balzac's short stories published by Oxford University Press (1964), A. W. Raitt lists 49 short stories in the *Comédie humaine*, wisely pointing out that this list is bound to be arbitrary "inasmuch as there can be no hard and fast dividing-line between a short story and a short novel" (p. 19). For reasons of convenience I accept Dr Raitt's list, adding only *L'Église*, even though it was finally published by Balzac as part of *Jésus-Christ en Flandres*.

Général in *Honorine*). These last four works thus become basically first-person narratives and could be included with the 12 works in which some variation of the first-person narrator is adopted at the outset. In this latter group there are also important distinctions to be made however; in six of the stories the 'je' narrator (who may be unidentified as, for example, in *Les Deux Rêves* or named as in *La Grande Bretèche*) recounts a story which he has learned about either from another character (*Un Drame au bord de la mer, Une Passion dans le désert*) or from an unidentified source (*Sarrasine*) or even by eavesdropping (*La Maison Nucingen*). The six remaining stories contain first-person narrators who have in some way been active in the events they relate, either from the beginning (Bianchon in *Étude de femme*; the unidentified narrator in *L'Église* and in *Le Message*), or as the action progresses (*L'Auberge rouge, Facino Cane* and *Z. Marcas*).

These groupings, though they demonstrate the diversity of approaches adopted, do not in themselves indicate the extent or the nature of the narrator's participation in the action; nor do they determine his relationship with the other characters or with the author. In *Facino Cane*, for example, the unidentified narrator is endowed with powers of divination and comprehension which lead to a peculiar kind of passionate involvement in events which are merely recounted to him; whereas Bianchon in *Étude de femme* adopts an air of humorous detachment in relating a story in which he played the leading role. And at any time a first-person narrator may be far more passive and objective than the third-person narrator so frequently employed in the *Comédie humaine* to provide commentary, assessment and judgment.[1]

Important distinctions must be made with respect to the extent of the involvement of the narrator (be he first-person or third-person) and the nature of his attitude towards events and persons. *La Paix du ménage* may be taken as an example of a work in which the narrator's role is primarily that of spectator. The story, which is told in the third person, opens with a brief preparatory summary

---

[1] As Wayne Booth has written: "To say that a story is told in the first or the third person will tell us nothing of importance unless we become more precise and describe how the particular qualities of the narrators relate to specific effects" – *The Rhetoric of Fiction* (Chicago, 1961), p. 150.

followed by a scene and a succinct recapitulation, after which the narrator adopts the position of a neutral observer and contents himself with recording conversation, actions and gestures which reveal the personalities and motives of the characters. The scene is a society ball; the plot concerns the successful attempt of Madame de Soulanges to recover from an admirer her diamond ring which her husband had given to his mistress. The characters are engaged throughout in a battle of wits and a game of concealment and decipherment. Only rarely is the reader given an 'inside view'; for the most part he, like the narrator and the other characters, is forced to interpret words, glances and gestures in an attempt to assess the situation and to predict the outcome of the tragi-comedy. A similarly discreet stance is adopted by the narrator in such works as *El Verdugo*, *Adieu*, *Les Comédiens sans le savoir* and *Un Homme d'affaires*; authorial commentary is rare, direct judgment withheld, and the stories seem to come unmediated to the reader.

The last two works contain groups of Balzac's reappearing characters whose personalities are perhaps so well known that they do not need presentation or evaluation. In other works the reappearing characters may function as narrators or as narrator-agents. Their presence adds authenticity and colour to the particular story, permits Balzac to withdraw from a position of direct responsibility, and confers the fiction of autonomy upon the created world. In *Autre Étude de femme* Balzac throws together a couple of dozen of his best-known characters, four of whom – de Marsay, Blondet, Montriveau and Bianchon – recount anecdotes or relate events from their own past, while the other characters provide comments and reactions as they listen to the four narrators. *Un Prince de la Bohème* adds a dimension to this device; as a result of listening to Nathan's account of the rakish adventures of La Palférine, one of the characters, the marquise de Rochefide, falls in love with La Palférine and her passion affects the outcome of the third part of *Béatrix*. As Claude-Edmonde Magny has pointed out, these examples reveal and affect "l'architecture cachée de l'édifice balzacien".[1] They also show the extent to which Balzac's characters can 'take over' from their creator and achieve a seeming independence of action and existence. It is as if,

---

[1] Mme Magny refers in passing to these examples in her chapter on Gide in *Histoire du roman français depuis 1918* (Paris, 1950), vol. I, p. 272.

having set the complex world of *La Comédie humaine* in motion and having created his enormous cast of reappearing characters, Balzac can afford to retire from the scene and, like some inscrutable divinity, watch and listen to his characters reminiscing about themselves and gossiping about one another.

By means of these narrative devices Balzac deliberately adopts a stance of apparent neutrality, and renounces his powers of intervention, overt manipulation and direct judgment. A *nouvelle* like *La Maison du chat-qui-pelote*, usually considered a typical Balzacian work, contains a more conventional use of the narrator who is present throughout as observer, commentator and judge. In his analysis of this work in his *Short Fiction in France*, Albert J. George provides a strong sense of the fundamental and apparently rather facile oppositions which Balzac established between the world of the draper Guillaume and that higher sphere to which Guillaume's daughter Augustine ascends as the result of her marriage to the painter de Sommervieux.[1] The basic plot is simple: because of her anachronistic upbringing in the stagnant sub-world of "la maison Guillaume", Augustine is unable to adapt herself to her new surroundings, and, after a brief period of felicity, she is destroyed by the effects of her husband's character and mode of existence; in the final words of the story which take up and weld together a whole series of familiar Balzacian metaphors used throughout: "Les humbles et modestes fleurs, écloses dans les vallées, meurent... quand elles sont transplantées trop près des cieux, aux régions où se forment les orages, où le soleil est brûlant" (I, 71). This figurative language suggests a thematic preoccupation running deeper than the concern with 'mésalliance' which Balzac, cashing in on his recently established reputation as a diabolically inspired marriage counsellor, appeared anxious to set up at the centre of the work.[2]

In mapping out the antipodes of the story Balzac makes it plain that the basic opposition is between the physical prison of the maison Guillaume and the liberating, heady world of Théodore. The house itself is closed, anachronistic, monastic, tyrannical; barred and shuttered, antediluvian, empty, it is governed by Guillaume's

[1] Albert J. George, *Short Fiction in France 1800–1850* (Syracuse, 1964), pp. 81–3.
[2] In the preface to the first edition of the 1830 *Scènes de la vie privée*, Balzac stressed the social value of his studies of marriage in the six stories (XI, 163).

"principes inexorables", and "pensée symétrique". The "hiero-glyphics" on its walls, the dress of its inhabitants, their physiogno-mies, their language, their gestures, all are signs conspiring, with typically Balzacian fervour, to point inwards to the void which threatens Augustine. Yet a second series of motifs, presented from a different, more sympathetic perspective – less evident and slower to emerge – suggests in M. Guillaume not only a tenacious will to endurance, but also a prudent solicitude for his employees, probity, even "bonté naturelle" (p. 41). There is a third view, also, provided, indirectly by Théodore, a sensuous view compounded of the amorous and the æsthetic, which travelling the façade of the house and glimp-sing the interior, sets up painterly "oppositions", creates almost supernatural illuminations, sees in Augustine "un ange exilé du ciel" (p. 31) and in general transposes the observed reality into a work of art, later to result in the two pictures which Théodore exhibits at the *Salon*. These divergent optics prepare for later misunderstandings of value and evaluation. A further set of uncer-tainties, now concerning the lovers uniquely, is opened up by the images of light and fire used in the portrait of Théodore – "grâce lumineuse," "feu sombre" (p. 20) – and the depiction of the dual nature of the effect of passion on Augustine: "un rayon de soleil était tombé dans cette prison" (p. 35), "cette pantomime [Théodore's amorous signals] jeta comme un brasier dans le corps de la pauvre fille qui se trouva criminelle, en se figurant qu'il venait de se con-clure un pacte entre elle et l'artiste" (p. 33); both these sets of images lead towards the final words of the text already quoted, in which the image of the sun is represented as a force of vivification and of destruction.

Taken together, all these views and images indirectly suggest value, outcome and judgment. Théodore's assessment of Augustine is revealed as superficial; inevitably she disappoints him, and he is in part guilty of her destruction. Augustine lacks the strength to survive the move from the centripetal world of her family to the centrifugal sphere of the prodigal artist; yet her predicament is real and wins sympathy from the author's delegate, an unknown admirer who, appearing in the last lines of the story, obliquely draws atten-tion to Augustine's innocence and her weakness, both of which are present in her character and are to some extent determined by her milieu. The story ends with Augustine's death, yet there is promise of continuation. Joseph Lebas, Guillaume's chief clerk, endures by means of the double mechanism of renunciation and transformation, operations which consistently favour the prudent throughout the *Comédie humaine*. Rejected by Augustine, urged to fall in with the "pensée symétrique" of M. Guillaume, Lebas marries Augustine's tranquil sister Virginie and undertakes to preserve, with some modification, the structure which he has inherited. Unlike the older Guillaumes who are forced upon their retirement to change their milieu, and find themselves "échoués sur un rocher d'or" (p. 58), Lebas and Virginie "[marchent] avec leur siècle" (p. 56), and discover a happiness which, while lacking the intensity of Augustine's two years of passionate felicity, has the virtue of endurance, and hence merits approbation.

Thus the narrator, by means of multiple perspectives and direct and oblique commentary, distributes sympathy and judgment more or less impartially. The basic oppositions within the story and the narrator's more emphatic statements might lead the reader to the view that Balzac's preferences are clear, his sympathy restricted and his condemnation irrevocable. But initial impressions are modified as the characters become more fully known through being seen in changing situations and from different angles. The modes of existence represented are all granted a certain validity and are endowed with a reality which emerges even when a particular character seems close to a stereotype. As Georges Blin has written: "Balzac sait bien que chacun de ses personnages a raison. Chacun sa vérité. Tout notre auteur est dans ce refus de choisir qui rend au vrai son épaisseur obscure."[1] In *La Maison du chat-qui-pelote*, as in many other works, Balzac's impartiality is not that of the mere observer, but rather that which comes from a deepening of perception and from a progressive revelation of value through knowledge of the characters' lives. It is in this context that it is appropriate to use the term realism to define not the faithfulness with which Balzac reproduces the exterior world but the fidelity with which he expresses the discovered reality of his characters.

---

[1] see Georges Blin, 'Chacun sa vérité. A propos de Balzac et de ses personnages', in *Revue Hebdomadaire*, II (1938), 99.

The narrator as detached observer, and the narrator as active
though impartial commentator give way, on occasion, to the narrator
as impassioned participant in the fictional world. For a discussion
of this third position it is convenient to examine *Facino Cane*, a
work in which the powers and actions of the first-person narrator
indirectly raise once again the whole problem of the relationship
between author, narrator and fictional world. Even though there is
no reason to read the story as autobiography as far as the events are
concerned, it is generally accepted that the extraordinary powers
claimed by the 'je' narrator in the prologue to the story are those
with which Balzac felt himself to be endowed:

> Chez moi l'observation était déjà devenue intuitive, elle pénétrait
> l'âme sans négliger le corps; ou plutôt elle saisissait si bien les
> détails extérieurs, qu'elle allait sur-le-champ au-delà; elle me
> donnait la faculté de vivre de la vie de l'individu sur laquelle elle
> s'exerçait, en me permettant de me substituer à lui comme le
> derviche des *Mille et une Nuits* prenait le corps et l'âme des
> personnes sur lesquelles il prononçait certaines paroles. (VI, 66.)

The remainder of the story is concerned with the reported quest of
the musician Facino Cane for unlimited quantities of money which
he knows to exist in Venice, and with his attempts to persuade the
narrator to accompany him. The blind, formerly incarcerated
Facino Cane, perpetual prisoner of his passion for gold, exerts a
fearful tyranny over the youthful narrator who, having *become*
Facino Cane ("mon âme passa dans [son] corps") (p. 69), imaginatively participates in the old man's recounted adventures and
finally cries out his eager assent to a proposal to renew the search,
the account of which had taken on in his imagination "les proportions d'un poème" (p. 77). Thus the narrator succumbs to that
"folie" which (in the dramatized prologue to the story) he has sensed
as a possible result of the practice of his extraordinary powers (p. 67).
Yet finally he resists his impulsiveness, and although his change of
heart is not explicitly motivated, its origins can be discovered in the
penultimate scene of the story during which, deeply moved, he
has witnessed a momentary change in Facino Cane himself. At the
conclusion of his passionate story, the old man plays a mournful
tune during which the narrator senses in Cane a momentary return

to a state of joyous innocence. The telling of the tale has led the old man to a glimpse of earlier felicity; the playing of the tune (during which Cane rediscovers his former talent as muscian) then causes him to relive for a moment his love affair with Bianca. Like Goriot who, dying, momentarily recaptures the innocent love of his daughters in the "paradis de la rue de la Jussienne" and lucidly assesses the stages of his fall to present degradation, so Facino Cane achieves a brief moment of joy and repose, which the narrator is privileged to glimpse. But, as in the case of Goriot, lucidity is followed by a final return to blindness: "Mais l'or reprit bientôt le dessus, et la fatale passion éteignit cette lueur de jeunesse" (p. 78). Facino Cane, yet another of Balzac's inspired somnambulists, describes himself in his final state as "éveillé comme en rêve" (p. 78). In doing so, he transposes the words of the narrator who at the beginning of the story has described the images generated by his extraordinary powers of sympathy as composing "le rêve d'un homme éveillé" (p. 67). The phrase is an admirable one to describe the whole of the *Comédie humaine* itself, evoking, as it does, its extraordinary mixture of hallucination and clairvoyance, wish-fulfilment and critical detachment, and suggesting, at the same time, the complexity of viewpoint which confronts the reader of Balzac's fiction.

In *Facino Cane* the central character finally re-enters the degraded realism of illusion and destructive desire ("Je suis robuste, et l'on est jeune quand on voit de l'or devant soi") (p. 78); the narrator, however, though close to the abyss, obliquely refuses his assent to join the old man in his search, and lives to tell the tale. His admiration for the single-mindedness of Cane's passion involved him so deeply in the old man's obsessive dream that his critical faculties were temporarily paralysed: as so often in the *Comédie humaine*, the "derviche" vanquishes the observer. This substitution represents Balzac's romantic immersion in the lives of certain of his characters, particularly those whose search is passionate and who create within and beyond the self a dynamic momentum. A list drawn from the whole of the *Comédie humaine* would include the sensual heroines – Louise de Chaulieu, Véronique Graslin, Marie de Verneuil; the titanic artists and thinkers – Frenhofer, Claës, Lambert; the amoral men of action – Vautrin, Nucingen, De Marsay. These characters,

apprehended from within and on their own terms, are admired for
the form of their endeavour and the momentum of their lives. They
assume perilous destinies which, while they may be open to criticism
on ethical grounds, are nonetheless exemplary of man's freedom to
create new modes of action and patterns of being. Those who aspire
to higher states of existence – social, intellectual, spiritual – demonstrate at least man's potential to be other than a mere creature of
habit, milieu and circumstance.

Undoubtedly Balzac is hypnotized by the momentum and 'poetry'
of his most forceful and absorbing characters to such an extent that
he appears incapable of judging them impartially. And yet there
are throughout his work recurring moments when the narrator, as
at the end of *Facino Cane*, disengages himself from even the most
passionate, wilful and anarchical destinies, and creates an interlude
of contemplative detachment. Such moments of transcendence occur
either at a time of movement from life to death (Goriot, Véronique
Graslin, Pons)[1] or at a crucial transitional stage from one mode of
existence to another. They may be experienced directly by the
character, or expressed in hypothetical terms by the detached
narrator. An example of the latter occurs in *Le Père Goriot* at the
moment when Rastignac is about to isolate himself from his past
idealism and fall in with the amorality of Parisian society. The
narrator, heretofore almost unfailingly sympathetic toward his hero
and closely involved in his actions, draws back and comments:

Rastignac, semblable à la plupart des jeunes gens, qui, par avance,
ont goûté les grandeurs, voulait se présenter tout armé dans la
lice du monde; il en avait épousé la fièvre, et sentait peut-être la
force de le dominer, mais sans connaître ni les moyens ni le but
de cette ambition. A défaut d'un amour pur et sacré, qui remplit
la vie, cette soif du pouvoir peut devenir une belle chose; il suffit
de dépouiller tout intérêt personnel et de se proposer la grandeur
d'un pays pour objet. (II, 1032.)

[1] In his *Mensonge romantique et vérité romanesque* (Paris, 1961), René Girard, though
he does not deal in detail with Balzac's work, quotes the passage from *Le Cousin
Pons* which describes the agony of the dying Pons (pp. 304–5). Girard draws
attention to Balzac's comparison of Pons' state of mind to that of a "joyeux
artiste" reconciled with the world, and argues that "la conclusion du *Cousin
Pons* est un *Temps retrouvé*" (p. 305).

In making this analysis the narrator might seem, perhaps, to be playing with mere abstract notions if the reader were not aware of other figures in the *Comédie humaine* in whom these qualities are fully realized – d'Arthez, Michel Chrestien, Joseph Bridau, Bénassis, Bianchon. Such characters are as rare, no doubt, as the moments which call them to mind, but they do exist as a perpetual indication of the heights of Balzac's world. And the Protean narrator, as he regains his position of commentator and judge, demonstrates his awareness of these heights, and opens up a perspective which leads to the difficult discovery of value.

F

Le Rouge et le blanc:
notes sur *le Lys dans la vallée*

JEAN GAUDON

Immédiatement après la lettre-prétexte de Félix de Vandenesse à Natalie de Manerville, *le Lys dans la vallée* comporte une sorte de prélude décrivant en une quinzaine de pages l'enfance du héros jusqu'à sa rencontre avec Madame de Mortsauf, le jour du bal donné en l'honneur du duc d'Angoulême, de passage à Tours. On y retrouve un certain nombre des traits qui caractérisent l'éducation du narrateur dans *Louis Lambert*, et, du même coup, quelques-uns des souvenirs les plus amers du romancier lui-même.[1] L'intérêt psychologique de ces notations à la première personne est évident: cette préhistoire du roman, décrite *a posteriori* par Félix lui-même, se veut justification. Elle contribue à introduire dans une histoire apparemment gratuite des relations de causalité; plaidoyer, elle est aussi une analyse.

Malheureusement, pour beaucoup de lecteurs, cet intérêt est quelque peu gâté par le ton excessivement lyrique, par un véritable hérissement de figures de style qui accaparent toute notre attention et distraient inutilement de l'analyse. On cite une ou deux phrases turgescentes. Balzac écrit si mal... Eternel malentendu auquel ont achoppé bien des spécialistes de Balzac, et des plus éminents.

Le Lys dans la vallée est certainement un des romans les plus construits de Balzac, un de ceux dans lesquels chaque détail est écho ou préfiguration, figure d'un ensemble poétiquement cohérent. Le prélude n'échappe pas à la règle. C'est là que les fils se nouent, que se forment les grands thèmes, qu'apparaissent les motifs qui vont orienter notre lecture. Rien qui ne soit, finalement, totalement déchiffrable.

La première anecdote rapportée par Félix concerne son amour

---

[1] Sur ce point l'édition de Moïse Le Yaouanc (Paris, 1966) est particulièrement précieuse.

précoce de la solitude, au sein d'un jardin. Sa jouissance, toute passive, reste élémentaire et consiste simplement à "jouer avec des cailloux à observer des insectes, à regarder le bleu du firmament" (VIII, 772). Cette vague prédilection va pourtant se métamorphoser en un goût des "contemplations" (p. 772) qui se fixera sur une étoile. Un jour où, "tranquillement blotti sous un figuier" (p. 772), il se livre à sa "passion", survient le premier conflict avec la mère. Accusé à tort d'une faute qu'il n'a pas commise, Félix est arraché à sa rêverie et "persiflé sur [s]on amour pour les étoiles" (p. 773). Une phrase de la mère terrible donne la mesure de l'incompréhension dont souffre l'enfant: "Connaît-on l'astronomie à votre âge?" Mais ni la moquerie ni les sévices ne viennent à bout de l'amour. Le martyre même renforce l'emprise de la passion et l'enfant passe de la contemplation à un monologue qui marque la naissance d'une nouvelle parole: "J'eus donc souvent le fouet pour mon étoile. Ne pouvant me confier à personne, je lui disais mes chagrins dans ce délicieux ramage intérieur par lequel un enfant bégaie ses premières idées comme naguère il a bégayé ses premières paroles" (p. 773). Le sens profond de ce passage apparaîtra quelques pages plus loin, au moment où Félix, qui a maintenant plus de vingt ans, vient d'obéir à un mouvement de passion en se jetant sur les épaules d'une femme inconnue. Ce geste totalement irrationnel, qu'il décrit lui-même comme une "métamorphose", entraîne la réapparition de l'imagerie sidérale et enracine le premier élan charnel dans le tuf des rêves d'enfance: "Tombée des steppes bleues où je l'admirais, ma chère étoile s'était donc faite femme en conservant sa clarté, ses scintillements et sa fraîcheur" (p. 786). Tout naturellement l'adolescent retrouve l'attitude de l'enfant contemplateur et va "[s]accroupir dans un coin du jardin pour y rêver au baiser qu'[il] avai[t] volé" (p. 786).

Le femme-étoile est aussi fleur. Fleur sidérale, grâce à l'image des "steppes bleues" qui préfigure une des plus belles strophes de *Booz endormi*, mais aussi fleur terrestre, lys. Dans le beau développement au cours duquel se trouve expliqué le titre du roman, c'est naturellement cet aspect qui passe au premier plan. Sans perdre ses connotations célestes, l'étoile devient fleur dans la vallée de l'Indre devenue, tout entière, jardin: "quand je m'assis sous mon noyer, le soleil de midi faisait pétiller les ardoises de son toit et les vitres de ses fenêtres. Sa robe de percale produisait le point blanc que je remarquai dans ses vignes sous un hallebergier. Elle était, comme vous le savez déjà, sans rien savoir encore, LE LYS DE CETTE VALLÉE où elle croissait pour le ciel, en la remplissant du parfum de ses vertus" (p. 788). A partir de là, le schéma de la rêverie amoureuse se superposera sans difficulté à celui de la rêverie enfantine, enrichie simplement d'une profusion d'images florales. Deux scènes, parfaites, en reprendront le rituel. La première, le soir du jour où ayant reconnu dans la châtelaine de Clochegourde la belle inconnue du bal, Félix reste longtemps assis sous la fenêtre de Madame de Mortsauf "où brillait une lumière" (p. 814), et se voue au culte de "cette fleur sidérale" (p. 814). La seconde, quelques jours plus tard, après le premier entretien amoureux qui suit la partie de tric-trac. Ici, le regard passe successivement de la "robe blanche éclairée par la lune" à la lumière de la chambre puis à "l'azur ensemencé d'étoiles" (p. 839), en un mouvement audacieux qui met "Henriette" hors de portée.

La trajectoire des images suit en effet de très près les figures qu'impose aux protagonistes le mouvement romanesque. Dans la rêverie de l'adolescent frénétique, en proie à "la grande fièvre du cœur" (p. 786), l'incarnation de l'étoile en femme était une chute. L'étoile était, on s'en souvient, "tombée des steppes bleues". Dans la perspective choisie par Balzac, il importait de l'y faire remonter, pour que Madame de Mortsauf ne soit plus, selon sa propre expression, "qu'une lueur élevée, scintillante et froide, mais inaltérable" (p. 973).

Le symbolisme utilisé par Balzac est aisément déchiffrable, mais il serait un peu puéril de reprocher au romancier un excès de système qui n'a visiblement pas suffi à empêcher certains lecteurs de déraisonner. L'étoile, quand bien même Madame de Mortsauf ne le rappellerait pas, est, de sa nature, froide et inaccessible. Quant au lys, il est, de tradition, un des accessoires privilégiés de la virginité, la fleur qui, dans la main de l'ange de l'Annonciation, affirme sans équivoque la virginité de Marie. Vierge pour son mari – on se demanderait si Jacques et Madeleine ne sont pas nés par parthéno-génèse s'ils n'avaient pas visiblement hérité de la syphilis de leur père – Madame de Mortsauf est vierge pour Félix. Cette robe blanche qu'elle met à l'intention de l'adolescent, pour être davantage

semblable à un lys,[1] est le signe d'une interdiction. Balzac tient
même tellement à ce thème qu'il substitute un instant au symbolisme
du lys une figure plus parlante encore. Lorsque Madame de
Mortsauf apparaît pour la première fois à Félix, telle la vierge dans
le jardin clos des enluminures, l'image qui la désigne est celle du
convolvulus: "Sans savoir pourquoi, mes yeux revenaient au point
blanc, à la femme qui brillait dans ce vaste jardin comme au milieu
des buissons verts éclatait la clochette d'un convolvulus, flétrie si
l'on y touche" (p. 789). Mais le lys des Annonciations a un autre
message à transmettre. En tant que symbole de la vierge-mère, il
résume toute la relation entre Félix et Madame de Mortsauf.

C'est parce qu'elle devient la mère de Félix, parce qu'elle fait
peser sur leur relation l'interdit de l'inceste que Madame de Mortsauf justifie, au niveau psychologique le plus profond, sa chasteté.
Félix, que la nature "avait fait aimant" (p. 772) a été dans son
enfance totalement privé d'amour maternel. Ses rapports avec sa
mère selon la chair sont ceux de "l'oiseau devant le serpent" (p. 780).
Aucune tendresse, aucun abandon, mais un mélange de négligences
et d'interdictions, qui se résume assez bien dans la défense faite à
l'enfant de rester au jardin le soir. Face à cette créature dure et
railleuse, Madame de Mortsauf apparaît comme la mère idéale, celle
qui non seulement ne s'oppose pas aux rêveries sidérales de Félix
mais qui va jusqu'à les incarner. Il n'est pas jusqu'à la différence
d'âge qui ne favorise l'identification. Cent fois au cours du roman,
ce rapport de mère à fils sera souligné, généralement par Madame
de Mortsauf elle-même. Elle enveloppe Félix "dans les nourricières
protections, dans les blanches draperies d'un amour tout maternel"
(p. 850), elle a pour lui "un peu de coquetterie", comme on en a
"pour le dernier enfant" (p. 859). Elle va jusqu'à envisager l'union
de sa fille, Madeleine, et de Félix, seul acte qui donnerait à la fiction
une réalité sociale.

Un tel jeu n'est pas dépourvu d'équivoque. Lors de la scène des
vendanges, lorsque Félix appelle Madame de Mortsauf 'maman', il
reçoit en échange de cette demi-plaisanterie "cette caresse de la
voix, le *tu* des amants" (p. 862). Bien que la comtesse conçoive son

---

[1] voir p. 972: "Pourquoi donc aimai-je à mettre une robe blanche? ainsi je me
croyais mieux votre lys; ne m'aviez-vous pas aperçue, pour la première fois, ici,
en robe blanche?"

rôle tout autrement que Madame de Warens, rien ne peut empêcher Félix de voir en elle "une mère secrètement désirée" (p. 914). Ce parti pris de chasteté fondé sur des interdits religieux et sociaux se trouve ainsi aiguisé et pour ainsi dire irrité par cette fiction utilisée par Madame de Mortsauf pour tromper le désir.

On pourrait s'étonner que Félix ne se cabre pas davantage devant un pacte qui comporte pour lui, en apparence, plus de frustrations que de bonheur. Ce serait faire trop bon marché, il me semble, de ce que la mère idéale apporte à Félix, ce pouvoir de vivre à retardement, à l'âge adulte, l'enfance heureuse dont il a été privé. Madame de Mortsauf donne en effet à Félix tout autre chose que l'amour éthéré, empreint de religiosité, qu'elle croit lui apporter. Elle lui rend la nature dont il a été sevré, et lui permet de s'épanouir au sein du grand jardin dont elle est l'âme, de la vallée dont elle est le lys. En cela aussi, elle est la mère, prenant le relais de l'autre, la mère naturelle. Cette opposition entre les deux mères s'exprime également par une opposition du clos et de l'ouvert qui contribue à renforcer le rôle joué par Madame de Mortsauf, dans l'initiation de Félix aux délices du temps retrouvé.

Le prélude du roman est, sur ce point, rempli de signes. La mère semble avoir comme principal souci d'enfermer l'enfant. Chez les Oratoriens de Pont-le-Voy où il a été à l'âge de sept ans "exporté" (p. 775), Félix connaît la claustration totale. Ses parents ne venant jamais le voir, même les jours de distribution de prix, il reste toute l'année prisonnier, rêvant d'un au-delà terrestre qui commence à la loge du portier, et d'un au-delà céleste qui représente une variation sur le thème de l'étoile. Même tonalité dans l'épisode parisien. L'au-delà terrestre y prend, certes, de la consistance, puisqu'il s'appelle Palais-Royal, mais il demeure tout aussi inaccessible. Accompagné dans ses trajets de la pension au lycée ou au domicile de Madame de Listomere, Félix n'est pas plus libre de ses mouvements qu'il ne l'était chez les Oratoriens. Trois fois, il cherche en vain à s'échapper. Un jour enfin, exaspéré, il décide de s'évader de la voiture du directeur de la pension, en en descendant au moment où Monsieur Lepître, qui est "gros comme Louis XVIII et pied-bot" (p. 780) y monte. C'est la liberté dans les rues de Paris, peut-être même la plongée dans l'enfer merveilleux du Palais-Royal. Las! Au moment même où Félix va mettre son projet à exécution, la mère terrible survient en chaise de poste et enlève l'enfant. L'escapade rêvée se termine dans la véritable voiture cellulaire qu'est pour Félix la chaise de poste maternelle. Rien d'étonnant si le bonheur de la contemplation s'accompagne, pour le jeune homme, d'une refus des clôtures humaines et si, par deux fois, les espaces étoilés sont opposés dans le roman à la touffeur de la chambre. Le lieu de l'amour ne peut être que la nature tout entière, vue de la terrasse de Clochegourde. Le style hautement figuré du début trouve ainsi sa justification. L'enfance de Félix, n'est-ce pas, à la lettre, la misére de l'arbre qui lutte pour la vie? Et n'est-ce pas d'épanouissement, au sens propre du terme, qu'il importe de parler? Cette écriture, après tout, n'était peut-être pas si grandiloquente. Elle avait une fonction. "A quel talent nourri de larmes devrons-nous un jour la plus émouvante élégie, la peinture des tourments subis en silence par les âmes dont les racines tendres encore ne rencontrent que de durs cailloux dans le sol domestique, dont les premières frondaisons sont déchirées par des mains haineuses, dont les fleurs sont atteintes par la gelée au moment où elles s'ouvrent?" (p. 771). Généralisée ainsi, l'image de l'arbre est en parfaite harmonie avec le grand roman de la nature qu'est *le Lys dans la vallée*.

La sainteté de Madame de Mortsauf, vierge, mère, martyre, capable de miracles, ne va pas cependant sans ambiguité. Il ne faut pas oublier que lorsqu'il rencontre enfin l'incarnation de son étoile, Félix vient de traverser une période tout occupée de rêveries érotiques. Le "monde oriental et sultanesque du Palais-Royal" (p. 779) y a joué un plus grand rôle que les chastes élans de l'enfance. La scène du bal ne se place donc nullement au niveau des contemplations sidérales. Elle est, dans une certaine mesure, la réalisation des désirs qui poussaient Félix à s'échapper de la pension Lepître, la saisie irraisonnée, frénétique, du fruit défendu dans une atmosphère de serre chaude et de suffocation. Le grand amour éthéré prend sa source dans l'éblouissement des lumières, les "tentures rouges", les "ornements dorés", au bruit des "cuivres ardents" de la musique militaire. La chaste Henriette porte une robe très décolletée qui découvre non seulement ses épaules, mais des "globes azurés et d'une rondeur parfaite... douillettement couchés dans des flots de dentelle" (p. 785). Celle qui sera la mère joue d'abord le rôle d'initiatrice qui semblait devoir être dévolu aux courtisanes du Palais-Royal: elle n'appartient pas à la nature ouverte, elle n'est ni lys ni étoile, mais pur objet de désir, dans une tente poussiéreuse où domine le rouge.

Balzac est infiniment plus discret sur ce second aspect du personnage, et il faut lire de très près le roman pour comprendre l'importance de cette scène. En dépit de sa gaucherie, de son inexpérience, de sa jeunesse, l'initié est ici l'initiateur, et s'attache, sans le savoir, l'objet de son désir par un désir pareil. Une phrase vertigineuse nous renseigne à mots couverts, dès la première visite de Félix à Clochegourde. Il s'agit une fois encore du sentiment de maternité qui domine la comtesse. Le fait que Félix est malingre et délicat permet à Madame de Mortsauf de l'associer à ses enfants: "Ce fut, comme je le sus depuis, le second lien qui l'attacha si fortement à moi" (p. 805). Quel était donc le premier?

La réponse vient beaucoup plus tard, dans la lettre que Félix ne lit qu'après la mort d'Henriette: "Vous souvenez-vous encore aujourd' hui de vos baisers? Ils ont dominé ma vie, ils ont sillonné mon âme; l'ardeur de votre sang a réveillé l'ardeur du mien; votre jeunesse a pénétré ma jeunesse, vos désirs sont entrés dans mon cœur.... Je ne me sentis plus mère qu'à demi" (p. 1018).

C'est dire que Madame de Mortsauf n'est pas ce personnage monolithique qu'elle s'efforce d'être et que la scène du baiser est véritablement la cellule initiale du drame. Cela posait au romancier des problèmes techniques extrêmement complexes. Moins habile, il nous eût présenté une femme déchirée entre l'amour et la vertu, consciemment ou inconsciemment, se trahissant à chaque pas par des actes manqués, vivant aux yeux du lecteur la torture de son âme. En cessant d'être tout à fait vertueuse, Madame de Mortsauf serait devenue une Phèdre provinciale, et le roman se serait perdu dans les sables d'une psychologie parfaitement conventionnelle. La blancheur du roman y eût sombré sans recours. Il fallait donc que le conflit cessât d'être psychologique et que l'âme de Madame de Mortsauf ne pût être, aux yeux des lecteurs, le lieu du combat entre le désir et la pureté. Dans le *Lys* Balzac a résolu ce problème d'une manière souveraine, en poète.

En un contrepoint discret, Balzac fait entendre, auprès de la note blanche, la note rouge, couleur de la passion imparfaitement

assouvie, couleur de la scène du bal. Il suffit d'un coucher de soleil
pour qu'éclate la symphonie du désir: "Un jour je la trouvai religi-
eusement pensive devant un coucher de soleil qui rougissait si
voluptueusement les cimes en laissant voir la vallée comme un lit,
qu'il était impossible de ne pas écouter la voix de cet éternel Cantique
des Cantiques par lequel la nature convie ses créatures à l'amour"
(p. 820). Un peu plus loin, une image d'une incomparable audace
combine les deux composantes de la passion qui lie Félix à Henriette,
et le jeune homme s'endort "dans des langes de pourpre" (p. 824).
Enfin, il y a les fleurs, l'admirable épisode des bouquets opposant
au lys solitaire une incroyable profusion de couleurs. En une page
d'un érotisme flamboyant, Balzac balaye toutes les pudeurs et fait
retentir le cri du désir à l'état pur: "Du sein de ce prolixe torrent
d'amour qui déborde, s'élance un magnifique double pavot rouge
accompagné de ses glands prêts à s'ouvrir, déployant les flammèches
de son incendie au-dessus des jasmins étoilés et dominant la pluie
incessante du pollen, beau nuage qui papillotte dans l'air en reflétant
le jour dans ses mille parcelles luisantes" (p. 858). Aussi la "blanche
tendresse" se trouvera-t-elle "troublée par des mouvements in-
domptés, et ce rouge désir de l'amour qui demande un bonheur
refusé dans les luttes cent fois recommencées de la passion contenue,
infatigable, éternelle" (p. 858).

Cette dernière phrase suffit à montrer clairement ce qui fait la
singularité du *Lys*. Balzac ayant substitué à la construction de type
dramatique une construction de type poétique a su aller jusqu'au
bout de son entreprise et écrire un livre qui fût tout entier figure:
figure de la longue rêverie d'un homme jeune sur le monde extérieur,
figure d'une relation amoureuse toute en nuances et en contradictions
qui ne peut nous être dévoilée *psychologiquement* que dans les
dernières pages du livre. Au lecteur attentif de retrouver, au niveau
des mots, le sourd cheminement des tensions et des déchirements.

Monde balzacien et monde réel:
notes sur *Illusions perdues*

JEAN GAULMIER

Les trois épisodes d'*Illusions perdues* sont très fortement liés: la localisation des scènes principales, Angoulême – Paris – Angoulême, ramenant le héros à son point de départ, donne l'impression, pleinement satisfaisante pour l'esprit, d'un cercle qui se boucle. Architecture à la fois simple et rigoureuse dans la manière dont Balzac traite les données spatiales. En va-t-il de même en ce qui concerne la durée? C'est à cette question que je voudrais répondre en examinant la chronologie de ce long roman, chronologie dont Mme S. Bérard a noté sans y insister la bizarrerie.[1]

Le roman commence "vers la fin de 1819" (IV, 167) avec le retour à Angoulême de David Séchard qui vient de terminer ses études à Paris. C'est alors qu'a lieu l'inventaire de l'imprimerie que le père Séchard cède à David. "Quelques jours après son installation dans l'imprimerie paternelle" (p. 480), David retrouve son ami d'enfance, Lucien de Rubempré, et s'offre à lui apprendre le métier de prote. De là, nous passons brusquement "en 1821, dans les premiers jours de mai" (p. 484) où se place la soirée poétique chez Mme de Bargeton. Pendant l'été de 1821, Lucien conquiert les bonnes grâces de Mme de Bargeton: "vers le commencement du mois de septembre" (1821) (p. 571), visite compromettante de Lucien à Mme de Bargeton, suivie immédiatement du duel Chandour-Bargeton, et "le lendemain matin" (p. 584), Lucien apprend de Mme de Bargeton sa décision de partir pour Paris. C'est donc à la fin de septembre, au plus tard, que "le Fernand Cortez littéraire" prend le chemin de la capitale. Or, le *lendemain* de leur arrivée, Louise et Lucien se séparent, sur les instances de du Châtelet, et celui-ci les

---

[1] S. Bérard, *La Genèse d'Illusions perdues* (Paris, 1961), t. II, p. 306: "Le roman qui débute en 1821 passe brusquement à 1822, puis à 1823; les âges et les dates de naissance des personnages sont l'objet de réjouissantes étourderies."

invite tous deux à l'Opéra: il aura une loge, car "au mois de juin, les
ministres ne savent que faire de leurs loges aux théâtres" (p. 600).[1]

L'arrivée de Lucien à Paris, au lieu de fin septembre, est donc
placée ici en juin (1821). "Le dimanche" suivant la soirée à l'Opéra,
Lucien, abandonné par Louise, se promène dans Paris; "le lendemain" (p. 625), après une conversation avec du Châtelet, il s'installe
dans un garni du quartier latin. Commence alors la vie pauvre de
Lucien pendant l'été (1821). "Par une assez froide matinée du mois
de septembre" (p. 637), Lucien visite les libraires. Puis il se lie avec
d'Arthez et le Cénacle: cela nous mène "au commencement du
mois d'octobre" (1821) (p. 657). A la fin d'octobre se placent la
visite de Lucien au petit journal, le resserrement de son amitié avec
Lousteau, sa conversation avec celui-ci, un soir au Luxembourg
(p. 672).[2] Le même soir (p. 683) s'ouvre une nuit torrentielle:
Lucien avec Lousteau visite le Palais-Royal, puis assiste à la représentation du *Panorama dramatique*, conquiert Coralie, soupe avec
les journalistes chez Florine, rédige son premier article et termine
la nuit avec Coralie... On comprend que de ces orgies il soit sorti
"ignoblement malade" (p. 742)! Tout cela s'est passé un vendredi
(p. 755). Le dimanche suivant, Lucien déjeune avec Lousteau, puis
va voir divers journalistes et finalement fait accepter ses *Marguerites*
par Dauriat. Nous arrivons ainsi, vraisemblablement, à la fin de
novembre 1821: alors a lieu la soirée à l'Opéra où triomphe Lucien.
Ensuite "Lucien vit pendant un mois son temps pris par des
soupers" (p. 809) et l'hiver est rempli de plaisirs: il s'agit de l'hiver
1821–2, si l'on en croit la p. 823 qui nous fait passer à mars 1822.
Lucien alors s'endette, tente de vendre son roman, se risque à jouer,
collabore vers avril au royaliste *Réveil*. En avril, Fendant et Cavalier
ont payé le roman de Lucien en billets à 6, 9 et 12 mois, mais
déposent leur bilan "à la fin du premier mois" (p. 870), c'est à dire
fin mai: à ce moment, Lucien se trouve réduit à faire trois billets
de mille francs chacun en imitant la signature de David (p. 873)
– mais dans *Souffrances de l'inventeur*, ces mêmes billets sont datés
du 10 février 1822 et échus le 30 avril (p. 919)! Coralie tombe

[1] Grosse inadvertance de Balzac: les députés ministériels "font leurs vendanges".
En juin! A. Adam (Paris, 1956, p. 169) note que dans le manuscrit Balzac avait
bien écrit "septembre".

[2] Discuter de poésie sur un banc du Luxembourg, un soir de fin octobre – début
novembre...

malade. "Au commencement du mois d'août" (p. 874), elle est perdue et meurt avant la fin du mois, le 27, d'après la lettre de Lucien à Eve (p. 939). Lucien passe *deux mois* dans l'accablement avant de repartir pour Angoulême, ce qui fixe son retour à la fin d'octobre 1822. La fantasmagorie parisienne a donc duré un an, de septembre 1821 à septembre 1822, ou 15 mois, si on place en juin l'arrivée de Lucien à Paris.[1]

Lucien, sur le chemin du retour, passe une semaine au moulin près de Mansles: sa rentrée à Angoulême devrait donc être fin octobre au plus tôt, ou mieux *début novembre*. Or nous apprenons que l'ex Mme de Bargeton et du Châtelet devenu préfet l'invitent à dîner le 15 septembre...[2]

On voit combien, à la serrer de près, cette chronologie est flottante. La durée réelle et la durée romanesque présentent une singulière discordance. Les aventures dramatiques de Lucien, le fourmillement des expériences du héros et des personnages autour de celui-ci suggèrent au lecteur une longue durée. Balzac a d'ailleurs soin de ne donner que très rarement des dates; il utilise le plus souvent des expressions vagues, telles que *le lendemain* ou *quelques jours après* – de sorte que le lecteur, pris par le récit, ne s'aperçoit pas que ce long roman en trois épisodes se borne en fait à l'évocation de quelques journées marquantes: dans le premier épisode, l'inventaire de la maison Séchard et la réception chez Mme de Bargeton; dans le second, la soirée à l'Opéra et cette nuit torrentielle où Lucien expérimente avec Lousteau les orgies de Paris; dans le troisiéme, le jour de septembre 1822 où, à la veille du dîner de Lucien à la Préfecture, David Séchard est arrêté pour dettes. Balzac ne retient que les temps forts dans l'existence de ses héros, ne s'attarde pas aux temps morts, cauchemar des romanciers laborieux qui cherchent, sans y parvenir, à faire coïncider réel et imaginaire. Composition dramatique dont Mme Bérard a bien vu qu'elle s'apparente à la technique du théâtre.[3]

Il est un autre domaine où l'on est porté à mettre en doute le prétendu "réalisme" de Balzac: celui de l'histoire. M. Jean Gaudon

---

[1] Un passage de *Souffrances de l'inventeur*, IV, 844, évolue à 18 mois l'aventure parisienne de Lucien.

[2] Que le retour de Lucien ait eu lieu fin septembre ou début novembre, on ne voit pas comment à cette date sa sœur pourrait lui faire manger des fraises! (*ibid.*, p. 970).

[3] Bérard, *op. cit.*, t. II, p. 16.

remarquait récemment à propos du *Père Goriot*: "A la différence
d'un Flaubert qui, dans l'*Éducation sentimentale*, choisit avec soin
ses dates, de manière à décrire les interférences entre les événements
historiques et la vie de ses personnages, ou du Hugo des *Misérables*
qui fait se retrouver tous ses acteurs sur la barricade, le 5 juin 1832,
les événements imaginaires décrits dans le *Père Goriot* sont totalement en marge de l'histoire dite événementielle."[1] Le fait est peut-
être plus frappant encore dans *Illusions perdues* dont le second
épisode prétend retracer la vie intellectuelle et politique de Paris
en 1821–2. Pour s'en convaincre, il suffit de feuilleter un journal
que Lucien devait lire puisque le roman fait plusieurs allusions à
son directeur, le *Drapeau blanc* de Martainville.[2] Ce journal, fondé
en 1818 sous la devise *Vive le Roi... quand même*, organe des ultras,
et d'ailleurs fort bien rédigé, affichait un dévouement aveugle à la
religion et aux Bourbons.[3] A se borner aux événements dont parle
le journal après l'arrivée de Lucien à Paris en juin 1821, on note
que le 5 juillet a été connue à Paris la mort de Napoléon:[4] comment

---

[1] J. Gaudon, in *Année balz.* (1967), p. 155. Cette étude sur *Goriot* aboutit à la mème
conclusion que la nôtre sur *Illusions perdues*.

[2] Alphonse Martainville (1776–1830) est représenté par Balzac comme l'un des
coryphées de la presse royaliste (*Illusions perdues*, IV, 845), l'homme le plus
abhorré des libéraux, le seul qui aimât Lucien (IV, 859–50), un excellent connaisseur du théâtre (IV, 857), le plus terrible antagoniste du Ministère (IV, 866), un
"courageux athlète" qui seul reste fidèle à Lucien (IV, 870).

[3] Chaque numéro du *Drapeau blanc* détaille les souscriptions – plus ou moins
spontanées – des villes de France pour l'achat du Château de Chambord à
l'intention de "l'enfant du miracle". Le 8 février, il donne un bulletin de santé
du petit duc de Bordeaux atteint de la varicelle. Les 13 et 14 janvier, le journal,
encadré de noir, contient un éditorial de Martainville sur l'anniversaire de
l'assassinat du duc de Berry, "effet du tigre populaire mal muselé". Sont fré-
quentes de petites nouvelles sur l'activité des Pères de la Foi et sur leurs missions.
Et ceci qui atteste le curieux fétichisme royaliste de Martainville: "23 mars
S.A.R. Mme la duchesse de Berry a daigné faire remettre un exemplaire de
l'*Imitation de Jésus-Christ*, orné de gravures et doré sur tranche, à M. Auguste
Lemoine qui, concurremment avec Mme Desmaries, a présenté a S.A.R. le
couvre-pied que la ville de Bordeaux offre à notre Henri..."

[4] *Drapeau blanc*, samedi 7 juillet 1821: "La mort de Buonaparte est officiellement
annoncée dans les journaux anglais du 4 courant. Voici dans quels termes le
Courrier donne cette nouvelle: Buonaparte n'est plus. Il est mort le samedi 5 mai,
à 6 heures du soir, d'une maladie de langueur qui le retenait au lit depuis plus
de 40 jours. Il a demandé qu'après sa mort son corps fût ouvert pour reconnaître
si sa maladie n'était pas la même que celle qui avait terminé les jours de son
père. Il a conservé sa connaissance jusqu'au dernier jour et il est mort sans
douleurs."
Drapeau blanc, 8 juillet 1821: "Il n'est donc plus cet homme dont la vie a si
longtemps tourmenté l'univers"... "La postérité dira qu'il est mort trop tard.

les amis de d'Arthez n'ont-ils pas été bouleversés par cette grande nouvelle? En 1821, la session parlementaire s'est terminée le 31 juillet, après le vote d'une loi importante prolongeant la censure:[1] en juin, députés ministériels et ministres se trouvaient donc à Paris. C'est en 1821 que s'est constituée en France l'organisation des Carbonari, organisation qui aurait dû retenir l'attention de certains membres du Cénacle, de Michel Chrestien par exemple: Balzac n'y fait pas la moindre allusion![2] Comment les écrivains, les libraires que fréquente Lucien ignorent-ils la nomination de Chateaubriand comme maître ès-Jeux Floraux (*Drapeau blanc*, 21 juillet) et la remise de son diplôme qui lui fut faite par "M. Victor Hugo, le plus jeune des maîtres de l'Académie des Jeux Floraux" (*Drapeau blanc*, 31 juillet)? Comment n'ont-ils pas été émus par le procès en Cour d'assises de Paul-Louis Courier,[3] poursuivi pour "outrage à la morale publique" et condamné le 28 août à deux mois de prison et deux cents francs d'amende plus les frais? Comment les journalistes de toutes tendances, de Lousteau à Martainville, n'ont-ils pas réagi devant le projet de loi aggravant les délits de presse et prorogeant la censure (3 décembre 1821)? Et surtout, comment sont-ils tous restés muets devant le procès sensationnel de Béranger, provoqué

Sans doute ses premiers pas ont été marqués par un attentat exécrable. Mais enfin, s'il avait eu la chance de mourir au combat... Cette mort qui aurait pu avoir du retentissement ne produit aujourd'hui qu'une impression médiocre," "Buonaparte n'a pas su mourir à propos"... "Qu'il n'y ait pas en France un seul cœur, une seule bouche qui profère le cri qu'a indiqué dans ses alarmes un honorable membre de la Chambre des Députés!"

Drapeau blanc, 9 juillet: "Les nouvelles de Ste Hélène ont produit sur les fonds publics un effet favorable. La rente 3% a monté a 78 F. Il ne s'est fait aucune affaire sur les fonds français parce qu'on s'attend a une grande hausse à la Bourse de Paris quand on y apprendra la mort de Buonaparte."

Le journal ajoute: "Les spéculateurs anglais se trompent à cet égard: ils ignorent que la vie ou la mort de Buonaparte est complètement indifférente à 99 centièmes des Français qui n'y prennent qu'un intérêt de curiosité." Et le *Drapeau blanc* du 11 août signale que 27 marchands d'estampes sont poursuivis en justice pour avoir vendu, sans autorisation de la police, des images relatives à la mort de *l'Homme du destin*.

[1] Le *Drapeau blanc* du 7 juillet 1821 contient un grand discours de Bonald sur la censure, appuyé, le 8 juillet, d'un article de Martainville: "Des lois fortes et rigoureuses sont les plus sûres garanties de la liberté..."

[2] Sous la rubrique *Rome 18 septembre*, le *Drapeau blanc* du mardi 9 octobre publie la bulle du Pape contre "l'association dite des Carbonari".

[3] P. L. Courier est pourtant cité dans *Illusions perdues* (IV, 692). C'était pour Balzac l'occasion de rappeler que son *Simple discours*, provoqué par l'achat du Château de Chambord (6 mars 1821) avait connu un immense succès (4 mai 1821).

par un article de Martainville dans le *Drapeau blanc* du 27 octobre? Béranger fut condamné le 9 décembre 1821 à trois mois de prison sur réquisitoire de Marchangy. Le 15 décembre a marqué la chute du Ministère Richelieu et son remplacement par le Cabinet Villèle: ce ministère où le duc de Montmorency dirige les Affaires Etrangères, Corbière l'Intérieur et Peyronnet la Justice, n'a certes pas pu choisir du Châtelet, vieux beau de l'Empire, pour en faire un comte et lui donner la préfecture de la Charente! Janvier et février 1822 – le moment de la fiévreuse activité de Lucien dans le journalisme – sont marqués par la discussion de la loi sur la presse, votée le 7 février, qui soumet les journaux à l'arbitraire du pouvoir: c'est au cours de cette discussion que Martignac affirme que les journaux ne présentent aucune utilité et ne sont que des entreprises industrielles: ni Léon Giraud, ni Finot ne protestent...

On pourrait multiplier les exemples. Ceux-là suffisent pour prouver que Balzac ne travaille pas sur documents pour ressusciter, 15 ans après l'avoir vécue, une époque dont il se rappelle l'atmosphère mais dont il a oublié les détails. Il travaille dans un élan, en poète et non en chroniqueur. Il n'a pas besoin des faits exacts, il en invente par analogie[1] et son univers est autonome. Ça et là, une mention rapide d'un personnage réel, MM. Didot dans l'imprimerie, Benjamin Constant au Palais-Royal, Martainville dans une discussion, suffit à donner à l'ensemble de son roman l'allure du réel. Mais, dit très bien Mme Bérard, "la réalité n'arrive chez Balzac à l'existence romanesque qu'au terme d'une vie secrète où elle perd souvent toute authenticité"[2]: pour saisissant que soit le monde créé par le "miroir concentrique" qu'est l'esprit de Balzac, suivant ce que, d'un mot heureux, M. Barrère appelle "réalisme imaginaire",[3] il faut se garder de le confondre avec le monde donné par l'Histoire: parmi les illusions perdues, nous rangerons celle, si tenacement affirmée par cent exégètes, d'un Balzac historien.

[1] L'expression est de Balzac dans la préface de *La Peau de chagrin* (1831), XI, 174.
[2] Bérard, *op. cit.*, t. II, p. 311.
[3] J. B. Barrère, *Mercure de France*, no. 308 (janvier 1950), p. 114.

Vers une édition critique de *la Maison Nucingen*: genèse et épreuves

ROGER J. B. CLARK

C'EST en 1834 que Nucingen apparaît pour la première fois dans le monde de *la Comédie humaine*, à côté de Goriot et de Vautrin. Si le personnage, tout en contribuant à la déchéance du vermicellier, ne jouait alors qu'un rôle relativement effacé, il semble s'être rapidement imposé à l'imagination de Balzac; car, quelques semaines à peine après la publication du *Père Goriot*, l'écrivain envisageait déjà de le faire revenir et nourrissait le projet d'une élaboration détaillée de son caractère. Et cette fois le célèbre banquier devait être promu du rang de simple comparse à celui de personnage principal – quitte à devenir par la suite un des géants de l'univers romanesque balzacien. La réponse que Balzac apporte, dans sa lettre du 11 mars 1835, à une question de Mme Hanska représente incontestablement le point de départ de la genèse de l'œuvre qui, après de nombreuses péripéties, devait voir le jour en septembre 1838 sous le titre de *la Maison Nucingen*: "Vous me demandez ce que devient Mme de Nucingen; elle sera, ainsi que son mari le personnage le plus comiquement dramatique de *Une Vue du Monde*, si longtemps annoncée par la *Revue de Paris*. C'est *la Faillite de M. de Nucingen*. Mais il faut du temps pour toutes ces conceptions, et surtout pour leur exécution".[1]

Malgré son peu de précision, la déclaration de Balzac n'est pas totalement indéchiffrable. Elle laisse en effet entendre que le romancier avait à l'origine l'intention de ne donner dans *Une Vue du monde* (ou *la Faillite de M. de Nucingen*) qu'une suite au *Père Goriot*,

---

[1] *L.H.*, t. I, p. 313. Sur le projet de publication d'un "article intitulé *Une vue du monde*" dans la *Revue de Paris* de mars 1832, voir *Corr.*, t. I, pp. 678–9, no. 422. Le titre est mentionné à plusieurs reprises dans l'Album de Balzac et également dans une lettre de mai (?) 1834 (*Corr.*, t. II, p. 501, no. 779). Ce projet, qui n'a pas abouti, ne regarde en rien le texte qui nous intéresse ici, Nucingen n'ayant vu le jour qu'en décembre 1834. Balzac reprend seulement un titre auquel il avait déjà songé et qui sera d'ailleurs rapidement abandonné.

traitée du point de vue des Nucingen, et en premier chef de celui de Delphine: la curiosité de Mme Hanska, alléchée par la conclusion en suite-au-prochain-numéro du *Père Goriot* ("Vous me demandez ce que *devient* Mme de Nucingen"), contribua à déclencher l'imagination du romancier – et c'est à cette curiosité qu'il s'apprêtait tout d'abord à satisfaire dans son œuvre nouvelle. L'idée de raconter les débuts de Nucingen, et surtout celle d'exprimer ses propres désillusions sur la situation économique et politique, ne semblent avoir joué qu'un rôle minime dans la conception initiale; elles ne germeront que plus tard, ainsi qu'en font foi les hésitations de Balzac quant au titre de son ouvrage et également l'évolution des épreuves de *la Maison Nucingen*.

Enchaînant sur sa declaration à Mme Hanska, l'écrivain évoque en septembre ou octobre 1835 "un très piquant article, *la suite de Goriot*", qu'il promet à la *Revue de Paris* "pour la fin du mois". Il ne peut s'agir que de la future *Maison Nucingen*.[1] La déclaration de Rastignac dans *l'Interdiction* (publiée au début de 1836) – "J'ai été roué, mon cher, dans l'affaire de monsieur de Nucingen, je te raconterai cette histoire-là" (III, 12) – montre que Balzac continue à penser au banquier et envisage déjà d'analyser sa stratégie financière. De là au sujet de *la Maison Nucingen*, le pas était facile à franchir.[2] Le 2 novembre, dans sa lettre à Alphonse Karr, Balzac s'engage à donner au *Figaro* (dont Karr était alors le directeur) "deux ouvrages de ma composition, intitulés *la Haute Banque* et *les Artistes*',[3] la publication du premier étant prévue pour avril 1837. Le changement de titre témoigne de l'élargissement des idées de Balzac quant à la portée de son œuvre, l'étude de certains problèmes économiques et la physiologie d'un certain secteur social venant se greffer sur l'examen d'un cas de faillite particulier. Le 19 novembre Émile de Girardin, craignant que le sujet de *la Torpille* ne déplaise aux chastes lecteurs de *la Presse*, acceptait à la place *la Haute banque* qui, entretemps, avait été remplacée au *Figaro* par *César Birotteau*.[4] Le projet d'une publication en feuilleton dans *la Presse* est évoqué à plusieurs

---

[1] *Corr.*, t. v, p. 852, no. 2818.
[2] Nous devons cette indication a l'amabilité de M. Anthony R. Pugh que nous remercions de tout cœur.
[3] *Corr.*, t. III, p. 170, no. 1153.
[4] *ibid.*, p. 194, no. 1164.

reprises dans les lettres que Balzac adresse à l'Etrangère en décembre 1836 et janvier 1837.[1] Le 6 janvier *la Presse* avait même promis, "d'ici au premier juillet prochain", *la Haute banque ou la Maison Nucingen et Cie*; inventé semble-t-il par Girardin pour battre le rappel des lecteurs du *Père Goriot*, le sous-titre, dont c'est là la première apparition, souligne bien le double objectif que Balzac se proposait d'atteindre.

Malgré les supplications de Girardin du 23 janvier ("Je crois devoir vous faire demander si vous pensez à *la Haute Banque*"),[2] du 3 mars[3] et du 8 mai 1837 ("Je vous prie de vouloir bien me mettre en mesure le plus tôt qu'il vous sera possible, d'acquitter cet engagement envers mon public impatient"),[4] l'ouvrage reste à l'état de projet jusqu'au début de l'automne, Balzac étant pris par un long voyage en Italie pour le compte de Guidoboni-Visconti puis par un renouveau d'enthousiasme pour *César Birotteau*. Entretemps *la Femme supérieure* était passée à *la Presse* (en juillet 1837) à la place de *la Haute Banque*.[5] Finalement, le 10 octobre, l'écrivain se déclare prêt à commencer: "Je me hâte de vous écrire car, demain, je me mets à faire *la Maison Nucingen, ou la Haute Banque* [sic] pour *la Presse*. C'est encore une 50e de colonnes qu'il faut avoir pondues pour la fin du mois"[6]. La rédaction, d'abord lente et pénible, semble avoir été enlevée rapidement dans les derniers jours d'octobre, puisque le romancier est en mesure d'annoncer l'envoi à Charles Plon du manuscrit de *la Maison Nucingen* dès le début de novembre.[7] La correction des épreuves, laborieuse et exhaustive, fut terminée vers le milieu du mois,[8] lorsque *César Birotteau*, pour lequel un nouveau traité venait d'être signé avec le *Figaro*, vint absorber toute l'énergie de Balzac.

La Maison Nucingen n'est cependant pas oubliée et Balzac, dans

[1] voir, par exemple, *L.H.*, t. I, pp. 465, 476.
[2] *Corr*, t. III, p. 231, no. 1191.
[3] *ibid.*, p. 259, no. 1221.
[4] *ibid.*, p. 278, no. 1236.
[5] Sur les démêlés de Balzac avec Girardin au sujet de *la Haute Banque*, voir l'article de M. René Guise, 'Balzac et le roman-feuilleton', pp. 294–5, *Année balz.* (1964).
[6] *L.H.*, t. I, p. 358. C'est là dernière apparition du titre *la Haute Banque* qui ne sera cependant pas abandonné, Balzac s'en servant comme titre de chapitre dans l'édition originale de *César Birotteau*.
[7] *Corr.*, t. III, p. 344, no. 1294.
[8] *L.H.*, t. I, p. 360: l'ouvrage est d'ailleurs daté de novembre 1837.

les lettres qu'il écrit à la fin de 1837 et au début de 1838, anticipe à la fois sur la publication en volume de son nouveau roman et sur la publication en feuilleton dans *la Presse*.[1] Le bon à tirer en est même donné à Girardin, sans doute avant la fin de 1837. En février 1838, l'écrivain, épuisé par l'énorme effort que lui avait demandé *César Birotteau*, s'éloigne de Paris pour un séjour en Berry suivi de la célèbre expédition aux mines d'argent sardes. Il ne sera de retour dans la capitale que vers le milieu du mois de juin. Dans l'intervalle Girardin avait décidé que l'insertion de *la Maison Nucingen* dans *la Presse* ne pouvait avoir lieu "par des considérations puisées dans les exigences d'un journal quotidien" (annonce rétrospective dans *la Presse* du 28 septembre 1838). Les raisons du refus de Girardin furent sans doute multiples. Il est vrai d'une part, vu l'ésotérisme de son sujet ainsi que le resserré de sa forme, que *la Maison Nucingen* correspond assez peu aux formules de l'esthétique feuilletonesque. Mais ce furent sans doute des facteurs plus intimes qui motivèrent Girardin. Il s'était peut-être reconnu, à tort ou à raison, soit dans le personnage de Nucingen, soit, comme l'affirme le vicomte de Lovenjoul,[2] dans celui de Ferdinand du Tillet, soit encore dans les deux personnages à la fois; car, comme l'a pertinemment montré M. Jean-Hervé Donnard, le physique et le caractère de Girardin se retrouvent dans du Tillet tandis que les machinations de Nucingen ne sont pas sans offrir une certaine ressemblance avec les opérations financières montées par le gérant de *la Presse* en 1837.[3] Ces allusions à peine voilées à ses propres spéculations durent forcément déplaire à Girardin; il en profita pour refuser un ouvrage qui aurait certaine- ment été assez mal reçu des habitués du feuilleton, amateurs de Sue ou de Dumas. C'est là d'ailleurs bien ce qui ressort du procès-verbal de l'affaire que rédigea Balzac lui-même: "Il se trouve que *la Maison Nucingen*, qui convient pour la longueur, pour la largeur, pour le prix, parle de choses trop épineuses qui ne cadrent point avec la politique du journal. *La Maison Nucingen* demeure sur les bras de l'auteur."[4]

---

[1] voir *Corr.*, t. III, p. 349, no. 1298 et *L.H.*, t. I, p. 563.
[2] dans sa note sur les épreuves de *la Maison Nucingen*: Lovenjoul, A. 125, f. A.
[3] voir, de M. Donnard, *Les Réalités économiques et sociales dans 'la Comédie humaine'* (Paris, 1961), pp. 306–18, et 'Qui est Nucingen?', *Année balz.* (1960), pp. 135–48.
[4] Préface de la première edition de *la Femme supérieure*, de *la Maison Nucingen* et de *la Torpille* (XI, 358).

La Maison Nucingen fut finalement publiée par Werdet vers la fin du mois de septembre 1838 dans une édition en deux volumes in-octavo qui comprenait en outre *la Femme supérieure* et *la Torpille*. La publication, annoncée dans les journaux parisiens (*le Constitutionnel, la Presse, les Débats, la Quotidienne* et *le Siècle*) du 24 ou du 25 septembre, fut enregistrée le 6 octobre par la *Bibliographie de la France*. Cette première édition était précédée d'une longue préface dans laquelle Balzac s'attaquait encore une fois au problème de la propriété littéraire et à celui, plus coriace, du rôle à jouer par l'État dans le subventionnement du domaine artistique.

L'ouvrage n'attira guère l'attention de la critique et les quelques commentaires que suscita *la Maison Nucingen* furent sans exception très défavorables. Les feuilletonistes dirigèrent leurs reproches avant tout contre la témérité de la préface et, en ce qui concerne le roman lui-même, contre le procédé du retour des personnages et contre l'impénétrabilité de son style. Ainsi, par exemple, ces deux coups de griffe caractéristiques, celui de la *Revue de Paris*[1] et celui de Théodore Muret dans *la Quotidienne* du 30 octobre:

> Pour ce qui regarde son nouveau roman, nous faisons grâce à M. de Balzac de nos trop justes censures. Ah! si M. de Balzac pouvait savoir quel est cet immense ennui de voir sans cesse revenir dans ses livres les mêmes figures avec les mêmes grimaces, les mêmes noms propres, suivis des mêmes sobriquets, comme il trancherait d'un seul coup la tête à tous ces personnages qui, depuis sept ans, s'agitent sans cesse sans arriver jamais, discutent sans fin, sans rien conclure.

> Nous ne pouvons, à notre grand regret, attacher plus de valeur à *la Maison Nucingen* et à *la Torpille*, autres histoires banales où M. de Balzac reproduit à satiété les noms et les personnages de ses précédents romans, surtout ceux du *Père Goriot*, œuvre d'immoralité et de cynisme que nous voudrions oublier, dans l'intérêt même de la réputation de son auteur.

La Maison Nucingen, que Balzac avait dédiée à Zulma Carraud, prit place en 1844 dans le tome III des *Scènes de la vie parisienne* (t. XI de *la Comédie humaine*).

---

[1] *Revue de Paris*, LVIII (1 octobre 1838), 229.

Les épreuves de *la Maison Nucingen* sont conservées à la bibliothèque Lovenjoul sous la cote A. 125: au total, sept jeux différents
reliés en un volume de 296 feuillets que Balzac offrit le 25 août
1839 à Edmond Duponchel, le directeur de l'Opéra.[1] Il s'agit là
sans aucun doute, comme l'affirme d'ailleurs le vicomte de Lovenjoul,[2] des épreuves corrigées par Balzac en novembre 1837 en vue
de la publication de son roman dans *la Presse* au commencement de
1838. Le texte Werdet de septembre 1838 diffère légèrement de la
dernière version de Lovenjoul A. 125: Balzac après son retour d'Italie
a donc revu son texte au moins une fois avant la publication en
volume. L'ouvrage ne subira après que de légères modifications: on
relève sur le Furne corrigé seulement un ajouté d'importance (le
passage, assez réactionnaire, sur le danger de la démoralisation du
peuple par les caisses d'épargne: v, 640) et, contribuant à relier plus
étroitement *la Maison Nucingen* au reste de *la Comédie humaine*,
quelques transpositions de noms de personnages (apparaissent en
particulier des allusions à Sinard et à Rabourdin).

Lovenjoul A. 125 a jusqu'ici assez peu attiré l'attention des
balzaciens – à tort semble-t-il car ces épreuves de *la Maison Nucingen*
présentent un intérêt certain. Elles constituent tout d'abord un
exemple typique de la technique de composition par adjonction
qu'avait adoptée Balzac. C'est là la méthode balzacienne par excellence
et la succession des sept séries d'épreuves de *la Maison Nucingen*
permet admirablement d'en suivre le rythme haletant, d'autant
plus que le travail sur épreuves semble s'être échelonné sur un laps
de temps relativement bref, trois semaines au maximum, les indications apportées par le romancier en tête de quelques-uns des jeux
soulignant clairement le train endiablé qu'il s'imposait.[3]

Un examen des épreuves de *la Maison Nucingen* permet également de constater que Balzac, voyant sa nouvelle s'allonger de plus

[1] *Corr.*, t. III, p. 684, no. 1574.
[2] Lovenjoul, A. 125, f. A.
[3] Ainsi, par exemple, en tête de la première épreuve (Lovenjoul, A. 125, f. 1):
"Charles [Plon], vite une autre épreuve faite sur du papier semblable mais
double car il faut que je consulte quelqu'un sur mon ouvrage." Il est impossible
d'identifier avec certitude le "quelqu'un" consulté par Balzac mais il pourrait
bien s'agir de Girardin. On relève une indication du même ordre en tête de la
sixième épreuve (Lovenjoul, A. 125, f. 214): "Charles donnez une révision pour
ce soir 4 heures (une double épreuve car il faudra recomposer en cicéro pour
achever le 2e volume de *la Femme supérieure* dont je vais envoyer *les bons à
tirer*)."

en plus, avait senti le besoin de l'aérer en la divisant en chapitres. L'écrivain découpe ainsi son texte en cinq parties lors de la correction du quatrième jeu d'épreuves et inscrit un titre pour chacun de ces chapitres: 'Les Cormorans' (mise en scène, présentation des quatre interlocuteurs, les deux premières liquidations Nucingen, v, 592-603: jusqu'à "–que je vais vous mettre en scène"); 'Théorie du bonheur' (la vie de Godefroid de Beaudenord de 1800 à 1825, pp. 603-11: "–je vous le dis, l'*improper* nous gagne"); 'l'Objet aimé' (Isaure d'Aldrigger jusqu'en 1826, histoire de sa famille, pp. 611-23: "–ni recevoir, ni aller dans le monde"); 'Cœurs assortis' (évocation du chassé-croisé amoureux Isaure-Godefroid, Malvina-du Tillet, pp. 623-31: "–je n'entrevois pas le mot de cette énigme"); 'les Petits Law' (la troisième liquidation Nucingen et ses répercussions: pp. 631-53). Puis, ayant ajouté sur la cinquième épreuve de substantiels développements à la fin de sa nouvelle (notamment tout le passage sur les troubles de Lyon: pp. 636-8), Balzac, en revoyant le sixième jeu, sousdivisa la conclusion de *la Maison Nucingen* en deux parties: 'les Petits Law' (début de la troisième liquidation Nucingen, discussion générale de problèmes économiques ajoutée en grande partie sur les quatrième et cinquième épreuves, pp. 631-43: "–et regardant ses auditeurs surpris"); "la Liquidation Nucingen' (la troisième liquidation Nucingen, ses répercussions: pp. 643-53). Divisions et titres de chapitres (inédits jusqu'à ce jour) sont cependant supprimés par le romancier sur la dernière série d'épreuves.

Si le projet de publication en feuilleton dans *la Presse* explique en partie l'idée du découpage en chapitres, le désistement de Girardin ne peut être étranger à la décision finale de Balzac de revenir à un texte continu. Le schéma adopté par le romancier réfléchissait pourtant la structure interne de son récit, la division en chapitres suivant de très près le mouvement de la conversation des quatre cormorans, centrée autour d'un certain nombre de moments critiques. Chaque chapitre est en quelque sorte un tiroir, comme le remarque d'ailleurs Couture (p. 631), où nous est présenté un épisode ou un personnage différent, un moment de l'effroyable carrière de Nucingen; le rythme du tout est essentiellement péré-grinal, haché, rythme qui reproduit à merveille à la fois la tactique délibérément imprévisible du banquier ("il est impénétrable, on ne le voit jamais venir": p. 602) et la qualité de plus en plus avinée d'une conversation d'après-dîner. Et, en même temps, chaque chapitre nous fait pénétrer plus avant dans les terribles filets de Nucingen où se sont englués les différents personnages: l'unité de la nouvelle provient ainsi de la menace qui pèse sur Beaudenord, sur les d'Aldrigger, sur Claparon, sur Rastignac même, de la redoutable présence de Nucingen ou, mieux, de son *absence* bien plus sinistre (car Nucingen est physiquement absent du récit et c'est là du reste le secret de son succès),[1] qui plane sur toutes ses victimes, capable à tout moment de les abattre, et relie entre eux les différents épisodes de la nouvelle.

L'examen de Lovenjoul A. 125 contribue finalement à éclairer le sens de *la Maison Nucingen*, et en particulier le rapport qui l'unit à *César Birotteau*. Rappelons tout d'abord que les deux romans, écrits et corrigés concurremment, sont toujours allés de pair dans l'esprit de Balzac; dès le début il ne peut, dans sa correspondance, en évoquer un sans, tout de suite, mentionner l'autre.[2] C'est qu'ils constituent les deux volets d'un diptyque (*la Maison Nucingen* est le 'tableau correspondant' de *César Birotteau*: XI, 360) où sont explorés l'envers et le revers d'une même situation; la technique sera répétée plus tard, dans un tout autre domaine, quand Balzac juxtaposera *la Cousine Bette* au *Cousin Pons*. Les affirmations du romancier sont à ce sujet explicites. Il écrit ainsi, dans la préface de l'édition originale de *César Birotteau*, que "ces deux histoires sont nées jumelles. Qui lit *César Birotteau*, devra donc lire *la Maison Nucingen*, s'il veut connaître l'ouvrage entier" (XI, 345); et, dans l'envoi de *la Maison Nucingen* à Zulma Carraud, que "vous et quelques âmes belles comme la vôtre, comprendront ma pensée en lisant *la Maison Nucingen* accolée à *César Birotteau*. Dans ce contraste n'y a-t-il pas tout un enseignement social" (V, 592). La *Lettre à Hyppolite Castille* d'octobre 1846 souligne de nouveau la parenté entre les deux ouvrages, cette fois avec une glose de Balzac: "*Nucingen* et *Birotteau* sont deux œuvres jumelles. C'est l'improbité, la probité, juxtaposées comme dans le monde."[3]

---

[1] Et également le sens du titre: le baron, dans *la Maison Nucingen* du moins, ne s'impose guere à nous en tant que personne; énormément au contraire en tant que système, en tant que *maison*, c'est à dire dépourvu de toute humanité et ce toute personnalité. Nous voyons la toile mais pas l'araignée.

[2] voir, par exemple, *L.H.*, t. I, pp. 465, 477, 491, 503.

[3] *O.D.*. t. III, p. 651.

C'est sans doute de l'opposition abstraite probité-improbité qu'est
née l'idée première de la juxtaposition des deux œuvres. On a ainsi
d'un côté l'exploitant, de l'autre l'exploité, la grosse mouche qui
passe à travers la toile de la loi en face de la petite qui y reste,[1] car
"l'écrivain, ce grand rapporteur de procès, doit mettre les adversaires
face à face".[2] L'apologie de l'absolutisme royaliste découle logique-
ment de la constatation de cet état de faits, un gouvernement absolu
étant seul capable à la fois de "donner la vie à l'argent",[3] de garantir
la liberté commerciale, de venir en aide à l'opprimé[4] et surtout de
réprimer "les entreprises de l'esprit contre la loi".[5] Une même
orientation politique – l'idéal du pouvoir fort dans la main d'un
seul – se retrouve dans les deux ouvrages.

Mais, sous cette opposition morale à valeur universelle entre
l'improbité du banquier et la probité, d'ailleurs relative, du parfumeur, Balzac nous présente également le spectacle de l'affronte-
ment entre deux mondes socio-économiques; et, en nous faisant
assister à un moment précis dans l'évolution du système commercial
et économique, l'historien rejoint chez lui le moraliste. *César*

---

[1] *La Maison Nucingen*, v, 652.
[2] Préface à l'édition originale de *César Birotteau*: xi, 344.
[3] *César Birotteau*, v, 344.
[4] *ibid.*, v, 579.
[5] *La Maison Nucingen*, v, 633; toute cette conclusion pro-royaliste de *la Maison
Nucingen* a été ajoutée par Balzac lors de la correction du premier jeu d'épreuves.
    La nouvelle se terminait en effet sur la première épreuve par la "vérité
pécuniaire" de Bixiou. Plus tard, Balzac remaniera encore son dénouement,
ajoutant sur les troisième et quatrième épreuves, après la conclusion actuelle,
des attaques contre le journalisme qui laissent présager la célèbre campagne
d'*Un grand homme de province à Paris*. Il introduit ainsi, sur le troisième jeu, une
phrase ("Le journalisme est l'opération d'un chimiste, dis-je à ma voisine
étonnée, vous venez d'en voir les plus beaux précipités": Lov., A. 125, f. 126)
qui sera longuement commentée sur le jeu suivant: " – Quelle effroyable jeunesse, s'écria-t-elle! – Le journalisme est l'alchimie de l'intelligence, dis-je à ma
voisine étonnée; vous venez d'en voir les plus beaux précipités. Est-ce à dire que
ni la *vertu* ni l'*art* n'existent, parce qu'il y a des *gens* qui passent devant Raphaël
en causant d'affaires, ou qui ne saluent pas un honnête homme dans le malheur? Il
est en nous un sentiment du beau idéal; moralement, il produit la vertu, physiquement, il produit l'art. Chez ces gens là l'esprit a tout tué. Ils n'ont pas un ami,
pas une maîtresse. Ils dînent au Rocher de Cancale quand on se bat dans Paris;
ils suivent en tilbury les tapissières chargées de morts pendant le choléra; ils ne
savent pas ce qu'on trouve dans Raphaël... – Les pauvres gens! dit-elle. – Eh
bien! Tu les plains?" (Lov., A. 125, f. 168 et verso.) Tout ce developpement est
retranché sur la cinquième épreuve et Balzac revient au dénouement définitif
avec l'explication suivante: "J'ai supprimé la copie de la précédente épreuve.
Il n'y avait pas à conclure. Il faut laisser penser ce que j'y disais." (Lov., A. 125,
f. 213.)

Birotteau nous offre en effet l'image d'une structure artisanale gérée par la famille (mais moins déjà que dans *la Maison du chat-qui-pelote*, première étape de cette évolution), fondée sur le principe de l'échange concret et profondément ancrée dans le comptant, dans le visible. *La Maison Nucingen* au contraire dépeint la naissance du capitalisme moderne qui, régi par un système corporatif et donc foncièrement impersonnel, se base sur le principe de liquidité, sur un commerce invisible, abstrait, occulte même, ou qui du moins peut sembler tel aux non-initiés. "C'est le parallélisme du petit commerce et de la grande banque, et l'opposition entre le petit commerçant probe et le gros financier malhonnête";[1] opposition qui nous enseigne que le monde où le créancier était plus fort que le débiteur est en voie d'être remplacé, selon la vérité de Bixiou, par un monde où le débiteur a l'avantage sur le créancier.[2] Parallélisme et opposition économiques sont renforcés par le contraste entre les titres adoptés par Balzac, par, ce qui revient au même, la différence de présentation des deux protagonistes (Birotteau, l'homme par excellence qui cherche à se faire valoir, lourdement et essentiellement présent, Nucingen volontairement absent), et surtout, sur le plan formel, par le contraste entre la structure des deux ouvrages: la prévisibilité de Birotteau et du système qu'il incarne est ainsi soulignée par l'inexorabilité du rythme romanesque, tandis qu'au contraire le décousu, l'improvisé de *la Maison Nucingen* renforce l'apparente imprévisibilité de la méthode de l'Alsacien.

Malgré ces indéniables différences de situation et de caractère, Birotteau et Nucingen partagent un trait fondamental, le charlatanisme moral, qui donne à la juxtaposition des romans dont ils sont les héros sa véritable signification. Car, nonobstant l'insistance de son créateur et le retour obsessif de mots tels que 'probe', 'probité', 'sage', etc. (qui contribue à hypnotiser puis à leurrer le lecteur),[3] le bon César n'est pas totalement innocent; comme Nucingen il ne craint pas de se salir les mains et de duper le public. C'est ainsi qu'il n'a aucun scrupule à profiter de la bêtise de ses contemporains en

---

[1] Présentation de *la Maison Nucingen* par M. Pierre Citron dans l'édition du Seuil de *la Comédie humaine* (t. IV, p. 233).
[2] cf. *César Birotteau*, V, 484, et *la Maison Nucingen*, V, 652.
[3] La protestation de vertu est du reste tellement appuyée que l'on est en droit, sinon en devoir de s'en méfier.

mettant sur le marché une huile qui, comme le lui fait remarquer Vauquelin (v, 412-13), n'aura pas plus d'effet qu'une autre mais qui, appuyée par les boniments de son prospectus et avec l'aide d'une emphatique campagne de publicité, assurera au parfumeur un bénéfice de 1 fr. 50 par flacon, soit de 50%.[1] On voit mal ce qui distingue, du point de vue de la morale, le lancement d'un produit sans valeur et sa vente à un prix exorbitant de la distribution d'un dividende fictif, de l'emploi de valeurs mortes afin de désintéresser des créanciers ou bien du recours à la stratégie de la *part à goinfre*. Une lecture attentive de *la Maison Nucingen* justifie d'ailleurs cette assimilation des deux situations. Que l'on en juge par ce passage que Balzac ajouta à son texte lors de la correction de la troisième épreuve, c'est à dire au moment où il se remettait à *César Birotteau*, et où il nous semble impossible qu'il n'ait pas eu à l'esprit le cas du parfumeur: "Accaparer la marchandise est la pensée du boutiquier de la rue Saint-Denis *dit* le plus vertueux, comme du spéculateur *dit* le plus effronté. Quand les magasins sont pleins, il y a nécessité de vendre. Pour vendre, il faut *allumer* le chaland, de là l'enseigne du Moyen Age et aujourd'hui le Prospectus."[2] L'implication est la même dans le reste du discours de Couture:

Eh bien, consultez les plus honnêtes gens de Paris, les notables commerçants enfin,... tous vous raconteront triomphalement la rouerie qu'ils ont alors inventée pour écouler leur marchandise quand on la leur avait vendue mauvaise... Les plus vertueux négociants vous disent de l'air le plus candide ce mot de l'improbité la plus effrénée: *On se tire d'une mauvaise affaire comme on peut...* Des casquettes et de la rue Saint-Denis aux Actions et à la Banque, concluez![3]

[1] Voir à ce sujet le chapitre sur 'la Faillite Birotteau' dans le *Balzac homme d'affaires* de René Bouvier (Paris, 1930), pp. 59–86. Le passage qui suit donne une bonne idée du manque de scrupules dont fait preuve César: "Ainsi, demain, à sept heures, soyons à la fabrique, les noisettes viendront et nous ferons de l'huile, car il [Vauquelin] a beau dire que toute huile est bonne, nous serions perdus si le public le savait. S'il n'entrait pas dans notre huile un peu de noisette et de parfum, sous quel prétexte pourrions-nous la vendre trois ou quatre francs les quatre onces!" (v, 415). C'est là également le point de vue avancé par M. Bouvier-Ajam dans son article sur 'les Opérations financières de la Maison Nucingen', *Europe* (janvier-février 1965), voir surtout pp. 29–32.

[2] v, 638. Les italiques sont de Balzac.

[3] v, 638-9. Les italiques sont de Balzac.

L'erreur de Birotteau provient du fait qu'il s'est également engagé dans une spéculation étrangère à ses préoccupations spécialisées, pour laquelle l'expertise lui fait défaut; et, comme le fait remarquer Claparon, "il lui arrive ce qui arrivera toujours à ceux qui sortent de leur spécialité" (v, 545). Il s'est en somme immiscé dans une affaire du genre de celles qui assureront la fortune de Nucingen, mais sans disposer des moyens et de la mentalité du banquier; ainsi, au lieu de s'en tenir à une entreprise concrète, où il aurait pu parfaitement réussir (comme le prouve Popinot), César se fourvoie dans les détours du "commerce abstrait". C'est ce qui explique la distinction entre la spéculation concrète, dont il comprend admirablement (?) le mécanisme (on peut en juger par la description très détaillée qu'il en donne à sa femme: v, 339), et la Spéculation abstraite devant laquelle il reste bouche bée (c'est là la portée de la scène avec Claparon dans la seconde partie du roman: v, 523-4). On apprécie alors toute la défiance de Constance et la différence de son attitude envers les deux aventures: "Quant à ton affaire de la Madeleine, je m'y oppose formellement. Tu es parfumeur, sois parfumeur, et non pas revendeur de terrains" (v, 338).

On en revient donc en définitive, pour rendre compte de la juxtaposition des deux romans, moins à l'opposition de départ entre la probité de Birotteau et l'improbité de Nucingen qu'au contraste sous-jacent entre l'intelligence et l'inintelligence, entre la supériorité intellectuelle, clef de voûte de la fortune du banquier, et la stupidité qui perd le parfumeur. De là l'admiration que Balzac ne peut s'empêcher d'accorder à "cet illustre baron [qui] s'est élevé sur l'abîme où d'autres auraient sombré" (v, 601), au Napoléon de la finance qui "ne saurait inventer une mauvaise affaire" (v, 641) – à l'encontre de son créateur qui en avait inventé d'innombrables (Nucingen, comme tant de héros de la Comédie humaine, est dans une certaine mesure une réalisation idéale des ambitions du romancier). L'homme supérieur balzacien (c'est à dire l'homme lucide, sachant diriger sa volonté et dominer ses passions), de par sa supériorité même, s'élève au-dessus des lois qui régissent le commun des mortels: "Son génie embrasse tout... La Banque envisagée ainsi devient toute une politique, elle exige une tête puissante, et porte alors un homme bien trempé à se mettre au-dessus des lois de la probité dans lesquelles il se trouve à l'étroit" (v, 602). De là également l'ambiguïté de l'attitude de Balzac envers son parfumeur, l'admiration pour le courage dont fait preuve César au cours de son calvaire coudoyant un certain mépris: mépris pour son manque de lucidité, pour son "incapacité... à remonter la chaîne des inductions par lesquelles un homme supérieur arrive aux causes" (v, 390), pour son impuissance à dominer ses antécédents paysans et son désir de paraître.[1] Et, en fin de compte, si Balzac nous présente ainsi le petit esprit en face de la tête forte ("en éclairant la profondeur de son caractère et les ressorts de sa grandeur, on pourra comprendre comment les accidents commerciaux que surmontent les têtes fortes deviennent d'irréparables catastrophes pour de petits esprits": v, 340-1), c'est qu'il entend, en juxtaposant *la Maison Nucingen* à *César Birotteau*, illustrer un enseignement social qui forme l'une des constantes thématiques de *la Comédie humaine*; il veut nous montrer, une fois encore, que seuls les êtres d'exception peuvent s'aventurer sans danger dans la jungle parisienne, qu'il n'y a que "les esprits d'élite, les gens d'une force herculéenne auxquels il soit permis de quitter le toit protecteur de la famille pour aller lutter dans l'immense arène de Paris".[2] Le précepte s'applique aux pères aussi bien qu'aux fils, aux vieux comme aux jeunes.

[1] La comparaison s'impose à cet égard entre les antécédents de Nucingen et ceux de Birotteau. Sur Nucingen, Balzac est d'un laconisme quasi gidien: nous savons seulement de lui qu'il est le fils "de quelque juif converti par ambition" (v, 601). Nous sommes au contraire beaucoup plus précisément renseignés sur les parents de César (V, 341), sur son père, closier des environs de Chinon, et sur sa mère qui mourut en le mettant au monde. Il y a dans ce contraste de quoi faire rêver les psychanalystes...

[2] Préface à la troisième partie d'*Illusions perdues*, XI, 342.

Balzac's *Les Chouans* and Stendhal's *De l'Amour*

F. W. J. HEMMINGS

IN March 1841 a certain Désiré Laverdant, returning by the over-
land route from India to France after a five years' absence, posted a
long letter from Naples to the French consul at Civitavecchia. He
reminded Stendhal of their earlier meeting in 1832; profiting from
a letter of introduction furnished by Mme Ancelot, Laverdant had
been able to wait on him, though he supposes that, after so long a
lapse of time, the occasion is unlikely to have remained in Stendhal's
memory. In the interval he has been turning over in his mind the
possibility of composing a monograph on the writer of whom he is
proud to count himself one of the most ardent admirers. His primary
purpose would be to ensure that Stendhal should receive proper
credit for all those ideas which he has been responsible for putting
into circulation, but which have been shamelessly appropriated by
others, for, as Laverdant adds: "bien des glaneurs et compilateurs
(M. de Balzac en tête) se sont parés à vos frais impunément".[1]

Stendhal seems to have answered this letter, to judge by a note
in his handwriting that appears at the top of it; but, unhappily,
the reply he sent has not come down to us. As for Laverdant, he
must have shelved his project which would have been, at the time,
difficult to put into operation. In fact, he never appears to have
published anything on Stendhal: certainly nothing on this interesting question of the literary debt Balzac may have contracted towards
his elder. The late François Michel did take the trouble to search
through the files of *La Démocratie pacifique*, the Fourierist organ
in which Laverdant published a large number of articles of literary

---

[1] Laverdant's letter has been published in Stendhal, *Correspondance*, édition établie
et annotée par Henri Martineau et V. Del Litto (Paris, Bibliothèque de la
Pléiade, 1968), vol. III, pp. 585–7.

criticism from 1843 onwards. He found Stendhal's name mentioned only twice, and only in passing.[1]

At the same time it does appear that Désiré Laverdant may well have been the first to realize what valuable results a systematic study of the intellectual interchanges between Stendhal and Balzac might yield. The next student to have looked at the question was, it seems, the Anglo-Welsh critic and symbolist poet Arthur Symons;[2] at all events it was he who made the first attempt at drawing up a list of the passages in which Balzac actually names Stendhal as the author of some opinion, theory, or observation of note. He communicated his findings to Adolphe Paupe, who summarized them in a chapter, 'Stendhal et *la Comédie humaine*', of his *Vie littéraire de Stendhal*.[3] Arthur Symons drew attention to three passages where Balzac mentions Stendhal, always in the most eulogistic terms. In *Étude de femme* there is the following sentence: "Un homme d'esprit, Stendhal, a eu la bizarre idée de nommer *cristallisation* le travail que la pensée de la marquise fit avant, pendant et après cette soirée."[4] (The *marquise* referred to is Mme de Listomère, somewhat flustered – if the word can be used of a lady of rank – by the receipt of a love-letter from Eugène de Rastignac which that scatter-brained playboy had sent to the wrong address.) Next, Symons quotes from *La Maison Nucingen*: "Un des hommes les plus spirituels et les plus profonds de cette époque, Stendhal, a très bien caractérisé l'*improper* en disant qu'il est tel lord de la Grande-Bretagne qui, seul, n'ose pas se croiser les jambes devant son feu, de peur d'être *improper*."[5] Finally, he recalls the passage in *La Muse du Département* where Dinah de la Baudraye, after four years' cohabitation with Etienne Lousteau, is said to have experienced "toutes les nuances [de l'amour] découvertes par notre esprit d'analyse et que la société moderne a créées; un des hommes les plus remarquables de ce

---

[1] see s.v. *Laverdant* in Michel's *Fichier stendhalien*.

[2] As far as I have been able to discover, Symons published only one essay on Stendhal, which appeared in the *English Review*, October 1917. It is clear from this that his appreciation of Balzac was greater: "Stendhal substituted the brain for the heart as the battle-place of the novel: not the brain as Balzac conceived it, a motive force of action, the mainspring of passion, the force by which a nature directs its accumulated energy: but a sterile sort of brain, set at a great distance from the heart, whose rhythm is too faint to disturb it."

[3] Paris (1914) pp. 191-4.

[4] I, 1052.

[5] V, 606.

temps, dont la perte récente afflige encore les lettres, Beyle (Stendhal) les a, le premier, parfaitement caractérisées."[1] Later in the same passage Balzac enumerates these *nuances*, these "manières d'aimer", referring his reader once more to what he calls the "définitions de Beyle".

There are, of course, a few other allusions to Stendhal in *La Comédie humaine* which Symons missed. Paupe himself – acknowledging Daniel Muller as the source of his information this time – pointed out that in the page he devotes in *Massimilla Doni* to the boxes in Italian opera houses, Balzac tells us that "la causerie est souveraine absolue dans cet espace, qu'un des écrivains les plus ingénieux de ce temps, et l'un de ceux qui ont le mieux observé l'Italie, Stendhal, a nommé un petit salon dont la fenêtre donne sur un parterré."[2] Finally – and it would appear that Pierre Jourda was the first to draw attention to this passage[3] – in *Un prince de la Bohème* Balzac, referring to the inhabitants of that mythical realm, Bohemia, informs us that "ils ont mis en pratique, sans le savoir et sans l'avoir lu peut-être, le livre *De l'Amour* par Stendhal; ils ont la section de l'amour-goût, celle de l'amour-passion, l'amour-caprice, l'amour cristallisé, et surtout l'amour passager."[4]

One curious fact emerges as soon as one gathers together all these allusions to Stendhal scattered through *La Comédie humaine*: Balzac never once refers to his great contemporary as a novelist. Stendhal is "un des hommes les plus spirituels et les plus profonds de cette époque", "un des hommes les plus remarquables de ce temps", "un des écrivains les plus ingénieux de ce temps". Furthermore it would seem that, as far as Balzac was concerned, Stendhal deserved mention for two works only. The story of the ultra-decorous English aristocrat who would not dream of crossing his legs even if he were sitting alone before his own hearth is drawn from *Rome, Naples et Florence*, though it is perhaps worth noting that where Balzac, repeating the story, uses the Victorian word *improper*, Stendhal contents himself with the slightly milder French equivalent *vulgaire*.[5] Similarly, *Rome, Naples et Florence* seems to have been

[1] IV, 189. [2] IX, 337.
[3] 'Balzac lecteur de Stendhal', *Le Divan*, no. 253 (1945), 42–3.
[4] VI, 824.
[5] *Rome, Naples and Florence*, ed. V. Del Litto (Lausanne, 1961), p. 127.

H

Balzac's source for his comparison between an opera box and a drawing-room; writing about the Scala, Stendhal had observed: "on fait la conversation dans les deux cents petits salons, avec une fenêtre garnie de rideaux donnant sur la salle, qu'on appelle loges."[1] Apart from these two, the other references are all to Stendhal as the author of *De l'Amour*; even when Balzac does not mention the work by name, it is clear that he has it in mind, either in respect of the theory of crystallization it enshrines or of Stendhal's categorization of the various types of love.

It is, indeed, highly probable that *De l'Amour* was the first of Stendhal's books that Balzac came across. His *Physiologie du mariage*, authorized for publication in 1826 and partly composed by that time, bears signs already, as Maurice Bardèche has shown,[2] of an assiduous reading of *De l'Amour*, in particular of the sections dealing with girls' education. In addition, we know that Balzac collaborated with Horace Raisson in the confection of some, if not all, of the various *Codes* published under Raisson's name in the late 1820s, one of which, the *Code galant ou Art de conter fleurette* (1829), reproduces, with due acknowledgment, the whole of Stendhal's chapter on the medieval *cours d'amour*.[3] There is thus no lack of evidence that Balzac's reading of *De l'Amour* antedated considerably his first meeting with the author, which as his biographers tell us took place some time in 1830, in the house of their mutual friend the painter Baron Gérard.[4]

De l'Amour has never, as far as I am aware, been cited in connection with *Le Dernier Chouan*, a work which was announced in the *Bibliographie de la France* on 28 March 1829, and thus preceded by nine months the appearance of the *Physiologie du mariage*. Professor Maurice Regard, in the introduction to his invaluable edition of *Les Chouans*, admittedly stresses the Stendhalian atmosphere of the work, but only in order to demonstrate that *Les Chouans* incorporates certain techniques and qualities that will make their appearance later in Stendhal's novels, in *La Chartreuse de Parme*

---

[1] *Rome, Naples and Florence*, ed. V. Del Litto (Lausanne, 1961), p. 35.

[2] see Bardèche's edition of the *Physiologie du mariage préoriginale* (Geneva, 1940); and also his *Stendhal romancier* (Paris, 1947), pp. 98–9.

[3] see Claude Pichois, 'Balzac, Raisson, Chasles et *De l'Amour*', *Le Divan*, no. 291 (1954), pp. 420–4.

[4] H. J. Hunt, *Honoré de Balzac, a biography* (1957), pp. 40–1.

in particular. The character of Marie de Verneuil, "cette âme énergique et passionnée," he writes, "préfigure admirablement les héroïnes de Stendhal. Rêveuse et violente, calculatrice, coquette, follement séduisante, elle est comme une sœur aînée de la Sanseverina." Similarly the Marquis de Montauran, "le Gars", "est aussi étranger au monde de la Vivetière que l'est Fabrice à la cour de Parme. Cet amant, qui demande à Marie la permission de lui parler aussi longtemps qu'il peut tenir un charbon enflammé, a des mots que n'eût pas désavoués Fabrice: 'Ces gens-là m'ont volé un moment de bonheur.' "

Professor Regard draws our attention, further, to the very similar way in which, in *Les Chouans* as in *La Chartreuse de Parme*, the action can be said to develop. Each novel, he writes, "se compose de deux parties séparées par un certain temps et dont le lien est plus psychologique que dramatique. Le combat de la Pèlerine est un prélude qui nous donne une atmosphère sauvage et dangereuse dont nous avons besoin pour nous trouver à la hauteur de ce qui va suivre. La bataille de Waterloo sera à la même place dans le roman de Stendhal et produira le même effet." The editor of *Les Chouans* suggests that Balzac may well have been remembering his own early novel when he wrote his long critique of *La Chartreuse* in *La Revue parisienne*; that would explain why Balzac said he would have preferred "à propos de Rassi 'au moins une petite scène d'intérieur', qu'il eût voulu aussi 'le côté physique dans la peinture de quelques personnages', des retours en arrière naturellement, et tout cela nous montrerait que *la Chartreuse* dans son esprit procédait des *Chouans*."[1]

It would not enter into anyone's mind to dispute Professor Regard's conclusions; but it is possible to attack the question from the other end, as it were. We cannot be sure that Stendhal ever read *Les Chouans*, whereas we are certain that Balzac had not only read *De l'Amour* by the time he came to write *Les Chouans*, but can almost be said to have soaked himself in it.

To search *Les Chouans* for direct reminiscences of *De l'Amour* would probably be a waste of time. The only passage which one might be tempted to interpret in this way occurs in chapter xii (a chapter to which we shall have occasion to allude again later). Marie de Verneuil, accompanied by her maid Francine, is travelling from

[1] *Les Chouans*, ed. Maurice Regard (Paris, 1957), pp. xxvii-xxviii.

Alençon to Mayenne in the mail-coach, which is also transporting the young naval officer she met the previous evening in the hostelry at Alençon and the woman who passes as his mother, Mme du Gua. The coach is being escorted by a detachment of republican soldiers under the command of Captain Merle, who for the time being is taking his orders from Mlle de Verneuil.

A league out of Mayenne they are set upon by a band of Chouans. The attack is not pressed seriously; the purpose was merely to allow one of the assailants, the Chevalier de Valois, to get close enough to the young Du Gua to be able to whisper a few words in his ear. The naval officer is, in fact, none other than "le Gars" whom Marie has instructions to contact, in other words the Marquis de Montauran, the guiding spirit of the royalist insurrection in Brittany; the warning conveyed him by the Chevalier was that his bewitching travelling companion is possibly a vamp sent by Fouché to destroy him. His attitude towards the young woman changes abruptly; astonished and resentful at first, she soon guesses the reason for his sudden coolness. The few words that she exchanges with Merle are sufficient to convince her of the true identity of the young man who, shortly before, had been paying court to her so charmingly; nevertheless she decides against having him arrested on the spot, preferring to keep him in a state of agonized suspense. Balzac describes her behaviour in the following words:

> Son regard, empreint d'une perfidie moqueuse, montrait les soldats au jeune chef d'un air de triomphe; en lui présentant ainsi l'image de son danger, elle se plaisait à lui faire durement sentir que sa vie dépendait d'un seul mot, et déjà ses lèvres paraissaient se mouvoir pour le prononcer. Semblable à un sauvage d'Amérique, elle interrogeait les fibres du visage de son ennemi lié au poteau, et brandissait le *casse-tête* avec grâce, savourant une vengeance tout innocente, et punissant comme une maîtresse qui aime encore.[1]

The suggestion Maurice Regard makes is that this simile may have been drawn from *The Last of the Mohicans*; a plausible hypothesis, given Balzac's well-attested admiration of the romances of Fenimore Cooper. The original title he chose for his work, *Le*

VII, 882-3.

Dernier Chouan, was almost certainly intended to echo the title of the French version of Cooper's masterpiece, *Le Dernier Mohican*. Elsewhere in his novel, he is at pains to establish parallels between the customs and habits of the redskins, as described by the American novelist, and those of the Bretons of 1799. In his second chapter, for instance, he asserts that "l'absence complète de nos lois, de nos mœurs, de notre habillement, de nos monnaies nouvelles, de notre langage, mais aussi la simplicité patriarcale et d'héroïques vertus s'accordent à rendre les habitants de ces campagnes plus pauvres de combinaisons intellectuelles que ne le sont les Mohicans et les Peaux-Rouges de l'Amérique septentrionale, mais aussi grands, aussi rusés, aussi durs qu'eux." And a little further on, Balzac adds: "C'étaient des Sauvages qui servaient Dieu et le roi, à la manière dont les Mohicans font la guerre."[1]

It is, however, arguable that the comparison of his heroine with "un sauvage d'Amérique" who "interroge les fibres du visage de son ennemi lié au poteau" may have been suggested to Balzac, not by anything he read in Fenimore Cooper, but rather by a passage in *De l'Amour* consisting of a long excerpt from Volney's *Tableau du climat et du sol des États-Unis* or, more exactly, from one of the articles appended to this work, entitled 'Observations générales sur les Indiens ou Sauvages de l'Amérique du Nord'.[2] Here, Balzac would have read that "le sort ordinaire des prisonniers de guerre est, non pas seulement d'être brûlés vifs et mangés, mais d'être auparavant *liés à un poteau* près d'un bûcher enflammé, pour y être pendant plusieurs heures tourmentés par tout ce que la rage peut imaginer de plus féroce et de plus raffiné." Two further details in Balzac's account reinforce the parallel between the situation he is describing and Volney's relation of the barbarous behaviour of the Red Indians. First, the fact that it is a woman who is tormenting a man, "obéissant peut-être," observes Balzac, "à cet instinct qui porte la femme à jouer avec sa proie[3] comme le chat joue avec la

---

[1] *ibid.*, 778, 780n.

[2] *De l'Amour*, édition établie et commentée par Henri Martineau (Paris, 1957), pp. 112-13.

[3] The MS. of *Les Chouans* (Collection Lovenjoul) shows that Balzac originally wrote "son captif" instead of "sa proie" – a significant variant, since Montauran cannot be described as in any sense Marie's 'captive'; but it is understandable, if Balzac had one eye on this page of *De l'Amour* as he was writing, that he should have used such a word in a moment of distraction.

souris qu'il a prise"; it is noteworthy that Volney mentions that one circumstance in particular has impressed every European who has had the opportunity of witnessing these atrocious scenes of torture, viz. "la fureur des femmes et des enfants, et leur plaisir atroce à rivaliser de cruauté". The second point that Volney stresses is the stoical determination with which the tortured brave dissimulates his sufferings. He writes of the "sang-froid inaltérable du prisonnier qui non seulement ne donne aucun signe de douleur, mais qui brave et défie ses bourreaux par tout ce que l'orgueil a de plus hautain, l'ironie de plus amer, le sarcasme de plus insultant". This is a feature meticulously reproduced by Balzac; the only modifications he has introduced are those necessary to make it clear that we are concerned, at this point in *Les Chouans*, with moral, not physical torture:

> Le jeune général souriait de l'air le plus calme, et soutenait sans trembler la torture que mademoiselle de Verneuil lui faisait subir; son attitude et l'expression de sa physionomie annonçaient un homme nonchalant des dangers auxquels il était soumis, et parfois il semblait lui dire: "Voici l'occasion de venger votre vanité blessée, saisissez-la! Je serais au désespoir de revenir de mon mépris pour vous."[1]

One last observation in favour of what is being advanced here. The passage from Volney is quoted by Stendhal in the thirty-eighth chapter of *De l'Amour*: this chapter is headed 'De la pique d'amour-propre'. At the point Balzac has reached in his narrative, his heroine was suffering, precisely, from a violent "pique d'amour-propre". She was aware that she had made some impression on her handsome fellow traveller; she then observes that, suddenly and inexplicably, his manner towards her becomes cold and remote; what could be more mortifying for the young woman's pride? It is almost as if Balzac, realizing that he needed at this stage to dramatize the emotional state described by Stendhal under the name of "pique d'amour-propre", opened his copy of *De l'Amour* at the relevant chapter, and finding there Volney's narrative, incorporated it in all its particulars in the form of a prolonged and brilliant metaphor.

[1] VII, 883.

Is this the only occasion in *Les Chouans* when the author seems to have recourse to *De l'Amour*? Almost certainly not; for it can be readily seen that the entire love-story underlying the historical novel represents an exact demonstration of Stendhal's theory of the birth and growth of love, as convincing a demonstration, actually, as any that can be found in Stendhal's own novels. The central argument of *De l'Amour* is that love (*l'amour-passion*) is a matter of losing and recovering confidence. The two poles between which the lover (or his mistress) wavers are those of trust and mistrust or, to put it slightly differently, of security and insecurity. A measure of insecurity is indispensable to keep passion alive: "toujours un petit doute à calmer, voilà ce qui fait la soif de tous les instants, voilà ce qui fait la vie de l'amour heureux".[1] But the doubts have to be dissipated – even if only temporarily – to permit the process of crystallization to start up again.

This sequence – first crystallization, doubt, second crystallization – as described by Stendhal in his chapter entitled 'De la naissance de l'amour', will be faithfully observed by Balzac in the account he gives of the burgeoning of passion between his two lovers. For Marie, the first crystallization occurs after her initial encounter with Montauran in the coaching inn. "Combien de fois n'ai-je pas vu cet homme dans mes rêves," she exclaims in the privacy of her bedroom. "Oh! comme sa tête est belle et quel regard étincelant!"[2] For any reader of *De l'Amour*, a classic case of love at first sight, of the *coup de foudre* occurring precisely in the conditions Stendhal had laid down:

> L'âme, à son insu, ennuyée de vivre sans aimer, convaincue malgré elle, par l'exemple des autres femmes, ayant surmonté toutes les craintes de la vie, mécontente du triste bonheur de l'orgueil, s'est fait, sans s'en apercevoir, un modèle idéal. Elle rencontre un jour un être qui ressemble à ce modèle, la cristallisation reconnaît son objet au trouble qu'il inspire, et consacre pour toujours au maître de son destin ce qu'elle rêvait depuis longtemps.[3]

Marie de Verneuil, as we realize when we learn her past history, is literally in the situation stipulated by Stendhal for the experience

[1] *De l'Amour*, p. 94.   [2] *Les Chouans*, p. 853.   [3] *De l'Amour*, p. 52.

she is undergoing; it is she, this "âme... ennuyée de vivre sans aimer";
truly she has "surmonté toutes les craintes de la vie" and has grown
"mécontente du triste bonheur de l'orgueil".

Her passion, before long, becomes a shared passion, for within
a few hours the young nobleman 'crystallizes' in his turn; this
happens during the short walk the couple take up a hill while their
coach lumbers behind. The conversation he has with the fair stranger
awakens his curiosity and stimulates a violent interest in her; having
conducted her back to her seat in the coach, the disguised Chouan
leader contemplates her in silence and, says Balzac, "l'amant en
vint bientôt à cette phase de la passion où un homme trouve dans
les défauts de sa maîtresse des raisons pour l'aimer davantage"[1] – a
piece of psychological observation that sounds as if it has been directly
inspired by one of Stendhal's descriptions of the process of crystallization: "même les petits défauts de sa figure donnent de l'attendrissement à l'homme qui aime".[2] A little later, the marquis is
assailed by *doubts*: again, according to the text-book, the inevitable
sequel to the first crystallization. These doubts, as we have already
seen, were implanted by his friend and companion in arms, the
Chevalier de Valois, in the course of the brief skirmish on the high-
road between the *chouans* and the *bleus*. Marie, observing the sudden
indifference of her lover towards her, is led similarly to doubt the
reality of the dawning passion she imagined she had detected in
him. That same evening, at the Château de la Vivetière, she is not
merely disdained and cold-shouldered by the marquis, but subjected
in his presence to an abominable outrage; it is then that the love
she first felt turns to bitter hatred for, as Stendhal tells us in *De
l'Amour*, "la haine a sa cristallisation; dès qu'on peut espérer de se
venger, on recommence de haïr".[3] When Montauran, without
attempting to protect her or to interpose his authority, allows Mme
du Gua to insult her in front of the royalist leaders, to tear open her
bodice and expose to their sight a "gorge palpitante", Marie can
feel nothing but a burning desire for vengeance:

L'homme qui lui avait témoigné tant d'amour avait donc entendu
les plaisanteries dont elle venait d'être accablée, et restait le
témoin glacé de la prostitution qu'elle venait d'endurer lorsque

[1] *Les Chouans*, p. 872. [2] *De l'Amour*, p. 39. [3] *ibid.*, p. 18.

les beautés qu'une femme réserve à l'amour essuyèrent tous les regards! Peut-être aurait-elle pardonné à Montauran ses sentiments de mépris, mais elle s'indigna d'avoir été vue par lui dans une infâme situation; elle lui lança un regard stupide et plein de haine, car elle sentit naître dans son cœur d'effroyables désirs de vengeance. (p. 911.)

According to the sequence established by Stendhal in *De l'Amour*, the period of doubt that follows the first crystallization will normally be succeeded by a second crystallization. Once again, this is exactly what happens in *Les Chouans*. The ardour that Montauran displays at the ball of St James, and above all his action in plucking a burning coal from the fire and begging Marie to listen to him for so long as he can endure to hold it in his hand, all this convinces her that his love is genuine: "Je suis aimée, dit-elle, j'ai reconquis l'estime de l'homme qui représente à mes yeux le monde entier, je puis mourir." (p. 999.)

The hypothesis of a direct influence of *De l'Amour* on *Les Chouans* encounters one grave objection, which is this: Why should it be supposed that Balzac needed to delve into Stendhal's treatise in order to trace the progress of his two lovers' mutual passion? If the path this passion follows happens to coincide with the general itinerary plotted by Stendhal, might this not simply mean that each of these two great "students of the human heart" had reached identical conclusions based on their separate experiences? Was Balzac, in short, so ignorant of the psychology of love as to be incapable of reconstructing the process himself?

But no such claim is being made here. It has to be remembered that *De l'Amour* exhibits a specifically Stendhalian image of love; the observations which illuminate and enliven the book were personal to Stendhal, the psychological substructure on which it depends is one that he had inherited from his masters the ideologists. The passion of love, with which he is concerned, can — and does — present itself in many ways, in ways different from those that Stendhal knew.

In his later novels, Balzac shows that he understood this. It is only in *Les Chouans* that one will find so faithful an illustration of Stendhal's theories. The girls and young women who appear in his subsequent novels, Eugénie Grandet, Ursule Mirouet, Hortense Hulot, even Rosalie de Watteville, fall in love in a much more straightforward, much less complicated way; they 'crystallize' once and for all, without requiring to pass through the intermediary stages of doubt, desire for vengeance, and forgiveness, so as to reach the haven of the 'second crystallization'. The point is that these young ladies are purely Balzacian heroines, whereas Marie de Verneuil, his first vibrant feminine creation, is better described as a Stendhalian heroine making an exceptional appearance in a novel by Balzac.

Balzac and Stendhal:
a comparison of electoral scenes

COLIN SMETHURST

For some years now Balzac and Stendhal specialists have been
urging the interest and usefulness of an exhaustive comparison of
the connections between these two writers. A certain amount of
work establishing the direct or indirect personal or literary connections has already been done,[1] and in this essay we should like to
sketch a brief comparison of each author's treatment of a common
theme, namely general elections. We shall use Balzac's *Albert
Savarus* and *Député d'Arcis* and Stendhal's *Lucien Leuwen* as the
basis of our study.

The interest of just such a comparison has been noted in passing
by Professor Hunt[2] and in a more general way by Paul Valéry in
his prefatory essay to *Lucien Leuwen*. The latter observes that: "le
parallèle de Balzac et de Stendhal, – si l'on prenait quelque intérêt
à cet exercice, – pourrait se concevoir et se poursuivre assez raison-
nablement. Ils opèrent l'un et l'autre sur la même époque et la
même substance sociale. Ce sont deux observateurs imaginatifs du
même objet."[3] In the three novels mentioned the two writers are
dealing, not only with the same society, but with the same aspect
of that society: elections under Louis-Philippe.

It is not however a case of a direct influence of the one author
on the other. *Lucien Leuwen* was written and corrected during the
period May 1834 – November 1836, but did not see the light of day
until well after Balzac's death. Although the first conception of the
Député d'Arcis also dates, curiously enough, from late 1834 or early
1835, Balzac did not do anything about the project until April or

---

[1] see notably R. de Cesare, *Stendhal Club*, no. 3; P. Citron, *Année balz.* (1966);
V. D. L.[itto], *Stendhal Club*, no. 41; H. Martineau, *Le Divan*, no. 257; R.
Martineau, *Le Divan*, no. 256; A.-M. Meininger, *Année balz.* (1965 and 1966).
[2] *Balzac's Comédie humaine* (1959), pp. 312 and 407.
[3] *Lucien Leuwen* (Paris, 1927), ed. H. Debraye, préface p. xi. All subsequent
references to *L.L.* are to this edition.

May 1839 and finally published the unfinished work in 1847. *Albert Savarus* was written and published between the end of April and the end of June 1842. Any influence, therefore, of the one author on the other can only be via the other works of Balzac and Stendhal. Such small instances as have been discovered or suggested[1] are not linked with the electoral episodes in these novels. This discussion is thus limited to the coincidences and differences provoked in each author's imagination by the literary treatment of an identical theme, and the light they shed on each writer's approach to elections.

The distinguishing feature of elections under the Restoration and July monarchies was the high property qualification, or *cens*, required of both candidates and voters. Until 1815 the electorate was nominally very large, though election to the National Legislature was indirect and in fact controlled by Napoléon. From 1848 onwards universal adult manhood suffrage was the rule. It is only in the period 1815–48 that we find a very restricted electorate sending its representatives directly to the National Assembly. The electorate increased slowly from 171,000 in the June 1834 elections to 220,000 in those of July 1842. About 75–80 per cent of the electorate voted. Balzac and Stendhal were writing in a period when the actual votes cast for the election of 459 deputies increased from 129,000 in 1834 to 173,000 in 1842.

An average constituency would have about 350 electors actually voting. This number naturally varied a good deal. In the poorer constituencies which thus furnished fewer heavy taxpayers the tax requirements often had to be lowered in order to bring the registered number of voters up to the figure of 150 required by law. In general, the poorer constituencies were easier to manipulate than, say, the Parisian constituencies which had over 2,000 voters who, from the government's point of view, voted badly. Hence the government concentrated its ballot-rigging activities in the provinces where the vote was relatively easier to swing.

There is, then, a certain significance in the fact that both Stendhal and Balzac show the government's agents, Lucien Leuwen and Maxime de Trailles in the *Député d'Arcis*, operating in the pro-

---

[1] see Stendhal's marginalia printed *passim* in Debraye, *op. cit.*; H. Martineau, *Le Divan*, no. 257; and J. Pommier, 'A propos d'Albert Savarus', in *Balzac et la Touraine* (Tours, 1950).

vinces. Equally both authors show the government's successful influence in moderate-sized constituencies. In the *Député d'Arcis* a campaign meeting attended by 67 voters is sufficient to disturb very seriously the administrators of Arcis. There is, of course, no description of the poll in the unfinished *Député*, but from a passing reference in *Cousine Bette* (VI, 330) we see that Beauvisage is the deputy for Arcis, which indicates the defeat of Giguet and the triumph of the ministerial influence. In addition there is a series of unpublished jottings on the title page of the manuscript of the *Député d'Arcis*[1] which shows Balzac trying to establish possible voting patterns and ending with a total poll of 342 or, in another variation, 360. Whatever the implications these figures may have for the plot and characters of the novel (and they may be interesting), they suggest an electoral register of 380–400.

Balzac fixes on a slightly larger figure in *Albert Savarus*. In the preliminary voting for the presidency of the election we find a total of 207 votes cast (I, 837-8), but it is also known that there are 160 voters who, at this stage, are holding back, giving a total of 367 voters and, we may infer, a voting register of probably around 400 names. This estimate seems to be slightly inflated two pages later when the abbé de Grancey calculates that 130 votes will go to Savarus, who replies that another 75 are needed to win. 205 votes for a majority implies 400 to 409 voters in Besançon and a correspondingly larger number on the electoral register.

It would probably be wrong to try to tie these figures to any specific constituency; indeed Balzac warns the reader against making any such comparison: "La ville d'Arcis-sur-Aube n'a pas été le théâtre des événements qui en sont le sujet. L'Arrondissement d'Arcis va voter à Bar-sur-Aube, il n'existe donc pas de député d'Arcis à la Chambre." (XI, 422.) However, we do find that in 1839 the electoral register of Bar-sur-Aube had 392 names on it, and that of Besançon (*intra muros*) – the constituency being fought in *Albert Savarus* – in 1839 had 365 names, which demonstrates how close Balzac was to actual figures.

The two elections described in Part II of *Lucien Leuwen* have rather higher electorates. The first constituency has 613 electors and an estimated poll of 400 – a rather low poll, for which no specific

[1] Collection Lovenjoul, A. 55, f. B.

reason is given. Here the government influence carries the day. The second constituency of Caen (or Ranville) is a rather special case. It has, according to Stendhal, 1,280 voters, which would make it the largest provincial constituency in the France of 1834. Stendhal seems to have entertained doubts about the figures he quotes for, among his marginal notes, we find: "Electeurs inscrits... 1280. A vérifier. Est-ce le nombre convenable pour le bureau, par exemple, de Bourges?"[1] In fact, barely 200 people voted in the 1834 elections for Bourges (*intra muros*). The marginal note is typical of those in *Lucien Leuwen* where Stendhal shows his semi-commitment to the factual basis of his portraits: he realizes the problems of getting his facts more or less right, reminds himself to check them, and then does nothing about it. It can be said in his favour that Stendhal was in a curious position for describing political life under Louis-Philippe in that up to September 1835, by which date virtually the whole of *Lucien Leuwen* was written and corrected, he had spent only seven months in the France of Louis-Philippe. Of these seven months three and a half were at the very beginning of the régime, leaving a bare three months in France in late 1833 for Stendhal to experience the régime directly. Hence the large number of notes in the margins of *Lucien Leuwen* reminding himself to check this or that detail on his return to Paris, or to write to friends for information. The external sources for *Lucien Leuwen* are to be found in the newspapers Stendhal read in Rome and Civitavecchia and the conversations with friends, particularly in the embassy at Rome. The source of much of the actual tone of the electoral episodes is to be sought in the personal experiences of Stendhal, not under the July monarchy, indeed, but rather during the Restoration or even earlier. One can see it, for example, in his observations on the election of the abbé Grégoire in the Isère in 1819,[2] or his relations with the Préfet of the same Département during the period of 1814 when Stendhal was assisting in trying to galvanize the administration within a very short space of time using just such high-pressure methods as Lucien employs in the Caen-Ranville episodes of the novel.

On this question of the size of the electorate in our three novels, then, Balzac is closer to the facts, more 'realistic' if one uses a very

---

[1] *L.L.*, vol. iv, p. 383.
[2] see Stendhal, *Correspondance*, Pléiade edition, vol. i, pp. 989–91.

narrow definition of the term. But the unlikely size of the electorate in the Caen-Ranville election covers the perhaps more important truth that in a large electorate the governmental influence is relatively smaller than in the rotten boroughs such as Balzac's Arcis. For in the Caen-Ranville election the opposition candidate wins the seat. He is prevented from gaining a landslide victory only by the desperate and brilliant efforts of Lucien.

The relatively restricted electorates of the 1830s turn out to be a great convenience for the political novelists of the period, as they can still deal quite correctly with the electoral process in terms of individual personalities or at least small groups, and hence employ the traditional or well-established methods of the novelist, and do not have to invent new techniques to deal with mass phenomena. The analyses of power they provide are equally applicable to today's circumstances but the direct influence of the individual is no longer so clearly visible.

When we turn from this aspect of the background of the elections to the descriptions of the actual elections in the novels we find a good measure of agreement on the part of each author, an agreement all the more striking in view of the differences in access to information on the régime mentioned above.

In both cases the official or ministerial candidate is a nonentity. The difference comes in each novelist's treatment of these candidates. Balzac spends a certain amount of time delineating the dull M. de Chavoncourt and his history as a constitutional monarchist in *Albert Savarus*, and spreads himself even more fully in the *Député* in describing the future ministerial candidate Philéas Beauvisage, "ce général du tricot", a comic grotesque of sublime stupidity, though endowed with a certain commercial acumen. Stendhal, on the other hand, is temperamentally unable to plunge himself into the substance of provincial life and spend time on elaborating portraits of people whom he tends to dismiss as fools. He sidesteps more or less neatly by assuming a complicity with the reader: "Nous ne ferons pas à notre lecteur l'injure d'indiquer les vingt raisons qui..."[1] or, "Nous supprimons ici huit ou dix pages sur les faits et gestes de M. Fléron préparant les élections; cela est vrai, mais vrai comme la Morgue, et c'est un genre de vérité que nous laissons aux romans

[1] *L.L.*, vol. i, p. 123.

in-12 pour femmes de chambre. Retournons à Paris…".[1] The official candidates in *Lucien Leuwen* are mere shadows. In one case, "Blondeau est un imbécile qui de la vie n'a porté ombrage à personne", though he, like Beauvisage, has a certain commercial cunning. An ironmaster, he has sent cash to a nephew in Paris, "pour faire des démarches en faveur du maintien du droit sur les fers."[2] In the other election the Préfet's candidate is only known as "M. Gonin, pamphlétaire employé par le gouvernement."

Stendhal portrays the elections essentially through the eyes of the administration. The candidates and indeed the voters have no human existence. It is significant that the most detailed portraits at the two elections in Part II of *Lucien Leuwen* are those of the two Préfets, MM. de Riquebourg and Boucaut de Séranville. In these episodes the only other character described at any length is that of the general commanding the garrison at Caen, General Fari. Thus, Stendhal's portrait of elections is almost entirely drawn from the officials' viewpoint, or that of the outsider visiting the provinces like a tourist in a foreign country, whereas Balzac's descriptions are conceived mainly from the provincials' viewpoint. This is not entirely so, however, for in the *Député d'Arcis* Balzac obviously wanted the reader to understand at the same time both the provincial and the Parisian perspective. The provincial viewpoint does nevertheless predominate in the only section of the novel Balzac actually wrote. The government's electoral agent in this novel is, for example, described as "l'étranger" or "l'inconnu". Such an appellation is naturally inconceivable in *Lucien Leuwen*. This difference does not prevent Stendhal and Balzac from agreeing on the sort of pressures or practices common in elections under Louis-Philippe.

We have seen that the official candidates are mere ciphers. It follows, and both writers show this, that there is an almost total lack of ideological content in the various candidatures. The composite picture emerging from both novelists' election scenes is one which shows the representatives of central government as willing to enter into bargains to what would nowadays be regarded as the left or the right of the political spectrum, with the sole and important proviso that the candidates emerging from such bargains should not constitute a serious threat once elected to the Chambre des Députés.

[1] *L.L.*, vol. III, p. 182.   [2] *ibid.*, vol. IV, p. 55.

At Caen, Lucien, representing the Minister of the Interior, makes a private deal with the country legitimists via the clerical influence in order to exclude a strong liberal candidate, This link between the clergy and the legitimists is underlined in *Albert Savarus,* but their weight is brought behind a candidate – Savarus himself – who has shown publicly his allegiance with the 'liberal' businessmen of Besançon, but is privately a convinced legitimist. The Préfecture opposes Savarus, not on the specifically political grounds that he is a liberal or a legitimist, but because he is a man of talent and an excellent orator. It is not the fact that he is a liberal or a crypto-legitimist that worries the administration, but the fact that he has a will of his own.

Both authors show most clearly the extent of government influence in elections, influence which, in this golden age of ballot-rigging, effectively blurs the distinction between the administrative and political function of an agent like the Préfet or Sous-Préfet. There was no pretence and certainly no intention on the part of the Ministry of the Interior of remaining aloof from electoral affairs and its instructions were explicit. Casimir Périer's circular to Préfets before the elections of July 1831 set the tone for the rest of the régime: "Pour moi, Monsieur le Préfet, je vous dirai sans détour l'intention générale du gouvernement. Il ne sera pas neutre dans les élections. Il ne veut pas que l'administration le soit plus que lui…".[1] The support and influence that could be brought to bear in one way or another by the Ministry of the Interior was enormous. The Préfet dispensed patronage, offered bribes, obtained dismissals from official posts, attacked or supported candidates personally or through their relatives. Stendhal is much more explicit about the forms and motives of this corruption, largely, it seems, because of the nature of his own administrative experience and of his consequent perspective on elections already mentioned. In Part II of the novel he provides character-sketches of two Préfets, much in the style of the popular *Physiologie* or of the *Proverbes* of an author like Théodore Leclercq, showing the craven attitude of one Préfet and the ill-disguised ambitions of another, but each with his own plan of organized corruption.

The actions of M. de Riquebourg, who would hardly stop at

[1] quoted by G. D. Weil – *Les Élections legislatives depuis 1789* (Paris, 1895), p. 155.

I

bloodshed in order to obtain a 'good' result at the elections, are inhibited only by the influence of a member of the peerage, M. d'Allevard, who has the ear of the Minister and exercises his own patronage directly in the constituency without passing by way of the Préfecture.[1] Thus the Préfet can be caught between two fires. Balzac's Antonin Goulard, the Sous-Préfet at Arcis, finds himself in just such a position, with a future not yet fully assured, and wondering which way to leap. The government, and particularly the Préfet, has not yet given him clear instructions, he is fearful of the influence of the Comte de Gondreville, and could still if he wished support the opposition candidate, Simon Giguet, who is an old school-friend . . . but "Avant de tomber, le Ministère actuel peut me destituer. Si nous savons quand on nous destitue, nous ne savons jamais quand on nous renomme." (VII, 666.)

In cases of really doubtful elections both authors show how the government sends a special representative with virtually dictatorial powers. This is the case of Maxime de Trailles in the *Député d'Arcis* and of Lucien Leuwen. *Albert Savarus* does not include such a character, largely because the centre of interest in the novel is elsewhere. Having noted this point, which is a fairly banal fact of political history, we should stop to analyse its importance to each novelist in the general economy of the novels and as indicative of a whole series of attitudes towards political life.

In Part I of *Lucien Leuwen* elections are mentioned incidentally on several occasions and there is of course a good deal of wry political comment; but once Lucien falls in love with Mme de Chasteller the political content of the novel temporarily drops to zero. An interesting example of this is in the ball given by the Marquise de Marcilly.[2] The evening is at first presented as a legitimist occasion celebrated by provincial *ultras*, the whole treated by Stendhal with a tone of mockery and ridicule: "Madame la marquise de Marcilly, veuve d'un cordon rouge, se crut obligée de donner un bal; mais le motif de la fête ne fut point exprimé dans le billet d'invitation; ce qui parut une timidité coupable à sept ou huit dames pensant supéri-eurement, et qui, pour cette raison, n'honorèrent point le bal de leur présence."[3] Then follows the description of the treatment meted out

---

[1] *L.L.*, vol. IV, pp. 48–9.   [2] *ibid.*, vol. I, pp. 280-97 and vol. II, pp. 241 ff.
[3] *ibid.*, vol. I, p. 260.

to Lucien's colonel, despised because he commands a *juste-milieu* regiment. Even the dress of the ladies is shown as representing a political stand. Stendhal goes on to remark the vanity of these provincials, their constant harping on their connections with and devotion to the Bourbons. The whole occasion is seen in political terms. Lucien, by recognizing this vanity and ridiculing their politics, feels superior to them and in control of the situation. At this moment Lucien sees Mme de Chasteller who has just arrived at the ball: "Tout le brillant courage, tout l'esprit de Lucien disparurent en un clin d'œil."[1] In fact the *courage*, the *esprit*, referred to are Lucien's political comments, his sense of superiority resulting from a condemnation of the political vanity and stupidity of his fellow guests. The presence of Mme de Chasteller totally destroys this superiority, and replaces it by love alone: "Au lieu de cette disposition satirique et malheureuse, depuis une heure Lucien n'avait pas assez d'yeux pour voir, pas assez d'âme pour admirer."[2]

From this point the political content in the novel diminishes very rapidly and noticeably, disappearing almost entirely for ten chapters. Love destroys the political element in Lucien's character. Indeed from chapter 13 of the novel to the end of the Nancy episodes it is legitimate to see the political and satirical elements as obstacles only, or hindrances, to the pursuit of the ideal love. Stendhal is perfectly aware of his tendency to exclude politics and social matter once he is launched on a description of the growth of love, and makes strenuous efforts to prevent this happening. A clear example is the brutal insertion of the short chapter on the suppression of a strike in an industrial town.[3] These few pages are brilliantly conceived, but are only included with all sorts of mental reservations on Stendhal's part: "*Plan*, 18 mai. Ce jour-là, les arrêts; le lendemain, il marche contre les ouvriers. Dans l'embryon, la colonne vertébrale se forme d'abord, le reste s'établit sur cette colonne. De même ici: d'abord l'intrigue d'amour, puis les ridicules qui viennent encombrer l'amour, retarder ses jouissances..."[4] Politics, then, are "les ridicules qui viennent encombrer l'amour", and the negation of true love. Turning to the electoral scenes in the novel, we find they are marked by the total disappearance of this true love or the

[1] *L.L.*, vol. I, p. 266.   [2] *ibid.*, vol. I, p. 276.   [3] *ibid.*, vol. III, pp. 13–21.
[4] *ibid.*, vol. III, p. 322.

discussion of anything approaching love. The abortive affair with
Mme Grandet is in a totally different category from that with
Bathilde de Chasteller. For Stendhal, true love cannot exist in a
political context. Lucien's experiences as the special envoy of the
government during the elections have a very useful educative or
maturing effect on the hero, helping him to come to terms with the
world, but this education is only achieved at the expense of the
search for the ideal love, and provides a commentary on Stendhal's
famous dictum that "La politique au milieu des intérêts d'imagination, c'est un coup de pistolet au milieu d'un concert!"

Balzac's use of the same historical fact (the government's sending
a special envoy to supervise elections and obtain a 'good' result) is
exploited in a totally different way from that of Stendhal. In the
Député d'Arcis Balzac's envoy, Maxime de Trailles, is using his
mission in order to seek marriage and a fortune. For him, marriage
and politics are on the same plane. It could be objected that Maxime
is a cynic and not to be placed in the same category as Lucien
Leuwen and his conception of love and marriage. When, however,
we examine Balzac's two candidates, Simon Giguet and Albert
Savarus, we find just such an equation in their minds, too, and begin
to realize that this is something essential to Balzac's conception of life.

Simon regards his candidature as the means to a successful
marriage to Cécile Beauvisage and future riches. But, one might
object again, Simon is a provincial lawyer with woolly liberal views
but fairly limited talents and not to be compared to Lucien. In the
portrait of Albert Savarus, however, we are presented with somebody
of great intelligence, capable of great intensity of passion, and he,
too, equates love, marriage, riches and politics and is even encouraged
to this end by his spiritual bride. Francesca Colonna has told Albert
to make "une brillante fortune... L'illustration est un pont-volant
qui peut servir à franchir un abîme. Soyez ambitieux, il le faut."
(I, 788.) He has chosen to stand as a candidate in the hope of taking
advantage of his position to enrich himself, be made a peer and,
finally and as a legitimate result of all this, to marry the woman he
idolizes.[1] For Stendhal, politics and specifically elections are the

---

[1] It is not necessary here to go into the detail of the way in which this corresponds
to Balzac's own wishful thinking, but it is clear that it does so to a very large
degree.

negation of love, where for Balzac election as deputy is a means of expressing love, love which can be a divine thing, but no more so than ambition, fame and fortune.

Both writers agree in large measure on the corrupt practices indulged in by the government under Louis-Philippe. Both show how candidates under Louis-Philippe strove to persuade the alienated legitimists to sink their conscientious objection to swearing allegiance to the régime and use their vote to swing an election, much as a Communist might be asked to support one 'moderate' candidate against another in France today. Both show the continuing and semi-secret influence of the clergy upon this legitimist vote. Both show the commercial and industrial middle-class flexing its muscles and beginning to think of refusing the governmental candidate or at least starting to impose their own conditions for supporting such a man.

We have tried to show one or two interesting differences of approach to the description of these electoral scenes, the most significant being undoubtedly the importance of politics relative to other aspects of life in the world picture of each author. Independently of such an analysis, however, each author provides us with a general impression, an atmosphere in which his political descriptions are bathed. Stendhal's election episodes leave us with a feeling of almost panic urgency. There is a sense of half-suppressed violence and revolt, symbolized by the smashing of windows after Mairobert's election, a feeling of the brittleness of such a State. Balzac impresses us, rather, with a sense of process, of alliances forming and slowly evolving over generations. There are sudden swirls of excitement like the candidature of Albert Savarus in Besançon, but in the end the province casts out this foreign body and continues its organic growth and development.

Stendhal and Balzac as
connoisseurs of Italian art

DONALD ADAMSON

NOTHING is more remarkable in the history of nineteenth-century literature than the fact that Mérimée and Balzac were virtually alone in their defence of Stendhal's novels. Besides praising him in *Massimilla Doni*, *La Maison Nucingen* and *La Muse du Département*,[1] Balzac hailed his *Chartreuse de Parme* as "un livre où le sublime éclate de chapitre en chapitre".[2] Nor was the appreciation one-sided: Stendhal considered Balzac to be the greatest of living novelists, and had a particular regard for some of the shorter provincial stories, such as *Le Curé de Tours*.[3]

On a personal level, too, a warm (if intermittent) friendship existed between the two men. They first met, it seems, in the late summer of 1830, appropriately enough at one of the Wednesday evening parties given by François Gérard.[4] Stendhal was 16 years Balzac's senior in age, and many years his senior at these parties; but as novelists, they were equally unfledged.

The two men continued to enjoy Gérard's hospitality, and also met at Astolphe de Custine's and Madame Ancelot's receptions.[5] As Madame Meininger has suggested,[6] Stendhal may even have called on Balzac's deep knowledge of Touraine in May 1837, just as he was about to set off on the trip to the Loire valley of which he has left an account in *Les Mémoires d'un Touriste*.[7] When, therefore, Balzac wrote: "j'avais rencontré deux fois M. Beyle dans le monde,

---

[1] IX, 337: "l'un de ceux qui ont le mieux observé l'Italie"; V, 606; IV, 189.
[2] *Revue Parisienne*, 25 Sept. 1840; *O.D.*, vol. III, p. 374. This eulogy did not appear until 18 months after the novel's publication.
[3] *Mémoires d'un touriste*, Divan, vol. XIII (1), p. 83, 27 April 1837. All subsequent references to Stendhal's works (unless otherwise stated) are to the Divan edition.
[4] A. Maurois, *Prométhée, ou la Vie de Balzac* (Paris, 1965), p. 411.
[5] M.-L.-V. Ancelot, *Les Salons de Paris. Foyers éteints* (Paris, 1858), pp. 65–6.
[6] A.-M. Meininger, 'Balzac et Stendhal en 1837', *Année Balz.* (1965), pp. 143–55.
[7] Divan, vol. XIII (1), pp. 390–463.

en douze ans, jusqu'au moment où j'ai pris la liberté de le compli-
menter sur *la Chartreuse de Parme* en le trouvant au boulevard des
Italiens," apropos of a chance encounter in 1839, he was in fact
over-simplifying the matter: perhaps he did not wish to admit to
too close a friendship, in case his warm praise of *La Chartreuse de
Parme* might be thought to savour of partiality.[1]

The evidence of their writings is enough to suggest that both
men were deeply and fairly constantly interested in the visual arts,
especially painting, and particularly Italian art – although Balzac
was by no means solely interested in the Italians (witness Rembrandt,
Poussin and Murillo, for example); Stendhal, on the other hand,
paid far less attention to the paintings of the Dutch, Flemish,
German and Spanish schools. Before meeting Stendhal in the summer
of 1830, Balzac had probably had occasion to read *Rome, Naples et
Florence* and *Promenades dans Rome*, for we know that on 15
December 1829 he purchased the second edition of *Rome, Naples et
Florence* (published in 1827) and the first edition of *Promenades
dans Rome*, which had appeared in the preceding September.[2] So
soon after buying these books, Balzac must have been overjoyed to
meet and converse with their author, and no doubt to learn much
about Italy from him – for Italy was a country Stendhal had known
and increasingly appreciated from as early as June 1800.

The painting, sculpture and architecture of Italy must have been
one of the principal subjects on which Stendhal used to hold forth,
in his own inimitable vein, at the evening parties of Gérard,
Custine and Madame Ancelot. Whether or not Balzac had actually
read *L'Histoire de la peinture en Italie* in 1830 (and of this we
cannot be certain), he would have made good this deficiency by
joining the attentive circle of Stendhal's listeners. In fact, he would
have more than compensated for the deficiency – for had not the
publication of the book been ignominiously discontinued, owing to
its failure to sell, when in addition to the two volumes already
produced, another four volumes were on the way? All that Stendhal
had intended to publish on the schools of Bologna, Rome, Venice

[1] *O.D.*, vol. III, p. 404. Does this mean that they first met in 1827? Such a meeting would certainly have been possible, in the sense that they were both in
Paris at the time, but to the best of our knowledge Balzac was not yet launched
into Parisian society in 1827.
[2] *Corr.*, vol. I, p. 481, n. 1.

and Parma, but which an accident of commerce had prevented from seeing the light of day, would have been available to Balzac in the direct exchanges of their meetings in 1830, 1833 perhaps,[1] and certainly from 1836[2] onwards.

Before outlining the nature of the ideas and knowledge which Stendhal may have imparted to Balzac, it is necessary to trace his own points of contact with Italian art, the depth of his knowledge of it and his indebtedness to previous connoisseurs. Stendhal first arrived in Italy, at the age of 17, early in June 1800 – at a time when Balzac was barely a year old. But before travelling to Milan to take part in Napoleon's second Italian campaign, he had spent six months in Paris, ostensibly to study at the newly founded military academy of the École Polytechnique. Between 10 November 1799, the day of his arrival in Paris from Grenoble,[3] and 7 May 1800, when he left for Italy, he would have had ample opportunity of visiting the Napoleonic Louvre.

One of Napoleon's most grandiose ambitions was to create in Paris a "muséum central des arts", a collection of all that was most abiding in the painting and sculpture of the West, to be housed in the Louvre with the art collection of the former kings of France as its nucleus. The conquered territories would be compelled to hand over their choicest works of art, not simply to appease the victor's predatory instinct, but to bring together in one place a representative collection of the best all schools and all centuries had to offer. In this way merits could be compared, and the canons of Ideal beauty (as enunciated by Winckelmann and Mengs[4]) appreciated as never before. It was fitting that France, the new Attica, should be the centre to which all cultivated people would turn, rather than Rome, the decadent survival of barbarous superstition.

[1] Stendhal arrived in Paris on 11 September 1833 and stayed till 4 December; he and Balzac may well have met at Gérard's parties in October or November.
[2] cf. R. de Cesare, 'Stendhal et Balzac au *Cercle des Arts*', *Stendhal Club*. April 1959, pp. 227–8; *idem*, 'Un incontro fra Stendhal e Balzac nel 1836', *Studi sulla letteratura dell'Ottocento in onore di Pietro Paolo Trompeo* (Naples, 1959), pp. 120–44.
[3] *Vie de Henri Brulard*, Divan, vol. I (2), p. 179.
[4] J. J. Winckelmann, *Gedanken über die Nachahmung der griechischen Werke in der Malerei und Bildhauerkunst* (Friedrichstadt, 1755), pp. 8–9, 24–5; *Geschichte der Kunst des Altertums* (Dresden, 1764), pp. 141–212. A. R. Mengs, *Gedanken über die Schönheit und über den Geschmack in der Malerei* (Zürich, 1774), especially pp. 29–40, and pp. 75–119, where he extols Raphael, Titian and Correggio.

But though Paris, not Rome, was to be the cultural centre of the modern world, Italy – and especially the Papal States – would clearly provide the enlarged Louvre with the most, and the best, paintings and statues. Commissars followed Napoleon during his Italian campaigns, deciding which paintings and sculptures should be surrendered. They began their work in Parma, Milan, Bologna and Rome in 1796.[1] Further consignments – from Florence, Turin, Venice, Modena and Palermo, though not (for some unaccountable reason) from the conquered territory of Naples[2] – arrived in Paris at fairly regular intervals from 1798. By 1802 the new collection was largely complete, though it was not set out in its full splendour for another eight years.[3]

It was here, rather than in Italy itself, that Stendhal became acquainted with the works of Raphael, Titian, Leonardo and the schools of Bologna and Parma, following his return to Paris in 1802. Amongst the 'indigenous' Raphaels he would almost certainly have seen *La Belle Jardinière*, *Balthazar Castiglione* and *Joan of Aragon*; but the expropriated masterpieces – *The Transfiguration*, *The Vision of Ezekiel* and *The Madonna of Foligno* – would have been more dazzling still, at any rate in the general opinion, if not in Stendhal's own.

Less was confiscated of Titian's work, but of the indigenous paintings *The Young Man with the Glove* and *Alfonso of Ferrara and Laura di Dianti* were amongst the very finest exhibits; *Mona Lisa* and *The Virgin and Child with St Anne* (the *enigmatic* Leonardos) were indigenous, not confiscated;[4] and, no less than the sixteenth-century chief of the school of Parma, Correggio, the main Bolognese artists of the seventeenth century – Domenichino, Guido Reni, Albani and Guercino – were represented in abundance. Though there is little awareness of their huge importance in either *Henri Brulard* or the letters and diaries prior to 1811, we have Stendhal's own admission in *Henri Brulard* that even as a very

---

[1] C. H. M. Gould, *Trophy of Conquest. The Musée Napoléon and the Creation of the Louvre* (1965), pp. 44–6.

[2] Gould, *op. cit.*, pp. 47–8. Cf. [anon.], 'Napoleone, Canova e l'Ercole Farnese', *Napoli Nobilissima*, III (1923), 175.

[3] Gould, *op. cit.*, pp. 46, 59 n. 1, 103.

[4] for details see *Notice des tableaux... du Musee* (Paris, 1815), nos. 1132, 1125, 1140, and *Notice des tableaux... du Musee Royal* (Paris, 1816), nos. 1021, 1071, 930, 932.

young man at Grenoble he was exceptionally responsive to the visual arts, or rather to their eroticism.[1]

His own hierarchy of values in painting[2] resembled the artistic preferences expressed at the Louvre: the conquerors brought home Raphaels, Correggios and Domenichinos in great numbers, and these were the artists whom Stendhal particularly admired. The central museum, which he saw on innumerable occasions between 1802 and 1811 (even helping to inventory it in 1810–11), seems to have exerted as strong an influence on his categories of taste as any tour of Rome or Florence.[3]

Not until August 1811, however, when he was aged 28, did the really decisive moment come in the history of Stendhal's art appreciation – despite visits to Berlin and Vienna in 1806 and 1809. Between August and November 1811 he returned to Italy after an absence of almost a decade: he viewed the galleries and churches of Bologna, Florence, Rome and Naples for the first time, and (on his second visit to Milan) studied the exhibits at the recently opened Brera Gallery. For the first time the diary and letters convey positive appreciation. Stendhal was enraptured with the four 'Sibyls' painted by Baldassare Franceschini[4] in the Niccolini chapel of Santa Croce, Florence; in the same chapel he was transfixed for two hours before Bronzino's painting of *Christ in Limbo*.[5]

From the visits to Milan, Bologna, Florence, Rome and Naples came *L'Histoire de la peinture en Italie*.[6] At first, he did not intend

---

[1] Divan, vol. I (1), p. 216.

[2] *Correspondance* (Paris, Bibliothèque de la Pléiade, 1962–), vol. I, p. 625; Stendhal to P. Périer-Lagrange, 8 Dec. 1811.

[3] The Italian paintings at the Louvre could hardly have impressed him before 28 June 1804, however: "je vais le dimanche 12 messidor au Musée," he writes on that day. "Je conçois la peinture bien autrement perfectionnée qu'elle ne l'est. Je conçois peints les tableaux que j'ai dans l'imagination" (*Pensées. Filosofia Nova*, Divan, vol. XVIII (1), p. 296). Cf. *Journal*, Divan, vol. XXXII (3), p. 368: "j'admire de plus en plus le tableau de Raphael qui est au Luxembourg" (25 June 1810). He had not felt so enthusiastic about Raphael in 1805 (*Correspondance*, vol. I, p. 191).

[4] Stendhal refers to Baldassare Franceschini (1611–89) as Volterrano. Balzac may have retained the name Franceschini for use in *Le Père Goriot*.

[5] *Journal*, Divan, vol. XXXII (4), pp. 335–6, 27 September 1811.

[6] As early as 10 June 1810 he was planning a book that would have dealt with painters, poets and musicians – the painters being largely Italian (*Journal*, Divan, vol. XXXII (3), p. 357).

anything more than to provide a translation of Lanzi's art history[1] – a fairly free translation, however, which would permit him to include the occasional comment. But as the year 1812 slipped by, the work grew in scope: with the aid of other commentators[2] – particularly Amoretti, Bossi, Condivi and Vasari[3] – Stendhal broke away completely from his original mentor, and produced a work which, though riddled with plagiarism and not laid out after any particular pattern, is nevertheless the work of an inquiring and highly individual mind. After various setbacks, including the loss of the original MS. during the retreat from Moscow, the book was finally completed in 1817 – enriched by visits to Parma (October 1811[4]), Dresden (July-August 1813[5]) and Venice (July 1815[6]). As ill-starred in its publication as in its beginnings, *L'Histoire de la peinture en Italie* proved to be a commercial failure: only two out of the six projected volumes actually appeared in 1817. *Écoles italiennes de peinture*, the text of the abandoned volumes III-VI, was not published until 1932. A further deposit of Stendhal's ideas on art is to be found in *Idées italiennes sur quelques tableaux célèbres*, the book which he wrote in 1839 in collaboration with his friend Abraham Constantin – and which Balzac may have read, since it accords with many of his own preferences.

How deep is Stendhal's knowledge of Italian art, as evidenced by *L'Histoire de la peinture en Italie*, *Écoles italiennes de peinture*, the travel books and miscellaneous writings? Despite his conventional tributes to Raphael ("la simple et divine physionomie des vierges de Raphaël",[7] he is the equal of Mozart,[8] "il est parvenu à rendre

[1] L. A. Lanzi, *Storia pittorica della Italia dal risorgimento delle belle arti fin presso al fine del XVIII. secolo*, 3rd edn. (Bassano, 1809), 6 vols.

[2] cf. *Histoire de la peinture en Italie*, ed. P. Arbelet (Paris, 1924), vol. I, pp. xxxv–xlv.

[3] C. Amoretti, *Memorie storiche su la vita, gli studi, e le opere di Leonardo da Vinci* (Milan, 1804), especially pp. 152–67; G. Bossi, *Del Cenacolo di Leonardo da Vinci* (Milan, 1810); A. Condivi, *Vita di Michelagnolo Buonarroti*, 2nd edn. (Florence, 1746); G. Vasari, *Vies des peintres, sculpteurs et architectes les plus célèbres*, trs. G. G. Bottari (1804).

[4] *Correspondance*, vol. I, 619; Stendhal to P. Périer-Lagrange, 24 October 1811. Here he would have seen the Correggios to which he refers twice in *La Chartreuse de Parme* (Divan, vol. XXIII (1), p. 148; vol. XXXII (5), p. 259).

[5] *Journal*, Divan, vol. XXXII (5), pp. 197–9.

[6] *ibid.*, pp. 272–86. Cf. R. Dollot, 'Stendhal à Venise', *R.L.C.*, vii (October-December 1927), 667–99.

[7] *Journal*, Divan, vol. XXXII (4), p. 69.

[8] *Promenades dans Rome*, Divan, vol. XXI (1), p. 22.

sensible ce que la voix du plus grand poète ou sa plume n'aurait pas pu rendre"[1]), Correggio is undoubtedly his favourite artist: "Raphaël lui-même a été surpassé par le Corrège."[2]

To a degree unequalled by any other artist, Correggio is the painter of female grace and voluptuousness ("cette tendresse et cette délicatesse que le seul Corrège a possédées et qu'aucun peintre n'est parvenu à imiter, ni même à copier"[3]) – but the gracefulness of Correggio is not only to be found in the content of his paintings, it is reinforced by his style: his skilful blending of colour, juxtaposition of light and shade, and use of aerial perspective. Hence, the unique effect of spaciousness and visual harmony, quite independent of the subject portrayed.[4] Hence also the almost magical remoteness: "ses tableaux... semblent recouverts de six pouces de cristal."[5] But despite the sincerity and warmth of Stendhal's tributes, they hark back to the taste of the eighteenth century, as expressed by Cochin, de Brosses and Arthur Young.[6]

On the other hand, in his admiration of the school of Bologna (and particularly Domenichino and Guercino) Stendhal is – as in his fondness for Raphael – the child of his age.[7] But he is not always behind or abreast of contemporary taste: he is even sometimes ahead of it, and never more so than in his attitude towards the Florentines. He rightly acknowledges Masaccio's epoch-making contribution to Italian art: "Masaccio est plutôt le créateur que le rénovateur de la peinture."[8] Ghirlandaio he considered supreme as a painter of frescoes.[9] Stendhal's view of Leonardo's *Last Supper*[10] is refreshingly

[1] *Écoles italiennes de peinture*, Divan, vol. XXII (1), p. 210; hereafter *E.I.P.*
[2] *Histoire de la peinture en Italie*, Divan, vol. XII (1), p. 291; hereafter *H.P.I.*
[3] *E.I.P.*, p. 24.
[4] *ibid.*, p. 8.
[5] *H.P.I.* (1), p. 159.
[6] C.-N. Cochin: *Voyage d'Italie*, 3 vols. (Paris, 1758). Cf. R. Michéa, 'Cochin devant les Corrège de Parme, et le renouvellement du goût', *Études italiennes* (1934), pp. 216–24. Although Stendhal agreed with Cochin in admiring the school of Bologna, he had the lowest opinion of Cochin's actual book: *Correspondance*, vol. I, p. 622; Stendhal to P. Périer-Lagrange, 29 October 1811. See also C. de Brosses, *Lettres historiques et critiques sur l'Italie*, 3 vols. (Paris, 1799); Y. Bezard, 'Le Président de Brosses et le Corrège, ou l'amateur enthousiaste', *Études italiennes* (1934), pp. 211–15; and A. Young, *Travels during the Years 1787, 1788 and 1789*, 2nd edn. (London, 1794), vol. I, p. 264 (9 December 1789).
[7] cf. J.-J. Seznec, 'Stendhal et les peintres bolonais', *Gazette des Beaux-Arts* (March 1959), pp. 167–78; G. Raimondi, 'Stendhal e i Bolognesi', *Palatina* (January-March 1966), pp. 74–8.
[8] *H.P.I.* (1), p. 15.   [9] *ibid.*, pp. 180–4.   [10] *ibid.*, pp. 226–40.

sensitive, and the pages devoted to Michelangelo's *Last Judgment* are amongst the finest he ever wrote: "c'est un morceau de génie", was Delacroix's opinion.[1] His progressive outlook does not take in the Duecento, however, although nowadays we consider that the foundations of modern painting were laid in the century of Cimabue and Duccio: "j'avouerai sans peine que les peintres les plus remarquables du treizième siècle n'ont rien fait de comparable à ces estampes coloriées que l'on voit modestement étalées à terre dans nos foires de campagnes."[2] And the same dislike, only very slightly attenuated, applies to Giotto, Simone Martini, Orcagna and other artists of the fourteenth century.

Turning to Balzac, we see that the first point of difference between the two novelists is that Balzac was very much the younger man. Stendhal had seen the Napoleonic Louvre while Balzac was still only in his cradle; from 1811 onwards he made repeated visits to Italy; he saw Rome 34 years before Balzac did; by 1815, when Balzac gained his first impression of the Napoleonic Louvre, Stendhal had been to almost all the great picture galleries that were then in existence in Europe, including those of Rome, Florence, Dresden and Vienna, and had virtually completed his history of Italian painting. Though Balzac planned a journey to Italy in June 1834,[3] his first sight of the peninsula did not in fact come until 1836, when he spent a mere fortnight in Turin[4] on a business visit which allowed him no opportunity to admire works of art, despite the fact that he found time for a few purchases. His journey to Venice,[5] Milan,[6] Bologna and Florence in February–April 1837 gave Balzac his first direct acquaintance with some of the greatest Titians, Giorgiones, Guido Renis and Domenichinos and (still more awe-inspiring to behold) Raphael's *Sposalizio* and *Maddalena Doni*. Not

[1] *H.P.I.*, (2), pp. 276–301; F.-V.-E. Delacroix, 'Sur le *Jugement dernier*', *Revue des Deux Mondes* (1 Aug. 1837), 342 n. 1.

[2] *H.P.I.* (1), p. 16.

[3] *L.H.*, vol. i, p. 208.

[4] cf. H. Prior, 'Balzac à Turin', *Revue de Paris* (15 Jan. 1924), 360–404.

[5] cf. H. Prior, 'Balzac à Venise', 1837', *Revue de France* (1 Dec. 1927), 385–417.

[6] cf. H. Prior, 'Balzac à Milan, 1837', *Revue de Paris* (15 July 1925), 283–302; *ibid.* (1 Aug. 1925), 602–20.

until 1846 did Balzac finally visit Rome – but many of its great
pictures he had already seen in Paris in 1815.

To what extent can it be said that the much more experienced
and knowledgeable Stendhal, who had spent over eight years of his
life in Italy by the time he first met Balzac, influenced the younger
man? And how far, in any case, do Balzac's taste, knowledge and
critical appreciation extend? Unlike Stendhal, Balzac did not write
art criticism as such: we must gather his attitudes from the literary
references, both his asides and his visual borrowings.

Balzac worships Raphael (even in the apprentice novels[1]); he also
worships the school of Bologna, but pays no more than lip-service
to Correggio. Like Stendhal, he is neglectful of the Primitives, but
unlike him, he attaches enormous importance to the Venetians.
Titian, "ce peintre souverain", "ce roi de la lumière", has Frenhofer's unqualified admiration.[2] Balzac considers that Titian's *Alfonso
of Ferrara and Laura di Dianti* is one of the "plus immenses chefs-
d'œuvre de l'art".[3] Magus's painting of *The Entombment* is transferred (via the Louvre) from the collection of Charles I.[4] Giorgione,
whose brilliant colouring foreshadows Frenhofer (so much so that
Poussin mistakes one of Frenhofer's early works for a Giorgione[5])
is represented in the galleries of both Pons and Magus.[6] Sebastiano
del Piombo sums up the whole magic and power of Venetian art,
besides combining (as Balzac tells us in *Le Cousin Pons*[7]) the colour
of Bellini and Titian with the Florentine draughtsmanship of his
second Roman master Michelangelo, and even equalling Raphael
in grace and purity. Pons's *Chevalier de Malte en prières*, one of
his four greatest masterpieces, is a direct transposition of a similar
subject (hardly, alas! by Sebastiano – such upgradings are the privilege of the novelist) which Balzac had acquired in Rome in the
spring of 1846.[8]

Balzac, it will be noted, is mainly attracted by the early Venetian
Cinquecento; Bellini, Veronese and Tiepolo hold fewer charms;
despite the fact that he had been to the Scuola di San Rocco, he is
not even enamoured of Tintoretto, who admittedly was almost
unknown until popularized by Ruskin in *Modern Painters* and *The
Stones of Venice*. Balzac's devotion to Venetian art, dating from his

[1] *La Dernière Fée*, I, 61.   [2] IX, 400.   [3] *Le Cousin Pons*, VI, 654.   [4] VI, 637.
[5] IX, 399, 410.   [6] VI, 593, 631.   [7] VI, 651.   [8] *Corr.*, vol. v, no. 2411.

first *important* journey to Italy (in 1837),[1] is in marked contrast to Stendhal's relative lukewarmness – to which Mérimée has given us the clue.[2]

But the art of Italy does not merely consist of its painting, incomparable though this may be. In architecture, Stendhal loves straight lines rather than arches; thus, he dislikes Gothic architecture (much preferring the Classical simplicity of San Clemente and Santa Sabina). He also dislikes the complications of Baroque, preferring Michelangelo to Bernini.[3] Balzac agrees with these attitudes, though he is a little friendlier towards the Gothic style, whose massive proportions occasionally leave him spellbound. In sculpture, Stendhal reiterates his liking for Classicism or neo-Classicism. Michelangelo's *Pietà* is, in his view, less impressive than *The Last Judgment*. He much prefers Canova, whom he made a point of meeting on his first visit to Rome in 1811:[4] in particular, he admires the tombs of the Archduchess Maria Christina (Augustinerkirche, Vienna), Alfieri (Santa Croce, Florence) and Clement XIII.[5] Balzac is no less fond of Canova, though he rates his *Vénus sortant du bain* and *Madeleine pénitente* more highly than the tombs.[6] As befits an admirer of Raphael, he is also extremely impressed by the sculpture of Classical Greece, much of which he saw in 1815.

How then did Stendhal and Balzac use their knowledge creatively? Professor Seznec has studied[7] Stendhal's indebtedness to Guercino in *Le Rouge et le Noir*, pointing out that the career of Julien Sorel, the ordinand turned soldier for a day, was already epitomized in Guercino's *St William of Aquitaine taking the Monastic Habit*, which Stendhal must have seen and perhaps even inventoried whilst it was sequestered at the Louvre. (Even as late as 1830, Stendhal was unaware of the painting's restitution to Bologna.[8]) Julien's portrait[9]

---

[1] Balzac resembles Stendhal in the fact that his second Italian journey was the first important one from an artistic point of view.

[2] P. Mérimée, *Œuvres complètes*, vol. IV (Paris, 1928), p. 185.

[3] cf. M.-H. Foix, 'Stendhal et l'architecture romaine', *Communications présentées au Congrès stendhalien de Civitavecchia (IIIe Journée du Stendhal Club)* (Paris, 1966), 107–12.

[4] *Journal*, Divan, vol. XXXII (5), pp. 21–2.

[5] *ibid.*, (4), p. 332; *Promenades dans Rome*, Divan, vol. XXI (1), p. 50.

[6] V, 1093–5; VI, 337.

[7] *Gazette des Beaux-Arts*, LIV (1959), especially pp. 174–6.

[8] *Le Rouge et le Noir*, Divan, vol. XXIV (1), p. 321 n. 1.

[9] Divan, vol. XXIV (1), pp. 30, 45, 47.

may also owe something to Domenichino,[1] and so too may Fabrice's
– though it is likely that the principal debt is elsewhere.

Not only, however, does Guercino epitomize the priest-cum-
soldier, and Domenichino inspire (to some extent) the physical
portraits of two young heroes: there is a still deeper indebtedness
to Italian art. At the close of *Le Rouge et le Noir*, after Julien has
been guillotined, Mathilde de la Mole is shown contemplating her
lover's head. Fouqué

> entendit Mathilde marcher avec précipitation dans la chambre.
> Elle allumait plusieurs bougies. Lorsque Fouqué eut la force de
> la regarder, elle avait placé sur une petite table de marbre, devant
> elle, la tête de Julien, et la baisait au front...

> Un grand nombre de prêtres escortaient la bière et, à l'insu de
> tous, seule dans sa voiture drapée, elle porta sur ses genoux la
> tête de l'homme qu'elle avait tant aimé...

> Restée seule avec Fouqué, elle voulut ensevelir de ses propres
> mains la tête de son amant...[2]

A painting which Stendhal must almost certainly have seen, and
very possibly inventoried during his time as Inspector-General of
Crown Furniture, was Bernardino Luini's *Salome Receiving the Head
of St John the Baptist*: "Salomé, fille d'Hérodiade, reçoit dans un
bassin la tête de S. Jean-Baptiste qui lui est présentée par un
bourreau dont on ne voit que le bras."[3]

It is unnecessary to dwell on the marked similarity between this
late Florentine painting and *Le Rouge et le Noir*. But was the debt
to Luini himself or to the same subject painted by some other artist –
for the 'Salome' theme was extremely popular in sixteenth- and
seventeenth-century Italy. Professor Seznec has indicated[4] the
possible inspiration of Guercino – and indeed, a Guercino *Salome* is
recorded at the Louvre in 1816,[5] but not before. It is therefore

---

[1] G. Natoli, 'La peinture italienne et les personnages de Stendhal', *Journées
stendhaliennes internationales de Grenoble* (Paris, 1956), pp. 194–5.
[2] Divan, vol. XXIV (2), pp. 494–5.
[3] *Notice des tableaux... du Musée Royal*, no. 1055.
[4] Seznec, *art. cit.*, p. 174.
[5] *Notice des tableaux... du Musée Royal*, no. 886.

K

rather unlikely that Stendhal would have seen Guercino's version
during his lengthy stays in Paris between 1802 and 1811. But what
of the so-called Strozzi,[1] ambitiously recatalogued in 1816 as a
Giorgione,[2] and now thought to be by Titian's pupil Polidoro
Lanzani? Or even one of the Primitives which Napoleon brought
to Paris – Angelo Gaddi's fourteenth-century *predella*[3] showing
both St John the Baptist's execution and Salome presenting the
saint's head to her mother? Here is a situation in which one, several
or all of the above paintings could have inspired the literary image,
but the two likeliest influences are Luini and Lanzani.

Le Rouge et le Noir is in many ways a Romantic novel. It is,
therefore, no coincidence that 'Salome' was one of the supremely
Romantic themes of the Cinquecento and Seicento, comparable to
Cristofano Allori's *Bianca Capello* (Uffizi) and *Judith and Holofernes*,[4]
or Guido's *Beatrice Cenci* (Palazzo Barberini, Rome) and *St Mary
Magdalene*[5] – or even the *Medusa's Head* at the Uffizi, which early
last century was thought to be by Leonardo but is now firmly
attributed to Caravaggio, and of whose "tempestuous loveliness of
terror" Shelley has written in a memorable line. The Romantics
felt an attraction towards these paintings not only because – like
their predecessors in the sixteenth and seventeenth centuries – they
were in rebellion against a neo-Classical tradition, but because of a
congenial similarity of subject-matter spanning the centuries. Themes
such as 'Judith and Holofernes', 'St Mary Magdalene' and 'David with
the Head of Goliath' appealed to the sensationalism and violence
which was one of the facets of nineteenth-century Romanticism.[6]

Stendhal's second great masterpiece is also indebted to Italian art,
but whereas *Le Rouge et le Noir* owes much to Luini and Lanzani,

[1] *Notice des tableaux... du Musée*, no. 836.
[2] *Notice des tableaux... du Musée Royal*, no. 875.
[3] *Notice des tableaux des écoles primitives... exposés dans le Grand Salon du Musée
Royal* (Paris, 1815), no. 57. L. Hautecœur, *Musée national du Louvre*, vol. II:
École italienne et école espagnole (1926), no. 1302.
[4] *Notice des tableaux... du Musée*, no. 781. It is now at the Palazzo Pitti. Balzac
believed he owned a Florentine painting of 'Judith'; Stendhal admired a painting
of the same subject which he mistakenly ascribed to Domenichino.
[5] *ibid.*, nos. 997, 1000, 1001. *Notice des tableaux... du Musée Royal*, nos. 904, 905.
Hautecœur, *op. cit.*, no. 1448.
[6] Hebbel, for example, wrote two plays inspired by such artists as Allori and
Luini: *Judith* (1840) and *Herodes und Mariamne* (1848). A third play was entitled
Maria Magdalene (1843).

La Chartreuse de Parme is (he says) indebted to Correggio: "Tout le personnage de la duchesse Sanseverina est copié du Corrège (c'est-à-dire produit sur mon âme le même effet que le Corrège)," Stendhal confessed to Balzac.[1] More important still, there is a debt to Italian painting as a whole: "A mesure que j'avançais dans *la Chartreuse*, je portais des jugements sur ce livre tirés de *l'Histoire de la peinture…*"

And indeed, when we examine the portrait of Gina Sanseverina, we find that the visual inspiration comes from wider sources than Correggio. At first sight, it would seem that Leonardo has provided the model: "la duchesse avait… un peu trop de la beauté *connue* de l'idéal, et sa tête vraiment lombarde rappelait le sourire voluptueux et la tendre mélancolie des belles Hérodiades de Léonard de Vinci."[2]

But where are Leonardo's paintings of 'Herodias'? Though many such subjects were commonly attributed to him in the first half of the nineteenth century, they are attributed now to his pupils Bernardino Luini and Cesare da Sesto. The very title of the paintings has since been rectified: instead of 'Herodias' we now read 'Salome', for St Mark's Gospel makes it very plain that an executioner "brought [the Baptist's] head in a charger, and gave it to the damsel: and the damsel gave it to her mother".[3]

Are these the 'Salomes' which appear to have inspired *Le Rouge et le Noir*? The matter would present little difficulty except that none of the Luinis, Guercinos, Lanzanis and Gaddis that were to be seen at the Louvre in the years 1815/1816 were actually thought to be by Leonardo himself. The Guercino was called a Guercino; the Lanzani a Strozzi (1815) or a Giorgione (1816); the Angelo Gaddi was attributed to that artist's father Taddeo; the Luini was ascribed to Andrea Solario (another of Leonardo's pupils). Where, then, could Stendhal have seen 'Salomes' which at that time, if not today, were actually thought to be by Leonardo himself? Rigollot writes of 'Salomes' by Leonardo in the galleries of the Uffizi, Dresden, Vienna and Rome – all of which places Stendhal had

---

[1] *Correspondance*, Divan edition, vol. XXIX (10), p. 277; draft of a vanished letter from Stendhal to Balzac, 29 October 1840. Cf. alternative draft, *Correspondance*, Pléiade edition, vol. III, pp. 394, 396.

[2] *La Chartreuse de Parme*, Divan, vol. XXIII (2), p. 53. Cf. *Promenades dans Rome*, Divan, vol. XXI (2), p. 104; (3), 17–18.

[3] Mark vi, 27–8.

visited long before 1838.[1] It is these paintings to which he is presumably referring, two of which (at the Uffizi and the Kunsthistorisches Museum) are now thought to be the work of Luini.[2] But the significant fact is that Luini's paintings of 'Salome' – from whichever gallery – are of crucial importance in determining the nature of both *Le Rouge et le Noir* and *La Chartreuse de Parme*. They also seem to have inspired the portraits of Mathilde de la Mole and Madame Grandet.[3] (According to Lieutenant Robert, even the Marquise del Dongo resembles a 'Salome'[4]).

Nor does the portrait of Clélia Conti have any direct affinity with the school of Parma. She is "une jeune fille encore un peu trop svelte que l'on pouvait comparer aux belles figures du Guide",[5] as (for example) the female figure in Guido's *Atalanta and Hippomenes*, which in Stendhal's day was at the Museo Nazionale, Naples, but is now in the Capodimonte gallery. Madame de Chasteller[6] and even perhaps Madame de Rênal also seem to be drawn from Guido. Bologna, therefore, has influenced the portraits of virtuous women, whereas the Florentine Cinquecento has inspired the 'Salomes' of *Le Rouge et le Noir*, *La Chartreuse de Parme* and *Lucien Leuwen*. Why then does Stendhal speak of an identity between Gina Sanseverina and Correggio? And how did *L'Histoire de la peinture en Italie* mould his writing of *La Chartreuse de Parme*? The questions are interrelated (though the chapters on Correggio are in fact in *Écoles italiennes de peinture*[7]). Stendhal's meaning is that *La Chartreuse de Parme* is an artistic transposition, rather than a mere conversion of appearances, gestures or attitudes: his novel emulates the style of Correggio, with his suavity and voluptuousness, his "magie des lointains"[8] and his chiaroscuro. Just as Correggio heightens both joy and pathos by means of the alternation of light and shade, so Stendhal intensifies climacteric moments by suppressing details elsewhere.

[1] M.-J. Rigollot, *Catalogue de l'œuvre de Léonard de Vinci* (Paris, 1849), pp. 8–12.

[2] A. Ottino della Chiesa, *Bernardino Luini* (Novara, 1956), nos. 50, 244.

[3] *Le Rouge et le Noir*, Divan, vol. XXIV (2), pp. 34–5, 102; *Lucien Leuwen*, Divan, vol. XI (2), p. 330. In the same novel, Mme de Sainte-Aulaire would have been inspired by 'Salome'/'Herodias' (*Romans et Nouvelles*, 2 vols. (Paris, Bibliothèque de la Pléiade, 1952), vol. I, pp. 1520–1).

[4] *La Chartreuse de Parme*, Divan, vol. XXIII (1), p. 11.

[5] Divan, vol. XXIII (2), p. 53.

[6] *Lucien Leuwen*, Divan, vol. XI (1), pp. 60, 71; (2), pp. 57–8.

[7] Divan, vol. XXII (2), pp. 7–75.

[8] *H.P.I.*, p. 181. In this perfection, Correggio follows Ghirlandaio.

Compared with *Le Rouge et le Noir* and *La Chartreuse de Parme*, Balzac's novels are not so directly inspired by the personalities of individual artists: Raphael's *Transfiguration* may, however, have had some bearing upon the general character of *Séraphîta*, and his *Maddalena Doni* may have influenced the outlines of Balzac's *Massimilla Doni*. A more conclusive example of the way in which an artist's life and work leave their impress upon the outlines of a novel occurs in Balzac's early story *La Peau de chagrin*. The very name of the novel's hero, Raphaël de Valentin, points to the twofold image underlying the work: Valentin from Goethe's *Faust*, Part I, with all its associations of the fatal pact (not to mention the duel); and Raphael, the divine artist, who according to Vasari[1] died of an excess of love – just as Balzac's Raphaël dies striving to consummate his love for Pauline.[2] (Balzac was well aware of the Fornarina legend.[3])

Quite apart from the fundamental influences on structure and theme, a large number of visual reminiscences are clearly derived from Italian painting; there are also some borrowings from the sculpture of Michelangelo and Canova. Raphael is foremost in his visual influence upon the *Comédie humaine*, particularly when his madonnas (as in the *Belle Jardinière* and *The Presentation in the Temple*, both of which paintings Balzac could have seen at the Louvre as a young man[4]) inspire the features of ideally beautiful women: Agathe Rouget, Esther Gobseck, Massimilla Doni, Pierrette Lorrain.[5] Raphael's *Joan of Aragon* inspires the dresses of women at Lady Dudley's ball and the portraits of Diane de Cadignan and Dinah de La Baudraye.[6] A further visual model is a painting which in Balzac's day was thought to be a Raphael, but which we now know is by Parmigianino: *Portrait d'un jeune homme dont la tête est appuyée sur la main*;[7] it moulds the features of Hélène d'Aiglemont's

---

[1] G. Vasari, *Vies des peintres, sculpteurs et architectes les plus célèbres* (trans. G. G. Bottari), vol. II, (Paris, 1804), pp. 115–16. Cf. A.-C. Quatremère de Quincy, *Histoire de la vie et des ouvrages de Raphaël* (Paris, 1824), pp. 383–4.

[2] IX, 245–7.

[3] IX, 152; *Splendeurs et Misères des Courtisanes*, V, 699. *Secrets de la Princesse de Cadignan*, VI, 25.

[4] *Notice des tableaux... du Musée Royal*, no. 1027; *Notice des tableaux... du Musée*, no. 1126.

[5] III, 854; V, 687–90; IX, 327, 340; III, 749.

[6] II, 97; VI, 29; IV, 86.

[7] *Notice des tableaux... du Musée Royal*, no. 1022. Stendhal was already aware of this picture on 28 July 1805 (*Journal*, Divan, vol. XXXII (2), p. 256).

eldest son Gustave, and (though here the debt is unacknowledged) Louis Lambert and Emmanuel de Solis.[1]

In a rather similar manner to Parmigianino's *Portrait of a Young Man*, Titian's *Young Man with a Glove*[2] exerts a powerful influence upon the minds of the Romantic generation: it inspires the portrait of Emilio Memmi,[3] and also (we may suspect) Stendhal's Julien and Fabrice. Another debt to Titian is in the portraits of opulently beautiful young women: Suzanne du Val-Noble and Flore Brazier[4] are as lovely as any of his 'Venuses'. Through the medium of painting, the system of correspondences even extends to architecture: the Frari Church, Venice, becomes the Memmi family's chapel.[5] Another of the many paintings which help to shape the *Comédie humaine* is a work which was also deeply admired by Shelley, Guido Reni's *Beatrice Cenci*. In *La Femme de trente ans*[6] Julie d'Aiglemont's portrait is modelled on Beatrice, whose sufferings no doubt recall Pierrette's. But Balzac's greedy assimilation of the Italian masters stops short of Guercino or Correggio. Domenichino himself is only *represented* in the *Comédie humaine*.[7] He does not seem to have inspired any portraits. Balzac is more reserved than Stendhal in his attitude towards the schools of Bologna and Parma.

Which of the two novelists was the more perceptive, and what did Balzac gain from Stendhal? All too readily, both men fall into the habit of reading personal ideas, moods and attitudes into the paintings they are viewing. Both have more enthusiasm than discernment (witness Balzac's collecting activities,[8] or Stendhal's disappointment that Bronzino's *Christ in Limbo* was not, as he had originally thought, by Guercino[9]). Balzac certainly draws on the thesaurus of Italian painting and sculpture to a far greater extent than Stendhal ever does in his novels: in *Le Rouge et le Noir*, *La Chartreuse de Parme*, *Lucien Leuwen* and *Lamiel*, the acknowledged debts to particular paintings or statues are very few and far between. Moreover, Balzac is better able than Stendhal to convey to the reader his tremendous enthusiasm for Italian art. But against this must be set the fact that, although neither of the men is primarily

[1] II, 790; X, 369; IX, 557–8.   [2] *Notice des tableaux... du Musée Royal*, no. 1080.
[3] IX, 319.   [4] IV, 220; III, 1010–11.   [5] IX, 318   [6] II, 837.   [7] III, 965, I, 959.
[8] L.H., vol. III, pp. 167, 250, etc.
[9] *Journal*, Divan, vol. XXXII (4), p. 336, 27 Sept. 1811.

concerned with tactile values, Stendhal does seem to be rather more perceptive in his appreciation of artistic technique.

Admittedly, many of his aesthetic notions are eccentric and outdated. Apropos of the Bronzino which he had thought was a Guercino, he notes in his Italian diary: "il me faut de l'expression, ou de belles figures de femmes."[1] The erotic element in painting which had appealed to him even when he was a schoolboy at Grenoble also accounts for many of his later preferences: but though our own generation is equally, if not more, responsive to eroticism, we have learned (except perhaps with some of the works of D. H. Lawrence) to separate this erotic appeal from the peculiarly artistic merits of a book or painting. Consequently, we are not attracted towards Bernardino Luini or Correggio by the voluptuous qualities of their 'Salomes' or 'Madonnas'.[2] Nor is Balzac entirely exempt from this failing: whatever qualities we admire in the *Sposalizio* today, they are not the 'grace' and 'celestial purity' on which he lays so much stress.

A second outdated notion (this time, peculiar to Stendhal) is the importance of *expression*, to which he even refers in his comment on *Christ in Limbo*. This was a feature of eighteenth-century aesthetics which he still championed in the age of Corot and Delacroix. A painter's merit consists in the extent to which he has succeeded in portraying tense states of mind in abnormal situations: the expression on Salome's face as she receives St John the Baptist's head from the executioner, or on St Mary Magdalene's face as she contemplates the instruments of Christ's passion. As with the voluptuousness of Correggio, Stendhal is again concerned with contingent, rather than essential, qualities of painting – but stylistic success has now been transferred from Raphaelesque perfection (which Balzac understood and admired) to the age-old dilemma of making the tragic truth of history or legend – whether it be St Mark's Gospel, Suetonius or Euripides – humanly and artistically probable. Corneille and Racine wrestled with this dilemma, but not Balzac.

What elements in Stendhal's aesthetics are of enduring value?[3]

[1] *ibid.*
[2] It is perhaps relevant to note that photography was only invented in the year of *La Chartreuse de Parme*'s appearance.
[3] cf. A. Ledent, 'L'Esthétique de Stendhal', *Revue Internationale de Philosophie* (January, 1949), 88–107.

First, reacting against Winckelmann and Mengs, he stresses that the appreciation of art is relative, that what may seem beautiful in one generation may seem ugly in the next; in this, of course, he follows the Idéologues. Secondly, he foreshadows Baudelaire, Verlaine and the symbolists in his constant equation of music and painting – as if all the arts were but facets of one underlying reality. Thirdly, as Professor Coe has strongly insisted,[1] Stendhal is no ignoramus in the technical aspects of painting. He was perhaps less aware than Balzac of the contribution which colour can make to a painting (hence his unresponsiveness to the Venetians); indeed, his own novels are bare of colour. But in his appreciation of colour as a component of form he had scarcely any equal amongst his contemporaries, and in fact foreshadows Cézanne. He condemns the linear perspective which had been based on form alone. The use of chiaroscuro and the subtle merging of one colour into another produce that *aerial* perspective which, as in *La Chartreuse de Parme*, creates a sensation of spaciousness and distance. In these insights Stendhal surpasses Balzac – except that *Le Chef-d'œuvre inconnu* also discusses colour as a component of form.

What then (if anything) did Stendhal contribute to the *Comédie humaine* in the way of aesthetic awareness? A few details, perhaps, such as the two types of female beauty to be found in the women painted by Raphael,[2] or Michelangelo's use of Sebastiano del Piombo to combat Raphael's ascendancy.[3] But not such perplexing details as Balzac's entirely mistaken notion that Giulio Romano had no hand in *The Transfiguration* or that Raphael painted this picture for Francis I.[4] (The source of these ideas is still undiscovered.) Nor did Balzac assimilate to any extent the idea of *correspondances* between the arts, or the relativity of taste, or the pre-eminent importance of expression. Perhaps the greatest of Balzac's debts to Stendhal – besides a vicarious acquaintance from as early as 1830 (or 1827?) with many of the great art treasures of Italy – is the artistic philosophy expounded in 1837 in the third edition of *Le Chef-d'œuvre inconnu*:

[1] R.N.C. Coe, 'Quelques réflexions sur Stendhal paysagiste', in *Première Journée du Stendhal Club* (Lausanne, 1965), pp. 35–48.
[2] *Promenades dans Rome*, Divan, vol. XXI (1), p. 86; *L'Hôpital et le peuple*, X, 1082.
[3] *E.I.P.* (1), p. 147; (2), pp. 99–100; *Le Cousin Pons*, VI, 651–2.
[4] Prefaces to *Le Livre mystique* and *La Femme supérieure*, XI, 273, 356.

La Forme est... un truchement pour se communiquer des idées, des sensations, une vaste poésie...[1]

La nature comporte une suite de rondeurs qui s'enveloppent les unes dans les autres. Rigoureusement parlant, le dessin n'existe pas![2]

Where did such ideas originate? They were not present in the first edition of 1831, nor in the second of 1833. Could they have come from Delacroix, who certainly shared these opinions?[3] But he and Balzac were never particularly friendly, and quickly drifted apart after their early meetings in 1829–30. Or from Gautier? But his published writings bear little resemblance to Balzac's theories.[4] On the other hand, Stendhal and Balzac were living within a few miles of each other between the years 1836 and 1839. We have seen that they met occasionally, and many other opportunities must have occurred for meetings of which we have no knowledge. The possible indebtedness of *Le Chef-d'œuvre inconnu* to *L'Histoire de la peinture en Italie* is a fruitful subject for investigation.

[1] IX, 395.
[2] IX, 400.
[3] F. Fosca, *De Diderot à Valéry, les écrivains et les arts visuels* (Paris, 1960), pp. 65–7.
[4] *ibid.*, pp. 65–5 Cf. however P. Laubriet, *Un Catéchisme esthétique, le 'Chef-d'œuvre inconnu' de Balzac* (Paris, 1961), pp. 106–12. Laubriet points out that there are a few similarities of style between *Le Chef-d'œuvre inconnu* and Gautier's journalistic art-criticism, and also suggests that Gautier may have relayed some of Delacroix's ideas to Balzac.

A propos d'une lettre inédite:
Balzac et le marchand de linge
de Francfort

ROGER PIERROT

ON a déjà étudié les fournisseurs de Balzac dont les noms tiennent tant de place dans sa *Correspondance*. A l'occasion de la communication d'une lettre inédite, voici quelques notes concernant Doctor, un marchand de linge à Francfort.

Balzac lui rendit visite pour ses premiers achats pendant les quelques jours passés à Francfort, en compagnie de Mme Hanska, au début de mai 1847. Peu après le départ du romancier qui regagnait Paris, Mme Hanska écrivait à sa fille: "Il a fait des commandes de linge ici, ce qui a rendu bien fiers les Francfortois."[1] Les Francfortois pouvaient en effet être étonnés – ou fiers – de voir Balzac dédaigner l'artisanat parisien pour commander des draps, mais il avait écouté Mme Hanska qui trouvait tout trop cher à Paris et, ayant des prétentions à l'économie, lui avait conseillé d'acheter en Allemagne.[2]

Le 13 mai, Balzac était rentré à Paris, il y avait retrouvé tous les soucis de l'installation de sa maison de la rue Fortunée, où rien n'était achevé. Le 20, il confiait à Mme Hanska: "Depuis 8 jours je n'ai pas eu le temps d'écrire 2 mots à Doctor."[3] Le 8 juin, les draps étant enfin arrivés, Balzac devait piteusement faire part de sa déception:

> Vous savez le désastre des draps de Doctor; ils sont trop courts d'un mètre et il manque un lez, il faut que je calcule les quantités, et qu'il me renvoye de la toile; si ces draps-là ne vont pas au lit de la coupole qui je crois est un peu moins long et un peu moins large que celui du 1er étage.

[1] Marcel Bouteron, *La Véritable image de Mme Hanska* (1929), p. 30. *LH.*, vol. IV, p. 579.
[2] Le 29 juin et le 21 novembre 1846, il avait été question de se fournir à Dresde (*L.H.*, vol. III, pp. 247 et 496).
[3] *L.H.*, vol. IV, p. 20.

Dans les circonstances où je me vois, la commande [...] à Doctor est de trop.[1]

Avant d'acheter des draps en Allemagne, il aurait sans doute été bon de prendre les mesures des lits, de ne pas oublier qu'il y a différentes manières de les faire d'un pays à l'autre et qu'Outre-Rhin, on n'a pas coutume de les border!
Le bilan du désastre est fourni le 22 juin:

Tous les draps sont à refaire, même ceux achetés par la scélérate de Chouette. Il faut pour le lit de la chambre rouge, des draps de 3 mètres de longueur sur 2 mètres de largeur. Je vais essayer de vendre les draps que n[ous] avons et d'en commander d'autres, à Doctor avec l'argent que j'en ferai. Il est impossible de border des 2 côtés, et je suis très mal couché. D'autre part, il est impossible de rien changer au lit, car il n'est que bien pour les 2 gros l[ou]ps que vous savez. J'attends avec impatience, le lit d'en bas pour savoir si les draps peuvent y aller. Et je me dis aussi qu'à la campagne, à Moncontour, il y aura des lits d'amis, et que des draps sont toujours bons. Mais commander 12 paires de draps à Doctor, c'est tout à fait hors de mes moyens! J'aurai bien de la peine à lui payer mon linge en 7bre quand je viendrai. Vous qui faites de la toile, vous devriez en faire, chère drapière!...[2]

Ensuite, nous n'entendrons plus parler de Doctor et de ses draps jusqu'au 11 février 1848. Revenant de Wierzchownia, Balzac passa par Francfort, d'où il annonça à Mme Hanska:

J'ai vu Doctor. Doctor a enflé le mémoire, les chemises sont à 28 fr. et il ne peut faire celles de Georges qu'à 30 fr., car il jure ses grands dieux qu'il est en perte avec moi. Comme il doit faire les chemises de Georges dans la plus belle façon des miennes, je ne crois pas que 24 fr. de plus fassent de la peine à la chère Annette pour cet effet si essentiel. Les mouchoirs auront un M. et un G. mariés surmontés d'une couronne. Il ist convenu que s'il a une occasion de les faire passer sans que la Douane les voye, il les enverra à Berditcheff à Halpérine; sinon, je les prendrai en juillet, et les apporterai. J'ai soldé 900 fr. à ce dit sieur Doctor...
Ah! j'oubliais! Doctor refera vos 6 p[aires] de draps commandées,

[1] L.H., vol. IV, pp. 33-4.   [2] ibid., p. 59.

dans la dimension que je lui enverrai. Il reprend les 6 paires que
j'ai à Paris, et moyennant une très légère différence, il me donnera
en échange des Draps de la dimension que je veux. Ainsi, moyennant ces 6 paires que j'ai trouvées, les 6 que je renverrai et les 6
nouvelles paires, il y en aura 18 paires de la dimension voulue.
Ce qui me semble fort honnête.

Il m'a parlé d'oreillers brodés qui sont de cette même commande
de vous, je lui ai dit d'attendre les dimensions et de nouveaux
ordres que vous me donnerez par votre première lettre. Ai-je bien
fait? Il y a aussi dans cette commande des *peignoirs* et des *couver-
tures de lit* brodées, il faut 6 mois pour les faire, j'ai dit d'attendre
également v[otre] réponse là-dessus.[1]

Dans Paris en révolution, les soucis accablent Balzac; le 31 mars,
il soupire: "Quel regret j'ai aux draps de Doctor!... Dans quels draps
je suis."[2] Le 28 avril, il a reçu des nouvelles de son fournisseur:
"Doctor m'a écrit que le linge de *Zorzi mio* est fini, et il me demande
si je le prendrai toujours en passant en juillet. Dieu de bonté!... si
je me mets en route, il faut bien des événements!"[3]

Après un certain délai, Balzac lui répondit, par cette lettre inédite
et non datée:

Mon cher Monsieur Doctor,
C'est moi qui vous paierai les chemises que je vous ai commandées
pour le comte G. Mniszech, et je ne sais pas encore si je m'en
chargerai, je ne pourrai vous le dire que dans deux mois; quant
à mes draps, il faut me les envoyer, paire à paire, par des occasions
à Paris, rue Fortunée n° 14; j'avais tout-à-fait oublié v[otre]
lettre, à cause de mes occupations, et j'étais aussi chargé par Mme
la c[omte]sse Hanska de vous dire de ne rien faire pour elle, sans
ses ordres nouveaux, car vous devinez bien que les événements
ne sont pas ordinaires. Ainsi, gardez chez v[ous] les chemises
jusqu'à nouvel ordre, et envoyez-moi les draps, paire à paire, et
lavez-les, s'il le faut.

Agréez mes complim[ents]
de Balzac.[4]

[1] *L.H.*, vol. IV, pp. 186-7.   [2] *ibid.*, p. 287.   [3] *ibid.*, p. 327.
[4] Nous remercions bien vivement M. Jean Devyver qui nous a fort aimablement
communiqué une photocopie de cette lettre dont l'original fait partie de sa
collection d'autographes.

Nous laisserons de côté les chemises du comte Mniszech.[1] Quand Balzac quitta à nouveau Paris pour l'Ukraine en septembre 1848, aprés avoir mentionné l'arrivée de nouvelles paires de draps ne convenant pas davantage, il laissa à sa mère un trop long relevé de ses dettes, où Doctor figure pour 480 fr.[2] Il passa par Francfort où il prit livraison de la commande du gendre de Mme Hanska.

Un heureux hasard permettra peut-être d'ajouter un jour un nouvel épisode aux relations de Balzac avec son fournisseur; écrivant en avril 1849 à Heinemann, fondé de pouvoir de la banque Rothschild à Francfort, il le chargeait de remettre à son "ami Doctor" une lettre qui n'a pas été retrouvée.[3]

Il nous paraît probable qu'elle concernait encore les draps commandés par Balzac.

Enfin marié, mais regagnant la France bien malade, Balzac fêta la Saint-Honoré à Francfort, le 16 mai 1850. Peut-être prit-il enfin livraison de sa commande à cette occasion![4]

---

[1] *L.H.*, vol. IV, pp. 361, 407, 535, 545, 549, 556.
[2] *Corr.* t. V, p. 375.
[3] *ibid.*, p. 538.
[4] Dans la lettre envoyée par Balzac et sa femme à Anna Mniszech le 16 mai 1850, il n'est pas question de Doctor (*L.H.*, vol. IV, pp. 565-68).

Jules Janin et Balzac

HENRI J. GODIN

Né à Saint-Etienne (Loire) le jeudi 16 février 1804, Jules-Gabriel Janin, fils d'avoué, fit ses premières études dans cette ville. Brillant élève, il passa ensuite au Collège Royal de Lyon où il eut comme condisciples Edgar Quinet, Armand Trousseau et...Lacenaire. A quinze ans il fut envoyé au Collège Royal de Louis-le-Grand, à Paris, pour y terminer ses études secondaires. Il y connut Cuvillier-Fleury, Lerminier et Sainte-Beuve auquel il devait succéder à l'Académie Française le 7 avril 1870.

En 1822, Janin était bachelier. Au sortir du Collège il alla s'installer avec sa grand'tante au no. 30 de la rue du Dragon où il se mit à donner des leçons particulières à deux francs l'heure. Il ne manqua jamais d'élèves. "Je n'ai jamais conçu qu'un homme pût rencontrer dans son chemin tant d'imbéciles."[1] Le soir il allait au théâtre. Invité un jour par un ami de rencontre, promeneur de chien comme lui dans les jardins du Luxembourg,[2] il passa une délicieuse soirée à l'Opéra-Comique et fut emmené souper ensuite chez une chanteuse. Emerveillé, Janin voulut connaître la profession de son ami: il était journaliste. Ce soir-là Janin avait découvert sa propre vocation.

Il débuta au *Courrier des théâtres* en février 1825; passa à *la Pandore*, puis à *la Lorgnette* et enfin se proposa, en 1827, au directeur du *Figaro*, Le Poitevin 'Saint-Alme', qui l'engagea sur sa bonne mine à 45 francs par mois.

Bientôt sollicité par d'autres journaux, Janin collaborera à *la Quotidienne*, au *Messager des chambres* et au *Mercure du XIXe*

---

[1] J. Janin, *Contes nouveaux*, Préface, t. IV (1833), p. 67. Cette préface autobiographique sera reproduite avec certaines variantes (*v. infra*) dans *les Catacombes*, vol. I (1839).

[2] J. Janin, *Histoire de la littérature dramatique* (*H.L.D.* par la suite), t. V (1858), pp. 24–9.

siècle. M. Bertin l'accueillit au *Journal des débats* en novembre 1829,[1] et il y resta presque jusqu'à sa mort en 1874.

Rappelant ce qu'étaient les célébrités littéraires au temps où il entrait lui-même dans le journalisme, Janin écrivait dans sa préface aux *Contes nouveaux*: "Alfred de Vigny, qui commençait avec toutes sortes de peines, était obscurément annoncé chez les libraires du quai de la vallée; Alexandre Dumas, commis obscur perdu dans un bureau rêvait tristement une célébrité qu'il n'a pu réaliser que six ans plus tard."[2] Chose curieuse, reprenant cette préface à la demande de l'éditeur des *Catacombes*, en 1839, Janin substitue à la phrase relative à Alexandre Dumas ces mots se rapportant à Balzac: "M. de Balzac, cet homme de tant d'esprit, publiait, et en vain, depuis dix ans un roman nouveau tous les huit jours, rêvant tristement une célébrité qu'il n'a pu réaliser que six ans plus tard."[3]

La modification du texte est significative. On ne peut y lire qu'un hommage, empreint de nostalgie pour une amitié d'autrefois mais dénué de toute rancune. Janin, qui se crut toujours beaucoup plus vieux qu'il n'était,[4] jugeait-il opportun, à cette date, de mettre fin à une brouille dont il ne tirait pour sa part aucune satisfaction? Que s'était-il passé entre eux au cours de dix années?

Balzac et Janin durent faire connaissance entre 1824 et 1825 lorsqu'ils fréquentaient tous deux les rédactions des mêmes journaux. Il est matériellement impossible qu'ils se soient rencontrés chez Me Guillonnet-Merville, ainsi que l'affirmait Eugène de Mirecourt.[5] Quand Balzac faisait son stage au 42 rue Coquillière, en novembre 1816, Jules Janin n'était même pas arrivé à Paris, et Balzac avait quitté l'étude depuis quatre ans quand Janin sortit du Collège Louis-le-Grand. Il ne fut jamais clerc de notaire et encore

---

[1] "M. Bertin l'aîné, mon second père. Il venait de m'adopter, comme un des siens; il venait de m'ouvrir, paternellement, *le Journal des Débats* où, depuis trente années, j'ai trouvé le travail et le pain de chaque jour..." J. Janin, *Barnave*, préface à l'édition de 1860, p. 26.

[2] I, p. 187.

[3] Werdet n'avait pas dû s'apercevoir du changement, car il déclarait dans l'Avertissement aux *Catacombes*: "Nous réimprimons, sans y rien changer, la préface des *Nouveaux Contes*" (p. 5).

[4] "je suis déjà dans cet âge où l'on s'étonne des morts qu'on a laissés derrière soi!..." *Contes nouveaux*, t. I, p. 170.

[5] *Les Contemporains* (Paris, 1856), p. 18. "Eugène de Mirecourt, pamphlétaire assez peu digne de créance...", Clément-Janin (neveu du critique), *Drames et comédies romantiques* (Paris, 1928), p. 135.

moins saute-ruisseau, comme l'a prétendu André Billy.[1] C'est vraisemblablement grâce à leur relation commune avec Le Poitevin que Balzac et Janin se lièrent d'amitié. On sait combien Balzac avait dû subir l'ascendant de 'Saint-Alme' qui flairait partout les jeunes talents dont il pourrait user à son avantage. Janin ne tarda pas à comprendre qu'il pouvait, quant à lui, très bien se libérer de son influence. Sans doute fut-ce là la cause initiale d'un antagonisme de l'aîné pour le cadet. Cette belle facilité d'invention, nuisible finalement à Janin, était ce que Balzac lui enviait le plus. On conçoit qu'un tempérament comme le sien fût prédisposé à la rancune: tout avait été dur pour lui, comme l'implique la phrase de Janin dans *les Catacombes* – dix ans de labeur avant de se découvrir du génie![2] Janin, lui, sans tâtonnements, presque sans effort, allait aux nues dès son premier roman.

Il est remarquable que la célébrité soit venue à Janin et à Balzac la même année: le 2 mai 1829, paraissait, sans nom d'auteur, *l'Ane mort et la femme guillotinée*, deux mois après *le Dernier Chouan ou la Bretagne en 1800* et quelque sept mois avant *la Physiologie du mariage*. Mais tandis que *le Dernier Chouan* languissait à la devanture des libraires, *l'Ane mort* faisait fureur. Il en parut quinze éditions.[3] Ce succès immédiat dut chagriner Balzac, encore qu'à la fin de l'année les deux jeunes romanciers aient pu s'estimer de force à peu près égale. Il est permis de supposer que leurs relations étaient alors des plus cordiales. Une lettre de Janin à Balzac, vraisemblablement du début de 1830, écrite à la suite d'un accident de cheval ou de voiture, fait preuve d'une très franche camaraderie.[4]

Janin ne publia aucun article sur *le Dernier Chouan*,[5] mais une fois intronisé aux *Débats*, il fit une bruyante publicité à *la Physiologie du mariage*. Les épithètes *brutal* et *infernal* appliquées au

---

[1] *Vie de Balzac* (1944), t. I, p. 33. Répété par André Maurois, *Prométhée ou la vie de Balzac* (Paris, 1965), p. 39.

[2] 'Balzac, dont la rancune était tenace, et qui était, selon sa jolie expression, "toujours au lendemain de l'injure qu'on lui avait faite..." ', Georges Adenis, *Le Courrier balzacien*, no. 10, décembre 1950, p. 211.

[3] Et même un vaudeville de Théodore N [...] joué au théâtre du Panthéon au début de juillet 1832. V. le compte rendu de Janin dans *le Journal des Débats* du 2 juillet: "A la fin de la pièce, la femme guillotinée n'est pas guillotinée, elle se marie avec son séducteur comme la Claudine de Florian."

[4] *Corr.*, t. I, no. 275.

[5] M. Regard dit à ce propos: "Janin avait sans doute promis de faire un compte-rendu qu'il ne fit pas." *Les Chouans*, Garnier, p. xvii.

L

livre de Balzac étaient bien calculées pour exciter la curiosité du public.[1] Mais, par ailleurs, on sentait déjà que Janin ne donnait pas une approbation entière à ce genre de littérature et qu'il guettait l'occasion d'en attaquer le pourvoyeur.

En attendant, on s'en tenait à un échange de bons procédés: à l'article sur *la Physiologie* en répondra un de Balzac sur *l'Ane mort*, à la parution d'une seconde édition le 12 décembre, chez Delangle. Le 5 février 1830, Balzac faisait dans *le Voleur* une esquisse fort jolie de l'auteur soi-disant 'inconnu' de *l'Ane mort* où tout le monde pouvait facilement reconnaître Janin:

> Je vois un jeune homme qui pourrait faire honneur à la femme d'un banquier. Son front avait la pureté, la blancheur, l'innocence que les romanciers supposent toujours à leurs héroïnes; sa figure était fraîche; rien n'accusait les travaux arides de l'esprit, ni ces nuits passées devant une lampe confidente et amie du silence et de la poésie. Ses yeux brillaient d'un feu moqueur, sa voix était sardonique; il avait les cheveux noirs, et sa chambre éclatait de luxe et de magnificence.[2]

Dans une conversation rapportée avec l'auteur, Balzac le raille d'avoir terminé son histoire en 29 chapitres. Il en propose donc un trentième. C'est l'autopsie du cadavre de la femme guillotinée que Janin n'avait pas songé à faire.

Cet *Ane mort* qui fit tant de bruit, c'était, en plein romantisme, la parodie du romantisme, le coup de grâce donné au roman dit 'frénétique'. Un jeune homme poursuit de ses attentions une jeune fille qui ne l'aime pas. Il la voit, Manon dégradée, arrêtée pour homicide, violée en prison par son geôlier et guillotinée après avoir donné le jour à son unique enfant.

Lors de la sixième édition, en 1842, Janin nous révèle la véritable intention de son livre. Il nous déclare que "pour n'être pas dupe de ces émotions fatigantes d'une douleur factice, j'avais voulu m'en rassasier une fois pour toutes et démontrer invinciblement aux âmes

---

[1] *Journal des Débats*, le 7 février 1830.
[2] *O.D.*, t. I, p. 211. L'allusion au luxe et à la magnificence nous rappelle que Janin avait tout récemment quitté la rue Madame, au moment où Harel passa de l'Odéon à la Porte-Saint-Martin, pour s'installer au 6 de la rue de Tournon dans un rez-de-chaussée de l'ancien hôtel de Théroigne de Méricourt. Il y vécut avec la marquise de la Carte.

compatissantes, que rien n'est d'une fabrication facile comme la grosse terreur.''[1] Puis, en 1854, revenant derechef sur son premier roman, Janin précise: "Ce livre abominable était pour ainsi dire un perpétuel démenti à tout ce qui fait peur, à tout ce qui fait rêver, à tout ce qui est le vague et l'idéal; si bien que, en ce temps-là, l'auteur fut chassé du camp des poètes, absolument chassé, et qu'il se vit forcé, par la nécessité même de sa propre condamnation, d'entrer dans le camp des critiques.''[2]

Ce que Janin visait, dans *l'Ane mort*, c'était évidemment le Balzac des premières années, celui du *Vicaire des Ardennes*, non moins que le Vicomte d'Arlincourt, Dinocourt, Soulary, Nodier et Hugo même, ainsi que tous les disciples d'Anne Radcliffe et de Maturin.[3]

Balzac dut bien le comprendre mais ne s'en formalisa pas. Il était bien plus intéressé par le thème de *l'Ane mort*. Mais en y ajoutant un chapitre, il trahissait, à son insu, le secret de sa propre méthode: féconder son imagination par l'insémination des idées de ses confrères et, en temps voulu, donner naissance à des créations nouvelles assez puissantes pour faire oublier leurs origines et usurper la place de leurs modèles dans la littérature.[4] Après *l'Ane mort* allait commencer chez Balzac un processus complexe de gestation. A la manière de certaines femelles de kangourous qui espacent à volonté la naissance de leurs petits à la suite d'une seule rencontre avec leur pére, Balzac développait à intervalles ses idées préalablement fertilisées, laissant croire ainsi (comme le croient au sujet des kangourous les aborigènes australiens) à quelque naissance virginale.

A peine le compte rendu fantaisiste de Balzac sur *l'Ane mort* avait-il paru que Janin publiait, toujours sans nom précis d'auteur, son second roman, *la Confession*.[5] Balzac en parlera dès le 14 avril

[1] Paris, Ernest Bourdin, p. vi. [2] *H.L.D.*, t. III, p. 100.
[3] Maurice Bardèche commente le roman en ces termes: "Le héros cherche l'horreur pour l'horreur et s'attache complaisamment à cette recherche et le lecteur y voit partout une satire: celle d'une génération blasée par trente ans d'horreurs radcliffiennes, puis par dix ans d'horreurs romantiques, incapable d'émotions littéraires et artistiques, paralysée par une sorte de stupidité du goût." *Balzac romancier* (1943), p. 209.
[4] "Balzac cherche volontiers des thèmes de romans dans les romans d'autrui." M. Le Yaouanc, *le Lys dans la vallée*, Garnier, p. xxxv. Janin avait finement pressenti la méthode balzacienne dès son compte-rendu de la *Physiologie*: "Il voulut faire l'*Art du mariage*, par émulation."
[5] Chez Mesnier, 1830, 2 vol. in-12. "Par l'auteur de l'*Ane mort*."

1830 dans le *Feuilleton des Journaux politiques*, no. 7. Non moins attentif au message de *la Confession* qu'à celui de *l'Ane mort*, il se montrera vivement impressionné par ce témoignage de la faillite spirituelle de son époque. "Ce livre", écrit-il, "est une pensée profonde et philosophique dramatisée. Cette pensée la voici: Pour l'honnête homme coupable, il n'y a plus de consolation possible aujourd'hui."[1] Le héros, Anatole, dans une sorte d'orgasme semiconscient, tue sa femme le soir de ses noces. On croit à une apoplexie; mais Anatole se sent coupable et part à la recherche d'un prêtre catholique digne d'entendre sa confession et prêt à lui donner l'absolution. Il ne le trouvera qu'après une série d'aventures qui ont pour but de montrer l'indifférence en matière de religion dans laquelle est tombée la France.

L'année suivante, le 10 janvier 1831, dans *le Voleur*, Balzac comparait les ouvrages de 1830 à ceux de 1730 et faisait ainsi l'éloge de quelques-uns de ses contemporains: "*L'Histoire d'une belle grecque* est-elle seulement comparable à *l'Ane mort* de Jules Janin?"[2] Il rappelle ensuite *la Confession*, plaçant ce roman ainsi que *l'Histoire du roi de Bohême* de Nodier dans les ouvrages de l'école du désenchantement; puis il ajoute: "L'auteur anonyme de *la Physiologie* prend plaisir à nous ôter les illusions de bonheur conjugal, premier bien des sociétés. La *Confession* achève le livre de M. de Lamennais, et proclame que la religion et l'athéisme sont également morts, tués l'un par l'autre." Il n'a qu'une réserve à formuler: "Ce livre, dont la pensée première est hardie, manque d'audace dans l'exécution." C'est l'indication qu'il songe déjà à faire mieux lui-même.[3]

Janin renvoie la balle avec courtoisie, mais non sans fermeté, lorsque paraît *la Peau de chagrin*. C'est le célèbre article du 14 août

---

[1] *O.D.*, t. i, p. 410.

[2] *Lettres sur Paris*, *O.D.*, t. ii, p. 113.

[3] M. Bernard Guyon écrit à propos des commentaires de Balzac sur Stendhal, Janin et Nodier: "En ce qui concerne Nodier et Janin, il est fort probable que la camaraderie a inspiré en partie les appréciations du critique. Nodier était alors un homme influent et Janin, jeune débutant, un rival qu'il fallait ménager." *La pensée politique et sociale de Balzac* (Paris, 1948), p. 768.

Geneviève Delattre commente elle aussi les réflexions de Balzac sur *l'Ane mort* et *la Confession* dans son livre *Les opinions littéraires de Balzac* (1961), p. 391, et remarque que "le style de Janin est en cette même année 1830 ridiculisé dans le conte inachevé des *Deux Amis* et dans *Des mots à la mode*." Le mot "ridiculisé" nous semble un peu fort.

1831, dans *l'Artiste*, où figure le passage si souvent cité que Balzac pastichera dans *Illusions perdues*: "Vous entendez un grand bruit; on entre; on sort; on se heurte; on crie; on hurle; on joue; on s'enivre; on est fou; on est fat; on est mort; on est crispé; on est tout balafré de coups, de baisers, de morsures, de volupté, de feu, de fer. Voilà *La peau de chagrin*. C'est un livre de brigand qui vous attend au coin d'un bois."[1] C'est, comme le dit M. Barbéris, un article de camarade, mais il est clair que les deux écrivains, sans chercher délibérément à se nuire, ne se ménageront plus.

De mauvaises langues vont indisposer Balzac contre Janin. Une lettre de Rabou, vers la fin de 1831, prévient Balzac qu'on le déteste "cordialement" aux *Débats* et qu'il faut s'unir pour "démolir *Barnave*."[2] Susceptible comme il l'était, Balzac dut prendre l'avertissement au sérieux. Rien ne prouve, cependant, qu'une campagne anti-balzacienne se préparât aux *Débats*. Janin semble alors satisfait des relations existantes et continue de glisser dans ses articles et livres le genre de réclame que lui et Balzac avaient sans doute promis de se faire mutuellement en toute circonstance. 1832, c'est l'année du choléra à Paris. Janin écrira sur ce sujet trois articles: les 16 et 23 avril et le 26 septembre, qu'il recueillera ensuite dans ses *Contes nouveaux* en 1833 sous le titre *Histoire du choléra*.[3] Dans l'article du 23 avril 1832, il raconte les inquiétudes d'une dame qui se croit atteinte de la maladie et qui fait venir un "docteur noir". Celui-ci la regarde et lui déclare qu'elle n'a pas encore le choléra mais qu'elle pourrait bien l'attraper si elle restait dans son état de dépression nerveuse. Pour la consoler et en guise d'ordonnance, il lui recommande de lire des contes:

> Faites comme les Florentins, madame; si je ne vous conseille ni de boire, ni de chanter, donc au moins lisez des contes. Justement M. de Balzac vient d'en faire de nouveaux, encore plus graveleux que ceux de Boccace: hâtez-vous donc, profitez du choléra pour les lire; le choléra porte avec lui son excuse. Quand le choléra sera parti, vous serez obligée de lire ces contes en cachette, si vous

[1] P. Barbéris 'L'accueil de la critique aux premières grandes œuvres de Balzac (1831–1832),' *Année balz.* (1968), p. 167.
[2] *Corr.* t. I. no. 375, p. 613. *Barnave*, par J. Janin, parut chez Mensier en 1831, 4 vol. in-12.
[3] III, pp. 1–73.

les lisez: donc lisez les *Contes drolatiques* de M. de Balzac, madame, et consolez-vous.[1]

Content de cette page, sans doute, Janin la reproduisit en 1853, avec quelques variantes, rappelant ainsi un gai souvenir exempt, semble-t-il, de toute animosité envers Balzac.[2]

A l'époque où paraissait le dernier des trois articles de Janin sur le choléra, Balzac était à Aix, au fond de la Provence. Il n'en oubliait pas pour cela son rival et n'avait de cesse qu'on lui envoyât son tout dernier ouvrage. Il écrivait à sa mère: "Prie donc Everat, l'imprimeur, de me donner un *Debureau*, et joins-le à mon paquet. Il saura ce que cela veut dire."[3] Cette lettre est du 16 septembre. Or *Debureau. Histoire du théâtre à quatre sous, pour faire suite à l'Histoire du Théâtre-Français*, de Jules Janin, ne parut officiellement chez Gosselin que le 29 septembre!

Ce fut vers le début de 1833 que se refroidirent les rapports entre Balzac et Janin. L.-J. Arrigon a raconté, d'après le *Journal* du comte Rodolphe Apponyi, la fameuse soirée du 15 mars chez Madame de la Bourdonnaye où Janin, en veine de rosserie, avait impitoyablement raillé le pauvre Balzac qui s'était embrouillé en racontant une histoire invraisemblable.[4] C'est à partir de ce moment-là que Balzac va prendre ombrage et faire part à Madame Hanska de ses griefs envers Janin:

> Janin est un gros petit homme qui mord tout le monde. La préface de *Barnave* n'est pas de lui, mais de Béquet, un rédacteur du *Journal des Débats*, homme spirituel, sans conduite, qui s'était caché chez lui pour échapper à ses créanciers. Béquet est mon camarade de collège; il est venu, lui déjà vieillard par suite de ses excès, pleurer chez moi pour la première fois de sa vie. Janin

---

[1] III, p. 47.

[2] *H.L.D.*, t. I, p. 419: "Justement M. de Balzac vient de publier tout exprès pour les cholériques des *contes drolatiques*! le choléra est une excuse à lire ces sortes de choses. Hâtez-vous de les lire aujourd'hui, de peur que, la santé publique de retour, les contes drolatiques ne vous soient défendus demain."

[3] *Corr.*, t. II, p. 533. V. sur *Debureau H.L.D.*, t. I, pp. 400–9. Janin avait *inventé* ce comédien du Théâtre des Funambules pour remplir son feuilleton et tout la belle société parisienne se rua pour le voir: "les esprits les plus délicats, les plus beaux messieurs et les plus belles dames de ce faubourg Saint-Germain, naguère ressuscité par M. de Balzac dans ses *Scènes de la vie privée*, envahirent ce taudis de la Melpomène vulgaire." (p. 406.)

[4] *Les années romantiques de Balzac* (1927), p. 258.

lui avait pris une pauvre cantatrice dont lui, Béquet, faisait son bonheur. La *Chanson de Barnave* est de Musset, l'infâme chapitre du viol des filles de Séjan, est d'un jeune homme nommé Félix Pyat.[1]

C'est chercher, avec beaucoup de malveillance, des sujets fort mesquins de médisance. Janin était très lié avec Béquet. Il fit, au lendemain de sa mort dans la clinique du Dr Blanche, un élogieux article, reproduit dans *les Catacombes*.[2] A l'enterrement de Béquet n'assistaient que ses deux frères, Antony Deschamps et Jules Janin. Quant à Félix Pyat, ami intime de Janin, fouriériste et futur communard, il devait, en 1844, être condamné à six mois de prison et à mille francs d'amende pour avoir diffamé Janin dans un article du *Journal de la réforme* (4 janvier).

Janin, cependant, ne pouvait soupçonner que Balzac nourrissait à son égard une aversion grandissante. Il continuait à le traiter avec sa bonhomie goguenarde habituelle, lui lançant des dards pour la plupart inermes. Ce fut le cas dans un de ses articles les plus caractéristiques au moment des vacances de 1833.[3] A la fin de juillet, Janin se disait en villégiature sur les bords de la Seine, loin de Paris, quand il fit la connaissance d'un certain lieutenant Godart. Celui-ci s'avisa un beau jour de faire au salon un véritable procès des contes et nouvelles dont il croyait le public d'alors repu. Quand donc s'arrêterait ce déluge de romans et de nouvelles? Janin, se prétendant visé par la critique du lieutenant, se dresse à la défense du conte, mais Godart ne se montre nullement convaincu: les meilleurs contes sont écrits depuis des siècles, on n'a que faire de nouveaux. Il divise les conteurs en trois catégories: celle des femmes (Balzac), celle de la marine (E. Sue), et celle du moyen âge (bibliophile Jacob). De Balzac, il déclare:

M. de Balzac est le chef de la catégorie des femmes; c'est M. de Balzac qui a inventé les femmes. Dieu! que de femmes sont sorties du crâne de M. de Balzac! La femme pleine de cœur, la femme

[1] *L.H.*, I, pp. 52–3 (29 mai 1833).

[2] *Journal des Débats*, 1er octobre 1838, et *les Catacombes*, t. IV, p. 177. La préface de *Barnave* n'était pas de Béquet mais de Théodose Burette à qui sont dédiées *les Catacombes*. V. *H.L.D.*, t. I, pp. 153–64.

[3] 'La cent millième et une et dernière nouvelle nouvelle', *Revue de Paris*, t. LIV (septembre-octobre 1833).

sans cœur, la femme de trente ans, la femme de quinze ans, la femme veuve, la femme mariée; il n'est question que de femmes chez M. de Balzac... M. de Balzac, c'est une femme manquée, une femme avec de la barbe et des moustaches.[1]

Janin se récrie de nouveau après avoir entendu les tirades sur Eugène Sue et le bibliophile Jacob et s'étonne que le lieutenant ne sache admirer "ces chefs-maîtres-conteurs pour lesquels la curiosité contemporaine n'a pas assez d'oreilles."[2] Mais Godart rétorque: "Peste soit de vos contes, monsieur, et de vos auteurs," et il invite la même compagnie pour le lendemain en promettant de fabriquer à son intention un conte selon la bonne formule: une femme, un adultère, une mort funeste. Ce conte sera le dernier conte de tous les contes, la nouvelle la plus nouvelle de toutes les nouvelles. Le lecteur attendra la livraison suivante de la *Revue de Paris* avec impatience et lira le récit du lieutenant Godart intitulé: *le Cercueil*. Il ne manquera pas d'y voir un très habile pastiche de la *Grande Bretèche*. Janin, bon diable, ajoute en dernier paragraphe: "Puisse cependant le lieutenant Godart, bonnes gens qui avez du temps à perdre et des larmes à répandre, ne vous avoir pas tout-à-fait dégoûté [sic] des contes, des nouvelles nouvelles et des conteurs!"[3]

Balzac laissera longtemps couver son ressentiment. Chose curieuse, c'est un accès de jalousie non littéraire qui ranimera le volcan. Il s'en ouvrira à Madame Hanska en janvier 1836, lui annonçant qu'il a rompu "les dernières et faibles relations de politesse avec madame de Castries. Elle a fait sa société de MM. J. J. et Ste-Beuve, qui m'ont si outrageusement blessé."[4] Nous sommes à la veille de ce procès qui mettra aux prises Balzac et la *Revue de Paris*. Celle-ci sentant sa cause mauvaise dans l'affaire de la prépublication du *Lys dans la vallée* dans la *Revue étrangère* de Saint-Pétersbourg, se chercha des alliés parmi ses plus illustres collaborateurs. Jules Janin fut de ceux qui signèrent une 'Déclaration' d'appui pour Buloz. Balzac s'en prit publiquement à Janin dans la première préface du *Lys*:

M. Janin prétend [*Revue de Paris*, 29 mai 1836] que, pour éviter la contrefaçon, il n'y a pas de meilleur moyen que celui de livrer

[1] *Revue de Paris*, t. LIV (septembre-octobre 1833), p. 27.
[2] *ibid.*, p. 29.   [3] *ibid.*, p. 86.   [4] *L.H.*, t. I, p. 389.

ses manuscrits à l'étranger, comme M. Buloz a livré les miens...
Si j'avais le temps, je coifferais M. Janin avec ses propres articles
publiés dans la *Revue*, à propos de sa polémique contre les contre-
façons; mais je l'engage à les relire, et il avouera que je ne saurais
être aussi éloquent dans ma propre cause qu'il l'a été contre les
misérables qui prenaient dans ce temps-là le chemin le plus court
pour arriver à son *Chemin de traverse*.[1]

Ces propos n'avaient probablement rien de bien blessant pour
Jules Janin. Pour nous ils sont révélateurs du fait que Balzac avait
lu le *Chemin de traverse* de Janin dès sa publication chez Ambroise
Dupont, fin mai 1836. Il n'allait certes pas l'oublier et en tirerait
bientôt un important parti.

Les circonstances et les hasards de sa vie ont toujours été pour
Balzac l'œstre de la création littéraire. Harcelé par les journalistes,
ne se voyant que des ennemis dans la Presse, Balzac voulut se venger
de façon mémorable: *Un grand homme de province à Paris* allait,
une fois pour toutes, révéler au public les coulisses sordides du
journalisme.[2]

Janin dut se sentir touché au vif car sa riposte dans la *Revue de
Paris* de juillet 1839 fut cinglante. Dans un de ses meilleurs articles,
il accuse Balzac d'avoir depuis longtemps voué aux journaux et aux
journalistes la haine la plus implacable. Pour Balzac, dit-il, la Presse
c'est l'hydre de Lerne dont il voudrait d'un seul coup abattre toutes
les têtes. Et Janin de défendre avec ferveur la profession des journalistes dont font partie les plus hautes intelligences, les esprits les plus
élevés et les plumes les plus distinguées d'Europe: "cela est triste
de voir sa noble et chère profession attaquée même dans ses ténèbres,
même dans ses accessoires les plus futiles et les plus inaperçus, et
attaquée par quoi, je vous prie? Par un livre sans style, sans mérite
et sans talent." Janin avait auparavant vigoureusement plaidé la
cause des héroïnes ingénues de 20 ans contre les femmes de 30 à 40
ans préférées de Balzac. Il blâme le romancier d'avoir corrompu la
saine moralité des mères de famille et de les avoir insidieusement
conduites sur la pente du vice. Enfin, bien que reconnaissant en
Balzac un des maîtres du roman moderne et le traitant d'*illustre
romancier*, il le voue, ainsi que son œuvre, à un oubli total.

[1] xi, 320–1.　[2] H. J. Hunt, 'Balzac's Pressmen', *F.S.*, xi (1957), 230-45.

La guerre était déclarée. Madame de Girardin se rallia à Balzac et prit sa défense dans la *Presse*, où elle avait inauguré, le 28 septembre 1836, ses fameux *Courriers de Paris*. Le 12 novembre 1839, elle donnait chez elle une lecture de sa pièce *L'École des journalistes*, où la profession est une fois de plus ravalée.[1]

L'article de Janin suscita même, longtemps après, une réaction rageuse chez le grand admirateur de Balzac que fut Zola. Celui-ci met en doute la bonne foi du critique et l'accuse de ne pas avoir exprimé ses propres sentiments mais de s'être fait l'instrument servile des rancunes de la *Revue de Paris*. Il ne cherche aucunement à réfuter les arguments de Janin: il ne sait que l'insulter grossièrement: "Grand Dieu! est-ce des *Illusions perdues* que parle le prince des critiques? Mais, vous ne connaissez pas seulement votre principauté, vous barbotez! Après un jugement pareil on aurait dû vous asseoir sur votre couronne comme sur une chaise percée."[2] Il y avait une certaine lâcheté dans cette invective.

Janin eut beau jeu quand il revint à la charge à l'occasion de la représentation de *Vautrin*, le 14 mars 1840. La réception fut des plus tumultueuses et malgré les efforts de Frédérick-Lemaître, la pièce tomba. Le lendemain les représentations étaient interdites par le Ministre de l'Intérieur. Avec quelle joie Janin se gausse de Balzac dans son feuilleton: "On n'a pas voulu entendre la plus petite moitié de cette pièce de *Vautrin* par pitié pour l'ancien esprit de M. de Balzac!"[3] Et plus tard, le souvenir de *Vautrin* restait si présent à sa mémoire qu'en rendant compte de *Mercadet le Faiseur*, il ne pouvait s'empêcher d'y faire allusion en ces termes: "Et *Vautrin*, quelle école! On lui fit l'honneur d'en avoir peur, on le supprima... Or ce Vautrin est un *faiseur*, Quinola est un autre *faiseur*, Mercadet est un troisième *faiseur*. Eh quoi! toujours des *faiseurs*, rien que des *faiseurs*!"[4] C'est dans ce même article que Janin s'en prend à

[1] Charles Léger, *Balzac mis à nu* (Paris, 1928), pp. 104–7. La pièce venait d'être reçue par la Comédie Française mais elle allait être interdite par la censure. "Victor Hugo est là, et Balzac, et Ballanche, Alphonse Karr, Jules Janin, Roger de Beauvoir... Puisqu'on dit du mal des journalistes, Custine est content. Balzac aussi." Marquis de Luppé, *Astolphe de Custine* (Monaco, 1957), p. 215.
[2] Zola, *Le roman expérimental* (Paris, 1880), p. 346.
[3] *Journal des Débats*, 16 mars 1840.
[4] *Critique dramatique*, t. IV (Librairie des Bibliophiles, 1877), p. 65. L'article reproduit est celui qui suivit la reprise de *Mercadet* au Gymnase, le 23 août 1851. "Le *Mercadet* a réussi... Mais soyez tous avertis, les uns et les autres, que de toutes les œuvres posthumes de M. de Balzac, le *Mercadet* seul pouvait réussir." (p. 72.)

l'amour de l'argent chez Balzac: "Il aime le *faiseur* parce qu'il aime l'argent! Il y a de l'argent dans tous les livres de M. de Balzac. C'est son rêve, l'argent; c'est son Apollon, l'argent; c'est sa muse, l'argent!"

Le fond de la querelle Balzac-Janin, c'est l'antagonisme éternel des romanciers et des critiques. Chacun d'eux a défendu avec le maximum d'acharnement sa profession, ce qui n'était que naturel et de la meilleure guerre; mais ce que Janin ne put jamais pardonner à Balzac, c'est d'avoir abusé du roman pour flétrir la Presse. Janin se fit alors le champion des journalistes outragés conscient des "exigences de la terrible et décevante profession du journaliste."[1] Dès 1833, il se déclarait "heureux et fier d'être un des hommes de cette presse, moi indigne! Depuis tantôt huit ans, j'y ai travaillé nuit et jour avec tout le zèle dont je suis capable."[2] On conçoit quelle fut sa fureur quand parut la *Monographie de la presse parisienne*. Cette fois son attaque est plus personnelle, plus mordante que de coutume. Reprenant le thème de Jules Sandeau dans son livre *Vie et malheurs d'Horace de Saint-Aubin*, il se moque du Balzac qui, pendant six ans, a écrit sous un faux nom des livres que personne ne voulait lire. Il termine rageusement son article: "On ne veut à aucun prix des romans de sieur Horace de Saint-Aubin; on n'en veut à aucun prix. L'antichambre même, ce grand dévoreur de livres, n'accepte pas les livres qui sortent de cette fabrique clandestine."[3] Dans ce même article il lançait ses foudres contre *la Comédie humaine*, "ce rendez-vous de romans, qu'il appelle *son œuvre!* un labyrinthe inextricable dans lequel avec la plus vive intelligence et la plus ferme volonté il est impossible de se retourner et de se reconnaître."

C'est en cette année 1843 que Balzac médite une fourberie qui fera rire le public aux dépens de Janin. Dans *la Muse du Département*, il fait lancer par Lousteau le fameux billet:

Madame la baronne de la Baudraye est heureusement accouchée d'un garçon.
M. Étienne Lousteau a lep laisir de vous en faire part.
La mère et l'enfant se portent bien.

[1] *Barnave*, édition de 1860, p. 27. [2] *Contes nouveaux*, t. I, p. 146.
[3] *Journal des Débats*, 20 février 1843.

C'était Janin qui avait conçu l'idée de ce curieux faire-part au temps où il était l'amant de la Marquise de la Carte, fille du statuaire Bosio. Arsène Houssaye,[1] Albéric Second,[2] et Jean Gigoux,[3] ont rappelé le luxe extravagant où Janin et la Marquise filèrent pendant deux années le parfait amour. Ils eurent deux filles, l'une née en 1833 et morte en bas âge, l'autre décédée à l'âge de vingt ans.[4] C'était pour célébrer la naissance de la première que Janin aurait fait imprimer le faire-part qui inspira Balzac:

Madame la marquise de la Carte est heureusement accouchée d'une fille. M. Jules Janin a le plaisir de vous en faire part.

Janin n'a jamais commenté cette allusion à un épisode de sa jeunesse. Il n'a jamais reconnu qu'il avait été portraituré dans le personnage de Lousteau ou d'aucun autre dans *la Comédie humaine*. Et pourtant il avait tout lieu de se sentir blessé par les paroles que Balzac attribue à Nathan: "Ce billet prouve que Lousteau manque de cœur, de bon goût, de dignité, qu'il ne connaît ni le monde, ni la morale publique, qu'il s'insulte lui-même, quand il ne sait plus qui insulter." Fatigué sans doute de la polémique, attristé par son procès à Félix Pyat et la mauvaise presse que cela lui avait attiré, Janin laisse tomber Balzac, sans pour cela cesser de l'admirer dans son for intérieur. Il regrettera bientôt le géant des lettres avec lequel il avait eu l'honneur de lutter et lui rendra un généreux hommage posthume.[5]

Julien Lemer a raconté avec quelle véhémence Janin défendit Balzac, quelques jours après sa mort, le 21 août 1850, chez le banquier M. Benoît-Fould. Le frère du maître de la maison ayant demandé à Janin quel était cet enterrement suivi d'une si nombreuse assistance qui lui avait barré le passage sur le boulevard? N'était-ce pas le convoi funèbre d'un faiseur de romans, d'un homme de lettres?

Ça! s'écria Janin en se levant, la lèvre frémissante, le teint animé, l'œil brillant d'indignation, le geste hautain, la voix vibrante, ça!

[1] *Confessions*, t. IV (Paris, 1885), p. 300.
[2] *Le Tiroir aux souvenirs* (Paris, 1886).
[3] *Causeries sur les artistes de mon temps* (Paris, 1885).
[4] Clément-Janin, *Candide*, no. 566, 17 janvier 1935.
[5] *H.L.D.*, t. III, p. 22; t. IV, pp. 167–82; t. V, p. 125.

ça! monsieur Achille... c'était tout simplement un des plus grands hommes, un des génies les plus profonds, une des intelligences les plus vastes de notre époque... Tenez pour certain que le vingtième [siècle] trouvera, après vous, [dans son œuvre] d'immenses trésors que vous aurez méconnus. Car je vous le dis, en vérité, Balzac est un de ces hommes sublimes qui, pour me servir de la poétique expression de Béranger, ont le plus richement "ensemencé les champs de l'avenir".[1]

Madame Janin, aussi surprise et émue que tous ceux qui assistaient à cette soirée, courut à son mari et l'embrassa tendrement. Elle savait, dit-elle, "à quelle violence d'attaques réciproques l'ardeur de leurs polémiques les avait entraînés l'un et l'autre, à quel point Balzac nous avait blessés." En effet, Janin aurait pu se plaindre d'avoir été, en mainte occasion, pillé par Balzac. Il aurait pu tout aussi bien se vanter d'avoir été son inspirateur. Il préféra garder le silence, savourant peut-être le plaisir d'avoir aiguillonné chez Balzac ce sentiment de jalousie qui activait en lui le processus de la création littéraire. C'était souvent ainsi que se développaient ses idées embryonnaires. Une rage d'émulation, mêlée à un désir de vengeance, lui faisait prendre la plume pour donner une manifestation éclatante de son talent supérieur, dût-il abandonner provisoirement une œuvre commencée dans un ordre logique. *La Torpille*, par exemple, avait eu pour but de porter un coup double: montrer à Hugo que la courtisane amoureuse pouvait trouver plus d'un poète, et à Janin qu'il n'avait pas su tirer le maximum d'effet de son corrupteur, le baron de la Bertenache, du *Chemin de traverse*, sans compter qu'une quatrième édition de *l'Ane mort*, parue en 1837, rendait vraiment trop populaire cette Henriette qui se prostituait même condamnée à mort.[2] N'est-ce pas le *Chemin de traverse* qui suggéra à Balzac le thème d'*Un grand homme de province à Paris* ainsi que les premières pages d'*Un début dans la vie*?[3] Quant à la scène fastueuse de confession publique du *Curé de village*, n'est-elle pas la grandiose illustration du concept de l'irrésistibilité de l'aveu, fondement

---

[1] Julien Lemer, *Balzac, sa vie et son œuvre* (Paris, 1892).
[2] voir notre c.r. de *la Torpille*, éd. Jean Pommier, in *F.S.*, XIII (1959), 172.
[3] voir nos c.r. d'*Illusions perdues*, éd. Antoine Adam, in *F.S.*, (1957), 178 et d'*Un début dans la vie*, éd. Robert et Matoré, in *F.S.*, (1951), 365.

psychologique de la *Confession* de Jules Janin?[1] Rappelons également
que Ginette Fainas a montré ce que *Massimilla Doni* devait au conte
de Janin *Gabrielli*, et Pierre Citron les évidents rapports entre
Gambara et le *Dîner de Beethoven*, de Janin.[2] Il reste certainement
d'autres emprunts à dépister.[3]

Il est incontestable que Balzac a beaucoup profité de la vie et de
l'œuvre de Janin, mais, bien entendu, il ne s'en est pas vanté. S'il
a cherché à noircir son rival aux yeux de Madame Hanska, c'est
sans doute parce qu'il craignait que celle-ci ne lût les livres de Janin
et comprît à quel point Balzac lui était redevable. Un jour que
Madame Hanska lui avait signalé un article où Janin faisait son éloge,
il avait répondu, avec une insigne mauvaise foi:

> Je ne lis jamais les journaux, en sorte que j'ignorais ce que vous
> me dites de Janin qui est un fort mauvais drôle. Quelques per-
> sonnes m'avaient dit, en passant, que les journaux et Janin surtout
> m'avaient beaucoup loué, à propos d'une petite pièce, prise dans
> *la Recherche de l'Absolu*, et tombée. Mais je suis, vous le savez,
> aussi indifférent au blâme qu'à l'éloge des gens qui ne sont pas
> les élus de mon cœur, et surtout aux opinions du journalisme et
> de la foule, en sorte que je ne saurais rien vous dire de cette
> conversion d'un homme que je n'aime ni n'estime, et qui
> n'obtiendra jamais rien de moi. Comme je ne connais ni ses amis
> ni ses ennemis, j'ignore les motifs de cette louange qui, d'après
> ce que vous m'en faites savoir, me paraît perfide.[4]

Balzac affiche ici une indifférence envers Janin qu'il voudrait
communiquer à son amie; mais indifférent il ne le fut jamais. Il a
eu la hantise de Janin: il l'a tour à tour admiré, envié et haï. La
complexité même de ces sentiments lui a troublé la conscience car

---

[1] voir notre article 'Variations littéraires sur le thème de la confession', *F.S.*, v.
(1951).

[2] 'Jules Janin inspirateur de Balzac. Une source inattendue de *"Massimilla Doni"* ',
Année balz. (1961), p. 223; 'Autour de "Gambara", II: "Gambara", Strunz et
Beethoven', *Année balz.* (1967), p. 169.

[3] M. François Bilodeau vient récemment d'établir un rapport de parenté entre
Henriette (*l'Ane mort*) et Fœdora (*la Peau de chagrin*): "En fait, le personnage de
Fœdora ne forme pas le portrait d'une personne mais il incarne la Société. En
ce sens, il offre une certaine parenté avec la 'femme dans cœur' dont Janin
avait fait l'histoire dans *l'Ane mort*; il appartient à la même volonté de condemnation de la société." – *Balzac et le jeu des mots* (Montréal, 1971), p. 211.

[4] *L.H.*, t. I, pp.576-7. (20 janv. 1838).

il savait sa destinée inexorablement traversée et marquée par Janin. Il en souffrit à la fois dans son amour-propre et dans son rêve brisé d'aséité.

Faut-il en vouloir à Janin de s'être trouvé mêlé ainsi à la vie de Balzac? On aurait tort, en vérité, vu que, finalement, c'est Balzac qui l'a emporté sur son adversaire. Souhaitons donc que tous ceux qui semblent s'être donné le mot pour casser du sucre sur le dos du Prince des Critiques reviennent à de meilleurs sentiments.[1] Le temps de la haine est passé.

[1] Surtout M. André Wurmser dans son livre *la comédie inhumaine* (Paris, 1964), qui voit un Janin "vénal et cynique" et qui le traite de "fielleux hypocrite" et de "petit esprit". André Billy s'est converti à Janin avant de mourir: "Charmant Janin! Grand méconnu!" – *Le Figaro litteraire*, 7-13 avril 1969.

Baudelaire and Balzac

GARNET REES

In an amusingly combative article published in 1934,[1] Randolph Hughes drew attention to the fact that no critic had yet attempted any methodical analysis of the influence of Balzac on Baudelaire, although the existence of such an influence had long been acknowledged. This challenge has still not been accepted although a number of articles and chapters have explored and enlightened this important and diffuse subject. Margaret Gilman's *Baudelaire the Critic*[2] indicates some possible lines of investigation. Jean Prévost devoted a concise and suggestive chapter to 'L'Influence de Balzac' in his brilliant book on Baudelaire[3] and Claude Pichois in 'Autour de la Fanfarlo'[4] developed some of these ideas on Balzac's mark on Baudelaire in this early writing. We owe the most acute assessment of this problem so far published to P.-G. Castex in a study combining impeccable erudition with great literary sensitivity. His article on 'Balzac et Baudelaire'[5] opens up all kinds of fruitful approaches. Since the publication of this article, Pierre Citron's book on *La Poésie de Paris dans la littérature française de Rousseau à Baudelaire*[6] has examined the nature of the treatment of Paris in the work of the two writers. In this volume destined to honour a great English *Balzacien*, there is perhaps room for some further discriminations.

It is known that Baudelaire had an abundant knowledge of Balzac's work, that he was one of the poet's "premières liaisons littéraires". He took all the then published volumes of what was to become *La Comédie humaine* with him on his long sea voyage in 1841. His

[1] 'Baudelaire et Balzac', *M.F.* (1 Nov. 1934), 476–518.
[2] New York, 1943.
[3] *Baudelaire: Essai sur l'inspiration et la création poétiques* (Paris, 1953).
[4] *M.F.* (1 Dec. 1956), 604–36.
[5] *Revue des sciences humaines*, 59 (1958), 139–51.
[6] Paris, 1961, 2 vols.

M

references to Balzac are respectful and full of admiration: he is
"cher", "grand", a "prodigieux météore", a "grand génie".
"Savant", "inventeur", "observateur", he is also a visionary and,
above all, "un créateur de méthode". It has already been observed,
notably by P.-G. Castex, that Balzac is revered by Baudelaire for
two distinct reasons. Not only is he a great novelist and creator,
but he is also an exemplar of the Writer by his force, his enormous
creative powers and his incarnation of the *volonté*. Further, in his
early lack of success, Balzac joins that other tattered saint, Edgar
Allen Poe, in Baudelaire's private calendar. But Balzac conquers the
obsessions and problems which overlaid Baudelaire, by his genius
and his vast powers of concentration. That Baudelaire attached a
primary and increasing importance to the discipline of work is
evident, and a letter to his mother in 1851 specifically links the
gospel of work to Balzac:

> J'avais il y a quelques jours entre les mains, des papiers de
> jeunesse de Balzac. Personne ne pourra jamais se figurer combien
> ce grand homme était maladroit, niais et BETE dans sa jeunesse.
> Et cependant il est parvenu à avoir, *à se procurer*, pour ainsi dire,
> non seulement des conceptions grandioses, mais encore immensé-
> ment d'esprit. Mais il a TOUJOURS travaillé. Il est sans doute
> bien consolant de penser que par le travail on acquiert non seule-
> ment de l'argent, mais aussi un talent considérable. Mais à 30 ans,
> Balzac avait depuis plusieurs années pris l'habitude d'un travail
> permanent, et jusqu'ici je ne n'ai en commun avec lui que les
> dettes et les projets.[1]

Seven years later he writes again to his mother:

> Je n'ai pas le courage, je n'ai pas le génie de Balzac, et j'ai tous
> les embarras qui l'ont rendu si malheureux.[2]

In 1851, Baudelaire had written in an article on Pierre Dupont the
following lines:

[1] *Corr. gén.*, t. I, p. 142. All quotations from Baudelaire are from the *Œuvres
complètes*, revised edition (Paris, Bibliothèque de la Pléiade, 1961), and the
Correspondance générale, 6 vols. (Paris, Conard, 1953).
[2] *Corr. gén.*, t. II, p. 120 (11 janv. 1858).

C'est un fait singulier que cette joie qui respire et domine dans les œuvres de quelques écrivains célèbres, ainsi que l'a judicieusement noté Champfleury à propos d'Honoré de Balzac. Quelques grandes que soient les douleurs qui les surprennent, quelques affligeants que soient les spectacles humains, leur bon tempérament reprend le dessus, et peut-être quelque chose de mieux, qui est un grand esprit de sagesse. On dirait qu'ils portent en eux-mêmes leur consolation.[1]

If Baudelaire's work notably lacks this quality of joy it is, in part at least, due to the fact that he never succeeded in imposing on himself this interior discipline which might have made him more impervious to the distractions of his life. The tragic jottings of the *Journaux intimes* reveal his preoccupation with work considered as salvation:

Plus on veut, mieux on veut. Plus on travaille, mieux on travaille, et plus on veut travailler. Plus on produit, plus on devient fécond.[2]

On mature reflection and with the sad experience of his own inability to transcend his weaknesses, Baudelaire's single stricture on Balzac is amended. In 1846 in the *Conseils aux jeunes littérateurs* he had written:

On dit que Balzac charge sa copie et ses épreuves d'une manière fantastique et désordonnée. Un roman passe dès lors par une série de genèses, où se disperse non-seulement l'unité de la phrase, mais aussi de l'œuvre. C'est sans doute cette mauvaise méthode qui donne souvent au style ce je ne sais quoi de diffus, de bousculé et du brouillon, — le seul défaut de ce grand historien.[3]

In *Fusées* he writes: "Travail immédiat, même mauvais, vaut mieux que la rêverie."[4]

In *Les Paradis artificiels* Baudelaire recounts the story of a gathering of a group of friends among whom was Balzac, in which the conversation turned to the effects of *haschisch*; he introduces the anecdote with these words: "Balzac pensait sans doute qu'il n'est pas pour l'homme de plus grande honte ni de plus vive souffrance que l'abdication de sa volonté." Baudelaire describes Balzac's lively curiosity on the subject but "l'idée de penser malgré lui-même le choquait vivement". The story continues:

[1] *O.C.*, pp. 612–13. [2] *Fusées*, p. 1265. [3] *Conseils*, p. 481. [4] *Fusées*, p. 1265.

On lui présenta du dawamesk; il l'examina, le flaira et le rendit sans y toucher. La lutte entre sa curiosité presque enfantine et sa répugnance pour l'abdication se trahissait sur son visage expressif d'une manière frappante. L'amour de la dignité l'emporta. En effet, il est difficile de se figurer le théoricien de la *volonté*, ce jumeau spirituel de Louis Lambert, consentant à perdre une parcelle de cette précieuse *substance*.[1]

For Baudelaire, Balzac is the lasting example of a man in whom the will is dominant and who possesses, in addition, the artistic means to transmit this dynamic force to all his characters. This is the tenor of that superb page of mature criticism devoted to Balzac in the article on Théophile Gautier which throws a brilliant flash of understanding on the novelist. Here the Balzac characters are truly seen as larger than life, bursting with an *ardeur vitale* and *chargées de volonté jusqu'à la gueule*. They all have the genius their creator himself had in abundance.

Joy, work, will and *énergie* are all characteristics which dominate the Baudelairien idea of Balzac the man and the writer. They are all characteristics which Baudelaire lacked – and knew he lacked. *L'Ennui* – "l'œil chargé d'un pleur involontaire" – , Time with its eroding action, the helpless figure in *La Cloche fêlée*:

> Moi, mon âme est fêlée, et lorsqu'en ses ennuis
> Elle veut de ses chants peupler l'air froid des nuits,
> Il arrive souvent que sa voix affaiblie
>
> Semble le râle épais d'un blessé qu'on oublie
> Au bord d'un lac de sang, sous un grand tas de morts,
> Et qui meurt, sans bouger, dans d'immenses efforts,

and the massed symbols of the *Spleen* poems which, by their number and diversity, overwhelm us totally, all haunt the *Fleurs du mal*.

> L'ennui, fruit de la morne incuriosité,
> Prend les proportions de l'immortalité

writes Baudelaire and when this confession and desolate self-portrait are set against the evocation of Balzac, both are enormously

---

[1] *Les Paradis artificiels*, p. 384.

illumined. Here there is no material influence of Balzac, indeed what is evident is an almost total incompatibility, but there is little doubt that Baudelaire's self-knowledge is made sharper and more cruelly lucid by his frequentation of Balzac. The best and most concise definition of *spleen* and *ennui* is that they are the opposite of Balzac's *volonté* and *énergie*.

———

ONE of the enigmas in Baudelaire's admiration for Balzac lies in the approving references to the novelist's method. How much one must agree with Margaret Gilman's remark that "an article devoted to Balzac is amongst the first of the articles one would like Baudelaire to have written"![1] One of the rare passages in which Baudelaire speaks directly of Balzac's method is to be found in the article *Les Contes de Champfleury* of 1848:

> Balzac est... un romancier et un savant, un inventeur et un observateur; un naturaliste qui connaît également la loi de génération des idées et des êtres visibles. C'est un grand homme dans toute la force du terme; c'est un créateur de méthode et le seul dont la méthode vaille la peine d'être étudiée.[2]

This, apart from the last words in the passage, is not particularly enlightening for it could be attached to the criticism of any great novelist as could the tribute to the "puissance de l'analyse racinienne" with which he elsewhere endows Balzac,[3] as well as Stendhal and Sainte-Beuve. We come nearer an understanding in this other anecdote retold by Baudelaire with evident pleasure:

> On raconte que Balzac (qui n'écouterait avec respect toutes les anecdotes, si petites qu'elles soient, qui se rapportent à ce grand génie?) se trouvait un jour en face d'un beau tableau d'hiver, tout mélancolique et chargé de frimas, clair-semé de cabanes et de paysans chétifs, — après avoir contemplé une maisonnette d'où montait une maigre fumée, s'écria: "Que c'est beau! Mais que

[1] Gilman, *op. cit.*, p. 53.
[2] p. 601.
[3] 'Notes sur "Les Liaisons dangereuses" ', p. 641.

font-ils dans cette cabane? à quoi pensent-ils, quels sont leurs
chagrins? les récoltes ont-elles été bonnes? *Ils ont sans doute des
échéances à payer?*[1]

The reaction of Baudelaire before this unidentified picture would
certainly not have been identical and it is difficult to imagine that
he would ever have arrived at the final italicized question but,
nevertheless, both writers share this curiosity about others. Both
pride themselves on this ability to share the preoccupations and
passions of other men and although it is a quality more clearly
essential to the novelist than to the poet, both define this gift in an
astonishingly similar and frank manner. Firstly, here is Balzac in a
well-known passage from *Facino Cane*:

> En entendant ces gens, je pouvais épouser leur vie, je me sentais
> leurs guenilles sur le dos, je marchais les pieds dans leurs souliers
> percés; leurs désirs, leurs besoins, tout passait dans mon âme, ou
> mon âme passait dans la leur. C'était le rêve d'un homme éveillé.
> Je m'échauffais avec eux contre les chefs d'atelier qui les tyrani-
> saient, ou contre les mauvaises pratiques qui les faisaient revenir
> plusieurs fois sans les payer. Quitter ses habitudes, devenir un
> autre que soi par l'ivresse des facultés morales, et jouer ce jeu à
> volonté, telle était ma distraction. A quoi dois-je ce don? Est-ce
> une seconde vue? est-ce une de ces qualités dont l'abus mènerait à
> la folie? Je n'ai jamais recherché les causes de cette puissance; je
> la possède et m'en sers, voilà tout.[2]

Baudelaire sees the same power as belonging to the poet although
his description is more self-conscious:

> Multitude, solitude: termes égaux et convertibles pour le poëte
> actif et fécond. Qui ne sait pas peupler sa solitude, ne sait pas non
> plus être seul dans une foule affairée.

> Le poëte jouit de cette incomparable privilège, qu'il peut à sa
> guise être lui-même et autrui. Comme ces âmes errantes qui
> cherchent un corps, il entre, quand il veut, dans le personnage de
> chacun.[3]

[1] 'Exposition universelle de 1855', p. 957.   [2] VI, 67.
[3] *Le Spleen de Paris*, pp. 243–4.

Again the Balzac passage has overtones of economic and social compassion which are absent from Baudelaire but, with this difference set aside, the two writers boast a similar power of intuitive understanding. Even if their aims diverge, the resemblance is striking and points towards a common acceptance of the imagination as arbiter of truth.

It is important at this point to remind ourselves that the two writers are using differing literary genres which are in entirely differing stages of development and critical acclaim. Baudelaire knows that poetry is an accepted, serious form of literature and that the only battles which need be fought on its behalf in the mid-nineteenth century are battles of definition and distinction of aim. The novel form, born without the privileges of long aristocratic lineage, is still mistrusted as something essentially frivolous and Balzac, apart from all his other preoccupations, is concerned with the establishment, amongst readers and critics, of the novel as a serious contribution to literature, philosophy and history. Jane Austen had earlier felt the same malaise:

> Although our [novelists'] productions have afforded more extensive and unaffected pleasure than those of any other literary corporation in the world, no species of composition has been so much decried. From pride, ignorance, or fashion, our foes are almost as many as our readers; and while the abilities of the mere hundredth abridger of the *History of England*, or of the man who collects and publishes in a volume some dozen lines of Milton, Pope and Prior, with a paper from the *Spectator* and a chapter of Sterne are eulogized by a thousand pens, there seems almost a general wish of decrying the capacity and undervaluing the labour of the novelist...[1]

and she summarizes the typical reactions of the lettered: "I am no novel reader; I seldom look into a novel; do not imagine that *I* often read novels...". In the first pages of *Le Père Goriot* Balzac wags a forbidding finger at the unsuspecting reader:

> Ainsi ferez-vous, vous qui tenez ce livre d'une main blanche, vous qui vous enfoncez dans un moelleux fauteuil en vous disant:

[1] Preface to *Northanger Abbey*.

Peut-être ceci va-t-il m'amuser. Après avoir lu les secrètes infor-
tunes du père Goriot, vous dînerez avec appétit en mettant votre
insensibilité sur le comte de l'auteur, en le taxant d'exagération,
en l'accusant de poésie.[1]

Baudelaire's perceptive observations on Balzac's "goût prodigieux
du détail, qui tient à une ambition immodérée de tout voir, de tout
faire voir, de tout deviner, de tout faire deviner"[2] are in no way a
criticism. They acknowledge at once the abundant qualities of a
novel formed by Balzac's prodigal gifts and the novelist's need to
confer on his work an authenticity of setting and circumstance which
was being withheld by readers and critics. Baudelaire was no
admirer of description for its own sake, as his severe strictures on
Sir Walter Scott reveal,[3] and he specifically forbade it to the poet:
"En décrivant ce qui est, le poëte se dégrade et descend au rang de
professeur; en racontant le possible, il reste fidèle à sa fonction."[4]

What Baudelaire saw unerringly as the supreme discovery of
Balzac's method is thus expressed: "Mais qui peut se vanter d'être
aussi heureusement doué, et de pouvoir appliquer une méthode qui
lui permette de revêtir, à coup sûr, de lumière et de pourpre la pure
trivialité? Qui peut faire cela? Or, qui ne fait pas cela, pour dire la
vérité, ne fait pas grand'chose."[5] The significance of this remark
for Baudelaire and for the poetry of his successors right into the
twentieth century is immense. Here is the authority for the image
of everyday life which, by the tensions of poetic form, can be
made to bear an immense amount of meaning and the charter for a
poetry which rejects exclusivity of vocabulary and subject. This
passage was written in 1859 when he was composing *Le Cygne*.
In this poem the weight of implication of the tragic results of moral
and physical exile is borne equally by the archetypal figure of
Andromaque and by the figures – trivial in any traditional poetic
context – of the swan, the "négresse amaigrie et phthisique" and
the shadowy gallery of sufferers. Of course the range of Baudelaire

[1] II, 848.
[2] 'Théophile Gautier', p. 692.
[3] "Oh! l'ennuyeux écrivain! – Un poudreux déterreur de chroniques! un fastidieux
amas de descriptions de bric-a-brac, – un tas de vieilles choses et de défroques
de tout genre...', *La Fanfarlo*, p. 489.
[4] 'Victor Hugo', p. 711.
[5] 'Théophile Gautier', p. 692.

is very considerably less than Balzac's. His was not the ambition to mirror an age in its bewildering variety and to attempt to explain its motives. Baudelaire lacked Balzac's certainties and rarely spoke in a tone of bold affirmation. His idea of beauty and significance is on an altogether smaller scale:

> Pourquoi le spectacle de la mer est-il si infiniment et si éternellement agréable?

> Parce que la mer offre à la fois l'idée de l'immensité et du mouvement. Six ou sept lieues représentent pour l'homme le rayon de l'infini. Voilà un infini diminutif. Qu'importe s'il suffit à suggérer l'idée d'un infini total? Douze ou quatorze lieues (sur le diamètre), douze ou quatorze de liquide en mouvement suffisent pour donner la plus haute idée de beauté qui soit offerte à l'homme sur son habitacle transitoire.[1]

But within this small scale there is room for the outgoing surge of Baudelaire's ideal of beauty – "quelque chose d'ardent et de triste, quelque chose d'un peu vague, laissant carrière à la conjecture"[2] – and for the clothing of trivialities in purple and gold.

For Baudelaire, Balzac is not an observer but a "visionnaire et visionnaire passionné" and it is in this vision that Baudelaire found in his elder a master and a leader. It is curious to recall how Rimbaud was later to honour Baudelaire in the same vein: "Baudelaire est le premier voyant, roi des poëtes, *un vrai Dieu*."

───────

It is not surprising that Balzac's visions of Paris should have had a great impact on the urban poet, although Paris serves a different purpose for the two writers. For Balzac it serves a novelist's ends, swarming with vivid characters, a jungle of rapacious creatures, a world which exaggerates with violence the extremes of wealth and poverty. It provides a kind of external hierarchy which gives a fourth dimension to the personages and, to the traditional means of character delineation by analysis, dialogue and action, adds a new depth of exploration by reference to possessions and status. Its tremendous reality adds veracity to the characters and reinforces

---

[1] *Mon cœur mis à nu*, p. 1290. [2] *Fusées*, p. 1255.

that authenticity which is Balzac's aim. For Baudelaire, Paris is a
poet's city, loved in his early years, hated as he grew older and
transferred his bitterness to it. It is not an economic or political
place but rather a depository of myths, reincarnated in the person
of the most ordinary passer-by. Pierre Citron analyses at length the
points of similarity and of difference in the treatment of Paris by
Baudelaire and Balzac in *La Poésie de Paris*, but I am more concerned
with the method of the two writers.

> La vie parisienne est féconde en sujets poétiques et merveilleux.
> Le merveilleux nous enveloppe et nous abreuve comme l'atmos-
> phère; mais nous ne le croyons pas... Car les héros de l'Iliade ne
> vont qu'à votre cheville, ô Vautrin, ô Rastignac, ô Birotteau...[1]

wrote Baudelaire in the *Salon de 1846* recognizing that epic quality
with which Balzac invests his characters, transforming them almost
instantaneously into figures in a contemporary mythology. For
Balzac too sees Paris with the eye of a poet as well as with the more
analytical eye of the historian. He is conscious that not all that comes
under his scrutiny is equally significant or endowed with poetic
potential: "Beaucoup de choses véritables sont souverainement
ennuyeuses. Aussi est-ce la moitié du talent que de choisir dans le
vrai ce qui peut devenir poétique."[2] The opening chapters of *La
Peau de chagrin* reveal to the greatest effect how the background of
Paris can convey both the novelist's truth to a clearly defined period
of time and the great potential for mystery which still lies dormant
even in the modern city. It is this which enables the novel to
predispose us to accept it at one and the same time, in Herbert J.
Hunt's words, as: "a fantastic novel, as fantastic as any of the
Thousand-and-one Nights so often quoted in connection with it, and
yet . . . a novel about contemporary society".[3] Balzac confers on even
the most commonplace aspects of Paris a sinister aspect:

[1] *Salon de 1846*, p. 952, P.-G. Castex refers to the discovery made by Claude
Pichois that Baudelaire struck out the name of Rastignac in Poulet-Malassis's
copy of the *Salon de 1846* and substituted the name of Raphaël de Valentin
which appears in the edition of 1868. Castex makes this comment: "Baudelaire
pourrait bien révéler par là que la décheance tragique de Raphaël le touche
davantage que l'ascension de Rastignac, et que le héros de *La Peau de chagrin*
lui paraît mieux illustrer les problèmes posés à la conscience de l'homme moderne" (*op. cit.*, p. 146).
[2] *Le Message*, II, 170.   [3] In *Balzac's 'Comédie humaine'* (1964), p. 39.

Quand les boutiques lui manquèrent, il étudia le Louvre, l'Institut, les tours de Notre-Dame, celles du Palais, le Pont-des-Arts. Ces monuments paraissent prendre une physionomie triste en reflétant les teintes grises du ciel dont les rares clartés prêtaient un air menaçant à Paris qui, pareil à une jolie femme, est soumis à d'inexplicables caprices de laideur et de beauté. Ainsi la nature elle-même conspirait à plonger le mourant dans une extase douloureuse.[1]

Thus is prepared the splendidly over-written vision of the Antiquary with Balzac's own gloss: "Cette vision avait lieu dans Paris, sur le Quai Voltaire, au dix-neuvième siècle, temps et lieu où la magie devait être impossible." But of course for Balzac this magic was always possible and it opened the way for Baudelaire's own recognitions. He is concerned with the avoidance of narrative and his evocations of Paris in his verse are more brief and pointed, full of a reserve of suggestion that causes resonance beyond the end of the poem. *Les Sept Vieillards* and *Les Petites Vieilles* show how the commonplace *rencontre* can be transformed; but this too is one of Balzac's gifts. It is not only the great set-pieces of the city in joyous or tragic mood which are memorable but also the smaller poetic insights and it is these lines that Baudelaire was to develop.

OTHER aspects of this topic have been discussed by other critics. The problem of the origin of the theory of *correspondances* as held by Baudelaire was examined by Jean Prévost in relation to *La Fanfarlo* which he judges to be very heavily influenced by Balzac. He concludes thus:

Peu importe la *Fanfarlo* dans l'œuvre de Baudelaire. Ce que nous avons voulu démontrer, c'est que la doctrine des *Correspondances* vient de Balzac; qu'Hoffmann et Swedenborg ne feront que compléter Balzac; et Baudelaire a pu ne les connaître que de seconde main. Ce que nous voulons surtout prouver, c'est qu'une telle doctrine est adoptée pour ses effets esthétiques, comme créatrice d'images nouvelles et d'ordre dans la fiction; elle est mythique, elle n'est pas mystique.[2]

[1] II, 21–2. [2] Prévost, *op. cit.*, p. 49.

P.-G. Castex develops the common themes to be found in the two writers (*correspondances, le guignon* and Paris) but sees the principal point of resemblance between them as "leur façon de poser les problèmes essentiels de l'existence humaine".[1] This is not a question of imitation but of Baudelaire's constant preoccupation with Balzac, of an admiration which lasted throughout his life as a writer. This is not a liberating moral influence for nothing could have lifted Baudelaire from his morass of guilt and despair; indeed the frequentation of Balzac enabled Baudelaire to see with more dreadful lucidity his own plight. Rather did it provide him with a constant source of joy, allowing Baudelaire to develop some of his most powerful effects and his view of the human condition.

[1] Castex, *op. cit.*, p. 146.

Balzac and the Latin-American novel

A. CAREY TAYLOR

AT the time when Balzac began to become known in Spain the Spanish novel had practically ceased to exist. In the latter part of the eighteenth century the most noteworthy productions were a few colourless historical novels or timid imitations of Rousseau's *Émile*. In the first half of the nineteenth century the position became even worse with one or two notable exceptions. The imitations of Scott's novels which were turned out by dozens of hacks were, in the words of a French critic, "des offenses au bon sens, au bon goût et aux réalités historiques".

It is not therefore surprising that the Spanish novel fell into such disrepute that it had few readers. The short-lived poet and critic of genius, Mariano José de Larra, is said to have asked: "Does no one read in Spain because no one writes, or does no one write because no one reads?"

The answer would seem to be that, in fact, no one read Spanish novels because there were none worthy of the name. But there were still some readers and the novels they read were translated from the French. The works of all the Romantics were read, both in the original and in numerous translations, often of very inferior quality. The principal favourites were Dumas, George Sand and Eugène Sue, whose novels can be absorbed without the slightest effort.

But Balzac also found many Spanish readers. *Le Père Goriot* was translated in 1838 (three years after its first appearance) and was closely followed by other volumes. By the time of his death more than 20 volumes of translations had been published. The reading of these French novels gradually improved the public taste and helped to create a demand for good Spanish novels.

In 1849, the year before Balzac's death, there appeared the first realist Spanish novel of the century, *La Gaviota*, by a woman writer, Cecilia Böhl de Faber (1796–1877), best known by her pen-name of Fernán Caballero. She greatly admired Balzac and her correspondence contains numerous references to him, usually accompanied by such flattering terms as "el profundo Balzac", "el gran Balzac", etc.

Almost at the very moment when a much younger generation of writers were discovering Balzac a conservative critic uttered a cry of warning against the great danger confronting Spanish literature if it allowed itself to be perverted by his example. In January 1867, Luis Carera wrote:

> Spanish literature is in great danger, and although my voice is weak, I must utter a cry of warning. After having . . . cultivated the system applied to the novel by Sue and Dumas père, now, penetrating into the corrupt regions of literature, it admires Balzac and studies his productions, believing that it will thus be able to raise our novel from its present state of decadence.[1]

But his warning went unheeded, and three years later the modern realist Spanish novel was created by Benito Pérez Galdós, born in 1843, and destined to be known as the Spanish Balzac. Two of his seniors, Alarcón and Pereda, though much less influenced by Balzac, were also fervent admirers of his work. Galdós began reading Balzac at an earlier age than these two writers, and this may explain why the influence exerted was so much greater in his case. On leaving the University of Madrid, he began to write as a dramatic and literary critic in *La Nación*. But he had no wish to take up criticism as a profession. At first he felt more inclined to become a dramatist than a novelist, and even wrote a play which was not accepted by the manager to whom he submitted it.

This period of hesitation was brought to an end in 1867 by a visit to Paris where he stayed for the whole summer. He soon found the bookstalls on the *quais*, and the first book he bought there was *Eugénie Grandet*, for which he paid a franc. This was his introduction to Balzac, all of whose works he immediately began to collect. "During that and my succeeding trips to Paris," he said, "I got together the whole collection of 80 odd volumes which I still keep

---

[1] *Revista Hispano-Americana* (26 Jan. 1867), 65.

with religious veneration." He not only collected these volumes, but he read them from cover to cover.

The reading of Balzac resolved Galdós's uncertainty and he decided to become not a dramatist but a novelist. Almost immediately he set about writing his first novel, *La Fontana de Oro*, which was published in 1870.

Like Balzac's first successful novel, *Les Chouans*, this was a well-documented study of comparatively recent history in a setting with which the author was thoroughly acqainted, relating as it did the political disorders in Madrid in the early 1820s. In this and later novels Galdos shows the same intimate familiarity with the history and topography of the Spanish capital as Balzac had with those of Paris.

This book revealed keen psychological insight in the study of character, a wonderful gift of portraiture and fine descriptive powers such as had been shown by no other nineteenth-century writer and marked Galdós as the first modern Spanish novelist (for we must remember that all the more successful novels of Alarcón and Pereda, and even of Juan Valera, their senior by nine years, were not published until several years later).

The happy accident that revealed the works of Balzac to Galdós while he was still in his formative years is a most important event in the history of the Spanish novel, for not only was Galdós the creator of the modern Spanish novel, but without his example even the most gifted of his contemporaries, and even of his seniors, would not have become true novelists. Henceforth, the influence of Galdós was as important in Spain as that of Balzac had been in France. Consequently, since Galdós had assimilated and put into practice many of Balzac's methods and techniques, many Spanish writers in whom it is impossible to detect the slightest trace of the direct influence of Balzac nevertheless owe a great deal to him.

In studying the successors of Galdós the problem is further complicated by the fact that the influence of Balzac is now reinforced, if not displaced, by that of Zola. For all the authors in the generation following that of Galdós more or less imitated the author of *Les Rougon-Macquart*; but some of them continued to express the greatest admiration for Balzac. In the countries of Latin America, however, the influence of Balzac is readily discernible for some time to come.

One of the earliest Latin-American admirers of Balzac was Domingo del Monte (1804–53), a Cuban of wide culture who devoted much of his time to combating the wilder excesses of Romanticism. After his marriage in 1834 he formed the habit of inviting the principal young writers to his house, and upon his return to Havana the following year his *tertulia* largely took the place of the defunct Cuban Academy. He and his friends read and discussed the latest publications, local or European, and exchanged comments on the works they were themselves preparing.

In 1837, José Zacarías González del Valle (1820–51), an extremely gifted young man, introduced to this circle his slightly older school friend, Anselmo Suarez y Romero (1818–78). The latter's reading of the MS. of his novel *Carlota Valdés* greatly impressed Del Monte, who wrote a glowing account of it to his friend, the poet José Jacinto Milanés (1814–63).

We have not been able to discover when Del Monte was first attracted to Balzac, but by 1838 at least he had acquired quite a number of his novels, and in July he lent González del Valle a volume of the *Scènes de la vie privée*, with instructions that he should send it on to his friend Suarez y Romero, who was then working as a tutor in the country. González del Valle told his friend that it was the best book he had ever read, that Balzac was a perfect model for any novelist who took his task seriously, and that his style was much to be preferred to the "estilo amanerado y falso" of Victor Hugo.[1] A fortnight later he asked Anselmo if he had ever come across a finer writer: "Has visto escritor más guapo?", and he was soon promising to send him further volumes.[2]

Other members of Del Monte's circle had also become acquainted with Balzac's works. On 29 August Milanés referred to him in a letter to Del Monte, and in December J. A. Echeverria reminded the latter of the theme of *La Recherche de l'Absolu*.[3]

Domingo del Monte was also interested in social problems and did all he could to persuade the Spanish authorities to set up a form of colonial government that would give the chief voice to the

---

[1] J. Z. Gonzalez del Valle, *La vida literaria en Cuba* (Havana, 1938), p. 50: letter dated 25 July 1838.
[2] *ibid.*, pp. 54, 55.
[3] D. del Monte, *Centón epistolario* (Havana, 1923–), vol. III, pp. 195, 252.

wealthier citizens of the island. These wealthy land-owners were beginning to understand that the mechanization of the work on the sugar plantations was making the employment of slave labour less and less necessary, and Del Monte played a leading part in the campaign for the abolition of the slave trade. He closely collaborated with Dr Richard R. Madden, the British member of the Mixed Arbitration Court set up by Spain and Britain to deal with questions arising from the slave trade. In order to enlist foreign sympathy for this campaign he had started compiling an album containing descriptions of the horrors of slave life, which Dr Madden would take back to England with him.

In discussing this proposal with his young literary friends he hit on the idea of including in this album a novel specially written for the purpose, and by September 1838 he had induced one of the most promising of their number, Suarez y Romero, to undertake this task.[1]

Del Valle continued to send on further volumes of Balzac to his friend, and to comment on them in his frequent letters to him. The young author used to send the rough drafts of his chapters to Del Valle, who corrected them and often discussed them with Del Monte. He was very pleased with the first chapter and thought that the description of the foreman was particularly successful; but he added some advice about Chapter II, part of which Suarez had read to him when they last met. In conveying the character and the mental states of the unfortunate hero, the slave Francisco, he should follow the example of Balzac, whose profound psychological insight allowed him to enter into the minds and hearts of his characters. Del Monte was also delighted by this first chapter, and thought that the excellent descriptions owed much to the influence of Balzac.[2]

Early in 1839 Suarez went to live on a sugar plantation, where he remained all that year, and it was there that he wrote the greater part of his book, which was composed, as it were, in the field. *Francisco*, the novel which resulted from this rather unusual collaboration, was finished before the end of 1839, and the text was entrusted to Dr Madden when he left for England. But, owing to the censorship, it was not possible to publish it in Cuba, and it first

[1] Del Valle, *op. cit.*, p. 57.
[2] *ibid.*, p. 68 (25 Sept. 1838); p. 78 (22 Oct. 1838).

N

appeared in 1880, in New York. However, it was passed from hand to hand in MS. and was also quoted at length by investigators of the conditions on the sugar plantations.[1]

This novel, which describes the sufferings of a slave who was driven to suicide, marks the transition between Romanticism and Realism in Cuba. Its sentimental treatment of the passions of the two lovers, Francisco and Dorotea, remains thoroughly romantic, but the descriptions of their masters and the scenes in the various parts of the sugar plantation clearly owe their realism to the example of Balzac. The author was also the first writer to exploit the great poetic beauty of Cuban folklore, whose songs and dances combined the traditions of Spain and Africa. The resulting picture of contemporary life served as an inspiration and a model for the school of realist novelists who continued to describe the horrors of slavery, and who criticized the urban society of their day.[2]

It is just possible that Peru's first novelist, Narciso Aréstegui (1824–69) owed something to Balzac. His *El Padre Horán*, published as a serial in the Lima newspaper, *El Comercio*, in 1848, is the story of a dreadful crime committed when the author was ten; and it has been thought that its graphic realism may have been due to the reading of Balzac. Luis Alberto Sánchez discusses this possible influence in his lengthy history of Peruvian literature,[3] and is inclined to reject it. But he admits that Aréstegui, who was known to have been a reader of Eugène Sue, may also have read Balzac, probably in translation, since he was a rough soldier without much education, and not a professional writer. However, the dates in Señor Sanchez's discussion are inaccurate and correspond neither to the first appearances of *Le Père Goriot* and of *Eugénie Grandet* in France nor to that of their Spanish translations.

The first major writer in Latin America who deliberately set out to imitate Balzac was Alberto Blest-Gana (1830–1920), the greatest Chilean novelist of the nineteenth century. He is one of the many authors whose whole career was changed by the reading of Balzac. Like so many young writers, he aspired to be a poet, and had already

---

[1] see A. Suarez, *Francisco, El Ingenio o las Delicios del Campo* (Havana, 1947), pp. 21–4.

[2] J. A. Portuondo, *Bosque Historico de las Letras Cubanas* (Havana, 1960), pp. 24–6.

[3] L. A. Sánchez, *La Literatura peruana* (Paraguay, 1951), pp. 216–18.

written a few narrative poems. But one day, as we read in a letter to one of his friends, "[after] reading Balzac, [he] made a bonfire of all his youthful rhymes [and] swore he would be a novelist or abandon the field of literature". He applied himself to the imitation of Balzac's methods with such success that his first short stories, published in 1858, aroused great interest, as a result of which the University of Chile decided to offer the prize at its next annual literary contest, not for a historical or critical work as it usually did, but for "a novel in prose, historical or of manners, the theme of which should be purely Chilean".[1]

The prize was awarded to Blest-Gana for his first novel, *La Aritmética en el Amor* (1860), the hero of which was a typically Balzacian *arriviste*. A few years later he wrote his masterpiece, *Martín Rivas* (1862), the first great Latin-American realist novel, which is a satire on the manners of the newly-rich and of the lower classes who ape the rich. In succeeding novels, he dealt with other social classes in city and country, so that his works have left us as complete a picture of Chilean society as Balzac had painted of the society of France. But he was not as great a writer as either Balzac or Galdós, his junior by 13 years and whose career was to be so similar to his own.

For, if Blest-Gana is known as the Chilean Balzac he might perhaps be better described as the Chilean Galdós, because of the way in which his example stimulated the growth of the novel in his country. The first novel published by a Chilean had only appeared in 1852 (just six years before Blest-Gana's short stories): *El Inquisidor Mayor o Historia de Unos Amores*. And the first result of the success of Blest-Gana's early novels was to create a growing appetite for novel reading, which was soon satisfied by a whole school of his imitators who studied various aspects of national life and history. Many of these novels were published in serial form in the daily papers, or else in 'parts'. They consequently had most of the defects of the long-winded and sensational *romans-feuilletons* so popular throughout the whole Western world in the nineteenth century. But the stimulus he had given to the creation of a national literature influenced a much later generation of twentieth-century

---

[1] Alfred Coester, *The Literary History of Spanish America* (New York, 1916), p. 225.

novelists, such as Eduardo Barrios (1884–1963), Joaquin Edwards Bello (1886–), etc.[1]

Florencio Mariá del Castilo (1828–63) has been called the Mexican Balzac, but Señor J. A. Leguizamón, whose word I must take, since I can find no other references to this writer, says that there are no signs of any direct influence.[2] An almost contemporary Mexican novelist, Ignacio Manuel Altamarino (1834–93), probably derived his realism from the example of Balzac, though it was tinged by an idealism that may have been suggested by Fernán Caballero. His best known novel, *Clemencia* (1869), contains a study of political life and *El Zarco* has as its sub-title: *Episodios de la vida mexicana en 1861–63.*

IN most Latin-American countries the Romantic movement lasted longer than in Europe; but a strain of realism is to be found in some of the principal novels of the period, whose authors owed something to Balzac.[3] Notable examples are *Amalia* (1851) by the Argentinian, José Marmal (1817–71), and *María*, thought to be the greatest Spanish-American novel, published in 1867 by the Colombian writer, Jorge Isaacs (1837–95). *María* is also in a certain sense a psychological novel, as is Blest-Gana's *Martín Rivas* (1862). For this particular aspect of his work, Isaacs was probably as much indebted to Balzac as was Blest-Gana.

THE further study of Balzac's influence in Spanish America is now complicated, as it was in Spain, by two new factors, the influence of Galdós and that of Zola, as we shall see when we turn our attention to Argentina. If Blest-Gana was known as the Chilean Balzac, Carlos María Ocantos (1860–1949) has been called "the Balzac of his native city", Buenos Aires. In his youth, cultivated people read the works of Balzac, Flaubert, George Eliot, Dickens, Zola and the

[1] Alfred Coester, *The Literary History of Spanish America* (New York, 1916), pp. 224–8; A. Torres-Rioseco, *La novella en a América hispana* (Berkeley, 1939), p. 198.
[2] *Historia de la literatura hispano-americana* (Buenos Aires, 1945), vol. II, p. 114.
[3] For the early influence of Balzac in Brazil, see A. Carey Taylor, 'Balzac and Manoel António de Almeida: the beginnings of Realism in Brazil', *R.L.C.*, XLI (April-June 1967), 195–203.

Goncourts, but romantic novels were still being produced by what local talent there was. Ocantos was not attracted by the scientific pretensions of Zola and owes little or nothing to this author; but his series of *Novelas argentinas* is, as it were, a small edition of the *Comédie humaine*. The 20 novels are linked by recurring characters and they provide a very full picture of every aspect of the life of the capital city and the great province of Buenos Aires in which it stands, and they could easily be divided into groups corresponding to Balzac's *Scènes de la vie parisienne*, and *Scènes de la vie de campagne*. Certain of them, such as *Pequeñas miserias*, *Riquez* and *Tulia*, which deal with moral and philosophical problems, correspond to the *Études philosophiques* and *Études analytiques*.

The title of *Pequeñas miserias* must surely derive from that of *Petites misères de la vie conjugale*, which, of course, was not a novel. This is not the only difference between the two books, since Ocantos only deals with a single aspect of marriage in his novel: the unfortunate consequences of a *mariage de convenance*. *Tulia* deals with the theme of excessive paternal affection and consequently reminds us of *Le Père Goriot*. But the treatment of the theme is very different in the two books, and Ocantos seems to make much more use of his personal observation and experience than of any literary sources.

Since the general idea of painting the life of his times could have been just as easily suggested by Galdós' *Novelas contemporaneas* as by Balzac's *Comédie humaine*, there is little, apart from the few slight resemblances in title or theme to which we have just referred, to help us decide which of these two sources was the more important. An American scholar, Theodore Andersson, contends that Ocantos continues the transmission of Balzac "only at second-hand", and that his work "derives directly from Galdós".[1] What is certain is that Ocantos's style is very different from that of Balzac, as also is the rigorous architectural symmetry to be found in his work. For example each of the 20 *Novelas argentinas* contains ten chapters of almost identical length. It is for this reason that a critic has said that Ocantos "creates a literary portrait of the Argentinian people with something of the heroic vision of a Balzac and the rigorous self-discipline of a Maupassant" – an author whose technique he greatly admired.[2]

[1] T. Andersson, *Carlos María Ocantos* (Princeton, 1934), pp. 87–90. [2] *ibid.*

The novels of another Argentinian, Roberto Jorge Payró (1867–1928), some of which describe the life of the *gaucho* and others of which are historical, may owe some of their realism to Balzac. But Payró was widely read and was also familiar with Dickens, Galdós and Zola. He was probably most influenced by Cervantes and Galdós, and one critic says that it was his ambition to be the Galdós of the Argentine.[1]

In Mexico we find a group of writers who were similarly influenced by Balzac, Galdós and even other Spanish writers. The first of these is Rafael Delgado (1853–1904), whose last novel, *Los Parientes ricos* (1903), clearly owes its title to Balzac's collective title *Les Parents pauvres*. His works and those of Emilio Rabasa (1856–1930) give a picture of Mexican life in the last part of the nineteenth century.

Another author in whom this combined influence may be detected is the Cuban Ramon Meza (1861–1911). But the most important member of this group is the Uruguayan Carlos Reyles (1868–1938), whose *La Raza de Caín* (1900) is one of the best Spanish-American naturalist novels. Mariano Azuela (1873–52), one of the greatest Mexican novelists, had a passion for Balzac and Zola in his youth. Their influence may be seen in the realistic detail of his early novels, but in his second manner he developed a poetic approach which owes nothing to them.[2]

As a result of this brief survey we see that in all the Latin-American countries, as in Spain and Portugal, and for that matter in most other countries, it was Balzac the 'realist', Balzac the forerunner of Naturalism, who made an impact on the rising generations of novelists: the more esoteric aspects of his work attracted little or no attention, and Strindberg is the only foreign writer I have so far discovered who was seriously influenced by such works as *Séraphîta*.[3]

[1] R. A. Arrieta, *Historia de la literatura argentina*, 6 vols. (Buenos Aires, 1958–60), vol. IV, p. 246.
[2] cf. J. R. Spell, *Contemporary Spanish-American Fiction* (Chapel Hill, 1944), p. 100.
[3] cf. A. C. Taylor, 'Balzac et les romanciers scandinaves', *R.L.C.* XXXVIII (1964), 203–37.

The changing study of Balzac

W. G. MOORE

I⟶ could be that Balzac is a writer about whom we know too much. Run your eye down any periodical or bibliography concerned with Balzac studies and you will be surprised at the number of facts which scholars think it important to establish. Enquiry into his life and work seems to be a prolific outcrop of 'literary' study. Much of this study has lost sight of the reason why the world of the 1970s knows about Balzac at all, that he is a novelist of genius. The genius (as some of us know to our cost) is hard to locate and define, but it might be well for scholars and teachers to revise their priorities.

Balzac wrote at a time when neither his readers, nor his critics, to say nothing of himself, were clear as to the scope and aim of fiction. The dilemma, as it has been called, of the novel did not end with the eighteenth century. Balzac's achievement was to enable the novel to do things it has never done, to invade provinces of experience till then thought to be unsuitable, and which since the vogue of Naturalism we have come to think 'natural' to the novel.

How was this done? The situation, the environment, of his novels and stories is so circumstantial that we can surely not refuse him keen powers of observation, of photographing on his mind the France of his day, Paris, provinces, houses, streets, churches, trades. So that it is a bit late in the day to agree with Baudelaire that we are dealing with a *visionnaire*. Yet his visionary powers, however we define them, were surely no less extraordinary than his visual memory. The way in which, as Henry James said (with the experience of a working novelist behind him), "he warms his facts into life" surely suggests a process of fusion, within the brain of the artist, of fact and vision (which as yet we are not able to explain). But even Henry James is not just to the fact of this artist's creation. If I may repeat myself: "We think he is describing a dining-room

when he is really describing the sort of people who live in it...
the landlady explains the lodging, in the sense of making it intelligible and more interesting than any actual lodging, and the lodging
implies the lodger by suggesting her outlook."[1]

Recent preoccupation with a late story has suggested these
thoughts, as an offering to a scholar whose contribution I hope to
try to make clear before I end this paper. About *Albert Savarus*
there exists quite a body of literature, informative rather than
critical: it tells us things which we do not need to know unless we
are studying Balzac's personality. The element of autobiography is
certain, but not important for any literary analysis.[2] One soon
becomes more interested in certain mysterious elements, which
seem to fit in to a pattern. If we could verify this, and discern the
pattern, we might find out something of the art of the novelist.

To begin with, there is Besançon, described as a typically dull
French town, as Issoudun is in *La Rabouilleuse*. Is this photography?
I think not. Pierre-Joseph Proudhon, who was probably living in
Besançon at the time of which Balzac wrote, does not suggest in
his letters that nothing was going on, nor that cliques were all-
important, nor that "nulle ville n'offre une résistance plus sourde
et muette au progrès". Why was Balzac keen to impose his view
of such a place? Why was it, for him, "nécessaire d'expliquer
Besançon en quelques mots"? The student thinks that this was done
in the interests of realism, of topographical accuracy. One student
told me that he thought Balzac was so determined to localize his
picture that he spares us no detail of what he had actually seen.
This is demonstrably inaccurate, and inherently unlikely. A novelist
is not writing a guidebook. There is an aesthetic reason for situating
Savarus in a sleepy town, as there is an aesthetic reason for starting
Goriot in the *pension* Vauquer. The cliques, the traditions, the
fantastic idleness of young ladies in such a society, all these are the
bedding, so to speak, of the "explosion" (Balzac's own word) in the
heart of an outwardly docile and naïve girl, which is the main motif
of the story. Scholars have been so preoccupied to identify auto-

---

[1] *Forum for Modern Language Studies*, III (1967), 178.
[2] "Son caractère autobiographique est un lieu commun de la critique balzacienne",
says Jean Pommier ('A propos d'*Albert Savarus*', *Balzac et la Touraine* (1950),
p. 155.)

biography that they have not noticed the care with which Balzac prepares and works out his molièresque theme. Yet his terms are explicit:

> L'éducation des filles comporte des problèmes si graves, car l'avenir d'une nation est dans la mère, que depuis longtemps l'Université de France s'est donné la tâche de n'y point songer... si vous les empêchez de penser vous arrivez à la subite explosion si bien peinte dans le personnage d'Agnès par Molière, et vous mettez cet esprit comprimé, si neuf, si perspicace, rapide et conséquent comme le sauvage, à la merci d'un événement...

This is in fact what we find. We are shown how the arrival of the mysterious and hardworking Paris lawyer (who *is* like Balzac) stirs the interest of the apparently colourless girl, so that she spies on him in church, in his own room – thanks to a summer-house which she induces her father to build in their (adjacent) garden – opens his letters, discovers his love life, and decides at all costs to ruin it. The pointers in the story are clear, for those who have not made up their minds that it is autobiography. They describe the curve of a story, the whole progress of "le désir d'une jeune fille jusque là sans désir". We are shown how "tout en machinant ces plans cette étonnante fille faisait des pantoufles à son père de l'air le plus naïf du monde" and how finally, having learned to copy the hand of Savaron, "aux véritables lettres de cet amant fidèle elle avait substitué trois lettres dont les brouillons communiqués au vieux prêtre le firent frémir, tant le génie du mal y apparaissait dans toute sa perfection."

It would be tedious to prove by comparison of passages that this is the main theme of the story. Any reader with the patience to analyse the structure will see that this modern incarnation of Molière's Agnès ruins Savaron's chances in the election, drives him to despair about his Italian countess and finally into the monastic seclusion and peace of the Grande Chartreuse.

These facts call for explanation. They do not allow us to say with any certainty that Balzac intended to write a Romantic version of *L'École des femmes.* Nor do they suggest that his main concern was to portray someone like himself in a light that would impress Mme Hanska. The most likely explanation seems to be that, while anxious to impress his countess with a self-portrait, he got caught

up in an exciting and potentially tragic theme and this created
exactly what a powerful novelist would create, a story which went
beyond his intention and which showed constant glimpses of creative
power. Only after much painful analysis did I find similar conclusions suggested by another scholar whose expertise in Balzac matters
far transcends my own:

> dans cette nouvelle qui n'était pas écrite pour conter son histoire...
> on ne se souvient plus que de cette fille effrayante... qui cache
> sous son visage ferme l'énergie implacable des jeunes filles de
> Stendhal. Cette petite sournoise est peut-être un des personnages
> les plus mystérieux de Balzac... personnage de tragédie... petite
> Parque aveugle... mélange étonnant de perversité, de profondeur
> et d'inexpérience...[1]

We are thus faced, if we work on these lines, with a widening
gap between intention and invention. This might perhaps yield
results if explored in Balzac. Recent work on *Le Cousin Pons*
suggests (but does not explain) that Balzac was induced to change
the dimensions of what started as a short story, and to turn it into a
full-length novel. In the difference between the project and the
perfected work may lie secrets as yet unexplored.

Is it not the experience of most readers of Balzac that he gives us
what seem to be incidental developments, passages of great force
which do not seem to be in line with his original intent, but which
in the circumstantializing, so to say, of the *récit*, invade the story?
The effective agents of a Balzac story would repay analysis, if only
we could agree on the vital passages in any given work. Perhaps
indeed the creator himself did not know where his story would lead
him, at what point it might spring into flame, what incidental
character or event might bring him up against the mystery which
is at the heart of all life. It was Bismarck, I think, who spoke of the
statesman as a sleepwalker, and in another image as drifting on the
current of events, unable to plot his direction, reduced to catching
at straws. Balzac seems to have thought the same about the artist.
Again I think that M. Bardèche is the only scholar who has ventured
into this field. In his first book he wrote as follows:

---

[1] M. Bardèche, *Une lecture de Balzac* (1967), pp. 255–7.

Il y a presque toujours chez Balzac un moment où il feint que le récit lui échappe... L'impuissance du conteur devant la réalité imaginaire... sur toute une vie, ou un fragment d'une vie, il laisse des zones de ténèbres, impénétrables au créateur lui-même ... c'est un des secrets de Balzac, un des plus rares, un des plus saisissants, que de conter ainsi dans les ténèbres de l'inspiration.[1]

This prompts us to ask what and where is the starting point of a Balzac story. As he spoke of them afterwards, his works were in many cases written to contain "une grande leçon". But this intent may have been latent in his mind, or may have arisen in the course of telling the story. The researches of M. Laubriet suggest that the story starts from an idea rather than from a fact or a picture:

Balzac ne part pas du réel pour composer, mais des idées... le roman est mauvais quand l'idée n'a pas trouvé son vêtement symbolique adéquat. Balzac n'a pas pour fin de reproduire le réel, mais de développer ou de vérifier des idées au moyen de ce réel... L'œuvre naît chez Balzac de la rencontre d'un thème abstrait, en général conçu le premier, et des éléments de la réalité qui l'expriment avec une totale et parfaite adéquation...[2]

This is an authoritative statement, but I would think that the question invites further investigation. The study of *Albert Savarus* in particular would seem to suggest something rather different; that Balzac's inventive power leads him into areas which his intention was far from contemplating. Some of his letters show him to be surprised and disconcerted by what he found he had written. One wonders, for example, whether the gold spread out before the bedridden Grandet, surely one of the finest scenes in fiction, was part of the story as planned, or an afterthought, or the elaboration of an original but vague intent. In any case we stand in need of more study of his technique of writing, and of the way it led him into the evocation of dark places. This would seem to be M. Bardèche's final judgment on *Albert Savarus*: "Cet emportement tragique, ce cas de 'possession' est unique sous cette forme dans les romans de Balzac. Mais on sent assez que l'invention de Balzac rôde souvent autour de tourbières aussi inquiétantes."

[1] M. Bardèche, *Balzac romancier* (1940 edition), p. 600.
[2] P. Laubriet, *L'Intelligence de l'art chez Balzac* (1961), p. 485.

It is only just to point out that new lines of inquiry into the nature of the inventive faculty in Balzac are not likely to surprise the recipient of this volume since they owe their impetus in great part to his labours. More than ten years ago Herbert Hunt described Balzac's activity in words which I think shed light on our present problem: "The continuous emission, from a radioactive centre, of particles varying in direction and penetrative force. . . . There is no rationally controlled advance towards a single goal, but simultaneous or closely consecutive surrender to divergent inspirations."[1]

May it not be to study of these divergent inspirations that we should look for the next break-through in Balzac studies?

[1] H. J. Hunt, *Balzac's 'Comédie humaine'* (1959), p. 59.

Part II

~~~~~~

FROM
CONSTANT
TO
ZOLA

Destutt de Tracy and the bankruptcy of sensationalism

COLIN SMITH

THOSE philosophers whose doctrines flourished in France from approximately 1790 to 1820, and who are known as the 'idéologues', are classified as sensationalists. Their philosophical views derive from the empiricist tradition of Locke and Condillac, and they were in search of an account of experience and consciousness which should be quite different from that associated with the rationalist tradition of the seventeenth century. In very general terms, that difference may be said to reside in the emphasis placed by sensationalists upon the subject as the recipient of the data of consciousness rather than as their source. I want to show that, in giving way to the voluntarism of Maine de Biran, sensationalism suffered not only a complete reversal of its inbuilt tendency to play down the notion of an autonomous self, which became reinstated, but that it expired largely through the bankruptcy of its own analysis of experience. Proudly empiricist, it proved more conservative than it knew, with the result that the fruitful science of phenomena was to be the long-term outcome of its successor movement, developed out of all recognition, if not inaugurated, by Maine de Biran, and coming to fruition in the phenomenological movement of the present century.

Condillac was the spiritual, or no doubt one should say the materialistic, ancestor of the ideologists, and if one is to place Maine de Biran outside the movement, despite his sympathy with it, we are left with Cabanis and Destutt de Tracy as its outstanding and most systematic representatives at the turn of the century. Cabanis' place is in the history of medical science, though his philosophical presuppositions were those of Condillac and his direct successors, so that it is in the writings of Destutt de Tracy that the distinctively philosophical exposition of sensationalism must be sought. It is my purpose to examine how far the notion of the sensation in the

Elémens d'idéologie conforms to the Cartesian desideratum of a clear and distinct idea, and is part of what one may call Newtonian, quantitative, atomism. In so far as it does inherit these traditions, its demise at a time of increasing concern with the qualitative would seem to be preordained. Destutt de Tracy was a voluntarist in so far as he was satisfied that the will provides evidence of a world external to the acting self (and therefore evidence of an autonomous self), but this self is never allowed to become a substantial thing. So the break between Destutt de Tracy and the main stream of nineteenth-century French philosophy, from which I venture to exclude positivism, was total.

Although anti-Cartesian in its postulates, Destutt de Tracy's philosophy shows a surprising resemblance to Descartes' in its general structure, though not in its rigour. In the volume of the *Elémens d'idéologie* devoted to logic, De Tracy seeks, as did Descartes, a self-evident basis of certainty, and finds it in the sensation. For him the *cogito* becomes a *sentio*. At this stage it is not very different from the Cartesian starting point either in its nature or its self-evidence, since it is an unchallengeable content of consciousness, although Destutt is very careful not to express it in this way, which would suggest that mind is a substance. The sensation, of course, is not intended to be an intuition, as is the truth of "I think, therefore I am". All the same, at this stage, which is prior to the distinction between self and external world, it is difficult to see what violence would be done to this initial grasp upon experience if one considered it to be intuitive.[1] The trouble with the word *sensation* is that it gives an entirely illusory impression of precision. The Cartesian *cogito* is a clear and distinct idea, an instantaneous apprehension of a basic truth. The notion of sensation, on the other hand, even if it does not presuppose a physical reality which is its source, anticipates the experience which it is intended to account for. If it does not, then, as Destutt de Tracy presents it, it relapses to the status of an intuition, as I have said, and moreover, takes on the further Cartesian characteristic of something unitary, which seriously distorts and even stultifies anything that could be thought of as constituting sense experience. In other words, as long as De Tracy does not invoke an object, or sense organs, or a body which mediates our experience of

[1] *Elémens d'idéologie*, 2e ed. (Paris, 1818), 3e Partie, *Logique*, p. 162.

a world – and he does not do so because his argument has not yet reached that stage – then the sensation is an intuition.

The obscurity of Destutt de Tracy's notion of sense experience, though a weakness which makes his thought an *impasse*, nevertheless has the virtue of forcing subsequent French philosophy into a radically different form. De Tracy explicitly rejects, consistently with Humean empiricism, "un sentiment vague de *conscience*, séparé de toutes mes affections positives". I know *myself*, he goes on, only through the impressions which I experience, and any "sentiment de conscience en général" is relegated to the realm of substantial forms and meaningless, metaphysical abstractions.[1] On the other hand it is difficult, as with most empiricists, to know what he understands by an "impression", and it must be admitted that he does not appear to have in mind anything instantaneous or in any way strictly bounded. Indeed he criticizes Condillac for his analytical approach to the role of sensation, seeming himself to favour some synaesthetic way of conceiving experience. Certainly he does not accept the sense of static touch as in any way privileged, as Condillac does. De Tracy puts forward the theory that *motility*, which is of course dynamic and related to time, is the particularly significant form of sense experience.

Being dynamic and temporal, and already, therefore, some way towards anticipating the *durée* which is at the core of Maine de Biran's idea of our experience of self, motility is, moreover, regarded as a kind of sixth sense which has no single means of sense perception at its disposal. This key activity, with its suggestion of a *combination* of immediate data of consciousness providing an access to meaningful experience, in spite of its air of going beyond analytical sensationalism and an atomistic psychology, in fact does not do so.

For Destutt de Tracy motility and will are invoked, or invented, not for the purpose of describing the basic experience of self, but for the purpose of accounting for the possibility of that experience; in other words, for the purpose of showing a way out of solipsism. Descartes maintains that our experience of the external world is validated by the goodness and non-deceptiveness of God. This has never seemed to me to be a good argument, and De Tracy's is no

---

[1] *Elémens d'idéologie*, 2ᵉ ed. (Paris, 1818), 3ᵉ Partie, *Logique*, pp. 226 ff.

o

better when he posits motility and the act of will, working against a resistant world, as evidence that there are beings, as he puts it, external to, and independent of, myself. This argument is set forth in chapter V of the volume on logic, and shows a development, as Picavet points out,[1] from an earlier treatment of the question, where movement alone suffices to acquaint us with our being in the world. Destutt de Tracy's later position is expressed as follows:

> Si nous continuons à suivre pas à pas la génération de nos idées, nous trouverons que dans un moment ou dans un autre cette sensation du mouvement de mes membres doit cesser par quelque cause étrangère à moi, quoique continuant à être désirée, et que par conséquent après quelques expériences plus ou moins répétées, je dois trouver refermée dans le souvenir de cette sensation l'idée *de n'avoir pas cessé par le fait de moi qui désirais la prolonger*, et par suite celle *d'avoir cessé par le pouvoir d'un* ÊTRE *autre que moi*, auquel être j'attribuerai postérieurement d'être la cause de toutes les sensations que je connaîtrai me venir de lui.

He goes on to emphasize that prior to the feeling of a desire for movement which remains unsatisfied, I have been aware of my will as one among other sensations (he slips rather too easily from need to desire, and thence to will) but that I was unaware of any possible limitation upon its expression. When, however, I recall a desire to use my limbs, but find myself unable to do so, or, at a certain point of the action, unable to continue to do so, then I am obliged to recognize the existence of a not-self. The objects of the external world are, therefore, not apprehended as corresponding to the deliverances of individual senses, but as made manifest by the operation of what one may call a composite, kinetic sense, closely related to touch but involving an additional element. This element is dynamic, and implies, I think, a time factor which, as we shall see, De Tracy elsewhere fails to incorporate clearly into his sensationalism. This failure forces him back into a quantitative quasi-Cartesianism from which Maine de Biran is able to escape. Thus, I want to emphasize, does De Tracy come near to providing a bridge to a philosophy of inner consciousness, and indeed gives a strong superficial impression of doing so, but this impression is illusory. I

[1] F. Picavet, *Les Idéologues* (Paris, 1891), p. 342.

believe that one important incidental reason for stressing this is that
it accounts in part for the curious ambivalence of Stendhal's position.
Stendhal's thinking was greatly influenced by that of Destutt de
Tracy, and the novelist is often forced into presenting experience
in terms of old-fashioned sensationalism and its implications, while
being at other times dissatisfied with an account of behaviour so
disjointed and mechanistic.[1]

Destutt de Tracy defends himself unsatisfactorily against the
charge that his solution of the problem of solipsism is no solution at
all. He airily dismisses Berkeley "and other sceptics" who, by
maintaining that one's feelings are modified by themselves, imply,
he thinks, that one can will and at the same time not will. But the
contradiction, in the context in which it is placed, is merely verbal
and apparent. There is no contradiction involved in supposing that
we may feel a desire and at the same time feel frustration. These are
feelings which can and do co-exist, and *qua* feelings neither points
to any necessary source beyond itself. Hume puts the matter with
characteristic clarity.

> That our senses offer not their impressions as the images of
> something *distinct*, or *independent*, and *external*, is evident;
> because they convey to us nothing but a single perception, and
> never give us the least intimation of anything beyond. A single
> perception can never produce the idea of a double existence, but
> some inference either of the reason or imagination... 'Tis
> absurd, therefore, to imagine the senses can ever distinguish
> betwixt ourselves and external objects.[2]

This equally sums up the gist of De Tracy's reasoning, except that
he considers that in the experience of frustration he has found a
special sort of sensation which does give evidence of something
beyond itself. There is in his argument a tacit assumption that the
self is autonomous, that it is, in his words, a "vertu sentante"[3]
which is independent in some way of those sensations which are
experienced as running counter to its pleasure-seeking impulses.

---

[1] see C. Smith, 'Destutt de Tracy's Linguistic Analysis as adopted by Stendhal',
M.L.R., LI, (1956), 512–21.
[2] David Hume, *A Treatise of Human Nature*, book I, section II.
[3] Shades of Molière!

Furthermore that this self is a substance, if only by virtue of a certain pleasureward orientation of its "vertu sentante". But this is not admitted. There is once more a parallel with Descartes' argument that the insufficiency manifested in my doubt is evidence of a being outside myself, in Descartes' case superior and divine. Even more is Destutt de Tracy's implicit assumption of a consistent will working upon an external reality parallel to Descartes' presentation, in the *Traité des passions*, of the will as at war with external forces, which may be no more than recalcitrant animal spirits, but none the less separate from the thinking and willing subject.

But there is a cruder inconsistency in De Tracy's answer to the sceptics and solipsists. "Le prudent Berkeley", he writes, did not deal with the difficulty posed by the question: "s'il existe à la fois dans la nature, seulement deux sceptiques, bien certains de cette seule chose, de se sentir douter, d'*exister doutans*, lequel des deux consentira à n'être qu'une modification de la vertu sentante et doutante de son camarade".[1] This is less succinct than Dr Johnson's kicking the stone to demonstrate that external objects really exist, and less witty than Voltaire's

> Pardonnez-moi, dis-je, en lui parlant tout bas,
> Mais je crois, entre nous, que vous n'existez pas!

Voltaire, however, was brushing aside the whole philosophical game of questioning the normal inferences from sensation. If one undertakes, as does De Tracy, to play that game, one must take the consequences, which are either to argue more painstakingly, or to fall into the scepticism of Berkeley, or to recognize the problem of solipsism and the reality of external objects as logically insoluble.[2]

Now the odd, and important, thing is that, having somewhat cavalierly rejected the 'sceptical' point of view, Destutt then half-concedes its validity by adding, correctly, that whether as sensationalists we believe in other beings or not makes no difference![3] This

---

[1] *Elémens d'idéologie*, 3e Partie, *Logique*, ch. VI.

[2] see Bertrand Russell, *The Problems of Philosophy*, paperback edn., (1967), p. 9 ff.

[3] "...la réalité particulière des êtres qui sont les causes premières de nos perceptions ne fait rien à leur exactitude... Il est donc avéré que la découverte qu'il existe des êtres distincts et indépendans de notre faculté de sentir, ne change rien du tout à la manière d'opérer de notre intelligence." – *Elémens d'idéologie*, 3e Partie, *Logique*, pp. 263 and 265.

admission is important because it leads on to the conclusion that correct inference and reasoning on the basis of sensations are more central to significant experience than sensations themselves. It is true that judgments are, for him, *sensations* of relation,[1] but it is at this point that the reductionism involved is shown at its most misleading. It is here that De Tracy is forced into attaching greater importance to relationships and their truth than to the status of the sensations themselves. There is nothing wrong with this as a method, and this is in essence what Destutt de Tracy is concerned with, but it involves an abandonment, or at least a depreciation, of the all-important primitive *sensation* as the decisive constituent of experience. The philosophy becomes intellectualist, and even pragmatical, and not a convincing account of the nature of consciousness, which it had given some promise of trying to present. Sensationalism is, after all, empiricism, and lays some claim to being sound psychology, or at least some kind of acceptable reduction of the body-mind dualism, but its tacit purpose has almost always been pragmatic, directed towards attaining utilitarian ends by objective means. No kind of philosophy is more laudable in its aims and, on the whole, in its effects, but through its exclusion of a substantial, subjective self, it has necessarily deviated from any attempt to turn consciousness back on itself, and has instead applied consciousness to the external world, and treated inner experience itself from the 'outside'. This analytical and objective approach which considers aspects of one's own experience as without any substantial unifying support, as composed of *partes extra partes*,[2] can be described as atomistic. It is this psychological atomism which sets a barrier between the thought of Destutt de Tracy and that of Maine de Biran and nineteenth-century voluntarism.

Destutt assumes 'the sensation' to be, if not precise, and it certainly is not that, at least a unitary experience. There is an implicit assimilation of a sensation to a sharp pain felt, or a flash of light seen, or an explosion heard. Though he probably would not

---

[1] "C'est uniquement la faculté spéciale de sentir entre une idée et une autre *le rapport du contenant au contenu.*"

[2] "La définition de l'objet c'est... qu'il existe *partes extra partes*, et que par conséquent il n'admet entre ses parties ou entre lui-même et les autres objets que les relations extérieures et mécaniques." M. Merleau-Ponty, *Phénoménologie de la perception* (Paris, 1945), p. 87.

have admitted it, I feel that his idea of a sense experience is reducible to something like this. At best, it seems to be the sense content of some determinate present, or 'now', which we are almost forced into conceiving as instantaneous. It is true that the sensation specially favoured by him is "l'impression qui résulte de l'action de mes muscles, et du mouvement de mes membres. Cette impression est bien certainement une pure sensation."[1] Nevertheless this "impression" must be spread over at least a short time, which means that there is necessarily a certain continuity in experience, of which he fails to take account. He evidently considers it unimportant, but it *is* important, because it impairs the watertight nature ascribed to each unitary sensation. The sensation has not the clearly defined boundaries implied by the difficulties he raises in connection with memory. He is thus tacitly accepting the conception of time put forward by Descartes in his Third Meditation:

> Car tout le temps de ma vie peut être divisé en une infinité de parties, chacune desquelles ne dépend en aucune façon des autres; et ainsi, de ce qu'un peu auparavant j'ai été, il ne s'ensuit pas que je doive maintenant être, si ce n'est qu'en ce moment quelque cause me produise et me crée pour ainsi dire derechef, c'est-à-dire me conserve. En effet, c'est un chose bien claire et bien évident à tous ceux qui considéreront avec attention la nature du temps, qu'une substance, pour être conservée dans tous les moments qu'elle dure, a besoin du même pouvoir et de la même action qui serait nécessaire pour la produire et la créer tout de nouveau si elle n'était point encore; en sorte que c'est un chose que la lumière naturelle nous fait voir clairement que la conservation et la création ne diffèrent qu'au regard de notre façon de penser, et non point en effet.

A sensation is such that we cannot really 'recall' it, we can only re-experience it, and even then it is not the numerically identical sensation.[2] As he puts it, "j'en sens le souvenir". The difficulties involved in this second-order "sensation" belong to another series of possible objections. Suffice it to say that he regards our sense of the pastness of the past as immediate, and that our awareness of the

[1] *Elémens d'idéologie*, 3e Partie, *Logique*, p. 216.
[2] *ibid.*, p. 183.

sensation of memory is transformed into a judgment (still a sensation!) by the fact of our positing *that* we are recalling it. Now it is in judgments that error is possible. We are certain of our present sensations, but we are not certain that we are correctly classifying a present impression as of the same kind as a previous one because, De Tracy implies, time is the great betrayer.

Stendhal, of course, in his autobiographical works,[1] is exercised by the problems posed by the recall – and anticipation – of sensations. He sometimes wants to relive experiences because merely to remember them is to distort them, and at other times, particularly in anticipation, he wants to dominate his prospective sensations, transform them in advance into *judgments* which will enable him to distance himself sufficiently from the stifling and pervasive *present* (when it comes) to be in a position to control his behaviour. As long as he is the passive recipient of sensations he lives in totally mortal instants. He looks for an impossible, simultaneous coincidence and detachment which will allow him both to live and conceptualize. Stendhal, however, is a novelist, interested in the variety of experience, and hedonistically hankering after the enjoyment of experience for its own sake. 'Ideology' for him is to have the function of ensuring enjoyment and excluding distress. He is dismayed by the transience of pleasure, and by the problems attendant upon that transience. Destutt de Tracy, consistently with his Scottish ancestry, is prepared to be more puritanical. He is not primarily interested in sensations as pleasurable moments which we are only too thankful to savour, but in the reliability and communicability of knowledge, of which sensations are the indubitable ingredients. Because of the intrinsic inability of sensations to engender knowledge, or even to constitute experience in the full sense, and of the impossibility of renewing any particular one, the crucial element in our objective knowledge of things has to be moved to some other part of our mental life, to judgment in fact. Of course, he lumps memory and judgments in with sensation, but we are not taken in by that.

It is nevertheless the case that his insistence that the judgment is a sensation, that in judging we *perceive* a relation (of container to

---

[1] e.g. in his *Journal*, Divan edition, vol. II, pp. 133 and 137, and in *La Vie de Henri Brulard, passim.*

contained), means that all our knowledge outside the present
moment is undermined by the unreliability of memory. The underlying discontinuity of experience as he conceives it is the reason for
his treatment of certain important parts of speech in his volume on
grammar.[1] Anything related to duration in the Bergsonian sense,
to time conceived otherwise than atomistically, to 'intellectual'
eternity in the sense in which this notion is presented in Ferdinand
Alquié's *Le Désir d'éternité,* is suspect. Abstractions, fictions,
qualities, non-episodic verbs, are all relegated to a derivative order
of pseudo-reality which is not quite respectable. It is, of course, a
case of logical positivism *avant la lettre.* What imposes these views
on Destutt de Tracy is his limited view of the nature of memory,
which is unintelligible to him because, although instants and sensations may be contiguous, they are discontinuous. The corollary of
this would seem to be that no memory is possible, but De Tracy
allows, as a fact of experience, that we do recognize events as
repetitions, or part repetitions, of what we have previously observed.
The difficulty is that this recognition is inexplicable and that therefore, it seems, the associations and inferences are felt to be unreliable.
It is these inferences which are all-important. Of our perceptions
he says that "leur justesse ne peut consister que dans leur *relation*".[2]
This is contrary to the denigrating attitude which he elsewhere
adopts towards abstraction, which is what a relation is. We now
find that the accuracy of the relation is what really matters. It is
necessary that our perceptions should be "bien liées entre elles",
which means that our present associations should be checked against
the elementary perceptions being associated.[3] Hence the importance
of signs as aids to memory and to the self bounded by its present
experience.

All this rather tortured philosophizing arises from a conception
of memory which is untenable. The theory of *two* memories, found
in Maine de Biran and Bergson, offers a way out of De Tracy's
difficulties, which stem from sensationalism, and are of two kinds.

---

[1] This is dealt with in my article in *Revue internationale de philosophie,* LXXXII
(1967), 475 to 485, 'Destutt de Tracy's Analysis of the Proposition'.

[2] *Elémens d'idéologie,* 3e Partie, *Logique,* p. 262. My italics.

[3] "Les dernières sont aussi certaines et aussi vraies que les premières, si nous
n'avons vu successivement dans chacune de celles qui les précèdent, que ce qui
y est réellement."

Firstly, after analysing experience into sensations, there is no possibility of reconstituting a thinking and recalling subject on the same basis, even less under the false pretence that under 'sensation' can be subsumed activities of the mind which are quite clearly *not* sensations. This is a futile reductionism which leaves the problem untouched. Secondly, the absolute insulation of sensation, as he conceives it, obliges him to posit other activities (which, though for him passivities *qua* 'sensation') are capable of accounting for the manifest quality and continuity of our mental life. By confining memory to the *modal* recall of Maine de Biran, and ignoring the *personal* memory, Destutt de Tracy is forced into an intellectualist account of experience. The descriptive treatment of consciousness, which had seemed a natural sequel to his tentative voluntarism, is not forthcoming.

The emphasis on a proper statement of *relation* pulls this whole philosophy away from the subtler empiricism which ideology had seemed capable of ushering in. Its natural and fruitful transformation is seen in the philosophy of Maine de Biran, and it is in his *Note sur les rapports de l'idéologie et des mathématiques* of 1803 that he perceptively shows how ideology must depart from its prejudice in favour of a mathematical reality[1] if it is to remain faithful to its mission. It is clear that he regards himself as upholding a tradition, not as an iconoclast. Nevertheless his argument shows the inadequacy and bankruptcy of atomistic sensationalism as expounded by Destutt de Tracy. Geometry, he says, presents us with objects of direct perception which, as signs, are homogeneous and lend themselves to accurate deduction. In this closed intellectual world "tout concourt à ménager des points de repos à l'attention, à assurer la fidélité de la mémoire...", which means that it offers that reliable grip upon reality which Destutt de Tracy had so painstakingly sought. It is, however, inappropriate for achieving the objective of ideology, which is "tout intérieur". The operations of consciousness are heterogeneous and qualitative; they do not lend themselves to a set of signs which can in any sense be substituted for them: "Rien ne garantit ici la fidélité de la mémoire; rien ne peut dispenser d'un examen profond, d'une réflexion assidue. Marche circonspecte, lente, mesurée et toujours réfléchie."

[1] To adapt Merleau-Ponty's expression, 'le préjugé du monde'.

Maine de Biran goes on, in the second part of this essay, not only to develop the argument that the analysis of consciousness must be recalcitrant to the use of unambiguous signs, but, with rare foresight, to foreshadow the demand that mathematics and the sciences themselves be disqualified from furnishing us with an unquestioned 'reality'; that they should themselves be placed, and their credentials assessed, in a wider context, a pre-reflective context, as we should now say. In this way the origins of the commonsense world will be revealed: " L'idéologie, qui a pour fonction de creuser jusqu'à cette origine, jusqu'à ces formes vraiment *génératrices*, pourra seule alors approfondir et raffermir les bases chancelantes de la certitude...".

I do not wish to fall into anachronism here by making Biran's essay into more than a tentative and partial anticipation of the introduction to *Phénoménologie de la perception*. The search for certainty now has an archaic air about it, and Merleau-Ponty's main purpose is to show it as a vain quest. There is still present in this essay of Maine de Biran a too-ready assumption that the axioms and conventions of mathematical thinking are rigidly fixed forever, and so, unsuited to his 'ideological' purpose, and even that mathematicians are incurious journeymen practitioners of their discipline. At the same time it is taken for granted that some sort of more subtle quasi-mathematical approach, some injection of *esprit de finesse* into *esprit de géométrie*, will provide the 'certitude' desired. The eventual abandonment by mathematicians of Euclidean space as the bedrock of geometry, or the Bachelardian 'rationalisme ouvert', are excusably not foreseen. But though he fails to anticipate a future not far ahead of him in which science is destined to be torn from its anchorage in eternal truths, no less than morality from eternal values, Maine de Biran does assume, well ahead of his time, the role of the critic of scientific presuppositions, of the non-scientist who can nevertheless situate objective thought in a context more basic and inclusive than itself: "...c'est précisément, parce qu'il n'a ni la prétention, ni les moyens d'agrandir actuellement le champ de la science, qu'il est plus propre à en raffermir la base, à en éclaircir les principes."

This essay of Maine de Biran, in cutting the Gordian knot of problems presented by eighteenth-century sensationalism, points the way clearly to the broader and deeper empiricism which finally finds its expression in phenomenology. What is implicit in this essay is well expressed by Merleau-Ponty:

> Le premier acte philosophique serait donc de revenir au monde vécu en deçà du monde objectif... de réveiller la perception et de déjouer la ruse par laquelle elle se laisse oublier comme fait et comme perception au profit de l'objet qu'elle nous livre et de la tradition rationnelle qu'elle fonde.[1]

[1] *Phénoménologie de la perception*, p. 69.

Constant's *Adolphe* read by Balzac and Nerval[1]

ALISON FAIRLIE

WHEN and how does a given book achieve its place in the canon of great works?[2] I propose here, not to trace the fortunes of *Adolphe*, but briefly to analyse two examples of fruitful contact between creative minds across a generation. Two great writers of the mid-nineteenth century made of this novel, in very different ways, a part of their mental substance: Balzac and Nerval. Both, in those years between the initial 'succès de scandale' of a supposed 'roman à clefs' and the late nineteenth-century rehabilitation of the 'roman d'analyse', react in a highly individual way to a work not yet part of an obligatory cultural tradition.[3] Both are of course characterized by their voracious use and personal assimilation of an exceptional range of material, whether from 'literature' or 'life'; in isolating one particular thread I shall be concerned less with details of 'sources' than with the interplay of instinctive affinities and critical judgments; and above all with the technique of theme and variations: the deliberate recalling of a past work both to provide a resonant sense of the permanence of human experience, and to serve as groundwork for provocative and personal developments.

[1] Page references in the text will be to Benjamin Constant, *Œuvres*, ed. Alfred Roulin (Bibliothèque de la Pléiade, 1957); Balzac, *La Comédie humaine*, ed. Marcel Bouteron (Bibliothèque de la Pléiade, 1951); Gérard de Nerval, *Œuvres*, ed. Albert Béguin and Jean Richer (Bibliothèque de la Pléiade, vol. I, 1966, vol. II, 1956.)

[2] Stimulating observations on different aspects of this question are made by A. M. Boase, 'Tradition and Revaluation in the French Anthology, 1692–1960' in *Essays presented to C. M. Girdlestone* (1960), pp. 49–63, and T. J. B. Spencer, 'Shakespeare the International Author' in *The Future of the Modern Humanities*, ed. J. C. Laidlaw (*The Modern Humanities Research Association*, 1969), pp. 31–50.

[3] A selection of comments by critics, from the date of publication onwards, may be found in E. Eggli and P. Martino, *Le Débat romantique en France, 1813–1830*, vol. I (Paris, Garnier, 1933); J.-H. Bornecque, *Adolphe* (Paris, Garnier [1955]); C. Cordié, *Adolphe* (Naples [1963]). Contemporary comments were strongly swayed by political considerations.

Several scholars have made penetrating observations on Balzac's references to *Adolphe*.[1] Space in the present article precludes exhaustive treatment of Balzac's attitude to Constant; I shall add to previous surveys one or two minor points of fact, and shall concentrate on *La Muse du Département*, the novel where Balzac deliberately chose the reading of *Adolphe* as a theme around which his characters were to produce their conflicting reactions.

Before *La Muse*, certain of Balzac's characters found in the reading of *Adolphe* a stimulus and a warning. Camille Maupin in *Béatrix* (1839) opened her career as a novelist by recounting her first tragic love-affair in a work which was "la contrepartie d'*Adolphe*". Her later giving up of the young man she intensely loves stems in part from her being haunted by the terrible lesson of the clinging older woman in Constant's novel.[2] In the *Mémoires de deux jeunes mariées* (1841–2), the young Louise de Chaulieu, fresh from her convent, reads love stories with indiscriminate appetite and finds many wearisome, but remarks that: "Deux livres cependant m'ont étrangement plu, l'un est *Corinne* et l'autre *Adolphe*." (I, 143). Balzac's sense of the novel's importance, and the

---

[1] J.-H. Bornecque, *ed. cit.*, quotes as "un jugement étonnamment peu connu" two passages from the discussion between Dinah and Lousteau in *La Muse du Departement*. H. J. Hunt in *Balzac's 'Comédie humaine'* (1959), p. 351, comments succinctly and suggestively on the unusual angle from which Lousteau is made to judge *Adolphe* and notes that references to Constant's novel occur here and there throughout *La Muse*. Jean Pommier in *'La Muse de Département* et le thème de la femme mal mariée chez Balzac, Mérimée et Flaubert', *Annee Balz.* (1961), pp. 191–221, provides, as always, basic and seminal discussion. Geneviève Delattre, *Les Opinions littéraires de Balzac* (Paris, 1961), gives an able summary of Balzac's main references to Constant (including his appearance in person in *Illusions perdues*) and briefly discusses the tone of *La Muse*. See also her excellent article 'L'Imagination balzacienne au travail: la lecture créatrice' in *Cahiers de l'Association internationale des Études françaises*, No. 15 (1963), 395–406. The present article will show why, while appreciating the penetrating and suggestive remarks of Mme Delattre, I should see differently her "tristes pantins", "cet échec", "simple avilissement des personnages". B. Guyon's *'Adolphe, Béatrix* et *La Muse du Département'* in *Année Balz.* (1963), pp. 149–75, provides a mine of information. On attitudes to *Adolphe* over 150 years, see the thorough conspectus by Paul Delbouille, '*Adolphe* sur le Chemin de la Gloire' in *Benjamin Constant: Actes du Congrès de Lausanne* (1967) (Genève, 1968), pp. 171–80 and the third part of his *Genèse, Structure et Destin d'"Adolphe"* ([Paris], Société d'Edition "les Belles Lettres", 1971).

[2] For a fuller discussion of the references in *Béatrix* see the critical studies mentioned in the preceding note. The tragic possibilities of the theme of the woman older than her lover are common to *Adolphe* and to many of Balzac's works. This particular form of intensification is less important in *La Muse*.

fact that it was not yet automatically a canonical work, emerge from a letter to the publisher Charpentier in 1838: "N'oubliez pas *Adolphe* dans votre collection."[1] Brief remarks in Balzac's writings other than his novels bring out the two qualities he admires in *Adolphe*. First, its concentrated analysis of the mainsprings of human feeling: "je ferai remarquer combien il y a peu de faits chez les romanciers habiles (*Werther, Clarisse, Adolphe, Paul et Virginie*). Le talent éclate dans la peinture des causes qui engendrent les faits, dans les mystères du cœur humain...".[2] Second, its symbolizing a vital aspect of the society in which it is set; it chooses not the accidental and temporary aspects, but "toute une face de cette société... quelque grand et vaste symbole".[3] Finally, in the *Avant-Propos* to the *Comédie humaine,* when he thinks of those great characters created by the human imagination to "faire concurrence à l'état civil", he sets Adolphe among his chosen list (I, 6).

But it is in *La Muse du Département* that he has made of *Adolphe* a vital element in the final structure of his novel, placing his references discreetly, deliberately and suggestively at key moments. He has in a sense used *Adolphe* as the equivalent of the classical authors' treatment of ancient and familiar myth: trebly suggestive in underlining the permanence of certain human experiences, in showing the recurrent struggle to avoid an inevitable outcome, and in setting against the echoes of the past new modes of expression and differing dénouements.

To Madame Hanska he wrote in March 1843: "J'espère que dans la fin de *La Muse,* on verra le sujet d'*Adolphe,* traité du côté réel,"[4] and the fourth part of his story was originally given the heading

---

[1] *Corr.,* 1391, vol. III, p. 470; letter dated [28 novembre, 1838]. I shall discuss below (p. 219) the importance of this letter (published after J. Pommier's and B. Guyon's articles) to the question of Gustave Planche's influence on Balzac's reading of *Adolphe.* Another letter refers to Constant: that from Louis Desnoyers (*Corr.,* 1693, vol. IV, p. 26) querying among 'dangerous' phrases that on an "orateur d'une finesse voisine de celle de Benjamin Constant". In the original publication of *Pierrette* in *Le Siècle* it was replaced by "une finesse à la Walpole", but the phrase was later restored (III, 740).
[2] 'Lettres sur la Littérature, le Théâtre et les Arts' published unsigned in the *Revue parisienne* (1840). *L'Œuvre de Balzac,* sous la direction d'Albert Béguin et de Jean A. Ducourneau (Club français du livre, XIV, 1964), p. 1053 (cf. also p. 1132).
[3] *ibid.,* p. 1149.   [4] *L.H.,* vol. II, p. 179.

Commentaires sur 'l'Adolphe' de Benjamin Constant.[1] Dinah
Piédefer gladly abandons her position as wife of the impotent M. de
Baudraye and the much-attacked 'superior woman' in second-rate
provincial society, to become the devoted mistress, in Paris, of the
journalist Étienne Lousteau: the theme of how devotion may become a deadly and stifling tie will emerge only in the second half
of the novel. But from the beginning, references to *Adolphe* serve
as an omen pointing to the sinister inevitability of breakdown and
bitterness in the relationship. First, in the predominantly comic
scene where Lousteau and Bianchon, guests in the provincial salon,
try, through terrifying anecdotes on adultery, to discover whether
Dinah has yet been unfaithful to her dwarfish husband. Discussion
brings to the fore a highly Balzacian theme: "Les inventions des
romanciers et des dramaturges sautent aussi souvent de leurs livres
et de leurs pièces dans la vie réelle que les événements de la vie
réelle montent sur le théâtre et se prélassent dans les livres."
(IV, 114.) Examples are quoted, culminating in: "Et la tragi-comédie
d'*Adolphe* par Benjamin Constant se joue à toute heure, s'écria
Lousteau." (It has been suggested that this insertion is meant to
stress the 'banalité' of the theme; less so, I think, than the menac-
ing inevitability of its outcome; it is also in keeping with Lousteau's
character that he should see *Adolphe* as a 'tragi-*comédie*'.) *Adolphe*
is again used as an omen of what is to come in one of those scenes of
multiple *sous-entendus* in which Balzac so excels. Dinah has arrived,
unannounced and pregnant, to join her lover in Paris, thus irrupting
into his plans for a profitable marriage; he asks Bixiou to come and
press him to that marriage, so that Dinah from the next room will
overhear and sacrifice herself. Bixiou stresses the blank prospects of
an illicit relationship between Dinah and Lousteau in the bare
phrases: "La Société, mon cher, pèsera sur vous, tôt ou tard. Relis
Adolphe" (IV, 166).

   This deliberate use of the portent reflects Balzac's preoccupation
with structure. The classical theatre had used dreams or oracles to
make the end implicit in the beginning, to convey a sense of
inescapable menace and of ironical struggle. Balzac, discussing
Stendhal's technique of construction in *La Chartreuse*, may also
have been struck by Stendhal's use, in his different novels, of the

[1] see Pommier, *art. cit.*, and Guyon, *art. cit.*

ambiguous omen. That the first, and highly suggestive, reference to *Adolphe* in *La Muse* is inserted as late as the *Furne corrigé* version shows him deliberately highlighting the effect planned much earlier in the 1843 letter.[1] The fact too that *La Muse* was written under special pressure and made use in the first part of much material from previous writings, may have made Balzac particularly keen, when revising, to stress its coherent construction.

But portents are a long-term matter, not immediately fulfilled. Lousteau decides to accept Dinah's devotion (speculating in part on her soon becoming a rich widow), and for a time they share a new 'lune de miel': here Balzac pauses to contrast their circumstances with those of Constant's novel:

> Un des traits les plus saillants de la Nouvelle due à Benjamin Constant, et l'une des explications de l'abandon d'Ellénore, est ce défaut d'intimité journalière ou nocturne, si vous voulez, entre elle et Adolphe. Chacun des deux amants a son chez soi, l'un et l'autre ont obéi au monde, ils ont gardé les apparences. Ellénore, périodiquement quittée, est obligée à d'énormes travaux de tendresse pour chasser les pensées de liberté qui saisissent Adolphe au dehors. Le perpétuel échange des regards et des pensées dans la vie en commun donne de telles armes aux femmes que, pour les abandonner, un homme doit objecter des raisons majeures qu'elles ne fournissent jamais tant qu'elles aiment (IV, 183).

These reflections would be true only of the first half of *Adolphe*; they suggest how closely Balzac interweaves his reactions to a seminal text, his deductions from personal experience, and his imaginative creation.

From the omen we move to the reaction. In face of all portents, Balzac's active characters set out to conquer their fate, to run counter to their reading. For Dinah: "Le roman d'*Adolphe* était sa Bible, elle l'étudiait; car, par-dessus toute chose, elle ne voulait pas être Ellénore" (IV, 192). From Furetière to Flaubert and beyond, deluded girls have attempted to copy fictional models with disastrous results;

---

[1] Pommier, *art. cit.*, called attention to the late stage at which this variant occurs. See also Guyon, *art. cit.*, for the different stages of insertion of references to *Adolphe* in *Béatrix*.

P

Balzac rejoices in presenting a reaction against the model, a reaction which ironically may prove equally disastrous. Dinah is no Emma Bovary to identify herself with each heroine in narcissistic pathos; she sets out to "ne pas être Ellénore", to excise every trace of reproach or tears (IV, 193).[1] To no effect. Both she and Lousteau cite their personal interpretations of the book as weapons in their intimate struggle. Dinah has seen its analysis of "le cœur humain", Lousteau its presentation of "toute une face de la société". When her patience is at last exhausted, Lousteau retorts:

> Vous avez beaucoup lu le livre de Benjamin Constant... mais vous ne l'avez lu qu'avec des yeux de femme... Ce qui tue ce pauvre garçon, ma chère, c'est d'avoir perdu son avenir pour une femme; de ne pouvoir rien être de ce qu'il serait devenu, ni ambassadeur, ni ministre, ni chambellan, ni poète, ni riche.

The crescendo here reflects the character expressing judgment, as it moves from social prospects to artistic success and culminates in the telling "ni riche"; Lousteau's view of Adolphe both indicates, in certain turns of phrase, his own superficiality and vulgarity ("un Allemand blondasse", "une jupe qu'on devance") and shows something of the swift if limited perceptiveness of the journalist: "Adolphe [est]... un cœur d'aristocrate qui veut rentrer dans la voie des honneurs, et rattraper sa dot sociale, sa considération compromise" (IV, 187–8).[2]

---

[1] "Bel exemple d'influence négative", writes Pommier, *art. cit.* The recurring treatment in Balzac of the "Ne pas être X" as applied to literary models would merit further treatment. An interesting example, combining omen, future reversal, and other suggestive undertones, occurs early in the *Mémoires de deux jeunes mariées*, where Louise, before her passionate involvement with her Hispano-Moorish adorer, reacts against Shakespeare's Desdemona (I, 161).

[2] "Consideration" is indeed a key-word in *Adolphe*. For discussion of the aspect of *Adolphe* which is here given lapidary form by Balzac, see A. Fairlie, 'The Art of Constant's *Adolphe*: the stylisation of experience' in *M.L.R.*, LXII (Jan. 1967), and 'L'Individu et l'ordre social dans *Adolphe*', in *Europe* (March 1968).

It would be interesting to analyse closely the cut-and-thrust of literary discussion between Lousteau, Bianchon and Dinah in the early salon scene; the bemused provincials ("On nous regarde! sourions comme si nous comprenions", IV, 123) in an atmosphere of pre-Verdurin display of cultural fashion, hear an analysis of the difference between the "contour net" of the "littérature de l'Empire" and the modern desire to "faire chatoyer les mots". Critical insights, modish clichés and personal prejudices or pretensions are skilfully and satirically interwoven. See also the comparison between Lousteau and Claude Vignon ("la distance qui sépare le Métier de l'Art"), IV, 178.

The end is both an echo and a reversal of *Adolphe*, and Lousteau is made to underline this: "Vous jouez en ce moment à la fois les deux personnages." Dinah reproaches him with the social stigma brought on her, but finds the strength to break decisively: "Votre Ellénore ne meurt pas"; and she returns to husband and high position.[1] Both novels, in very different tones, have their bitter postscript. Adolphe after Ellénore's death discovers how much he depended on those very bonds he longed to be rid of. Dinah, outwardly reconciled with respectable society, suffers from "une tristesse cachée mais profonde", finds that "Parfois les souvenirs de ses misères revenaient mêlés au souvenir de voluptés dévorantes" (IV, 202) and briefly gives in once more to her past lover. Later variants intensify the sardonic allusions implicit in her return to the fold.

Differences in tone and technique are too obvious to require extended comment. Constant has at his command the subtlest resources of retrospective analysis in the first person, reduces external events and settings to the minimum, achieves a unified tone of quiet tragic irony, and rounds off intolerable suffering by the stylized epitome of death. For Balzac, "Dans la nature, ces sortes de situations violentes ne se terminent pas, comme dans les livres, par la mort ou par des catastrophes habilement arrangées; elles finissent beaucoup moins poétiquement par le dégoût, par la vulgarité des habitudes..." (IV, 194). Balzac rings Dinah's destiny about with the rich comic detail of provincial pretentiousness, her own as well as that of others, and finds objective correlatives for the prospect of seduction in the difference between a silk and an organdie dress if crumpled in a carriage, and for the shared joy of lovers in elegant *toilettes* displayed at the Opéra, or for the irony of devotion in the drab black worn from self-sacrificial economy but provoking the disgust of the weary lover.

Beneath these differences lies for both authors a particularly penetrating sense of the complexity of that supposed entity, a human character. If, to recent theorists of experimental techniques for presenting the fluctuations of personality, Flaubert has at last

---

[1] Both irony and the art of construction are stressed when, speaking of her husband's new position and power, the devoted Clagny remarks (IV, 196): "Il satisfait tous les désirs que vous formiez à vingt ans."

been recognized as an ancestor rather than an Aunt Sally, yet pre-
conceptions regarding the Balzacian 'type' still die hard. In *La
Muse du Département*, the interventions, explanations or digres-
sions of the author are, for Balzac, unusually few (is there here a
reflection of Constant's art of concentration?); we are invited to
form for ourselves cumulative conclusions around two main characters who combine, as so often in Balzac, the mathematically and
aesthetically satisfying patterns of a basic inner logic with that
unpredictable interplay resulting from the reaction of human
complexity to fluctuating circumstance. To both Dinah and
Lousteau might well be applied Adolphe's fundamental dictum:
"Il n'y a point d'unité complète dans l'homme, et presque jamais
personne n'est tout à fait sincère ni tout à fait de mauvaise foi"
(p. 57).[1]

The Dinah of the middle of the book is the devoted victim of
Lousteau. But where Constant had emphasized the tragic depend-
ence of Ellénore and her lack of inner resources by giving her only
an "esprit ordinaire", Dinah has intellectual, artistic and practical
gifts – and above all strong personal ambition. In the early chapters
she "se convertissait par ambition" (IV, 14). If she flies to join her
lover in Paris, it is in part because the capital city has long been the
loadstone of her frustrated desires.[2] When she leaves Lousteau it
is for a husband who has with insect tenacity wormed his way to
the highest honours, and her key moment of decision, part that
of the victim at last turning on the faithless lover, part that of
the woman reverting to conventional values, is poised on the
unregenerate reflection that now she can lord it over the school-
friend whose scorn has so often wounded her: "Je suis comtesse,
j'aurai sur ma voiture le manteau bleu de la pairie, et dans mon
salon les sommités de la politique et de la littérature... je la
regarderai, moi!... Cette petite jouissance pesa de tout son poids au
moment de la conversion" (IV, 196). Like others of Balzac's survivor-
characters, she moves from her own form of haunting "recherche

---

[1] H. J. Hunt, *op. cit.*, p. 350, has a valuable discussion of the problem of coherence
of character.
[2] Sexual frustration in the first half of the book finds the *dérivatifs* of furniture-
collecting (cf. Pons) and of literary leanings. Frustration of ambitions for her
lover's success turns to the *dérivatif* of would-be maternal feeling for him
(cf. Bette).

de l'absolu" to learn to "se contenter de l'à peu près", but to the end, vanity and practicality, tenderness and sensuality recur and interact.

If Lousteau is the cynical profiteer and the drifting "velléitaire", we are yet made to see moments of fleeting sincerity or suggestive suffering. Like Adolphe, he embarks on seduction as a challenging exercise in technique, and is caught, as an already perceptive Dinah had threatened, in his own trap. Where to Adolphe the thought of a happy and respected marriage is no more than a late nostalgic dream (p. 92), Lousteau has a brilliant prospect, brought hallucinatingly alive in all its practical detail, snatched from him at the moment of achievement. Impulses of admiration or regret for suffering run sporadically beneath his calculating hold on Dinah.[1] His unsuccessful efforts in writing convey something of the torments of the artist, however ineffectual, faced by "les affres du style".[2] And, although he has nothing of Adolphe's tragic dignity, he is at times made to represent that central problem in Constant: the difficulty of distinguishing between different levels of scheming, rhetoric, self-persuasion, and immediate feeling.[3]

---

[1] Faced by the humility of his proposed pregnant bride, Félicie Cardot, "Lousteau fut ému, tant il y avait de choses dans le regard, dans l'accent, dans l'attitude" (IV, 158). On Dinah's tears at his cruel reception of her arrival in Paris, "Lousteau ne put résister à cette explosion, il serra la baronne dans ses bras, et l'embrassa", etc. (IV, 162). He marvels at her love: "je suis donc aimé pour la première fois de ma vie! s'écriait Lousteau" (IV, 171); like the early Adolphe he feels a woman can be easily cast aside when the moment suits, yet "Aussi Lousteau conçut-il pour elle une involontaire estime" (IV, 181). Later, facing her grief, he is "atteint au cœur par cette vivacité de sensitive" and provides a virulent self-analysis: "Je suis, littérairement parlant, un homme très secondaire... nous autres danseurs de corde...", etc. (IV, 188).

[2] see IV, 151, 175, 177, 188, 205, and compare the treatment of such characters as Wenceslas Steinbock and Lucien de Rubempré.

[3] Pommier's article raises possible parallels with *Madame Bovary*. For passages where the skilled use of both rhetoric and sensuality foreshadows Rodolphe Boulanger see IV, 118, 141, 149, 154, 157; cf. especially the real but egoistic regrets at a break which he had hoped for, 199. The selfish schemer predominates. But by the side of Constant's most probing passages on the power of self-persuasion through words, the difficulty of estimating degrees of sincerity, might be put the following: "Il y a des hommes... qui naissent un peu singes, chez qui l'imitation des plus charmantes choses du sentiment est si naturelle, que le comédien ne se sent plus" (IV, 177), or, after the fine rhetorical flourish in his last appeal ("Une goutte d'eau dans le désert, et... par la main d'un ange"), the comment "Ce fut dit moitié plaisanterie et moitié attendrissement." (IV, 207.)

The cry of Camille Maupin in *Béatrix* is frequently quoted by critics: "Adolphe, cet épouvantable livre de Benjamin Constant, ne nous dit que les douleurs d'Adolphe; mais celles de la femme? Hein! Il ne les a pas assez observées pour nous les peindre et quelle femme oserait les révéler?" But *La Muse* shows Balzac aware of Constant's two-sidedness, and is itself far from being written simply to take the woman's part. Each author has his own allusive technique. Adolphe's retrospective analysis sets the reader as much within Ellénore as within himself; Balzac, who has rejoiced in a reversal of roles, making the woman and the provincial finally stronger than the man and the Parisian, regards Dinah with a sardonic as well as an understanding eye. The balance between the two sides is held in Constant's tragedy by a desolate and critical sympathy for both, in Balzac's tragi-comedy by a fascinated contemplation of two opponents engaged in a struggle for survival.

One important aspect of Balzac's variations remains to be discussed. When Dinah studies *Adolphe* as her Bible she decides to avoid all those reproachful tears "si savamment décrites par le critique auquel on doit l'analyse de cette œuvre poignante, et dont la glose paraissait à Dinah presque supérieure au livre. Aussi relisait-elle souvent le magnifique article du seul critique qu'ait eu la Revue des Deux-Mondes, et qui se trouve en tête de la nouvelle édition d'Adolphe" (IV, 192). When Lousteau hurls his parting reproaches, he too refers to this article. Gustave Planche (who was mentioned by name in the first version of Dinah's remarks) had published it in the *Revue des Deux Mondes* in 1834 and included it in his *Portraits littéraires* of 1836; it was then placed in the Charpentier edition of *Adolphe* in 1839, republished in 1843, and continued to figure in Charpentier editions up till 1930. Several scholars have pointed out that Balzac is here indirectly attacking Sainte-Beuve, and have discussed the probable importance of Planche in recalling Balzac's attention to *Adolphe*, in 1839 (*Béatrix*) and 1843 (*La Muse*).[1] It is highly likely that Balzac read the article on its first publication in 1834; to the evidence other critics have adduced on possible contacts in 1839 and 1843 must now be added the letter

[1] See Pommier, *art. cit.*, and Guyon, *art. cit.*, and their references to M. Regard. For a penetrating study of Balzac and Sainte-Beuve, see J. Hytier, *Questions de littérature* (Geneva, 1967), pp. 111–40.

(quoted above, p. 211) where Balzac in 1838 suggests the Charpentier edition, here without mention of Planche.[1]

On Balzac's direct use of Planche, two further points are important. First that in the vital passage where Dinah decides to be the opposite of Ellénore (a passage which, as B. Guyon has shown, directly quotes not *Adolphe*, but Planche), Balzac uses one of the very few paragraphs from that critic which directly capture the spirit and mode of expression of Constant's book. For Planche's highly personal piece of criticism, while at the beginning excellently characterizing the subtlety of the work, is a thinly-disguised confessional, proceeding to a series of emotional elaborations on the supposed experience of Adolphe and Ellénore, where the critic startlingly endows the text with his own inapposite memories, rhetoric and moral conclusions. (Adolphe in youth is made to dream of the tears and trailing tresses of lively women wiping the sweat from his brow; Ellénore sees in sleep the ghost of her father with furrowed cheek reproaching her degradation; Adolphe is shameful because he "essuie sur les lèvres de sa maîtresse les baisers d'une autre bouche", and Ellénore "avilie" in forgiving him his waning love.)[2] The passage Balzac has selected is however a telling synthesis of the stage of Ellénore's growing reproaches. And, secondly, although he lets Dinah quote Planche almost word for word, the few changes Balzac makes are stylistically highly significant: he compresses the passage still further, and in particular rewords the clumsily comic phrase: "Dès qu'il fait un pas, il trouve devant lui un œil curieux qui attend sa réponse."[3]

Lousteau is made to accuse Planche of seeing only the woman's side. This is hardly a tenable accusation, but from Lousteau's

---

[1] Guyon points out that in both 1839 and 1834 Planche's edition of *Adolphe* appeared later than the relevant work of Balzac, but the two authors were in close contact. Balzac's letter to Charpentier notes (in view of the brevity of *Adolphe*) that it should be combined in one volume with a novel by some other author, and promises to reflect on what this should be. The eventual Charpentier edition added instead other works by Constant, and the Planche article.

[2] Ellénore's relation to the Comte de P., so quietly evoked with its insufficiencies in Constant, gives rise to such imaginings as: "Elle avait conquis l'amour d'un homme, elle avait posé sa tête sur son épaule, et dans ses rêves elle avait surpris le murmure de son nom; elle était fière et glorieuse...", etc. There is an extended evocation of a sobbing Adolphe scorned for his tears by a dominant and dry-eyed Ellénore, etc.

[3] Guyon quotes the relevant paragraphs from Planche, *art. cit.*, p. 167. Cf. IV, 193.

further remarks there comes a lapidary comment: "Ce livre, ma
chère, a les deux sexes... Dans *Adolphe*, les femmes ne voient
qu'Ellénore, les jeunes gens y voient Adolphe, les hommes faits y
voient Ellénore et Adolphe, les politiques y voient la vie sociale!"
(IV, 198.) The network of society, with its intrigues, its interventions,
its *idées reçues* and its false judgments, exercises to a particular
degree its ineluctable pressures on representative individuals in
both *Adolphe* and *La Muse*.[1]

Adolphe, then, is plainly no 'source' in the ordinary sense, but a
counter deliberately used. Its importance is twofold. First, in the
skilled art by which it becomes an allusive groundwork for Balzac's
own vigorous variations: references are placed at structurally
significant turning-points, and each also casts a revealing sidelight
on the character who utters it. Second, beneath the very obvious
differences of treatment or temperament, in the surprising, or
merely natural, affinities which unite two creative minds, each
intrigued or haunted by the contradictions and ambiguities that
underlie any stereotyped conception of 'character'.

———————

NERVAL makes no such use of *Adolphe* as an overt theme or structural device. But his scattered, yet very significant, references to the
novel show a still more personal response to what are perhaps its
two most fundamental suggestions.[2] Where so many critics, from
the time of publication to our own day, have stressed in Adolphe
the inconstant weakling, incapable of 'real love', Nerval notes in
his *Carnets de Dolbreuse* the essential passage from Chapter III
(p. 64) which both characterizes the delight of dawning love and
points forward to the years when Adolphe will be tied to Ellénore,
not merely in weariness or weakness, but in a prolonged tenderness
as persistent as his sporadic ambition or exasperation. Nerval's notes,
as transcribed by Jean Richer, read: "L'amour supplée aux longs

---

[1] Cf. the ironical detail of society's false judgments in *Adolphe* (discussed in the
articles mentioned in n. 2, p. 209) with for example Bianchon's comment on
"les tragédies qui se jouent derrière le rideau du ménage" – "je trouve la justice
humaine malvenue à juger des crimes entre époux;... elle n'y entend rien dans
ses prétentions à l'équité."
[2] I have not attempted here an exhaustive survey of Nerval's references to
Constant.

souv*enirs* par une sorte de magie. Toutes les autres aff*ections* ont beso*in* d'un passé, lui nous d*onne* la consc*ience* d'av*oir* vécu av*ec* un être nag*uère* étranger. B.C."[1] No theme could be more central to Nerval's own works than the search, beneath fluctuating and conflicting encounters and obsessions, for the means of uniting disparate experience whether from 'literature' or from 'life' within the converging parallels and consoling permanence of a shared past. Where Constant will distil from a multiplicity of real women one infinitely suggestive figure, Nerval's tales or sonnets will create three archetypes to represent his longings: the queen or saint as the ideal; the siren or actress as the fascinating and fallacious echo of that ideal in the real world; the fairy of naïve legend to suggest in a lovely and traditional countryside a possible but constantly elusive reconciliation with the nature of things. Behind all three is set the illuminating and shifting magic, constantly subject to disillusion and to re-creation, of a double past: historical and personal. That Nerval should note in Constant the analysis of the 'magic' means by which dawning love evokes imaginative memories is proof less of a 'source' than of a recognition of creative affinities.

Nerval's note on chapter iii of *Adolphe* stops at "naguère étranger", but the next phrases, with their sense at the same time of ecstasy and of impermanence, have obviously bitten into his memory. Constant had written: "L'amour n'est qu'un point lumineux, et néanmoins il semble s'emparer du temps. Il y a peu de jours qu'il n'existait pas, bientôt il n'existera plus..." (p. 64). In the *Lettres à Jenny Colon* Nerval distinguishes between two levels of love, and of the more moderate, which he longs to transcend, says: "C'est un point lumineux dans l'existence qui ne tarde pas à pâlir et à s'éteindre."[2]

In *Adolphe* the magic of the "point lumineux" is followed by the crescendo of irreparable errors. The theme of an obscure and haunting guilt is fundamental in the works of Nerval, and finds many individual means of suggestion.[3] That Constant's expression

---

[1] *Gérard de Nerval: Carnet de Dolbreuse.* Essai de lecture par Jean Richer (Athens, 1967), p. 91. This note corrects the faulty transcription given in the text, p. 65. (See also pp. 7 and 27, and Jean Richer: *Nerval. Expérience et Création* (Paris, 1963), p. 325.) The italics represent Richer's expansion of Nerval's abbreviations.

[2] *Œuvres*, vol. I, p. 771.

[3] Cf. the standard works of criticism on Nerval, and some brief remarks in A. Fairlie, 'Le Mythe d'Orphée dans l'œuvre de Gérard de Nerval', in *Cahiers de l'Association internationale des Études françaises*, No. 22 (March 1970).

of a parallel obsession has worked its way into his sensibility emerges all the more clearly from the quiet allusions made in journalistic articles to these pivotal phrases from Chapter IV of *Adolphe:* "Nous avions prononcé tous deux des mots irréparables; nous pouvions les taire, mais non les oublier. Il y a des choses qu'on est longtemps sans se dire, mais quand une fois elles sont dites, on ne cesse jamais de les répéter." (p. 71.) An article on a production at the Opéra, where Nerval discusses a husband's smug and scheming treatment of his wife, remarks: "N'y a-t-il pas, d'ailleurs, dans les blessures de l'amour-propre, ce quelque chose d'*irréparable* que l'auteur d'*Adolphe* peignit si bien?"[1] The break with the charming slave-girl of *Les Femmes du Caire* is prefaced by the phrase: "Il s'était dit entre nous un de ces mots *irréparables* dont a parlé l'auteur d'*Adolphe*."[2]

Beyond specific allusions, certain affinities link particularly closely, despite differences, the temperaments of Constant and of Nerval. First, their penetrating analysis of the artist's fundamental problem: that of words. For Constant: "Tous nos sentiments intimes semblent se jouer des efforts du langage: la parole rebelle, par cela seul qu'elle généralise et qu'elle exprime, sert à désigner, à distinguer, plutôt qu'à définir" (p. 1415), while for Nerval: "Il y a des années de rêves, de projets, d'angoisses qui voudraient se presser dans une phrase, dans un mot."[3] Second, a kind of instinctive physical retraction before the evidence of suffering in others: the Adolphe who, whatever his harshness in absence, is rendered powerless or momentarily tender when faced by the blank and shivering despair of a living woman, might be summed up by Nerval's phrase on Rétif: "une espèce de crispation nerveuse que lui fait éprouver le spectacle de la souffrance".[4] Third, and most important, the fundamental questioning of the 'reality' of any emotional experience. Both suffer from that 'dédoublement' which will become so much a part of nineteenth-century experience; each feels and expresses it with a particular and personal intensity. To Constant "cette analyse perpétuelle qui place une arrière-pensée à côté de tous les senti-

---

[1] *Œuvres complementaires de Gérard de Nerval*, vol. II, *La Vie du Théâtre*, textes réunis et presentées par Jean Richer (Paris, 1961), p. 655. A passing reference to *Adolphe* is also found in vol. III (1959), p. 153.

[2] *Œuvres*, vol. II, p. 286.

[3] *ibid.*, vol. I, p. 754.

[4] *ibid.*, vol. II, p. 1100.

ments, et par là les corrompt dès leur naissance"[1] is primarily intellectual: a product of the ratiocination drawn from both collective and personal experience. To Nerval, the threat is that of the imagination: the artist, unconsciously seeking to mould both others and the self to the demands of a stylized creation, meets either the stinging retort of the other: "Vous ne m'aimez pas! Vous cherchez un drame, voilà tout, et le dénouement vous échappe,"[2] or his own dawning realization:

> Nous ne vivons pas, nous! nous analysons la vie!... Suis-je bien sûr moi-même d'avoir aimé?... Nous ne voyons partout que des modèles à décrire, des passions à rendre, et tous ceux qui se mêlent à notre vie sont victimes de notre égoïsme, comme nous le sommes de notre imagination. (II, 1072.)

Other affinities could well be traced.[3] For both Constant and Nerval the analysis of an individual love consciously, if discreetly, carries the widest suggestions relating to the political, sociological or metaphysical assumptions of an age. Constant's comments on the wider implications of *Adolphe* remained unpublished in his lifetime; he had noted in a projected preface that "J'ai peint une petite partie du tableau, la seule qui fût non sans tristesse, mais sans danger pour le peintre" and had gone on to draw parallels between inconstancy or aridity in personal emotions and the political and metaphysical causes and results of such a division of the self.[4] Nerval, in *Sylvie*,[5] is able more directly to characterize the implications of the "époque étrange" of his youth, one of those "époques

---

[1] Fragments of projected preface, see J.-H. Bornecque's edition of *Adolphe*, *op. cit.*, p. 304.

[2] *Œuvres*, vol. I, p. 271. Nerval's frequent mockery at literary habits which demand either marriage or death as a *dénouement* (vol. II, p. 338, vol. I, pp. 79–80, etc.) might be compared with Balzac's observation quoted above, p. 215.

[3] Both comment on how differences of language may seem to break through stereotypes, Constant in the passage: "Elle parlait plusieurs langues, imparfaitement... Ses idées semblaient se faire jour à travers les obstacles, en sortir de cette lutte plus agréables, plus naïves et plus neuves; car les idiomes étrangers rajeunissent les pensées, et les débarrassent de ces tournures qui les font paraître communes et affectées." (p. 56); Nerval in the remark: "Il y a quelque chose de très séduisant dans une femme d'une pays lointain et singulier, qui parle une langue inconnue,... et qui enfin n'a rien de ces vulgarités de détail que l'habitude nous révèle chez les femmes de notre patrie." To Constant what counts is the apparent revivifying of ideas; to Nerval the stimulus of the unknown, allowing the imagination to weave its own dream. Both are brought back to the reality.

[4] *Adolphe*, ed. J.-H. Bornecque, p. 350.   [5] *Œuvres*, vol. I, pp. 242–3.

de rénovation ou de décadence" in which, as in *Adolphe*, against a background where systems so rapidly rise and fall, where all values are set at odds and questioned, inherited idealism and inherited cynicism find in personal destinies the concentration and the echo of the problems of society as a whole.

———

T<small>HIS</small> brief article has suggested only a few points of comparison and contrast; many more might be investigated. Both Balzac and Nerval, rather than 'borrowing' from Constant, have recognized in *Adolphe* themes which form part of their own most fundamental preoccupations. Balzac uses as a structural device the main outlines of its situation and dilemmas, then plays on them through parallels, reversals, and interpretations by individuals: his central concern is as always, with a play of forces. Nerval's fewer references are those of one who has more intimately absorbed details of analysis and expression; the details he recalls are those most vital to the delight and the despair at the centre of Adolphe's experience.

French literature is perhaps particularly characterized, throughout the centuries, by the joy, which both author and reader share, in an ability consciously to play on the resonances of the most suggestive authors of the past, while creating around them original variations and interpretations. To both Balzac and Nerval, countless other authors from many countries and ages will provide stimulus and substance. The individual reactions of these two writers to *Adolphe*, at a time before it was fully established in the canon of great works, suggest both their immediacy of response to subtleties of content and expression, and their own irreductible originality.

A note on the presence of Montaigne in the *Mémoires d'Outre-Tombe*

I. D. McFARLANE

MORE than once Chateaubriand has expressed his admiration for the Renaissance and those centuries that bridge the Middle Ages in their flower and the modern world:

> Dans les XIVe, XVe, XVIe et XVIIe siècles, la civilisation impar-faite, les croyances superstitieuses, les usages étrangers et demi-barbares, mêlaient le roman partout; les caractères étaient forts, l'imagination puissante, l'existence mystérieuse et cachée. La nuit, autour des hauts murs des cimetières et des couvents,... c'était au péril de sa tête qu'on cherchait le rendez-vous donné par quelque Héloïse. Pour se livrer au désordre, il fallait aimer véritablement; pour violer les mœurs générales, il fallait faire de grands sacrifices. Non-seulement il s'agissait d'affronter des dangers fortuits et de braver le glaive des lois, mais on était obligé de vaincre en soi l'empire des habitudes régulières, l'auto-rité de la famille, la tyrannie des coutumes domestiques, l'opposi-tion de la conscience, les terreurs et les devoirs du chrétien. Toutes ces entraves doublaient l'énergie des passions.

So wrote Chateaubriand in Stendhalian terms in an early book of the *Mémoires*.[1] And even in a pot-boiler such as the *Analyse raisonnée de l'histoire de France* he observed that "le siècle des arts en France est celui de François Ier en descendant jusqu'à Louis XIII, nullement le siècle de Louis XIV."[2] Time and again in the *Mémoire* he establishes parallels between his own times and events of the sixteenth century, very much as he had done in the *Essai sur les révolutions;* and he has an unmistakable liking for certain sixteenth-century historians such as Montluc and Tavannes. What attracted

---

[1] *Mémoires d'Outre-Tombe*, éd. Maurice Levaillant and Georges Moulinier (Paris, Bibliothèque de la Pléiade, 1951), vol. I, pp. 125-6. Hereafter referred to as *M.O.*

[2] *Analyse raisonnée de l'histoire de France*, Œuvres (Paris, 1858), vol. XXI, p. 108.

him above all was the vitality of the period, to be found also in the rich language to which his own style owes something.

Montaigne appeals to Chateaubriand in part because of his extraordinary linguistic vitality; but the recurrence of Montaigne's name over the years and in particular the frequent references in the *Mémoires* point to closer affinities between the two writers. Some critics would take Chateaubriand's familiarity with Montaigne back to his literary beginnings: Pierre Moreau sees in the essayist a lead to Raymond Sebond and his natural theology,[1] and a possible source of Chateaubriand's anti-rationalism, and J. Mourot has attributed to Montaigne's example something in Chateaubriand's refusal to organize the material of the *Essai sur les révolutions* too tidily, his desire, as the author himself said "d'éloigner de cet ouvrage tout esprit de système, en explorant avec candeur la vérité."[2] One might see in the *Essai* the exercise of the judgment on a series of elements which give us more insight into Chateaubriand than into the historical events he is discussing. However that may be, the only reference of an overt nature to Montaigne is bald and distant in tone: "Rabelais, Montaigne et Mariana étonnèrent les esprits par la nouveauté et la hardiesse de leurs opinions politiques et religieuses."[3] In the *Essai* it is Jean-Jacques Rousseau who makes the running, a very different state of affairs from what happens in the *Mémoires*. In a note added to the 1826 edition, Chateaubriand refers slightingly to "cet éternel *moi* et ce ton de confidence que je prends avec le lecteur",[4] but, given the date of this comment, it would

---

[1] P. Moreau, *Chateaubriand, l'homme et l'œuvre* (Paris, 1958), p. 158.

[2] J. Mourot, *Études sur les premières œuvres de Chateaubriand* (Paris, 1962), p. 186.

[3] *Essai sur les révolutions*, Book I, pt i, ch. 58. Without supporting evidence, this statement could be taken as a superficial generalization by one not particularly interested in the authors he mentions. The reference to Rabelais as an advanced thinker may surprise at this date, but J. Boulenger, *Rabelais à travers les âges* (Paris, 1925), pp. 74 ff., notes how c. 1790 several writers, in particular Ginguené, considered Rabelais as a sort of pre-Revolutionary figure.

[4] *Essai*, Book II, ch. 13. In another supplementary note to Book I, pt i, where he had originally pointed to "l'expérience des maux qui résultent de tout gouvernement", he wrote: "On a fait grand bruit de cette phrase, qui, si elle signifie quelque chose, veut dire seulement qu'il y a des vices dans toutes les institutions humaines. Ce n'est d'ailleurs qu'une boutade empruntée au doute de Montaigne ou à l'humeur de Rousseau." In the *Mémoires* Chateaubriand never refers to the "doute de Montaigne", and if he did at any stage see in the essayist an example of scepticism, he does not appear to make this a key factor in his later understanding of Montaigne.

seem to refer less to Montaigne than to Rousseau, if this tendency of which he complains is affected in any way by a literary example. Nevertheless, Montaigne is one of Chateaubriand's familiars quite early on: in a letter to Madame de Staël, dated 15 June 1801, we read: "Montaigne parle de ces jours de la jeunesse, où l'on a la tête pleine d'*oisiveté*, d'*amour* et de *bon temps*."[1] which shows that he has acquired the habit of quoting the essayist before embarking on the *Mémoires*. And if we turn to the last years of his life, we learn that, when he was engaged on the *Vie de Rancé*, the *Essais* were close at hand.[2]

External as well as internal evidence shows that it is in the *Mémoires* that Montaigne comes into his own. Chateaubriand's secretary, when he was ambassador in London, gives interesting details of his master's passion for Montaigne, of whom he was himself a devotee: "Il préférait à notre [sc. his secretaries'] compagnie des causeurs tels qu'Homère, Lucrèce, Camoens, Linné, Montaigne, ou même Ronsard."[3] But at one time, it was Montaigne who had pride of place: "C'était alors la lecture favourite de M. de Chateaubriand; et les *Essais* venaient de passer de ma petite bibliothèque dans les mains de l'écrivain, pour le distraire de ses travaux et de la diplomatie."[4]

During those months in London (January–September 1822) Chateaubriand was at work on the early part of the *Mémoires*. When he was appointed to Rome, he often referred to Montaigne's journey to Italy in the company of Marcellus who no doubt sharpened his master's appetite for that work. However, his interest was inspired by something deeper than the chance encounters of diplomatic life, and it is significant that, when attempts were made to boost sales of the first publication of the *Mémoires* in 1834, Chateaubriand's secretary Pilorge made what looks like an inspired statement:

Le secrétaire de M. de Chateaubriand... dit que les *Mémoires* ne sont pas précisément des mémoires dans le sens étroit du mot, mais un ouvrage varié à la manière des *Essais* de Montaigne, où

---

[1] *Correspondance générale de Chateaubriand*, ed. L. Thomas (Paris, 1912), vol. I, p. 50.
[2] M.-J. Durry, *La Vieillesse de Chateaubriand, 1830–1848* (Paris, 1933), vol. I, p. 319.
[3] Le comte de Marcellus, *Chateaubriand et son temps* (Paris, 1859), p. 71.
[4] *ibid.*, p. 98.

l'écrivain descend du ton de la poésie à des récits familiers, à des sujets philosophiques, à des lettres, des voyages, des épisodes, etc.[1]

In the *Mémoires* themselves, there are 18 quotations and eight allusions to the essayist, spread fairly evenly over the text as a whole, and there is also a quotation in a chapter that was subsequently rejected.[2] No other sixteenth-century author comes anywhere near this frequency; Rabelais, for whom Chateaubriand had a high regard, is mentioned or quoted six times, and Ronsard only four; so that Montaigne stands in a separate class. Compared with Chateaubriand's favourite authors in other centuries and countries, the essayist comes out very favourably. Among the classics, Homer and Vergil stand out alone in the frequency with which Chateaubriand turns to them; of the moderns, perhaps only Voltaire and Dante are quoted substantially more often than Montaigne. Many known favourite writers are mentioned or quoted over 20 times (Racine, Bossuet, Byron, Rousseau and Tasso), but of all these only two occur more insistently: Tasso and Rousseau. Even so, these two last are only marginally ahead of Montaigne (28/29 to 26 references), and it is noticeable that Rousseau, whose role in the *Essai sur les révolutions* was so prominent, has lost a good deal of his former prestige – a point which Chateaubriand himself makes more than once in the *Mémoires*. Statistics of this nature may have only a limited value, but they do give some indication of the hierarchy of favourite authors in a work so personal as the *Mémoires*; at the same time, tone and context must be taken into account.

Chateaubriand very rarely expresses a clear judgment on some aspect of Montaigne's work; one day he is surprised that the essayist should have been so exclusively bent on seeing what was left of ancient Rome as to neglect the present-day city around him;[3] elsewhere he remarks approvingly on the cast of his imagination.[4]

---

[1] quoted by M. Levaillant, *Chateaubriand, Madame Récamier et les Mémoires d'Outre-tombe* (Paris, 1936), p. 233.

[2] In the *Digression philosophique*, i (originally to be inserted in Part I, Book XI), Chateaubriand quotes: "La philosophie, dit Montaigne, n'est qu'une poésie sophistiquée", *M.O.*, vol. I, p. 1073.

[3] *M.O.*, vol. II, pp. 243–4.

[4] *ibid.*, p. 254; also vol. II, p. 840, where Chateaubriand refers to his "vivacité ordinaire d'imagination".

One passage is notable for the friendly tone that Chateaubriand adopts in spite of an apparent difference of opinion: "Mon pauvre Michel, tu dis des choses charmantes, mais à notre âge, vois-tu, l'amour ne nous rend pas ce que tu supposes ici. Nous n'avons qu'une chose à faire: c'est de nous mettre franchement de côté."[1] And even so, a perusal of the following text shows that the difference between the two is very much less than we are led to believe at the outset. Affective context is important in the passage where Chateaubriand recalls some of the daily routine of his childhood at Combourg and contrasts his father's strident voice with "la douce harmonie du son de laquelle le père de Montaigne éveillait son fils".[2]

The nub of the matter is naturally, where does Montaigne come in as a guide for Chateaubriand's own self-portrait? The difference hardly needs stressing: to begin with, Chateaubriand's anatomy of self was to be undertaken in great measure through the account he gives of others: "C'est ma propre vie que j'écris en m'occupant des autres",[3] and this conception of his relationship with his times marks a difference in perspective from the *Essais*, however concerned these may be on occasion with the problem of the relations between self and others. Here and there Chateaubriand declares his intention of not presenting the reader with a full self-portrait in all its revealing truth. He was anxious to leave to posterity a picture over which he had some control; for him the self was to have a certain aesthetic unity in which the element of dignity must play an essential role, and this portrait was not to be carelessly identified by others with some aspect of the times in which he lived; it is this thought that led him to comment on Mirabeau thus: "On ne voit plus le Mirabeau réel, mais le Mirabeau idéalisé, le Mirabeau tel que le font les peintres, pour le rendre le symbole ou le mythe de l'époque qu'il représente."[4] If such a process is to occur, the author must have some part in it! Nevertheless, whatever one may think of Chateaubriand's powers of self-deception in this field – the *Mémoires* are in part the creation of a legend for posterity – there is also a genuine desire to grasp the identity of his self; time and again, he returns to the theme of the self's inability to endure: "L'homme n'a pas une

[1] *ibid.*, p. 376.   [2] *ibid.*, vol. I, p. 84.
[3] *ibid.*, p. 1026. His intentions in 1809 were different (see below, p. 232).
[4] *ibid.*, p. 179.

Q

seule et même vie; il en a plusieurs mises bout à bout, et c'est sa
misère."[1] Or: "Personne n'est semblable à soi-même et n'embrasse
toute sa destinée."[2] There are indeed a number of companion
themes here which remind us of Montaigne's reflections: the
complexity of man,[3] his changing nature, his exposure to all sorts
of pressures and the role of fortune,[4] the need to resist the passions
which enslave,[5] the role that falsehood and 'songes' may have in
leading man to reality.[6] Indeed at one point Chateaubriand quotes
Montaigne in illustration of his own views on the irrational determination of our minds: "Il ne faut point de cause pour agiter nostre
ame; une resverie sans cause et sans subject la régente et l'agite."[7]
The two writers agree closely on the role of memory, that is cerebral,
not affective memory, which later Chateaubriand takes care to
differentiate and which plays a vital role in the structure of the
Mémoires. Like Montaigne he makes a point of despising the parrot-
like memory, like him he claims to have a very poor one: "Une
chose m'humilie: la mémoire est souvent la qualité de la sottise;
elle appartient généralement aux esprits lourds, qu'elle rend plus
pesants par le bagage, dont elle les surcharge."[8] But, like Montaigne
too, though on different grounds, he asks what life would be without
memory – and particularly in his own case, since, as he admits in
contrast to Montaigne's view of man, he yearns (*bée*) after time
past rather than after things to come.[9] Montaigne also comes to
mind in a passage where he wonders whether his memory is not
encouraging him to run on the narration of events beyond what is
relevant to his life or likely to interest his readers.[10] Finally, in this
connection, one may detect some similarities between the two writers
in their open, anti-pedantic views on education.

[1] *M.O.*, p. 103.   [2] *ibid.*, vol. II, p. 612.
[3] "L'homme n'est pas un et simple", *M.O.*, vol. II, p. 10.
[4] "Encore si l'homme ne faisait que changer de lieux! mais ses jours et son cœur
changent", *M.O.*, vol. I, p. 43.
[5] *ibid.*, pp. 76, 435 ff., etc.
[6] "... les passions et les vices vous relèguent dans la classe des esclaves", *M.O.*,
vol. II, p. 481. Chateaubriand also refers to "les passions modifiées par les
climats", *ibid.*, vol. I, p. 63.
[7] *ibid.*, p. 76.
[8] *ibid.*, pp. 49–50. Marcellus, *op. cit.*, p. 16, makes the comparison between
Chateaubriand and Montaigne and quotes the essayist, not in his attack on, but
in his defence of, the memory: "C'est un util de merveilleux service...".
[9] *M.O.*, vol. II, p. 157.   [10] *ibid.*, vol. I, p. 55.

Chateaubriand, then, has no intention of giving us a *portrait en pied*, though one may wonder whether the first chapter of Book XI (*Défaut de mon caractère*), in which Chateaubriand scrutinizes his character at greater length than usual and which he at least sketched out in London, was not written as it were in the shadow of *De la présomption*, at a time when Montaigne was his *livre de chevet*.[1] More normally, he claims that such self-examination is likely to bore the reader: "Tel est l'inconvénient des *Mémoires*, lorsqu'ils n'ont point de faits historiques à raconter, ils ne vous entretiennent que de la personne de l'auteur."[2] However much this view coincides with Chateaubriand's inner thought is a matter for conjecture; moreover he may have been aware of a relative poverty of inner life within himself. But he still had to commit himself on the way he was to present his self in the *Mémoires*, and here it seems that Montaigne emerges as a corrective to Rousseau. In the *Essai sur les révolutions* and other early works, the example and personality of Rousseau are pervasive; in the *Mémoires* Chateaubriand, conscious of the self he ought to commit to print, is very much more critical of his youthful idol, both on account of his way of life: "Je voulais dire adieu à la solitude d'un homme antipathique par ses mœurs à mes mœurs, bien que doué d'un talent dont les accents remuaient ma jeunesse"[3], and because of a fundamental vulgarity: "A travers le charme du style de l'auteur des *Confessions* perce quelque chose de vulgaire, de cynique, de mauvais ton, de mauvais goût."[4] Chateaubriand deplores the way in which Rousseau not only reveals aspects of his life damaging to his *dignité d'homme*, but seems to involve the reader in a certain complicity, in a willingness to condone these actions. One might have expected Chateaubriand to have criticized Montaigne for a frankness in domains liable to offend his susceptibilities, but this is never the

---

[1] *ibid.*, Book XI, ch. i, I, pp. 379–82. At the beginning of Book XI, Chateaubriand has written: "Londres, d'avril à septembre 1822. Revu en décembre 1846." Though these captions are not always accurate, there appears to be no over-whelming reason for doubting the accuracy of this one. Levaillant, summarizing the result of his earlier research, writes: "Il est donc aisé de se former une idée assez précise de cette première rédaction des *Mémoires de ma vie*. Entreprise en 1809, terminée postérieurement à 1822, et peut-être dès 1826, elle correspon-dait à l'actuelle première partie des *Mémoires d'Outre-Tombe*" (*M.O.*, vol. I, p. xii).

[2] *ibid.*, vol. II, p. 58.   [3] *ibid.*, vol. I, p. 307.   [4] *ibid.*, vol. II, p. 795.

case; and in 1809 his intentions in writing the *Mémoires* may have
been nearer those of Montaigne in 1803 or in the final shape they
took:

> D'abord, je n'entreprends ces mémoires qu'avec le dessein formel
> de ne disposer d'aucun nom, que du mien propre, dans tout ce
> qui concerne ma vie privée; j'écris principalement pour rendre
> compte de moi à moi-même... Je veux avant de mourir remonter
> à mes belles années, expliquer mon inexplicable cœur, voir enfin
> ce que je pourrai dire, lorsque ma plume sans contrainte s'abandon-
> era à tous mes souvenirs... Ce sera de plus un moyen agréable
> pour moi d'interrompre des études pénibles, et quand je me
> sentirai las de tracer les tristes vérités de l'histoire, je me reposerai
> en écrivant l'histoire de mes songes... Je suis résolu de dire toute
> la vérité. Comme j'entreprends d'ailleurs l'histoire de mes idées,
> et de mes sentiments, plutôt que l'histoire de ma vie, je n'aurai
> pas autant de raisons de mentir.[1]

When due allowance is made for the difference of Romantic tonality,
and for the fact that *Mémoires*, by their very nature of recall, must
engage different gears from those used in the journal or the essay,
this passage seems to show a desire for the fuller portrait and the
search for some *maîtresse forme* through time. Later, when self-
portraiture is under discussion, Chateaubriand sees the need for
adopting a tone that brings him on to the same footing with the
reader, and his advice is closer to Montaigne than to Rousseau:

> Quand on parle de soi en français, me disait M. de Chateaubriand,
> ce qui a toujours assez mauvaise grâce, soit que l'on raconte sa
> vie, soit que l'on donne son propre jugement sur les actes ou les
> ouvrages d'autrui, il faut baisser son style de plusieurs crans, et
> maintenir le ton familier de la conversation, qui admet les digres-
> sions, comme les réticences.[2]

Elsewhere, he writes: "Aucun défaut ne me choque, excepté la
moquerie et la suffisance."[3] Two faults which, as the cause of one's

---

[1] From the *Esquisse d'un mattre*, pp. 1–4, in *Souvenirs d'enfance et de jeunesse de Chateaubriand*: manuscrit de 1826 suivi de lettres inédites et d'une étude par Ch. Lenormant (Paris, 1874).

[2] Marcellus, *op. cit.*, p. 128; this may be compared with the statement by Pilorge quoted above, p. 227.

[3] *M.O.*, vol. I, p. 48.

being 'pris a jeu', make impossible the serenity of detachment, of which Alain spoke in his portrait of La Fontaine (one of Chateaubriand's 'dieux'). Indeed, what Chateaubriand respects primarily in Montaigne would seem to be that detachment, that refusal to let the *quant à soy* be invaded by passion or the outside world. Like Montaigne he underlines the existence of one's *arrière-boutique*: "Chaque homme renferme en soi un monde à part étranger aux lois et aux destinées générales des siècles"[1], a thought expressed in rather grandiloquent terms no doubt, but in its essence similar to Montaigne's.

This independence, this refusal to betray oneself reveals itself in certain comments on his political activity. I doubt whether one should make too much of a comparison between their political ideas: it is true that they both show dislike and distrust of the populace in political matters, both reveal on occasion a sentimental nostalgia for some form of primitivism – one recalls that Chateaubriand quotes Montaigne when he describes the pantomime of Mila[2] – and broadly speaking, both were in favour of enlightened monarchy in which the individual's liberty is respected; on the other hand Chateaubriand was perhaps more ready to accept that change, even uncongenial change in the direction of democracy and republicanism, was bound to come, and sooner rather than later. Where the two come together is in their view of the attitude that the individual should adopt towards the prince and statesmen he happens to serve, for both had had much experience of politics and civil commitment. Chateaubriand manifests an innate dislike of Court life which he attributes to his regional heredity: he refers to the fact that "l'éloignement pour la cour était naturel à tout Breton".[3] Nevertheless, in the second phase, as he sees it, of his life, there emerges a political animal, and here it is not easy to determine to what extent

---

[1] *ibid.*, p. 519.

[2] *ibid.*, pp. 247–8. Marcellus writes in this context: "En vérifiant plus tard sa citation des Iroquois de Montaigne, M. de Chateaubriand y ajouta deux petits paragraphes qui n'ont point figuré dans le feuilleton de la *Presse*, mais qui se trouvent dans l'édition in-8°; le premier, pour rire avec l'auteur des *Essais* aux dépens des Européens porteurs de hauts-de-chausses; le second pour annoncer Mila, la naïve Indienne. Elle a fait en effet son apparition dans les 'Bigarrures de ma jeunesse', que couvre assez singulièrement ici le grand nom de saint Clément d'Alexandrie...", *op. cit.*, p. 61.
M.O. vol. I, p. 19.

his self-proclaimed detachment is genuine; he reiterates his lack
of involvement, the absence of ambition which he believes to be his:
"Mille choses sont survenues; un second homme s'est trouvé en
moi, l'homme politique: j'y suis fort peu attaché."[1] And again
"... je ne réussirai jamais dans le monde, précisément parce qu'il
me manque une passion et un vice, l'ambition et l'hypocrisie".[2]
He certainly felt that it was his duty, as an ambassador, to carry out
his duties without placing his private self under any obligation to
those he served in a public capacity, and moreover he did not feel
it his concern to colour the truth of any political situation, as he
saw it, in the way his despatches reported it. Marcellus tells us how
on one occasion Chateaubriand countered his secretary's reluctance
by quoting Montaigne extensively:

> Au reste, il aimait à toute dire dans ses dépêches; et sa franchise
> ne se déguisait sous aucune réticence. Un jour que je m'étonnais
> de la liberté de son langage, il alla chercher dans sa chambre à
> coucher le Montaigne que je lui avais prêté et qu'il lisait dans son
> lit. Puis, après m'avoir fait réciter tout haut le passage suivant:
> Voilà la règle, me dit-il, ne dissimulons rien; c'est notre droit,
> c'est notre devoir.[3]

A man should give himself to his principles, not to his rulers. At
other times, Montaigne comes to the mind of the political Chateaubriand, who cites the example of the essayist's ability to continue
writing in such troubled times like himself,[4] and who compares
himself to Montaigne in that he refused to be bound by the chains
of party or system and in consequence incurred the displeasure of
both parties: "Pélaudé à toutes mains aux Gibelins j'étais Guelfe,
aux Guelfes Gibelin."[5]

The frequency with which Montaigne produces the apt quotation
for Chateaubriand's circumstances and purposes makes one wonder
whether the author of the *Mémoires* owes much to the style of the
Essais, over and above the general example of *décousu* he claims to

---

[1] *M.O.*, p. 107.   [2] *ibid.*, p. 102.
[3] Marcellus, *op. cit.*, p. 272. The Montaigne passage begins: "J'ai trouvé bien
étrange qu'il feust en la puissance d'un ambassadeur de dispenser sur les
advertissements qu'il doibt faire a son maistre...".
[4] *M.O.*, vol. I, p. 181.
[5] *ibid.*, p. 302.

find them in. He may have learned something from Montaigne in the proper use of quotations; Marcellus tells us how highly Chateaubriand valued the art of quotation:

> ... je n'ignore pas qu'il aimait les citations et qu'il en pratiquait et vantait fréquemment la méthode. Sa conversation en abondait quant elle dépassait les monosyllabes ou les lieux communs de la politesse: Il ne faut pas croire, me disait-il à Londres, que l'art des citations soit à la portée de tous les petits esprits qui, ne trouvant rien chez eux, vont puiser chez les autres. C'est l'inspiration qui donne les citations heureuses.[1]

and he went on to remark that the authors of the seventeenth century had been particularly notable in their use of quotation. Nevertheless, Marcellus comes nearer our purpose further on:

> Il y a eu peu de mémoires plus riches que celle de M. de Chateaubriand en souvenirs des autres antiques... Même au déclin de l'âge, s'il oubliait parfois le nom de l'écrivain, il retrouvait fidèlement la pensée et l'expression que le moindre trait réveillait dans son esprit: et parmi les prosateurs qui l'avaient aidé à grossir ce trésor, il faut mettre en première ligne Montaigne et Tacite.[2]

Chateaubriand's use of quotation in the *Mémoires* is less extended than Montaigne's, but it is still considerable enough to count as a characteristic of his style. In some other ways, Montaigne may have left a discreet mark on Chateaubriand's writing: in the aphorism of the moralist commenting on human nature,[3] also in his choice of vocabulary. There are occasional archaisms (e.g. the use of *quand et* for *avec*), and certain terms recall an earlier stage of the language.[4] According to Marcellus, Chateaubriand had firm views on the proper use of the epithet, which he saw best illustrated in the authors of the seventeenth century,[5] but his secretary also comments on a

---

[1] Marcellus, *op. cit.*, p. 286.   [2] *ibid.*, p. 302.
[3] Hardly the monopoly of Montaigne, but Chateaubriand's turn of phrase is sometimes reminiscent, e.g. "Chez moi l'homme public est inébranlable, l'homme privé est à la merci de quiconque veut s'emparer de lui..." (*M.O.*, vol. I, p. 287).
[4] Chateaubriand twice refers approvingly to Montaigne's use of *vastité* to describe cathedrals (*M.O.*, vol. I, p. 355; vol. II, p. 243).
[5] Marcellus, *op. cit.*, p. 209.

phrase in which he sees an echo of the essayist ("Mon Gil Blas, grand, maigre, escalabreux"): "Cette insulte à la fortune et ce portrait de Pélissier, rédacteur de l'*Ambigu*, sont un reflet de Montaigne, qu'on reconnaît à tant de vieux mots rajeunis."[1] Chateaubriand regards Montaigne as a linguistic descendant of Rabelais, to whom he awards a high place in the development of French literature.[2]

In all this, one will see not so much a major influence on any particular aspect of the *Mémoires* as a diffuse presence. Montaigne remains for Chateaubriand a sort of travelling companion, sometimes a kindred spirit, as a *moraliste*, as an example of the *dignité d'homme*, and of course as one who had the gift of the right remark for the right occasion. So far as one can see, Montaigne's companionship appears to have been lifelong, but in the *Mémoires* he acquires a rather more privileged position, as one might expect when Chateaubriand was passing from traditional fiction to autobiography and when he had outgrown a relatively uncritical admiration for Rousseau. In some measure, Montaigne would seem to be an example of attitudes which Chateaubriand claims to value in his survey of experience – the *quant à soy*, the sense of dignity, a proper detachment, a rejection of system, a search for a truth to self. Of course, the *littérateur* in Montaigne has a strong appeal for the gourmet of language one detects in Chateaubriand, but he is not unique in this respect; and certain interferences such as Chateaubriand's self-conscious concern for posterity and his self-deceiving vanity limit Montaigne's impact, hence my use of the word presence rather than that of influence. Chateaubriand had a considerable contempt for the scribblers in literature and saw in their proliferation evidence of corruption; indeed he quotes Montaigne in support of his view:

> Il devroit y avoir coertion des lois contre les escrivains ineptes et inutiles, comme il y [en] a contre les vagabonds et fainéants. On banniroit des mains de nostre peuple et moy et cent autres. L'escrivaillerie semble être quelque symptôme d'un siècle desbordé.[3]

[1] Marcellus, *op. cit.*, pp. 97–8.
[2] *M.O.*, vol. I, p. 408.
[3] *ibid.*, p. 411.

Somewhere, Chateaubriand remarks that "des auteurs français de ma date, je suis quasi le seul qui ressemble à ses ouvrages",[1] and he undoubtedly felt that there was a danger in the man of letters living at too great a distance from reality. When he made this hopeful statement about his own achievement, I wonder whether he was not in some measure affected by the presence of Montaigne in whom surely he sensed the right relationship between life and letters.

[1] *ibid.*, vol. II, p. 835. One final point: the two meet occasionally on the theme of death; both stress the significance of death in completing the pattern and meaning of life. In Chateaubriand, inevitably, the subject is coloured by a host of Romantic associations, but he does once quote Montaigne in this context, when reflecting on the utility or otherwise of travel:

> *Si je suis moult allé en bois, comme font volontiers les François*, je n'ai, cependant, jamais aimé le changement pour le changement; la route m'ennuie; j'aime seulement le voyage à cause de l'indépendance qu'il me donne, comme j'incline vers la campagne, non pour la campagne, mais pour la solitude. "Tout ciel m'est un, dit Montaigne, vivons entre les nôtres, allons mourir et rechigner entre les inconnus" (*M.O.*, vol. I, pp. 621–2).

From Correggio to class warfare: notes on Stendhal's ideal of 'la grâce'

RICHARD N. COE

ONE of the most characteristic (and, to the purist, one of the most infuriating) features of Stendhal's critical writing – particularly in his works on painting and on music – is his tendency to use certain technical or semi-technical terms, not only in an imprecise or patently incorrect fashion,[1] but often with a careless and nonchalant disdain for the normal boundaries of the subject he is discussing. What starts out as an innocuous term relating, say, to harmony, or to architectural form is often so overloaded with a whole range of social, moral, emotional or political implications, that the border-line between aesthetic judgment, ethical comment, ideological specu-lation and personal reminiscence is totally blurred. Outside his own professional field of literature, what interests him is seldom technique in its own right, but rather what Philippe Berthier, in his admirable analysis of the use of the term *chiaroscuro*, has called "le retentissement moral de la technique".[2] One such term is 'la grâce'.[3]

Stendhal uses the term constantly, in every sense and in almost every context, ranging from its simplest social connotation ("les grâces de la conversation"[4]), by way of significant character-assess-ment ("la grâce naïve de Fabrice"), to penetrating aesthetic com-ments which themselves will be the starting-point for far-reaching

---

[1] For instance, using the verb 'syncoper' in a sense which is appropriate to gram-mar, but impossible in music: 'to abbreviate a word or a construction'. (*Vie de Rossini*, ed. H. Prunières (Geneva, 1968), vol. I, p. 48.)

[2] Philippe Berthier, 'Stendhal et le clair-obscur', *Omaggio a Stendhal II: Aurea Parma* (1967), pp. 158–174.

[3] This essay is based primarily on Stendhal's critical writings 1801–26. It does not attempt to evaluate Stendhal's use of the term 'la grâce' in the context of seventeenth- and eighteenth-century aesthetics. In the substantially different version of the present study in the *Actes du 7ᵉ Congrès International Stendhalien de Tours*, such an evaluation has been attempted.

[4] In Stendhal's use of the term, there is no significant distinction maintained between 'la grâce' and 'les grâces'.

philosophical developments. The artists to whom the term is most
frequently applied are, in painting, Correggio (with Raphael as
runner-up); in sculpture, Canova; in music, Paisiello and, more
rarely, Cimarosa and Mozart; in the drama, Metastasio; and in prose
La Fontaine – the La Fontaine of *Les Amours de Psyché*. The concept is by no means always flattering: it is sometimes taken to
signify facility (as when applied to Sacchini), sometimes weakness;
it can mean effeminacy, or it can imply insipidity.[1] 'La grâce' can
be abused or misplaced, even by the greatest artists – for instance,
by Canova in his bust of Pope Pius VII;[2] and there is a constant
danger that it may serve simply to disguise a basically mediocre
capacity for emotional intensity.[3] Moreover, if Stendhal is always
careful to distinguish it from 'le gentil' and 'le joli' (Boucher is
"joli", whereas Correggio is "gracieux"), he does not always differentiate between 'la grâce' and elegance. Yet there are passages
where it appears to form an integral part of 'le sublime'[4] – a concept
which would have been totally foreign to aesthetic thinkers of an
earlier generation – and, more specifically, it plays an essential role
in Stendhal's famous formulation of "le beau idéal moderne".

Stendhal's second heading in his list of elements which contribute
to this "beau idéal moderne" is simply: "Beaucoup de grâces dans
les traits".[5] In the *Histoire de la peinture en Italie*, where this
definition is given, and where the contrast between "le beau idéal
antique" and its modern equivalent is worked out in detail, there
is no further attempt to analyse the exact significance of this blanket-
phrase: "beaucoup de grâces"; for once, however, this is not due to
Stendhal's deliberate vagueness, but to the fact that he had already
given his analysis at some considerable length in the *Première
lettre sur Métastase* – an important essay which had appeared in his
first published work, the *Vies de Haydn, Mozart et Métastase*
(1814/15), and which had in fact been composed at the same time
as much of the *Histoire de la peinture*.

---

[1] *Vie de Rossini*, vol. I, p. 238.
[2] *Salon de 1824*: in *Mélanges d'Art*, ed. H. Martineau (Paris, 1932), p. 131.
[3] *Vies de Haydn, de Mozart et de Métastase*, ed. H. Martineau (Paris, 1928), pp.
   217–18.
[4] "La grâce sublime [céleste] du Corrège" – the phrase is constantly reiterated.
[5] *Histoire de la peinture en Italie*, ed. P. Arbelet, (Geneva, 1969), vol. II, p. 117. In
   view of the arguments used later in this essay, it is perhaps worth noting two
   other headings "4. Beaucoup de gaieté. 5. Un fonds de sensibilité."

"Le commun des hommes méprise facilement la grâce"[1] begins Stendhal's apologia for the Italian poet-librettist, thus, from the very outset, equating 'la grâce' with the sensibilities of the Happy Few. 'La grâce' inspires no element of fear: it characterizes what is essentially a highly sophisticated and comparatively modern conception of art, not as a necessity, nor even as a utility (psychological, social or religious), but as a wholly superfluous luxury, whose first and perhaps only purpose, therefore, is to give pleasure, beginning with straightforward physical pleasure: 'la volupté'. It is not serious, if by serious we mean tragic: the limit of seriousness to which it can aspire is 'le pathétique' – as perfectly illustrated by the sort of emotions and situations exploited by Metastasio himself in his own libretti. It is the product of an artist who is completely master of his own medium; no sign of effort may betray itself, every line, note or brush-stroke must display a kind of nonchalant ease. If there is one factor which is destined infallibly to extinguish 'la grâce', it is "l'apparence de la difficulté vaincue".

Furthermore, if it can be said that 'la grâce' is the hallmark of a broad and general style in the arts, it is of a style or manner which is slightly feminine; and its appeal is less to men than to women ("moins courbées que les hommes sous le joug habituel des calculs d'intérêt"). In so far as the traditional concept of beauty ("le beau antique") implies a certain strength, 'la grâce' may not immediately be recognizable as beauty: it is not *striking* – Correggio, to the unpractised eye, is less striking than Titian. Above all, it embodies a certain virtue of passivity, almost of negativity: it is concerned not to give pain, not to offend, not to prick the bubbles of vanity, not to cause even too much mental activity. "[Métastase] semble dire aux spectateurs: 'Jouissez, votre attention même n'aura pas la moindre peine,'"–the reader, the listener, is to be *lulled* into pleasure; his intellectual co-operation is uninvited and unnecessary. He is to be consoled: the principal feelings evoked in him will be 'la tendresse' and 'le soulagement'. 'La grâce' is the expression of an attitude which is fundamentally optimistic; and its consequent weakness lies in its tendency to gravitate towards rose-coloured abstractions, far removed from all the petty, odious and disturbing realities of life.

---

[1] *Vies de Haydn...*, p. 333. All quotations in this paragraph and the following are taken from the *Vies*, pp. 333–40.

It has no use for details, it eschews "le petit fait vrai". It is all too liable to stylize its passions into broad and acceptable clichés – and yet, for all that, it is a high art-form, one of the highest in the modern world. It is the domain embellished, not so much by Raphael's madonnas, as by his arabesques in the Loggias of the Vatican, "ces amours à cheval sur des chimères". In a word, it is supremely decorative, the product of a world where (for some classes at least) there is economic security and there is leisure; a world which demands of its artists nothing more useful than the opium of pleasant dreams... "et jamais de dénouement malheureux".

In spite of its apparent comprehensiveness and its serious attempt at objective assessment, however, one has the feeling that this analysis somehow manages to miss the point. It never goes beneath the surface: it explains what 'la grâce' is, it does not make any effort to suggest *why* it is significant, still less why it is essential, either to nineteenth-century art, or to Stendhal himself.

Perhaps the best way to search out the underlying implications of 'la grâce' is to look for its opposite – to note the concepts which are set against it, to which it serves as contrast. In those passages of the *Histoire de la peinture* where "le beau idéal moderne" is contrasted with "le beau idéal antique", the corresponding concepts which contrast with 'la grâce' are those of 'la force' and 'l'énergie'. In the Metastasio definitions, the same notion is present, although formulated in broader terms: "le vulgaire n'estime que ce qu'il craint un peu".[1] In the context of Stendhal's thought as a whole, however, these concepts 'force', 'énergie', 'crainte', etc., appear as simple, particular manifestations of a very much more general preoccupation: a preoccupation with 'le sérieux'. From the *Filosofia nova* to *La Chartreuse* and *Lamiel*, this resentment of, and rebellion against 'le sérieux' represents one of the most persistent and obsessive motifs in Stendhal's thought; and the multiform ideal of 'la grâce', evolving in subtlety and in complexity from work to work accurately reflects at every stage the repugnance he feels for each new manifestation of 'le sérieux' which forces itself on to his attention. 'La grâce', from the outset, is the ideal which he sets up

[1] *Vies de Haydn...*, Stendhal is fond of this idea, and uses it on several occasions. In *De l'Amour*, he reverses it: "Je ne crains que ce que j'estime."

in opposition to his century: but in the end, it is something more also. It is the symbol of that vision which allowed him to realize his own fundamental seriousness as an artist without succumbing to the menace of 'le sérieux' as he felt and as he feared it.

More, perhaps, than any other writer of his generation, Stendhal had an intimation of that Great Victorian Seriousness (or of its Second-Empire and Wilhelmine equivalents) which was to descend like a great stifling eiderdown upon the arts and manners of Europe in the 1840s, and which was to reign supreme until the rebellion of the 1890s and the dawning of a new spirit of frivolity in the Belle Époque. The French Revolution had begun the whole thing by letting loose a great wave of Republican sincerity and high-mindedness, extinguishing for ever, as it hoped, the 'frivolity' of manners and morals that had prevailed under the old monarchies. The ideal was noble: but as time went by, it became apparent that the middle years of the nineteenth century were destined to inherit the worst of both worlds, wallowing in the solemnity of the newer, puritanical tradition, while at the same time maintaining and even emphasizing the inequalities, injustices and class-distinctions of the older way of life. Stendhal, with a sensibility deeply rooted in the culture of the eighteenth century, yet living out his experiences in the post-Revolutionary atmosphere of the nineteenth, irremediably divided within himself between his nostalgia for the older values of sophisticated dilettantism and his slightly puzzled and resentful admiration for the current emphasis on dedicated earnestness – Stendhal was acutely aware that an essential part of what was for him the beauty of the world was threatened with extinction; and his reaction was to rush to the defence of what he loved. Sometimes this defence was to take the form of a kind of aggressive petulance, as in the *Nouveau complot contre les industriels*; sometimes that of a retreat into fantasy, as in *La Chartreuse*; sometimes that of historical debate and rational analysis. But at all times the symbol, social, intellectual and aesthetic, of the values that he was defending against the dark flood of 'le sérieux' which threatened to engulf them, was 'la grâce'.

There is no doubt but that the revolution in sensibility which was to lead eventually to the dictatorship of the Great Victorian Seriousness in the nineteenth century was the direct consequence of major social and political upheavals in the state of Europe; and so the concept of 'la grâce' is likewise inseparable from its political and social context. Stendhal himself was perfectly well aware of this. His aesthetic writings are filled with political, social and historical analyses of the events of the preceding half-century, constantly returning to the theme of that "effroyable changement" which had transformed a gracious and supremely civilized style of living, whose very frivolity was the symbol of its sophistication, into an 'odious' society of money-grubbing and puritanical hypocrites. "Le parleur grossier qui, avec son accent de province, traite de la question des *capacités*", had replaced the glittering conversationalists of the salons of Madame Geoffrin and of Mademoiselle de Lespinasse; the tradition of French gaiety had evaporated, and the dismal march of events "nous a rapprochés du peuple le plus triste de la terre",[1] he noted in 1821–2, shortly after his return from Milan. Which government since 1780, he enquired with studied naïveté, "nous a valu l'affreux malheur de nous *angliser?*"; and he replied (on this occasion, at least) with the satirical paradox, that it could only have been the restored Monarchy under Louis XVIII, since all the others had too much energy, while even the solemnity of the Napoleonic epoch was redeemed by "les grâces de Madame Bonaparte".[2] As early as 1804 he had noted in the *Filosofia nova* that "nous nous sommes rapprochés des républicains", arguing further that "la *politesse* est un fruit nécessaire de l'égoïsme, qui lui-même vient d'un gouvernement monarchique", and concluding with admirably ingenuous logic that, since laughter is based on egoism, "donc la comédie est fille de la monarchie".[3] It was an identical analysis of historical events which was to lead him to formulate his theory of 'le romanticisme' as literature designed for a contemporary (and entirely non-frivolous) public: "Je prétends qu'il faut désormais faire des tragédies pour nous, *jeunes gens raisonneurs, sérieux et un peu envieux.*"[4] And in music too, it was the same view of a sociologically-based revolution in sensibility which he used to explain how the 'gracious' Italian melody of a Paisiello had gradually come

[1] *De l'Amour*, ed. D. Muller and P. Jourda (Geneva, no date), vol. I, pp. 8–9.
[2] *ibid.*, pp. 9–10.
[3] *Filosofia nova*, ed. H. Martineau (Paris, Le Divan, 1931), vol. I, p. 271.
[4] *Racine et Shakespeare I*. In *Stendhal: Racine et Shakespeare*, ed. B. Drenner (Paris, 1965), p. 25. My italics.

to be ousted in the public favour by the 'severe' Germanic harmony of a Simone Mayr.[1]

It is, in fact, in the *Vie de Rossini* that the most detailed account of this revolution is to be found.[2] Here, the analysis is at once more optimistic than in many other passages dealing with the same theme, and more complex. It is more optimistic because now Stendhal senses, perhaps for the first time, that the great bourgeois serious-ness of the politicians, the *industriels* and the *congrégations* may at the same time prove fertile soil for the ripening of a new Romantic seriousness, bred out of solitude and sincerity: "Toutes les fois que l'on trouve *solitude* et *imagination* dans un coin du monde, l'on ne tarde guère à y voir paraître le goût pour la musique."[3] But it is more complex, because Stendhal was realizing that the division of art and society into an epoch of pre-Revolutionary *grâce* and an epoch of post-Revolutionary *sérieux* was by no means as clear-cut as he had assumed, but rather represented an intricate series of stratifications. Not only were there two rival and incompatible groups of *esprits sérieux* who were destined to dominate the future: the utilitarian, money-making, Jeremy-Bentham-reading *indus-triels* and the serious-minded, saturnine young men, the "étudiants en droit et en médecine"[4] who constituted the potential Romantic generation; but there was also an intermediate generation, born like Stendhal himself in the early 1780s — the nouveaux-riches of the Napoleonic epoch, who combined a 'modern' seriousness about money with an 'aristocratic' frivolousness about the arts. Such people "portaient de la poudre", they admired Cicero, they were "abonnés à la *Quotidienne*"[5]... they were in fact the "Libéraux", who were at one and the same time the most ardent advocates of bicameral government (Stendhal's own utopian panacea for all politi-cal evils), and the implacable, last-ditch defenders of classical tragedy.

---

[1] *Vie de Rossini*, vol. I, pp. 154, 164, 170, 184, etc.
[2] *ibid.*, pp. 265–9.
[3] *ibid.*, p. 269.
[4] "*Jeunesse de 1822*. Qui dit penchant sérieux, disposition active, dit sacrifice du présent à l'avenir; rien n'élève l'âme comme le pouvoir et l'habitude de faire de tels sacrifices. Je vois plus de probabilité pour les grandes passions en 1832 qu'en 1772." – *De l'Amour*, vol. II, pp. 148–9 ('Fragments Divers', No. XXIII). In 1825, Stendhal began an address to these same "étudiants", but completed only a fragment (*Mélanges de Politique et d'Histoire*, ed. H. Martineau (Paris, Le Divan, 1933, pp. 193–8).
[5] *Vie de Rossini*, vol. I, p. 263.

R

If 'la grâce' then, emerges as the symbol of something that is endangered, if indeed it has not been already destroyed, by the great social revolution with which the nineteenth century opened, it is also part and parcel of Stendhal's own attitude towards *class*.

In spite of the notorious passage which he wrote in *Rome, Naples et Florence* in praise of convicts ("Ils ont la grande qualité qui manque à leurs concitoyens, la *force de caractère*"[1]), and in spite of one or two unforgettable portraits of working-class characters ("la Vivandière" in *la Chartreuse de Parme*[2]), Stendhal was anything but a total democrat. His sympathy for the workers was abstract, remote and very limited in range. His 'liberalism' tended much more towards government by an enlightened aristocratic oligarchy with middle-class participation than towards a proletarian, or even an 'American-style', middle-class republic. But here again, politics and aesthetics are inextricably interwoven: and while it is possible to argue that Stendhal's preference for 'la grâce' is motivated by its association with an aristocracy, it is equally valid to reverse the argument, and maintain that his political and social 'ducomanie' was rooted in his aesthetic appreciation of the *grâces* which the upper classes alone had the time, money and education to cultivate.

At all events, Stendhal's attitude to class is many-sided, and deserves a fuller study than is possible here. Even his use of the word shifts in meaning, depending on whether he is considering French or English social conditions. Discussing France, he tends still to use it in an older sense – the sense in which Diderot employed the term "les conditions" – meaning the professional rather than the economic categories of society. "Le gouvernement de la Charte", he observes, "sépare les diverses classes de citoyens par la haine"; later in the same passage, however, he satirically twists his use of the word to mean: "la *classe* des avocats, la *classe* des médecins, la *classe* des compositeurs de musique qui maudissent Rossini, la *classe* des vendeurs de croix et des opticiens qui en achètent."[3] But during the period 1817–21 in particular, he seems to have followed the evolution of social conflict in England with very close attention –

---

[1] *Rome, Naples et Florence*, ed. D. Muller, (Geneva, [1968]), vol. I, p. 161.
[2] See Tatiana Kotchetkova: 'A propos du "Chapitre de la Vivandière" de la *Chartreuse de Parme*', *Omaggio a Stendhal II. Aurea Parma* (1967), pp. 79–85.
[3] *Racine et Shakespeare II*, (see n. 4, p. 244), pp. 145–7 notes.

probably through the press, for in spite of his assertions, there is no real evidence that he ever visited Birmingham, Liverpool or Manchester before 1826 — and to have deduced from what he saw a concept of class conflict which is very much closer to the modern or Marxist variety.

Those years in England, it is to be recalled, were filled with the great depression after the Napoleonic Wars, whose influence blighted the whole social structure of early industrialism: it was the period of the Spa Fields rioting (2 and 9 December 1816), the Cato Street conspiracy and Peterloo — and here and there a fleeting reference, an inconspicuous footnote or jotting, betrays the eagerness with which he was following the course of events across the Channel. One such note at least reveals the fact that he had been reading reports of the trial of Watson and Thistlewood;[1] and this simple fact sheds a remarkable degree of light on his more familiar strictures on England as "un pays gouverné par des fous, au seul profit du petit nombre"[2] and as the seat of "la guerre à mort des riches contre les pauvres".[3]

Stendhal's comments on the early phases of the class struggle in England show at least this: that he was clearly aware of the implications of 'class' in the modern sense,[4] and quite realistic about his own position and his own attitudes. Consequently, his identification of 'la grâce' as the social, intellectual and emotional prerogative of the higher class-ranges in the social structure is strikingly significant. The fact that he refuses to recognize the inevitability of any class-distinction based exclusively on income[5] is irrelevant: 'la grâce' itself *is* a class-distinction. 'La grâce' is the product of education, leisure and sophistication, which in their turn are the consequences of possessing at least an ideal minimum income: "6.000 francs de

---

[1] *Rome, Naples et Florence en 1817 suivi de l'Italie en 1818*, ed. H. Martineau (Paris, Le Divan, 1956), p. 218. Dr James Watson (the elder) and Arthur Thistlewood, organizers and leaders of the Spa Fields meetings, are now accorded a significant place in the history of the British working-class movement. See E. P. Thompson, *The Making of the English Working Class* (1964), esp. pp. 632–6.

[2] *De l'Amour*, vol. II, p. 10.

[3] *ibid.*, p. 14.

[4] In *De l'Amour*, Stendhal tends to prefer the word *caste*, when he is specifically discussing England.

[5] "[A Milan] un homme qui vit avec quinze cents francs de rente parle à un homme qui a six millions, simplement et comme il parlerait à un égal (ceci passera pour incroyable en Angleterre)" – *Rome, Naples et Florence*, vol. I, p. 156.

rente".[1] His sensibility is penetrated through and through with values that, under eighteenth- and nineteenth-century social and educational conditions, could only be associated with a leisured aristocracy or upper middle class. Perhaps, if this had not been so, he would no longer have prized them: for after all, the very first definition of 'la grâce' was that it was the prerogative of the Happy Few. "Le banquier R*** me dit un jour: 'Je vois chez vous un élément aristocratique'," he recounts in *Rome, Naples et Florence*. "J'aurais juré d'en être à mille lieues. Je me suis en effet trouvé cette maladie."[2] As early as 1803 he was admonishing himself: "Ne pas prêter à des gens d'une classe des idées qu'on n'a que dans une autre classe. Les gens du peuple parlent-ils souvent du bonheur comme nous l'entendons?"[3] – and in *Des beaux-arts et du caractère français* he works out the same theme in an important variation which will later form the basis of an episode in *La Chartreuse*:[4] namely, the intimate relationship between class, clothes (as opposed to the nude, which is essential to "le beau antique"), love... and 'la grâce':

> Si la grâce dans la manière de porter les vêtements est pour nous une partie essentielle de la beauté, c'est que pour aimer nous avons besoin d'être compris de l'objet de nos vœux. Une jeune paysanne peut être plus belle que la Vénus de Canova; nous l'admirerons, mais si nous désirons l'amour, c'est celui d'une femme appartenant à la même classe de la société que nous.[5]

'La grâce' then, is at bottom the aesthetic reflection of Stendhal's deep-rooted involvement in the social and moral qualities of an idealized aristocracy. The "grâce naïve, inimitable" that he admires so intensely in Correggio, in Cimarosa, above all in Paisiello[6] – the same "grâce naïve" which, later, will characterize every gesture and every expression of Fabrice – is rarely an attribute of unvarnished nature. It is the sophisticated simplicity of a rich man: a work

---

[1] *De l'Amour*, vol. II, p. 161 ('Fragments Divers', No. LXI). Baudelaire approved of this idea, and quoted it in *L'Œuvre et la vie de Delacroix*.

[2] *Rome, Naples et Florence*, vol. I, p. 370.

[3] *Filosofia nova* (see n. 3, p. 244), vol. I, pp. 89–90.

[4] The contrast which is drawn between Fabrice's attitudes in love towards la Sanseverina and towards la petite Mariette.

[5] *Mélanges d'Art*, p. 164.

[6] See *Vie de Rossini*, vol. I, pp, 7–8, 233, 239, etc.

of art in itself. Equally clearly, this social-moral ideal is reflected in another aspect of 'la grâce': its lack of detail, its unpedantic carelessness, its studied negligence. In Stendhal's social-ethical code, 'la négligence' is equated with generosity, whose diametrical opposite, in the realm of *le grand Sérieux*, among the party-politicians and the industrial bourgeoisie, is 'la prudence'. But this careless, effortless nonchalance is again a virtue associated with an aristocracy: it is the contemptuous gesture of Don Juan giving his golden *louis* to the poor man "pour l'amour de l'humanité": it is not to be found in the prudent calculations of M. Grandet.

In art, an identical principle is developed. "Quelques négligences apparentes ajoutent à la grâce," observes Stendhal, thinking of Correggio: the 'prudent' painters of Florence "se les fussent reprochées comme des crimes".[1] In the footnote attached to this passage, he is even more explicit, as he is again in the *Vie de Rossini*: "Ce qui distingue le grand maître, c'est la hardiesse du trait, la négligence des détails, le grandiose de la touche... J'aime mieux une ébauche du Corrège, qu'un grand tableau fort soigné de Charles Lebrun."[2]

The importance of this aspect of 'la grâce' cannot be overstated. It is by the miracle of its 'négligences' that simple elegance merges with the Sublime; for it is precisely these same 'négligences' which leave room for the spectator's imagination to fill in what the artist has left unsaid. The soul is involved, where hitherto only the senses had been stirred; the soul 'embroiders' on the half-sketched canvas that the artist has provided, fills in the spaces in Ghirlandaio's "perspectives aériennes",[3] weaves patterns of "tristesse regrettante" about an aria by Zingarelli, holds conversations with Raphael's madonnas. For Stendhal, this is the celestial and perennial wonder of great art:

Parlerai-je de la *beauté*? Dirai-je qu'il en est, dans les arts, de la sublime beauté comme des beautés mortelles... A la faveur d'une parure ni trop flottante ni trop serrée, montrant beaucoup de

[1] *Histoire de la peinture*, vol. I, p. 161 and footnote.
[2] *Vie de Rossini*, vol. I, p. 228.
[3] See the author's 'Quelques réflexions sur Stendhal paysagiste', Sixième Journée du Stendhal Club (Lausanne, 1965), pp. 35–48.

leurs attraits, en laissant deviner bien davantage, elles ne sont
que plus séduisantes aux yeux du connaisseur...

– and, after the words "sublime beauté", Stendhal adds a footnote:
"Les négligences du Corrège."[1]

This aristocratic 'négligence' (described elsewhere as the gesture
of "l'homme riche et heureux qui jette un louis à une petite paysanne en échange d'un bouquet de roses"[2]) is not only, for Stendhal,
the hallmark of perfection; it leads him, as a critic, towards the
appreciation of a more 'open-ended' art than was usually thought
well of in the nineteenth century; and it may go a long way to
account for the characteristic 'négligences' of his own style.

To return, however, to the central theme of this study. Clearly,
the most immediately effective attribute of 'la grâce', considered as a
weapon to wield against the menace of *le grand sérieux*, is its gaiety:
its lightness of touch, the "grâces courtisanesques" of its choreo-
graphy, its refusal of all that is austere or pedantic or solemn or
puritanical, its "esprit... qui ajoute tant de grâce à la sensibilité, en
faisant qu'elle ne s'exerce que sur les sujets dignes d'intéresser".[3]
It is the splendid *grâce* of the *opera buffa* – its fusion of sublime
melodies "sur lesquelles l'imagination peut broder" with outrageous
comedy, which makes it "l'œuvre, jusqu'ici, où l'homme s'est le
plus rapproché de la perfection".[4]

But gaiety is *not* a nineteenth-century democratic quality. The
sérieux of politics, of elections "et les *peurs* qu'elles causent",[5] the
"farce lugubre" of "le passeport et l'attirail (*contre-*) révolution-
naire",[6] the "haine impuissante" ("cette fatale maladie du dix-
neuvième siècle") of party warfare "qui ne vous laisse plus assez de
gaieté pour rire de quoi que ce soit",[7] the guilt-feelings and the
cant, the lies and the hypocrisies – all this grows progressively more
nauseating to Stendhal as the years of the Restoration roll by. "En
1770, qui était payé pour mentir, en France?" he protests in *Rome,*

---

[1] *Histoire de la peinture*, vol. I, p. 49 and footnote.
[2] *Vie de Rossini*, vol. I, p. 135.
[3] *Salon de 1842. Mélanges d'Art*, p. 59.
[4] *Vie de Rossini*, vol. I, p. 64.
[5] *Rome, Naples et Florence*, I, p. 161, Cf. *Lucien Leuwen, passim.*
[6] *Racine et Shakespeare II* (see n. 4, p. 244), p. 194.
[7] *ibid.*, p. 135.

Naples et Florence. "Aussi était-on gai";[1] and in the *Vie de Rossini*, the cry reaches almost the pitch of despair: "On dirait que le rire est prohibé en France!"[2] And not only in France, but seemingly in every country in the world except Italy. As the old monarchies were gradually vanquished by the new democracies, so laughter was doomed to vanish, and art with it. What country had produced less art than the United States? The only government under which the arts and laughter could truly flourish was "un despotisme sans échafauds trop fréquents".[3]

Stendhal, then, set out in life with a compelling mission to recapture something of the lost gaiety of a bygone, non-democratic age: not the coarse, Rabelaisian guffaw, but the monarchical and distinguished laughter which consists in the ability "de plaisanter avec grâce sur tous les sujets".[4] For is not laughter itself an anti-democratic quality? It clearly is, at least in Hobbes' definition, which Stendhal accepts, for what is it but "le sentiment soudain de notre *supériorité sur autrui*"?[5] Hence his long-lasting ambition to be a new Molière; hence also the failrue of that ambition. Many reasons have been put forwrad to explain Stendhal's impotence as a comic dramatist, and yet there is scarcely any need to look beyond his own jottings for the year 1804. For comedy in the post-Molière tradition (and Stendhal could conceive of no other) meant dwelling on the ridicules and vices of characters in society. To achieve the sharp, staccato ring of pure laughter, it was necessary to plunge headlong into the filthy, odious and absurd realities of human nature. The poet's passion for the sublime came into violent conflict with the *bassesses* of nineteenth-century nastiness: "J'ai pu m'enthousiasmer pour les beaux caractères et les belles passions que j'ai vus jusqu'ici. Il n'est pas étonnant que je ne m'échauffe point pour les caractères essentiellement bas qu'il faut que j'étudie."[6] – and a few pages later he added significantly: "C'est l'amour de la gloire seul, qui peut me pousser à cette dissection repoussante."[7]

---

[1] *Rome, Naples et Florence*, vol. I, p. 250, footnote.
[2] *Vie de Rossini*, vol. I, p. 328.
[3] *Racine et Shakespeare II*, p. 146, footnote.
[4] *Histoire de la peinture*, vol. II, p. 323.
[5] *Filosofia nova*, vol. I, p. 306 and *passim. Racine et Shakespeare I*, p. 48.
[6] *ibid.*, vol. II, p. 102.
[7] *ibid.*, p. 217.

This was the paradox which not only made it inevitable that, in the end, Stendhal should abandon comedy, but which, eventually, impelled him to formulate his theory of 'la grâce'.

It was evident that a compromise was necessary. If 'le sérieux' could only be held in check by gaiety, but if, in the attempt to produce laughter, all that was sublime in Stendhal's soul was obliterated by the vulgarity of his subject-matter, then the cure was worse than the disease. What was required was a form or mood which, while still effective as an antidote to 'le sérieux', none the less managed to avoid the 'odieux' of comedy and the vulgarity of out-right laughter. This could only be a form of art which inspired, not 'le rire' but something having the character of 'la grâce': 'le sourire'. "Le poète comique me présente un jeune homme sem-blable à moi, qui par l'excès de ses bonnes qualités devient malheu-reux et qui par ces mêmes qualités devient heureux; *cela, me procurant la vue du bonheur, m'intéresse et me fait sourire.*"[1]

The passage I have italicized in this last quotation (which dates from 1804) contains the fundamental modification which Stendhal brings to the seventeenth-century conception of 'la grâce'. It is an idea which he will spend the rest of his life developing (cf. the famous dictum: "La beauté est une promesse de bonheur."). With-out it, he could probably never have become the writer we know.

The fatal weakness of traditional comedy, so Stendhal argues, is not only that it necessitates too close a contact with 'odious' reality, but also that, in order to make us laugh, it must appeal first and foremost to our vanity. But vanity and true sensibility are incom-patible. An appeal to vanity automatically excludes an appeal to sensibility. Only when the appeal to vanity is made secondary to the invitation to sensibility (i.e., when we *identify* ourselves with the hero instead of feeling superior to him), and only when the hero's misfortunes and misadventures spring from the "excès de ses bonnes qualités", instead of from his vulgarities and vices, will it be possible to conceive of a comedy which can dispel the gloom of 'le sérieux' without sacrificing every element of sublime emotion in the process. But, taking 'la grâce' to signify what Stendhal determined it to signify in his analysis of Metastasio, this new comedy will be, in a precise sense, "une comédie gracieuse". And

[1] *Filosofia nova*, vol. II, p. 267. (My italics.)

perhaps also "un roman gracieux" – for Stendhal's definition of the "jeune homme semblable à moi" who, "par l'excès de ses bonnes qualités devient malheureux..." etc., is a far more apt description of Lucien Leuwen, of Fabrice del Dongo and even of Julien Sorel than it is of Fabre d'Eglantine's *Philinte*, that mediocre and sentimental comedy that Stendhal had in mind when formulating his definition.

And from the discovery of a type of comedy which could embrace sensibility to the discovery of a type of emotion which could be profoundly serious without being *sérieux*, was but the shortest of steps. Paisiello and Cimarosa led directly to Mozart: the common element was 'la grâce'. To the "haine impuissante" of the Great Political Seriousness, Stendhal opposed the "tristesse regrettante" of his own romantic musings: to the *sérieux* of the *industriels* he replied with the monarchic, the aristocratic, the gracious *mélancolie* of *Don Giovanni*. With the discovery, during his sojourn in Italy and particularly during the years 1818–21, of the magic and mystery of 'la mélancolie', Stendhal brought his argument, as first adumbrated in the *Filosofia nova*, full circle. For if, from the outset, it was his primary objective, both as an artist and as a man, to defy the dreary menace of *le grand sérieux*, by the end he had discovered, by broadening and deepening his concept of 'la grâce', a way of expressing his own basic seriousness without fear that, by doing so, he might be contributing to those very same forces of cant, pedantry and pedestrianism that he so much detested. 'La mélancolie' was seriousness softened, redeemed and sublimated by 'la grâce'. It was to be found in the "grâce naïve" of those "chants majestueux, mélancoliques et rarement passionnés" which so deeply moved him listening to Rossini's *La Donna del Lago*,[1] no less than it was to be discovered in "la grâce et la mélancolie touchante" that emanated from Raphael's madonnas;[2] it was in the "sensation de grâce pure" which he could experience in Shakespeare's Imogen[3] and it dwelt perhaps most of all in Mozart's Doña Anna, who was "comme une maîtresse sérieuse et souvent triste, mais qu'on aime davantage, précisément à cause de sa tristesse".[4] It was Italy, it was love in Italy, it was love itself.

---

[1] *Vie de Rossini (Notes d'un Dilettante)*, vol. II, p. 290.
[2] *Histoire de la peinture*, vol. I, p. 240.   [3] *ibid.*, vol. II, p. 84, footnote.
[4] *Vie de Rossini*, vol. I, p. 46.

And so, in the last years of his life, we find Stendhal working out, in some of the finest of his novels, this underlying theme of 'la grâce', and exploring through his imagination the implications of some of the social, moral and political problems which we have discussed. For what is M. Leuwen *père* but an *industriel* trying to temper the prevailing *sérieux* of his class and age with the gay and elegantly frivolous graces of the courtier? And what is Fabrice but a *grand seigneur* who discovers how to be gracefully serious and gracefully melancholic, without for one instant sacrificing the most significant of his virtues: his inbred, elegant, courtier-like frivolity?

Le 'Dieu' de Lamartine
en 1820

J. B. BARRÈRE

> La foi se réveillant, comme un doux souvenir...
> – *Méditations poétiques*, XIV

Au seuil des *Méditations poétiques*, il ne faut pas manquer de lire attentivement l'*Avertissement de l'éditeur*. Il est d'autant plus intéressant qu'il est rédigé par Eugène Genoude, le traducteur de Job et le correspondant à Paris de Lamartine, "le premier, – dira ce dernier – qui ait vraiment fait passer dans la langue française la sublime poésie des Hébreux." Or donc, compétent en la matière, ce rédacteur bénévole signalait "la teinte originale et religieuse de cette poésie": "... Il y a au fond de l'âme humaine un besoin imprescriptible d'échapper aux tristes réalités de ce monde, et de s'élancer dans les régions supérieures de la poésie et de la religion." Il est superflu de faire remarquer que ces deux mots forment une *hendiadys* équivalant à *la poésie sacrée*, le titre même de la Méditation que Lamartine dédiera à Genoude. Sans doute était-ce là un habile moyen d'attirer l'attention des lecteurs sur une inspiration mise à la mode par *le Génie du Christianisme*. Elle attendait encore son chantre. Lamartine ne faisait pas mystère d'avoir calculé de l'être. Sur les deux douzaines de poèmes qui forment le recueil original, la moitié au moins s'orne de titres religieux[1] (ou traite de sujets philosophiques tout proches), en alternance avec ceux des poèmes qui forment le 'roman d'amour' des *Méditations*.

Sans doute est-il loisible d'en chercher la raison dans l'atmosphère particulière de dévotion créée autour de l'enfance du poète par sa mère. Mais il faut aussi tenir compte de l'ambiance générale de l'époque. Charles Nodier, qui écrivit la préface pour la 11e édition (1824), l'a souligné dans une opposition piquante: "Chez les anciens, ce sont les poètes qui ont fait les religions; chez les modernes, c'est

[1] Notamment II, IV, VI et VII, (IX), XII, (XIII), XIV, XVI, XVII, XX, XXI, XXII, XXIV.

la religion qui crée enfin des poètes."[1] Après les vicissitudes du christianisme qui "semble n'exister depuis longtemps que par tolérance", l'école romantique est apparue, "une école qui exprime la pensée la plus élevée... et cette école est chrétienne et ne pouvait pas être autre chose". Il n'oubliait d'ailleurs nullement de marquer le rôle de Chateaubriand dans l'expression littéraire de cette résurrection: "C'est alors que le christianisme se releva des ruines sanglantes sous lesquelles il avait paru enseveli, et manifesta, par la voix d'un de ses plus éloquents interprètes, qu'il était la religion immortelle. Alors reprirent leur ascendant ces sublimes théories religieuses auxquelles se rattachent toutes les hautes pensées...".

Lamartine, à coup sûr, quelque incertaine que fût devenue la foi de son enfance, ne pouvait négliger une mine aussi prometteuse – mais il fallait aussi qu'il en eût le goût –, et il semble bien qu'il considéra ces méditations religieuses, apparemment si ingénues, comme des exercices. Témoin l'effarant aveu à son ami de Virieu après la Semaine Sainte passée à La Roche-Guyon: "Je viens de faire les plus ravissantes stances religieuses... C'est original, pur comme l'air, triste comme la mort et doux comme du velours."[2] Quelle désinvolture d'amateur! est-on tenté de s'écrier. Ce mâconnais croit-il goûter un cru de sa vigne? Cette satisfaction ingénue donne-t-elle le ton d'une crise profonde par laquelle le poète prétend être passé? Quittant la Roche-Guyon le cœur léger et l'abbé duc de Rohan déconfit ("l'infini seul, dit celui-ci, peut donc le remplir [le cœur], et Dieu seul est l'infini"), Lamartine lui répond évasivement: "Il faut du repos, de l'espérance, de l'avenir, je n'ai rien de tout cela et j'ai tout le contraire... Mais je doute, je voudrais, je désire, j'espère plutôt que je ne crois fermement. Cela ne suffit pas pour décider d'une vie. Il faut un motif en rapport avec les actions."[3]

---

[1] Ed. Grands Écrivains, p.p. G. Lanson, 2 vols (Paris, 1915), t. II, p. 578.

[2] *ibid.*, t. I, Notice, p. 224.

[3] *Correspondance*, t. II, p. 26 (1819). Je note dans l'article de Sainte-Beuve sur *Les Feuilles d'automne* (*Extraits*, p.p. V. Giraud, éd. Hatier, p. 166): "On a déjà pu remarquer un envahissement analogue du scepticisme dans les *Harmonies* du plus chrétien, du plus catholique de nos poètes, tandis qu'il n'y en avait pas trace dans les *Méditations*, ou du moins qu'il n'y était question du doute que pour le combattre. Mais l'organisation intime, l'âme de M. de Lamartine, est trop encline par essence au spiritualisme, au verbe incréé, au dogme chrétien, pour que même les négligences de volonté amènent chez lui autre chose que des éclipses passagères." On peut accepter le diagnostic final, même en le prolongeant, sans souscrire pour autant au jugement touchant les *Méditations*.

On est tenté de mettre en doute un effort de croyance qui a besoin
de ces aises pour s'épanouir. Lamartine a beau protester de ce désir
de foi qui le soulevait – "Il y a longtemps que nous soupirons, Aymon
(de Virieu) et moi, vers cette conviction"[1] – on enregistre les soupirs
et l'on craint que l'élévation ne se borne au désir. D'autres, plus
forts, le bouleversent: c'est la passion involontaire pour Léna de
Larche, qui lui faisait confier plus tard à son ami Dargaud: "C'est
l'époque voluptueuse de ma vie, voluptueuse et immorale, entre
mon amour que je pleurais et mon mariage que je pressentais."[2]

Le mariage avec Miss Birch, en effet, sur le chemin d'une conversion inachevée, est peut-être l'étape la plus approchée du but
qu'il ait atteinte. Lui fournissait-elle ce "motif en rapport avec
les actions" dont il déplorait l'absence auprès du duc de Rohan?
On le dirait: "C'est par religion, écrit-il en confidence à son ami de
Virieu, que je veux absolument me marier et que je m'y donne tant
de peines." Et il ajoute, montrant par là que ses doutes sont loin
d'être entièrement disparus: "Enchâssons-nous dans l'ordre établi
avant nous... implorons de Dieu lui-même la force et la nourriture
qui nous conviennent spécialement; faisons-lui pour l'amour de
lui-même le sacrifice de quelques répugnances de l'esprit pour qu'il
nous fasse trouver la paix de l'âme,... *ergo* marions-nous!"[3] Singulier
enthousiasme qui se fonde sur un raisonnement de désenchanté! Et
Des Cognets de conclure avec assez de vraisemblance: "La conversion
formelle de Lamartine au moment de son mariage ne marque pas
le début, mais la fin de sa période de réelle ferveur chrétienne. Il a
souhaité la foi beaucoup plus passionnément qu'il n'en a joui
lorsqu'il a cru la posséder. Il était dans sa nature de demeurer
toujours une âme d'inquiétude et de désir." D'inquiétude, soit,
mais je craindrais, reprenant le mot de Du Bos, d'inquiétude un peu
complaisante.[4] Le vers 252 de *l'Homme* résume assez bien l'évolution spirituelle du poète, telle que de moins elle est évoquée dans
les *Méditations*:

Je rendis gloire au ciel, et le ciel fit le reste.

[1] *ibid.*, t. II, p. 8.
[2] J. Des Cognets, *la vie intérieure de Lamartine* (Paris, 1934), p. 100.
[3] *ibid.*, p. 113.
[4] Dans un très beau passage où le critique établit une correspondance entre le lac
du Bourget et le poète: "une mélancolie tant soit peu complaisante, voluptueuse
même...", *Journal* (Paris, 1949), t. III, p. 81.

C'est dire que la foi lui vint à force, comme disait Pascal, de
pratiquer l'agenouillement, ou plutôt l'élévation spirituelle: ce qui,
précisément, est l'objet de ce qu'on nomme la 'méditation'.[1] Or, le
sens de ce mot ne doit pas être perdu de vue dans la signification du
titre de ce recueil, quand il était neuf.

Il n'est pas dans mon intention de retracer ici l'évolution spirituelle du poète pendant ces années où il composa ces poèmes.[2] Toute
bouleversée d'élans et de dépressions, en relation avec sa vie sentimentale et même son était de santé, elle se prête mal à une stricte
détection et elle est plutôt constituée par des alternances irrégulières.
Mais on en connaît les termes. A l'origine, une mère qui se maria
comme on entre au couvent et garda l'habitude des méditations et
des lectures pieuses (elle se réjouit de l'orientation poétique de son
fils à ses débuts), une éducation chrétienne au collège de Belley,
chez les Jésuites, la fréquentation de l'abbé Dumont et de son oncle,
tous deux peut-être trop larges d'esprit pour y avoir bien présente la
lettre du dogme, et la lecture au moins en 1818 du premier volume
de l'*Essai sur l'indifférence* de Lamennais. A l'autre bout, si l'on
fait un saut, on trouve le libre penseur anticlérical de 1848, qui
s'efforce d'effacer les traces de sa foi passée lorsqu'il reprend les
carnets maternels pour en faire *le Journal de ma mère*.[3] Entre les
deux se place une époque d'exaltation des passions qui le fait
hésiter entre le chemin patient du bonheur spirituel et la piste de la
vie ardente, débat que reproduit assez bien *l'Enthousiasme*. Il n'en
garde pas moins le désir et l'habitude de composer des 'Méditations',
des 'Harmonies' et des 'Recueillements', qui, pour être qualifiés de
'poétiques', rendent néanmoins un son religieux impliqué par ces
titres. Dieu ou le sentiment de Dieu y est constamment "touché",
pour reprendre le mot de Valéry sur son M. Teste, ou même
caressé. Le dogme, en revanche, est absent. On croit avoir affaire à
une religiosité sincère, mais diffuse, faite d'élans en effet plus que
de convictions, et sans cesse troublée, aux prises avec les expériences

---

[1] Dans son essai sur Lamartine (Paris, 1965), M.-F. Guyard remarque que *l'Isolement*
transpose dans le registre sentimental les trois mouvements d'une méditation
religieuse: l'évocation du paysage rappelle la contemplation, le recours aux
souvenirs la réflexion, le vague élan final l'élévation.

[2] Voir le même recul dans la belle préface du même critique à l'édition des
Œuvres poétiques dans la Bibliothèque de la Pléiade (Paris, 1963), p. xii, pour une
raison analogue.

[3] voir là-dessus Henri Guillemin, *Connaissance de Lamartine* (Fribourg, 1941).

du cœur et les objections d'une raison voltairienne. Il ne s'agit pas de juger: qui se le permettrait?

————

Essayons de discerner d'après les mots – ce n'est pas aisé au milieu d'abstractions si suaves – ce que 'Dieu' représente pour le poète des *Méditations*.

Ce 'Dieu' est essentiellement d'abord le Dieu créateur et ordonnateur de l'univers. On ne s'étonne pas que, dans cette mesure, le jeune Lamartine reste assez proche du déisme du dix-huitième siècle, qu'il en ait été influencé ainsi que par une tradition paenïne gréco-latine, perpétuée par la poésie de discipline classique, qui figure Dieu dans le soleil. C'est l'esprit et c'est aussi la lettre de divers poèmes comme *Hymne au soleil, la Prière*. On lit dans le premier:

> Tu règnes en vainqueur sur toute la nature,
> O soleil!...

Ce vers, où Racine se décolore, est suivi de quelques autres où le poète rappelle que l'adoration du soleil est une réaction instinctive de l'homme primitif qui se retrouve dans tous les cultes. Tout sentiment personnel, toute sensation ne sont pourtant pas absents de cette formule abstraite et, sous les mots, peut se deviner une appréciation reconnaissante de la caresse réconfortante de l'astre et de sa nature divine:

> Il me semble qu'un Dieu, dans tes rayons de flamme,
> En échauffant mon sein, pénètre dans mon âme!...
> O soleil! n'es-tu point un regard de ses yeux?

Les méditations de 1819 développent ce thème seulement esquissé. Après le *Gloria* de la deuxième partie de *l'Homme* ("Gloire à toi..."), *la Prière* dégage de la contemplation nocturne et diurne le symbole d'une création luxuriante, dont l'hommage retourne au créateur. Résumé dans ce vers plat de tragédie post-classique, pourtant acte d'espérance:

> Oui, j'espère, Seigneur, dans ta magnificence...

ce sentiment s'appuie sur la perception admirative d'un ordre de l'univers, qui a quelque chose de vaguement platonicien:

> ...Celui qui...
> Des sphères qu'il ordonne écoute l'harmonie,
> Ame de l'univers, Dieu, père, créateur.

Cette appréhension de Dieu à travers la création se complète par une nuance d'optimisme dans le style du même siècle, que Lanson n'a pas manqué de souligner (dans *l'Homme*):

> Tout est bien, tout est bon, tout est grand à sa place.

Il est toutefois permis de se demander si cet acte de foi ne relève pas d'un désir plus que d'une conviction. Sans doute, le poète se déclare-t-il dans *l'Immortalité:*

> A genoux devant lui, l'aimant dans ses ouvrages,

tout comme le "vicaire savoyard" de Rousseau l'enseignait avant lui: "J'aperçois Dieu partout dans ses œuvres." Pourtant, il l'invoque trop souvent, dirait-on, il le presse trop de se montrer sous les traits de la nature pour qu'on soit fondé à y voir une certitude chrétienne. Dans *la Semaine Sainte*, la question "Roi du ciel, est-ce toi?", posée au pied de l'humble autel, s'attire cette réponse molle et ambiguë:

> Oui, contraint par l'amour, le Dieu de la nature
> Y descend, visible à la foi.

On comprend certes qu'il s'agit du sacrement destiné à perpétuer le sacrifice que le Christ offrit pour l'amour des hommes. Mais le Christ s'appelle ici le "Dieu de la nature". Dans *le Vallon*, le poète s'exhorte:

> Sous la nature enfin découvre son auteur!

et le rappel significatif de *l'Immortalité,*

> Dieu caché, disais-tu, la nature est ton temple!

trouve un écho dans la longue méditation de *la Prière* où la nature – "L'univers est le temple, et la terre est l'autel" – s'offre en hommage au créateur. Tout cela n'est pas très différent d'un panthéisme, également répandu au dix-huitième siècle, qu'un vers de *Dieu* (v. 47) atteste parfaitement: "Il est; tout est en lui..." Mais le poète sent le danger de s'y abandonner, qui est d'aboutir à un syncrétisme

naturaliste de nuance chrétienne; il l'affirme du moins, mais on peut
en douter. Lanson, tout en affirmant "le sens orthodoxe" de ce
poème, est obligé de reconnaître que les arguments invoqués par
Lamartine appartiennent aussi bien au rationalisme déiste qu'au
rationalisme chrétien. A l'exception du dernier vers, il n'est pas sûr
que Voltaire aurait pu renier le tour historique de ceux-ci:

> Voilà, voilà le Dieu que tout esprit adore,
> Qu'Abraham a servi, que rêvait Pythagore,
> Que Socrate annonçait, qu'entrevoyait Platon;
> Ce Dieu que l'univers révèle à la raison,
> Que la justice attend, que l'infortune espère,
> Et que le Christ enfin vint montrer à la terre!

Et sans doute précise-t-il dans *la Semaine sainte*, méditation tout à
fait contemporaine:

> Aux pieds d'un Dieu mourant puis-je douter encore?

Il n'en reste pas moins que, après l'avoir distingué du "Dieu par
l'imposture à l'erreur expliqué", formule obscure que la mention
des "crédules ancêtres" ne suffit pas à éclairer, il ajoute:

> Il est seul, il est un, il est juste, il est bon.

Ce qui ne s'accorde pas tout à fait avec le dogme de la sainte
Trinité. Les dénégations de Lanson n'empêchent pas de constater
que si, comme il est très probable, le poète n'a pas cherché à le
contredire, sa pensée religieuse reste au moins extrêmement vague.
Il faut attendre *le Crucifix* pour que le Christ prenne toute sa place:
"image de mon Dieu", "l'image du Sauveur".

   Lamartine ne cache pas d'ailleurs qu'il lui faut d'autres preuves
que celles de la terre. Dans le même poème de *Dieu*, il indique fort
bien les nuances respectives de ses manifestations:

> La terre voit son œuvre, et le ciel sait son nom!

Ainsi dans *le Vallon* aspirera-t-il à un autre soleil et à des

> Lieux où le vrai soleil éclaire d'autres cieux.

N'est-il pas de ces "nautonniers sans étoile" auxquels il conseille
d'aborder au port de la Roche-Guyon? Sur lui l'effet fut nul. Ce fait

s

donne à penser que cette foi est beaucoup plus un appel qu'une certitude.

Or cet appel, ou cet élan de spiritualité, est indéniable chez le poète. Sous une forme ou une autre, il est constamment attesté dans les vers des *Méditations*. Lamartine répète qu'il *aspire* à croire; dans *l'Immortalité*, cet élan le poussait avec Elvire:

> Vers cet être inconnu qu'attestent nos désirs.

On ne peut s'empêcher de songer au cri qu'arrachait à Jean-Jacques le sentiment de la paix retrouvée dans la solitude admirable de la nature: "O Grand Être!" Et dans *la Prière*, le poète déclare:

> Je te cherche partout, j'aspire à toi, je t'aime...

La combinaison de cet élan vers l'en-haut avec la recherche de Dieu dans la nature devait normalement le conduire à un regret des premiers âges.[1] C'est une nostalgie commune à beaucoup des sentimentaux, dont le potentiel de foi, si l'on peut dire, ne parvient pas bien à se fixer dans le cadre d'une tradition, qu'il s'agisse de Rousseau au dix-huitième siècle ou de Romain Rolland au vingtième: ils pensent que si la religion chrétienne s'était présentée à eux dans sa première nouveauté, ou s'ils avaient vécu au temps où, comme le poète dit dans *Dieu*,

> La nature, sortant des mains du créateur,
> Etalait en tous sens le nom de son auteur,

alors le doute n'eût pas été possible. Ainsi Musset dans *Rolla*. Au contraire, semble-t-il, Hugo n'éprouve pas ce besoin.

Il était dans la ligne des harmonies logiques de cet état que Lamartine cherchât à rejeter tout un passé de servitudes corporelles et intellectuelles qui nuisent à la libre expansion de l'élan spirituel et à l'union de la créature avec Dieu.

Bien qu'il n'ait lu le *Phédon*, à ce qu'on rapporte, qu'en 1822 avec Fréminville, il est évident que sa pensée a été touchée directement ou indirectement par la philosophie platonicienne ou du moins

---

[1] cf. *Voyage en Orient*, Introd.: "Mon imagination était amoureuse... des traces de Dieu dans l'Orient." Cf. dans une lettre inédite plus tardive de Monceaux, 18/12 (?): "Car au fond qu'est-ce qui importe[...]? Excepté de chercher Dieu et de le trouver. Or je crois qu'il y a des institutions entre Dieu et nous."

par ce qui en est passé dans la tradition chrétienne elle-même. Son imagination a été impressionnée par le mythe de la caverne ou du moins par l'un des multiples relais que cette allégorie a produit dans l'expression de la pensée humaine depuis lors, sans qu'il soit limitatif de s'en référer, comme Lanson, au *Songe de Scipion* de Cicéron. Le vers 76 de la IIe Méditation en constitue à son tour un nouveau, d'une approximation suffisante pour en appeler d'autres:

> Dans la prison des sens enchaîné sur la terre...

Le thème de la servitude corporelle, si répandu dans toute la tradition chrétienne, a inspiré au poète Lamartine quelques-unes de ses images les plus originales et certains de ses vers les plus vigoureux. Celui-ci, par exemple, dans *l'Isolement*:

> Il n'est rien de commun entre la terre et moi.

Et, dans *la Mort de Socrate*, cet autre:

> Cet adultère hymen de la terre avec l'âme.

Le motif qui l'exprime, *la prison du corps*, constitue l'un des plus constants modes d'expression du poète, avec son corollaire, les *chaînes*, qui, qualifiées de *corporelles*, semblent attirer la rime antithétique des *ailes*, comme dans *l'Immortalité*:

> Viens donc, viens détacher mes chaînes corporelles,
> Viens, ouvre ma prison; viens, prête-moi tes ailes.

Voici deux autres exemples, l'un extrait de *Dieu*:

> Oui, mon âme se plaît à secouer ses chaînes...
> Mon âme est à l'étroit dans sa vaste prison.

L'autre, du *Chrétien mourant*:

> De ce corps périssable habitante immortelle...
> Prends ton vol, ô mon âme! et dépouille tes chaînes.

On en trouverait d'autres en abondance dans ces poèmes. Elles font de la mort ce "libérateur céleste" (aussi "trait libérateur") qui affranchit l'âme de son esclavage. Il est certainement aussi difficile d'imputer une telle conception au platonisme que de la mettre au compte du christianisme, à l'exclusion l'un de l'autre, celui-ci ayant repris les images de la philosophie antique. C'est le même problème d'attribution déjà rencontré dans les arguments en faveur de l'existence de Dieu tirés de l'ordonnance universelle, qui relevaient aussi bien du théisme que du christianisme. Enfin, il n'est pas déplacé de faire remarquer que cette croyance à l'immortalité de l'âme s'impose à plus d'un titre dans le recueil de ces poèmes qui au même titre que des 'méditations' spirituelles, composent les rapports de deux amants séparés par la mort d'Elvire. Ainsi le *Credo* de *la Prière* fait-il un pendant nécessaire aux *Gloria* de *l'Homme*, exprimant le seul recours désormais loisible au poète – j'entends bien le poète, et non Lamartine:

> J'attends le jour sans fin de l'immortalité.

Le corps n'est pas seul à imposer ses chaînes; la raison a aussi les siennes. Bien que l'univers révèle Dieu à la raison, le poète des *Méditations* qui le répète n'est pas si sûr de celle-ci, tout imprégnée de Voltaire et de Rousseau. Dans sa correspondance, il parle des "répugnances de l'esprit" qui, s'il consent à les sacrifier, n'en existent pas moins à ses yeux. A plusieurs reprises, ses *Méditations* opposent la raison et la foi comme deux puissances inconciliables. Ainsi, dans *l'Immortalité*:

> Notre faible raison se trouble et se confond.
> Oui, la raison se tait; mais l'instinct vous répond.

Mais ce silence obstiné de la raison équivaut à un refus, et l'on se demande si 'l'instinct' sera toujours assez fort pour imposer sa 'réponse' positive. Dans *la Semaine sainte*, c'est le poète qui impose silence à sa raison:

> Que ma raison se taise, et que mon cœur adore!

Et dans *Dieu*, l'enthousiasme, autre variété irrationnelle, s'offre au poète:

> Et mieux que la raison, il m'explique le monde.

Dans tous ces témoignages, l'opposition, loin d'être réduite, demeure; elle disparaît seulement par la victoire souhaitée de la foi, non par leur accord final. Sans doute n'est-ce pas toujours aussi net. Parfois la raison semble appuyer les vœux du cœur. Est-ce pour faire pièce à Byron, qu'après avoir admis que la loi, "ignorer et servir", était "ce piège où la raison trébuche", le poète lance ce défi:

> L'hymne de la raison s'élança de ma lyre...

Le Désespoir, au contraire, laisse se plaindre la raison et le cœur dans une double protestation qui les met d'accord sur la traditionnelle objection du mal et du désordre, incompréhensible à l'homme, que la divinité semble patronner:

> J'ai vu partout un Dieu sans jamais le comprendre!
> J'ai vu le bien, le mal, sans choix et sans dessein,
> Tomber, comme au hasard, échappés de son sein...

En vain, la réponse de *la Providence à l'homme*, faite, on sait, "à contre-cœur", lui montre l'exemple de l'obéissance des plus grandes puissances de la nature, du soleil lui-même:

> Mais ton cœur endurci doute et murmure encore.

C'est le cœur, non la raison, qui résiste. Se taira-t-il? Son silence est pire que la bouderie de la raison, car il achemine le poète vers cet amour du néant, propre à la mystique indienne, dont, sans vraisemblablement la connaître encore, Lamartine s'est à sa manière rapproché parfois,[1] notamment à la fin de sa méditation sur *la Prière*:

> Dans ton sein, à jamais, absorbe ma pensée!

Et encore au début de *la Foi*:

> O néant! ô seul Dieu que je puisse comprendre!

Plus tard, dans son *Voyage en Orient*, Lamartine écrira: "L'Orient, pays de méditation profonde, d'intuition et d'adoration! pays où la grande idée qui travaille les imaginations en tous temps est l'idée religieuse. "Cette pensée ne lui est pas particulière en ce siècle où les écrivains, désespérant du christianisme, ont plus d'une fois tourné leurs regards vers cette source des religions (Nerval, par exemple). Mais Lamartine n'en est pas là en 1820, et l'on doit se borner à noter cette resemblance à peine ébauchée.

---

[1] voir le chapitre de R. Schwab, *la Renaissance orientale* (Paris, 1950).

Un tel appel, entre autres, laisse l'impression que la raison ne constitue pas le principal obstacle, qu'elle n'est ni si forte ni si imperméable aux miracles qu'il implore à la fin de *Dieu*:

> Viens! montre-toi toi-même, et force-nous de croire!

Cette exigence de croyant, apparentée, elle aussi, osera-t-on le dire, aux impératifs exaspérés de certains prophètes indiens (par exemple Ramakrishna), est aussi intéressante qu'insolite. Mais Lamartine a-t-il prévu l'objection qu'alors le mérite de croire serait inexistant?[1] Car le poète, à la différence du prophète, ne semble pas jaloux de s'en réserver le privilège; au contraire, il semble désireux de se compter au milieu d'une foule dont la présence divine exaucerait le vœu en confirmant son existence. Aussi n'est-ce pas une surprise que cet élan de spiritualité se fonde sur des arguments éprouvés aussi bien par les théistes que par les chrétiens et s'informe au moins à titre temporaire dans ce traditionalisme catholique dont délibérément le poète se réclame dans *la Foi* comme dans sa correspondance au moment de son mariage:

> De la terre promise l'immortel héritage,
> Les pères à leurs fils l'ont transmis d'âge en âge.[2]

Et, pour le "poète mourant", dont Lamartine, après tant de Gilbert, de Chénier et de Millevoye, a choisi d'emprunter la figure pour interprète de ses *Méditations*, la raison, au surplus, n'a pas de peine à s'incliner "aux portes du tombeau".[3] C'est ce que dit

---

[1] Hugo, au contraire, a insisté à plusieurs reprises sur cet aspect des relations de l'homme avec la divinité, notamment dans *la Bouche d'ombre* (v. 490 sq.): "l'homme doit ignorer":

> Sans quoi, comme l'enfant guidé par des lisières,
> L'homme vivrait, marchant droit à la vision...
> Où serait le mérite à retrouver sa route,
> Si l'homme, voyant clair, roi de sa volonté,
> Avait la certitude, ayant la liberté?

Teilhard de Chardin, on le sait, rejette cet argument où il voit un calcul indigne de la bonté divine et penche à attribuer cette occultation à une sorte d'incommensurabilité du fini a l'infini.

[2] Aussi, plus tard, dans *le Crucifix*: "l'héritage sacré". Cf. ce fragment de Lettre pastorale de Bossuet, cité par A. Gide dans ses *Lettres à Angèle* comme caractéristique du catholicisme, – et qui ne l'est plus: "Dieu a voulu que la vérité vînt à nous de pasteur en pasteur et de main en main sans que jamais on n'aperçut d'innovation. C'est par là qu'on reconnaît ce qui toujours été cru et par conséquent ce que l'on doit toujours croire."

[3] *Mélanges et lettres* (Paris, 1876), t. I, p. 506 (18 décembre 1842).

éloquemment, sinon très poétiquement pour le goût d'aujourd'hui, la conclusion de *la Foi*:

> Cette raison superbe, insuffisant flambeau,
> S'éteint comme la vie aux portes du tombeau;
> Viens donc la remplacer, ô céleste lumière!
> Viens d'un jour sans nuage inonder ma paupière;
> Tiens-moi lieu du soleil que je ne dois plus voir,
> Et brille à l'horizon comme l'astre du soir.

On comprend que, pour son époque, cette position d'aspirant croyant lui ait rallié les suffrages combinés des théistes, des catholiques de l'ordre et des mystiques de la croix. La sincérité frémissante du sentiment, dont persuadait la mélodie des vers, faisait oublier la confusion de la pensée, bien naturelle d'ailleurs. Car le poète ne prétendait pas offrir là un traité de théologie: il en était bien incapable, comme l'a joliment noté son contemporain X. Doudan, qui ne l'aimait pas trop: "Croyez-vous réellement que M. de Lamartine pense à faire un traité de philosophie? Je ne me figure pas bien toutes ces vapeurs brillantes se condensant en neige métaphysique, mais, après tout, cela se voit sur les montagnes."[1]

---

[1] *Ibid.*

The personal and the general in French Romantic literary theory

D. G. CHARLTON

A FREQUENT generalization in histories of French literature has been to the effect that whereas Classicist authors aspire to the general and the objective, the Romantics are above all preoccupied with the personal and the subjective. And linked with that has gone another contrast: whilst Classicism includes a cult of reason – seen as man's generalizing faculty – Romanticism is marked by a cult of emotion – seen as essentially individualistic and particular.[1] This view of the Romantics (and of the Classicists also, one may think) has been much qualified in recent decades – notably by works on social and political Romanticism by H. J. Hunt, D. O. Evans, Roger Picard and others, by several studies of their religious, moral and philosophical ideas, and by such suggestive *œuvres de synthèse* as Moreau's *Le Classicisme des romantiques* and Jacques Barzun's *Classic, Romantic and Modern*. None the less, we continue to identify the Romantics with self-expression, with emotional self-disclosure – and indeed the attacks of an Irving Babbitt upon their "emotional anarchy" have been renewed more recently by another Harvard scholar, Mr M. Z. Shroder, who deplores their "messianic pretension" and describes their image of the artist as "an unrealizable megalomaniac ideal of personal omnipotence".[2] Whilst this view may well be much too extreme, it is all the same needless to stress or to establish here that these authors do give a much larger place to the personal and emotional than most of their predecessors.

[1] In a very interesting discussion, 'Sur quelques définitions du romantisme', *Revue des sciences humaines*, fasc. 62–3 (1951), 93–110, Professor J. B. Barrère examines definitions given by historians from Brunetière and Lanson to Jasinski and Castex and concludes: "Ces définitions mesurées s'accordent à mettre l'accent, avec Croce, sur le sentiment, ou avec Goethe, sur la subjectivité: ce qui revient à peu près au même." (p. 101.)

[2] M. Z. Shroder, *Icarus: The Image of the Artist in French Romanticism* (Cambridge, Mass., 1961), pp. 48 and 247.

But I wish to emphasize here that this is only half of the truth and that their concern with the personal is complemented by more general, even universal concerns. Their interest in the self and their attention to man's emotions can be fully understood, I believe, only if seen in a broader context, as a part – albeit a crucial part – of far wider, more objective and more reasoned preoccupations. To establish properly such a thesis obviously demands the examination of their actual works – a massive task. This brief essay has a purely precursory aim and is limited to considering some of the Romantics' theoretical pronouncements. The sceptic has certainly the right here to point out that their writings may not necessarily conform to their statements of intent; in reply one can only submit that these statements may be suggestive and may point to aspects of their work to which we should attend.

The desire to produce a literature of wide, general and 'impersonal' relevance is manifested in three features in particular of the Romantics' declarations about their aims. First, they stress again and again that theirs is to be a literature of their own age and society. Bonald's celebrated formula: "La littérature est l'expression de la société" was widely accepted and led the Romantics to conclude that their own work should both express and seek to modify contemporary society. This emphasis is clear from Madame de Staël onwards and is influentially explored in her first major book, *De la littérature considérée dans ses rapports avec les institutions sociales* (to give its full title). "Les ouvrages qui appartiennent à la haute littérature [she there affirms] ont pour but d'opérer des changements utiles, de hâter des progrès nécessaires, de modifier enfin les institutions et les lois."[1] And *De l'Allemagne* reiterates the view that literature and especially poetry have throughout the ages been determined by "toutes les circonstances politiques et religieuses" of their time.[2] Nodier – a 'father' of the Romantics – takes up the same theme, as when he writes in 1821: "Convenons que le romantique pourrait bien n'être autre chose que le classique des modernes, c'est-à-dire l'expression d'une société nouvelle...".[3] As for his young friends,

---

[1] Madame de Staël, *De la littérature* (Geneva and Paris, 1959), 2 vols, vol. II, p. 318.
[2] Madame de Staël, *De l'Allemagne* (Paris, 1958–60), 5 vols., vol. II, p. 134.
[3] Cited from *Mercure du XIXᵉ siècle*, vol. II (1821), in C. M. Des Granges, *Le Romantisme et la critique: La Presse littéraire sous la Restauration, 1815–1830* (Paris, 1907), p. 214.

Hugo, by 1824 – well before the date of 1830 so often assigned to the birth of social Romanticism – was asserting "cette liaison remarquable entre les grandes époques politiques et les belles époques littéraires", was noting that "un mouvement vaste et profond travaille intérieurement la littérature de ce siècle", and was urging the poet to "marcher devant les peuples comme une lumière et leur montrer le chemin". "La littérature actuelle [he declared]... est l'expression anticipée de la société religieuse et monarchique qui sortira sans doute du milieu de tant d'anciens débris, de tant de ruines récentes."[1] And in the *Préface de Cromwell* also he was to argue at length that changes in literature follow from changes in society and in religious beliefs, instancing especially the Homeric age and the period since the establishment of Christianity. Vigny expressed parallel conclusions in his 'Réflexions sur la vérité dans l'art':

> L'étude du destin général des sociétés n'est pas moins nécessaire aujourd'hui dans les écrits que l'analyse du cœur humain... Ce que l'on veut... c'est, je le répète, le spectacle philosophique de l'homme profondément travaillé par les passions de son caractère et de son temps; c'est donc la VÉRITÉ de cet HOMME et de ce TEMPS...[2]

Lamartine established the same connection in 'Des destinées de la poésie'. Following the very early years of the nineteenth century, when literature was inhibited by scientific materialism, by "une ligue universelle des études mathématiques contre la pensée et la poésie", he argues: "la poésie était revenue en France avec la liberté, avec la pensée, avec la vie morale que nous rendit la Restauration."[3] And even Musset, in 'Un mot sur l'art moderne', favoured a contemporary literature – "tenant au siècle qui la produit, résultant des circonstances, quelquefois mourant avec elles, et quelquefois les immortalisant".[4]

---

[1] Hugo, *Œuvres poétiques*, vol. I (Paris, Bibliothèque de la Pléiade, 1964), pp. 273–4, 272, 277 and 274.

[2] Vigny, *Œuvres complètes*, vol. II (Paris, Bibliothèque de la Pléiade, 1948), pp. 19 and 22.

[3] Lamartine, *Premières Méditations poétiques* (Paris, 1903), pp. xxvii and xxxiii.

[4] Musset, *Œuvres complètes en prose* (Paris, Bibliothèque de la Pléiade, 1960), p. 884.

THE Romantics stressed not only the social relevance of their writing but also, secondly, its philosophical and religious significance – that is, once again, its more general import. Of Romantic literature Madame de Staël claimed in *De l'Allemagne:* "C'est notre religion et nos institutions qui l'ont fait éclore"; "elle exprime notre religion; elle rappelle notre histoire."[1] The next generation shared her view. Hugo could write of the poet: "Il doit ramener [les peuples] à tous les grands principes d'ordre, de morale et d'honneur."[2] Of his own theatrical aims he affirmed likewise: "Le drame ... doit donner à la foule une philosophie, aux idées une formule..."[3] and in the *Préface de Cromwell* he was even more far-reaching when he related his theory of the *drame*'s fusion of the *sublime* and the *grotesque* to the Christian idea of man as a combination of spiritual and bodily. "Le point de départ de la religion est toujours le point de départ de la poésie. Tout se tient."[4] Vigny took a similar stand when he declared in regard to the drama: "Si l'art est une fable, il doit être une fable philosophique"; in 'Dernière Nuit de travail' commenting on *Chatterton* he even identified his own age as "le temps du DRAME DE LA PENSÉE".[5] And one finds him affirming more widely still in his *Journal d'un poète:* "Il y a dans les œuvres d'art deux points de vue. L'un philosophique, l'autre poétique. – Le point de vue philosophique doit soutenir l'œuvre, drame ou livre, d'un pôle à l'autre...". It is in line with this claim that he should describe his own *Poèmes antiques et modernes* as "[des] compositions... dans lesquelles une pensée philosophique est mise en scène sous une forme Épique ou Dramatique".[6] As to Lamartine, he above all has been treated as a lyric poet writing from the heart about his own experience – much less often as a philosophical and epic poet, author of *La Mort de Socrate, Jocelyn* and *La Chute d'un ange*, not to add of the more philosophical poems found in even the *Premières Méditations*. Yet as he foresaw in 1834 the likely evolution of poetry, it was not lyric poetry in the normal sense that he envisaged: on the contrary, he proclaims: "la poésie sera de la raison chantée...; elle sera

---

[1] *De l'Allemagne*, vol. II, pp. 134 and 139.
[2] *Œuvres poétiques*, vol. I, p. 277.
[3] Hugo, *Théâtre complet*, vol. II, (Paris, Bibliothèque de la Pléiade, 1964), p. 556.
[4] *ibid.*, vol. I (1963), p. 416.
[5] *Œuvres complètes*, vol. II, p. 379, and vol. I (1964), p. 770.
[6] *ibid.*, vol. II, p. 1082, and vol. I, p. 3.

philosophique, religieuse, politique, sociale...; elle doit se faire peuple, et devenir populaire comme la religion, la raison et la philosophie."[1]

If the French Romantics tended to the general and impersonal in virtue, first, of the social significance they attributed to their art and, secondly, by their conviction that (in Coleridge's words) "no man was ever yet a great poet without being at the same time a profound philosopher", they did so thirdly, I believe, and in a rather different manner, in their view of poetic experience. This for them was not confined to emotion (as has sometimes been alleged) but was a cognitive process including intellectual and sensory components and bringing the whole personality into play. The Romantics in general rejected eighteenth-century rationalism, but that should not be confused with a rejection of reason. Their attack was not upon the intellect but upon the exclusive reliance placed on it, and on the scientific method associated with it, by some of the *philosophes*. They were fully aware that scientific rationalism played a large part in the thought of their day – in the Idéologues and the Positivists, for example – and they therefore naturally stressed the rights of intuition, feeling and the individual conscience: this last is, indeed, a part of their religious and political liberalism. Yet their intention, I suggest, was not to abandon the intellect but to complement it, to invoke a more complete epistemology that could find a place for the promptings of spiritual and occult experience, for the intuitive wisdom (as some of them believed) of primitive peoples and their mythologies, for the *esprit de finesse* as well as for reason and empirical knowledge. Theirs was an eclectic view of knowledge (perhaps not unconnected with that of their Eclectic philosophical contemporaries), a striving for a more total, all-inclusive apprehension of life.

This is a notion already implicit in their German precursor, A. W. Schlegel, who identified the *mélange des genres*, later propounded by Hugo, with Romantic literature:

La nature et l'art, la poésie et la prose, le sérieux et la plaisanterie, le souvenir et le pressentiment, les idées abstraites et les sensations vives... se réunissent et se confondent de la manière la plus intime dans le genre romantique.[2]

[1] *Premières Méditations poétiques*, pp. lix and lxi.
[2] cited by Ph. Van Tieghem, *Les Grandes Doctrines littéraires en France* (Paris, 1963), p. 180.

But its full expression is seen in Lamartine's famous definition of poetry:

> C'est l'incarnation de ce que l'homme a de plus intime dans le cœur et de plus divin dans la pensée, de ce que la nature visible a de plus magnifique dans les images et de plus mélodieux dans les sons! C'est à la fois sentiment et sensation, esprit et matière; et voilà pourquoi c'est la langue complète, la langue par excellence qui saisit l'homme par son humanité tout entière, idée pour l'esprit, sentiment pour l'âme, image pour l'imagination, et musique pour l'oreille![1]

One may also recall Hugo's description of the triple inspiration of the poet in the *Préface* to *Les Voix intérieures*:

> L'auteur a toujours pensé que la mission du poète était de fondre dans un même groupe de chants cette triple parole qui renferme un triple enseignement, car la première s'adresse plus particulièrement au cœur, la seconde à l'âme, la troisième à l'esprit.[2]

And here again, I believe, we see the Romantics' aspiration to render literature more universal – epistemologically, so to say, as well as in the range of experience – personal, political, moral and religious – which they sought to explore in their works.

———

Now it is clearly the case (and this essay does not at all seek to deny) that these aspirations to the general, impersonal and even universal are matched by a persistent concern with the personal and the expression of the self. This basic feature of the Romantics' work is too well known to require any substantiation here. What may perhaps be worth underlining, however, is that this 'individualism'

[1] *Premières Méditations poétiques*, p. xxxiv.
[2] *Œuvres poétiques*, vol. I, p. 919. Cf., three years later, the preface to *Les Rayons et les ombres*, *ibid.*, vol. I, p. 1018: "L'un des deux yeux du poète est pour l'humanité, l'autre pour la nature. Le premier de ces yeux s'appelle l'observation, le second s'appelle l'imagination." Cf. also Vigny's comment: "Le cœur existe bien, moralement parlant. On sent ses mouvements de joie et de douleur; mais c'est une chambre obscure dont la lumière est la tête. La mémoire et la pensée l'illuminent et y font paraître les sentiments. Sans la tête, ils s'éteignent." (*Œuvres complètes*, vol. II, p. 1127).

often stemmed less from self-centredness than from belief in the
value of the individual – of his inner experience, his political rights
and his religious and moral aspirations. These writers lived in an
age threatened by authoritarianism in religion and politics alike,
whether from the Catholic Right or from the new socialistic and
positivist prophets. In reaction the Romantics almost all stood for
personal rights, and whilst some began as Catholic royalists, they
all ended as political and religious liberals. At the same time, on
the philosophical front, they resisted the notion of the atheistic
philosophes and their successors that man is 'l'homme-machine' –
externally determined in all he does, without a soul – and they
defended against this mechanistic view the reality of the individual
self, a reality far transcending, they believed, men's need for
economic well-being and social order. I submit, in short, that their
individualism is a generalized rather than a self-centred individualism – and one may here recall the criticisms of 'l'odieux individualisme' made by Lamartine, Sainte-Beuve, and others at this time of
laissez-faire economic practice and their distinction between this
and the pursuit of a desirable 'individuality'.[1] The Romantic often
writes of his personal situation and problems, but he sees them as
widespread, common to at least the majority of men in his own age
and society. And we can here perceive that the apparently contradictory tendencies in Romantic literary theory towards the general
and towards the personal are in reality not in conflict but are interrelated. Georges Poulet has observed of the Romantics that their
withdrawal into the 'centre' of the self is followed by a return to
the 'circle' of the external world.[2] Likewise, at the level of theory,
they aspired to move from the personal to the general, as we must
now observe.

———

A FIRST example is offered by Madame de Staël in *De la littérature*.
She has developed her contention that poetry should "suivre, comme
tout ce qui tient à la pensée, la marche philosophique du siècle", but

[1] For a discussion of this distinction, cf. K. W. Swart, 'Individualism in the mid-
XIXth Century (1826–1860)', *Journal of the History of Ideas*, XXIII (1962), 77–90.
Cf. also A. Gérard, 'On the Logic of Romanticism', *Essays in Criticism*, VII (1957),
262–73 (mainly on the English Romantics).
[2] *Les Métamorphoses du cercle* (Paris, 1961), ch. vi and especially p. 138.

she then goes still further: "[L'imagination] peut exalter les sentiments vrais; mais il faut toujours que la raison approuve et com-
prenne ce que l'enthousiasme fait aimer... La philosophie, *en
généralisant davantage les idées,* donne plus de grandeur aux images
poétiques."[1] A similar purpose is seen in her two contemporaries,
Chateaubriand and Constant, in their statements about *René* and
Adolphe respectively. The former claimed that in writing *René* he
had wished, first, to depict a widespread passion of his age – *le vague
des passions* – of which a detailed analysis is given in the chapter
of *Le Génie du christianisme* that precedes the story; secondly, to
denounce "cette espèce de vice nouveau, et peindre les funestes
conséquences de l'amour outré de la solitude"; and thirdly, to "faire
aimer la Religion et en démontrer l'utilité". That is to say, whereas
many critics have stressed above all the autobiographical interest
of *René*, its author himself underlined its more universal importance
(and justifiably so in my view).[2] *Adolphe* is perhaps a less contentious
instance, though this novel too has sometimes been approached as
primarily autobiographical and personal. In the preface to its
second edition Constant posits two principal aims: to show the
dangers of superficial liaisons (a theme of obviously universal
relevance) and, secondly, he continues: "J'ai voulu peindre dans
Adolphe une des principales maladies morales de notre siècle, cette
fatigue, cette incertitude, cette absence de force, cette analyse
perpétuelle...".[3] Here again the portrayal of an individual, drawn
in good part no doubt from the author's own self, is explicitly
directed towards far more general themes – as is confirmed in the
novel's style, moreover, as particular description yields repeatedly
to almost abstract generalization.

To turn to their successors in the Romantic tradition is to find a
parallel insistence that is especially emphatic in Hugo. Thus in the
preface to *Les Chants du crépuscule* he could declare: "[L'auteur]
ne laisse même subsister dans ses ouvrages ce qui est personnel que
parce que c'est peut-être quelquefois un reflet de ce qui est général.
Il ne croit pas que son *individualité...* vaille la peine d'être autrement

[1] *De la littérature*, vol. II, pp. 361–3; my italics.
[2] *René* (Lille and Geneva, 1947), pp. 117 and 126–7. Cf. my article on 'The
Ambiguity of Chateaubriand's *René*', *F.S.*, XXIII (1969), 229–43.
[3] *Adolphe*, ed. G. Rudler (1950), p. xix.

étudiée."[1] A few years later in the preface to *Les Rayons et les ombres* he reiterated the point when writing of "cette profonde peinture du moi qui est peut-être l'œuvre la plus large, la plus générale et la plus universelle qu'un penseur puisse faire".[2] And in 1856 – the year before Baudelaire would address himself to his "hypocrite lecteur, mon semblable, mon frère" – Hugo asserted to his reader in the preface to *Les Contemplations*: "Ma vie est la vôtre, votre vie est la mienne... On se plaint quelquefois des écrivains qui disent moi. Parlez-nous de nous, leur crie-t-on. Hélas! quand je vous parle de moi, je vous parle de vous."[3] A preference for the general rather than the particular is evident in Vigny also. We earlier saw him affirm that literature should present "la VÉRITÉ de cet HOMME et de ce TEMPS" – "mais tous deux [he continues] élevés à une puissance supérieure et idéale qui en concentre toutes les forces".[4] And his *Journal* is quite unambiguous as early as 1824: "l'imagination donne du corps aux idées et leur crée des types et des symboles vivants qui sont comme la forme palpable et la preuve d'une théorie abstraite." And again later in life he makes his preference plain:

> Il y a plus de force, de dignité et de grandeur dans les poètes *objectifs* épiques et dramatiques tels qu'Homère, Shakespeare, Dante, Molière, Corneille, que dans les poètes *subjectifs* ou élégiaques se peignant eux-mêmes et déplorant leurs peines secrètes, comme Pétrarque et autres.[5]

Another particularly striking example is provided by Musset's *Confession d'un enfant du siècle*, a novel, like *René*, that is usually discussed as 'un roman personnel', as autobiographical evidence about the author's relationship with George Sand. Yet to look at Musset's successive intentions in writing the book is to find the transition from personal to general quite explicitly illustrated.

Musset's original purpose in writing this novel appears to have been personal and sentimental: to tell the story of his love-affair with George Sand and in doing so to exculpate and indeed idealize

[1] *Œuvres poétiques*, vol. I, p. 811.
[2] *ibid.*, p. 1020.
[3] *ibid.*, vol. II (1967), pp. 481–2.
[4] *Œuvres complètes*, vol. II, p. 22.
[5] *ibid.*, pp. 880 and 1121.

T

her. He wrote on 30 April 1834, shortly after returning from
Venice: "Je m'en vais faire un roman. J'ai bien envie d'écrire notre
histoire... Je voudrais te bâtir un autel, fût-ce avec mes os; mais
j'attendrai ta permission formelle."[1] (Not surprisingly George Sand
agreed, though her trust did not survive the period of waiting and
later we find her apprehensively requesting Buloz to check that the
book contained nothing detrimental to her.[2]) But, as he worked on
the book, his first aim was increasingly overlaid by the intention to
write a *Confession d'un enfant du siècle* – a title rather belatedly
chosen according to Paul de Musset[3] – and to examine "[la] maladie
morale abominable" which he discerns in many other young men
of his day as well as Octave. Hence, when he published in advance
in the *Revue des deux mondes* (15 September 1835) a 'Fragment' of
the book, he chose the novel's second chapter, the long analysis of
the *mal du siècle*. And when we turn to the novel itself, in the very
first, brief chapter, we find his own emphatic declaration:

> Ayant été atteint, jeune encore, d'une maladie morale abomi-
> nable, je raconte ce qui m'est arrivé pendant trois ans. Si j'étais
> seul malade, je n'en dirais rien; mais, comme il y en a beaucoup
> d'autres que moi qui souffrent du même mal, j'écris pour ceux-là,
> sans trop savoir s'ils y feront attention...[4]

He then gives his detailed discussion of the *mal du siècle* widespread
amongst his contemporaries before turning to the particular case
of Octave. And (though this present essay is deliberately excluding
discussion of the Romantics' actual works) one may recall to those
who would interpret this novel as mainly an account of the Musset–
Sand relationship the most basic facts about its arrangement.
Brigitte does not appear until little short of half way through it;
the lovers' first meeting in an edition (Garnier) of 320 pages comes
on page 133, and if Musset had held to his first plan to end the story
with the consummation of their love, the space given to their whole
relationship would have been a mere 41 out of 174 pages.

To conclude this brief consideration of the relation of the personal

[1] *Œuvres complètes en prose*, p. 1040.
[2] *ibid.*, p. 1043.
[3] P. de Musset, *Biographie d'Alfred de Musset: sa vie et ses œuvres*, 4e éd., (Paris, 1877), p. 146.
[4] *La Confession d'un enfant du siècle* (Paris, 1960), p. 1.

and the general in the literary theories of the Romantics, it is perhaps worth noting finally that the transition from the former to the latter was a feature singled out by contemporary critics favourable to the Romantics' work. Already in 1817, in the *Archives philosophiques, politiques et littéraires*, we find this declaration about 'the new poetry': "Quelles seront les sources de la poésie nouvelle? Les idées et les sentiments qui ont leurs racines et leur commencement d'existence dans le cœur de l'homme *ordinaire*... Tous les matériaux de la poésie se tirent de la nature commune à tout homme doué des facultés de l'homme."[1] (As Des Granges asks in citing this passage, "peut-on mieux définir la poésie *prochaine* de Lamartine, de Vigny et de Musset?") A little later, Charles de Rémusat writes of "the state of French poetry" in *Le Globe*, a journal which in 1825 was almost the leading exponent of Romantic attitudes:

> La poésie lyrique sort de la pensée, tout empreinte du sentiment de celui qui l'a conçue, pour se porter successivement sur tous les objets... Une telle poésie doit plaire à notre âge. En reproduisant des émotions personnelles, elle satisfait à ce besoin du naturel et du vrai, goût dominant de l'époque; et par son caractère de généralité... elle répond singulièrement à cette disposition de doute et de contemplation où nous jettent les doctrines et les événements du siècle.

And he concludes with words that are almost a summary of the central theme of this essay: "L'univers et un seul homme, l'infini et l'individu, tel est le contraste qui fait le fond de la poésie lyrique comme de la pensée humaine."[2] Or again, in the *Mercure du XIXe siècle* in 1830, Sainte-Beuve's *Consolations* are praised because their author "part d'un incident de la vie privée et domestique pour arriver aux régions les plus élevées du déisme, de la morale et de l'éclecticisme".[3]

And this reference to "l'éclecticisme" reminds us of the leading Eclectic philosopher of the day, Victor Cousin, whose impact upon the Romantics and their generation may have been much greater than is normally recognised.[4] In his influential lectures of 1817 and

---

[1] cited in Des Granges, *op. cit.*, p. 248.
[2] cited in Des Granges, *ibid.*, p. 288.   [3] cited in Des Granges, *ibid.*, p. 310.
[4] for a discussion of this point, cf. my article on 'Victor Cousin and the French Romantics', *F.S.*, XVII (1963), 311–23.

1818, in his article 'Du beau réel et du beau idéal' published in
the *Archives philosophiques* in 1818, reprinted in *Fragments philosophiques* in 1826, and expanded in *Du Vrai, du beau et du bien*
(1836), Cousin expounded precisely the relationship which has been
discussed here. He argues that "le caractère de la beauté extérieure
est double, comme l'opération qui s'y rapporte". It comprises an
'individual element' and a 'general element', of which he asserts:

> Le beau réel se compose donc de deux éléments, le général et
> l'individuel, réunis dans un objet réel, déterminé. Maintenant si
> l'on demande quel est l'élément qui paraît d'abord,... je répondrai
> que le général et le particulier, l'absolu et le variable, nous sont
> donnés simultanément l'un dans l'autre, et l'un avec l'autre.[1]

And as regards the artist or writer's creative and aesthetic experience, Cousin's view is no less close to the Romantics' claims we noted
earlier, for he stresses that the roles of intellect and feeling are
equally essential and must be harmoniously combined. Feeling is
"individuel, variable, relatif"; 'judgment' allows us to rise to the
general, absolute and even infinite:

> Ce jugement est un acte de la raison, de cette faculté merveilleuse
> qui aperçoit l'infini du sein du fini, atteint l'absolu dans l'in-
> dividuel, et participe de deux mondes dont elle forme la réunion...
> L'heureuse harmonie [du sentiment et du jugement] constitue ce
> qu'on appelle le goût, la faculté de discerner et de sentir le beau.[2]

Thus, Cousin suggests, we can pass through the "beau réel" to the
"beau idéal" – or as Hugo was to put it only four years later: "le
domaine de la poésie est illimité. Sous le monde réel, il existe un
monde idéal, qui se montre resplendissant à l'œil de ceux que des
méditations graves ont accoutumés à voir dans les choses plus
que les choses."[3]
    Wordsworth, in the well-known words of the preface to the
Lyrical Ballads, contended that "Poetry is the most philosophic of
all writing: . . . its object is truth, not individual and local, but

---

[1] Cousin, *Cours de l'histoire de la philosophie moderne*, 1ᵉʳᵉ série, vol. II (Paris, 1846),
   pp. 421 and 423.
[2] *ibid.*, pp. 420–1.
[3] *Œuvres poétiques*, vol. I, p. 265.

general, and operative".[1] If the argument of this essay is correct, the French Romantics were closer to his standpoint (and perhaps, one may add, to the German Romantic notion of, in Friedrich Schlegel's term, "eine progressive Universalpoesie") than has usually been acknowledged.

[1] Wordsworth, *Poetical Works*, vol. II (1944), p. 394.

'La blanche Oloossone':
some reflections on Romanticism
and Classicism

R. A. SAYCE

In *Du côté de chez Swann* Marcel's friend Bloch expresses contempt for Musset and for Racine:

> En m'entendant lui avouer mon admiration pour la *Nuit d'Octobre*, il avait fait éclater un rire bruyant comme une trompette et m'avait dit: "Défie-toi de ta dilection assez basse pour le sieur de Musset. C'est un coco des plus malfaisants et une assez sinistre brute. Je dois confesser, d'ailleurs, que lui et même le nommé Racine, ont fait chacun dans leur vie un vers assez bien rythmé, et qui a pour lui, ce qui est selon moi le mérite suprême, de ne signifier absolument rien. C'est: 'La blanche Oloossone et la blanche Camyre' et 'La fille de Minos et de Pasiphaé'. Ils m'ont été signalés à la décharge de ces deux malandrins par un article de mon très cher maître, le Père Leconte, agréable aux Dieux Immortels."
>
> Malheureusement, je ne pus pas apaiser en causant avec Bloch et en lui demandant des explications, le trouble où il m'avait jeté quand il m'avait dit que les beaux vers (à moi qui n'attendais d'eux rien de moins que la révélation de la vérité), étaient d'autant plus beaux qu'ils ne signifiaient rien du tout.[1]

The Musset line is misquoted: it is not "*et* la blanche Camyre" but "*à* la blanche Camyre" and, as we shall see, this word makes a great difference. The misquotation is entirely in keeping with Bloch's character but it is not out of keeping with Proust's, so whether it was deliberate or a slip is impossible to say. Proust in his early years certainly shared Marcel's admiration for Musset.[2] As

---

[1] *A la recherche du temps perdu* (Paris, 1960), vol. I, pp. 90–1.
[2] G. D. Painter, *Marcel Proust* (1959–65), vol. I, p. 51.

he grew older he came nearer to Bloch's view until in the essay on
Baudelaire of 1921 he comes to the rueful conclusion that "Musset
est malgré tout un poète de second ordre".[1] But he never abandons
him altogether.

The next question is the article by Leconte de Lisle. Was it ever
written or has Proust invented it? An article on Musset was announced as forthcoming in *Le Nain jaune* of 30 July 1864 but it
does not seem actually to have appeared.[2] The probability is that
Proust made it up, because he had already in *Jean Santeuil* written
a first draft of this passage which indicates a different source. Here
Rustinlor, the pretentious schoolmaster, plays the part of Bloch:
"Racine est un assez vilain coco... mais il y a dans *Phèdre* quelques
beaux vers comme celui-ci: 'la fille de Minos et de Pasiphaé', que
Gautier déclara être le seul beau vers qu'il eût jamais trouvé chez
Racine." Jean, like Marcel, is painfully surprised: "Le seul?
demanda Jean qui cherchait inutilement à deviner la beauté de ce
vers." And Rustinlor, like Bloch, has declared that the main thing
about verse is that it should be meaningless: "D'ailleurs des vers
purement extérieurs sont pour cela même infiniment supérieurs
aux vers qui signifient quelque chose."[3] This sends us off on another
trail, Gautier. In the Goncourt *Journal* for 11 May 1863 we read
how Gautier denounced Racine at a Magny dinner. His trenchant
remarks are very different in style from Bloch's, but the sentiments
are the same: "Racine? Il a deux beaux vers. Voici le premier:
La fille de Minos et de Pasiphaé. Seulement, il n'a jamais pu trouver
la rime: il a fait rimer *Pasiphaé* avec *liberté*, je ne sais pas quoi!"[4]
This seems to be what we are looking for, but the passage only
appears in the complete *Journal*, first published in the 1950s. How
did Proust, and others who have made earlier references, get to

[1] *Chroniques* (Paris, 1927; reprinted 1943), p. 230. See Laurence Le Sage,
Marcel Proust's Appreciation of the Poetry of Alfred de Musset', *F.R.*, XXI
(1948), 361–3; Jean Pommier, 'Musset et Proust', *Bulletin de la Société des Amis de
Marcel Proust*, No. 2 (1951-2), 59–77.

[2] Fernand Calmettes (*Leconte de Lisle et ses amis* (Paris, 1902), p. 106) seems to
suggest that the article appeared. However, a careful search of *Le Nain jaune*
for the relevant period has failed to reveal any trace of it. There is evidence in
Leconte de Lisle's correspondence of his dislike and contempt for Musset (e.g.
Irving Putter, 'Les idées littéraires de Leconte de Lisle d'après une correspondance inédite' *R.H.L.F.*, LXVI (1966), 457).

[3] *Jean Santeuil* (Paris, 1952), vol. I, pp. 127–8.

[4] *Journal* (Monaco, 1956–8), vol. I, p. 67.

know about it? Not, clearly, from the original bowdlerized editions
of the *Journal*.

Still, with Gautier we have almost reached Musset. We can now
look at the line in the *Nuit de mai* which, with "La fille de Minos",
has caused so much fuss:

> Inventons quelque part des lieux où l'on oublie;
> Partons, nous sommes seuls, l'univers est à nous.
> Voici la verte Écosse et la brune Italie,
> Et la Grèce, ma mère, où le miel est si doux,
> Argos, et Ptéléon, ville des hécatombes,
> Et Messa la divine, agréable aux colombes,
> Et le front chevelu du Pélion changeant;
> Et le bleu Titarèse, et le golfe d'argent
> Qui montre dans ses eaux, où le cygne se mire,
> La blanche Oloossone à la blanche Camyre.[1]

Here the main source is familiar: all these Greek names come from
Book II of the *Iliad*. Argos is Pelasgian Argos, Ptéléon is "Pteleos
couched in grass", Messa and its *colombes* is "many-doved Messe",
Pélion with its *front chevelu* is "Pelion covered with waving forests",
Titarèse with its silver gulf is "lovely Titaressus that poureth his
fair-flowing streams into Peneius: yet doth he not mingle with the
silver eddies of Peneius". Finally, *la blanche Oloossone* is τε
πόλιν τ'Ολοοσσόνα λευκήν, the white city of Oloosson, and *la
blanche Camyre* is ἀργινόεντα Κάμειρον, Cameirus white with
chalk (according to the Loeb translation). All the names are found
together in a couple of hundred lines of the *Iliad*. This would not
be conclusive in itself if they were the ordinary names of Greek
mythology, but most of them are very out-of-the-way indeed. When
we add the accompanying descriptions, especially the doves of
Messa and the whiteness of Oloosson and Cameirus, we see that
there is no other explanation than the influence of Homer on Musset.
But was this influence exercised directly or through a translation?
The standard translation of the time, Bitaubé's, has only "la blanche
Camire" in common with Musset, but that of Dugas-Montbel (1815)
has, as well as this, "Messa agréable aux colombes", and "la blanche

---

[1] *Poésies complètes*, ed. Allem (Paris, Bibliothèque de la Pléiade, 1957; reprinted
1962), p. 306.

ville d'Oloossone".[1] It looks as if Musset was at least partly inspired by this translation.

Sources are of value for the light they throw on the processes of poetic creation and the development of literary traditions. Here we can see, even in a Romantic poet, the possibility of creation from literary sources rather than directly from reality, in other words the possibility of an autonomous world of literature. Musset (like Racine) never went to Greece, and this after all rather fine picture is built up mainly (not, as we shall see, entirely) from Homeric reminiscences. All this is not to deny the other side, mimesis or the direct representation of reality, but we must appreciate the fact that literature can draw on its own resources.

We now come to the rather dismal chapter of commentators on this line. They all tell us that Oloosson is in Thessaly, not even on the coast, and that Cameirus is hundreds of miles away in Rhodes, so obviously they could not be reflected in the same water. A single example may suffice, Allem in the Pléiade edition: "Camyre est située sur la côte occidentale de l'île de Rhodes. Oloossone, ville de Thessalie, n'est pas au bord de la mer. Les deux villes ne pouvaient donc pas se mirer dans les mêmes eaux."[2] This sort of thing, which may reasonably be described as pedantry, misses the whole nature of imaginative creation: Musset has assembled his magically evocative names to conjure up a perfect, an ideal Greek land- and seascape, and it does not matter in the slightest where these places are on the map or what they are like in prosaic reality. Plain facts are very important in reading poetry, but we must know how to use them.

There is also something similar in Hugo's picture of the modern Greek town of Navarino in *Les Orientales*:

> Enfin! – C'est Navarin, la ville aux maisons peintes,
> La ville aux dômes d'or, *la blanche Navarin*,
> Sur la colline assise entre les térébinthes,
> Qui prête son beau *golfe* aux ardentes étreintes
> De deux flottes heurtant leurs carènes d'airain.[3]

---

[1] *Iliad*, trans. M. Dugas-Montbel (Paris, 1815), 2 vols: vol. I, pp. 66, 63, 70.
[2] Musset, *Poésies complètes*, p. 733.
[3] *Odes et ballades. Les Orientales* (Paris, 1912), p. 652.

Here we cannot speak with the same certainty as in the case of Homer, but Musset certainly read *Les Orientales*[1] and apart from the two coincidences of words there is a strong resemblance in the way the picture is made, the *facture*, which can be called Romantic. However, the true source of the line in its structure and poetic impact (as opposed to the Homeric names) is known to be an epigram of Chénier's (no doubt among the most beautiful lines in French poetry):

> Néère, ne va plus te confier aux flots
> De peur d'être Déesse et que les matelots
> N'invoquent, au milieu de la tourmente amère,
> La blanche Galatée et la blanche Néère.[2]

The word-order, the position of the Greek names, the repeated *blanche*, each time before the noun, all point to direct imitation. Chénier's poems had considerable influence on the young Romantics; the Néère epigram had already been quoted by Chateaubriand in the *Génie du Christianisme*.[3] So what looked at first like a straight imitation of Homer turns out to be more like an orchestration of echoes from at least three poets, Homer, Chénier, and Hugo.

We can now abandon source-hunting and approach the stylistic part of this enquiry. We have two lines, identical apart from a preposition and a conjunction, a difference which does not seem to matter much, different pairs of names, Galatée–Néère and Oloossone–Camyre, which make a fairly considerable difference phonetically but not otherwise – or so it would seem.

But before we proceed further it will be well to consider Chénier's historical position, his relation to the movement which art historians call neo-classicism, the painting of David and Prud'hon, the sculpture of Canova, the architecture of the British Museum or the Madeleine. The object of the movement was to remake the Renaissance, only better, to return to the genuine forms of ancient art in all its primitive simplicity, cutting away the florid ornaments and pretty frills which were becoming associated with the words baroque

---

[1] see Pierre Moreau, *Le Classicisme des romantiques* (Paris, 1932), p. 306.
[2] *Poems*, ed. Scarfe (1961), p. 21.
[3] Classiques Garnier (Paris, 1950), vol. II, p. 279.

and rococo. Looking from this point of view at the two identical lines, we see at once a major difference. Galatée and Néère are the names of sea-nymphs (or to be more precise of a Nereid whom Chénier treats as a goddess and of a mortal girl who runs the risk of a similar apotheosis); Oloossone and Camyre are the names of towns. In Chénier we have two female figures whose whiteness is the whiteness of flesh, of vague draperies perhaps, even of marble. We are forcibly reminded of the dazzling whiteness of Canova and even more of Prud'hon, who likewise concentrates all the attention on figures in the foreground, generally mythological, rendered in the same dominating white against a background of grey or *grisaille*. The *Venus and Adonis* in the Wallace Collection is a good example. The sea in Chénier is wonderfully present in the waves, the sailors and the bitter storm, but it is realized through conventional nota-tions (*flots*, a classical *mot noble*, and *tourmente*): we do not grasp it quite visually. In this respect Chénier is close to seventeenth-century Classicism and to Racine. In fact Racine uses the same rhyme in *Mithridate*, that superb sea-play:

> Les autres, qui partaient, s'élancent dans les *flots*,
> Ou présentent leurs dards aux yeux des *matelots*.[1]

But the word *blanc* only occurs once in the whole of Racine, half as many times as in this one line of Chénier's.[2] Again it is in *Mithridate*:

> Jusqu'ici la fortune et la victoire mêmes
> Cachaient mes cheveux *blancs* sous trente diadèmes.[3]

This, however, is hardly more than a metonymy for old age: it is completely lacking in any picturesque quality. Admittedly there is also a rather dull variant in *Alexandre*[4] and the effective use of *blanchissant* in *Iphigénie* and *blanchit* in *Athalie*.[5] Still, it remains true, as Cahen says, that "L'univers de Racine est à peu près

[1] ll. 1429–30.
[2] Pierre Guiraud *et al.*, *Index du vocabulaire du théâtre classique* (Paris, 1955–64).
[3] ll. 1039–40
[4] Grands Écrivains ed., 8 vols (Paris, 1865–73), vol. I, p. 595.
[5] *Iphigénie*, ll. 381, 1781; *Athalie*, l. 160.

dépourvu de couleurs".[1] Chénier's white, though monochromatic, acquires in comparison a vivid intensity from the powerful repetition.

With Musset we have moved into a different world. What we now see is the whiteness not of human figures but of two southern towns rising from the sea and reflected in it. Parallels are to be found not in the neo-classical painters of the human form but in the Romantic painters of landscape (for example Delacroix, Decamps, and Fromentin, especially the first two with their studies of towns in the eastern Mediterranean or North Africa). Taking Musset in conjunction with the Navarino description and similar passages in *Les Orientales*, it seems that such vivid evocation of exotic scenes is something not previously encountered in French poetry. But this is not all. In Chénier the whiteness is entirely contained in the two adjectives, in Musset it is extended and supported by the swan (or perhaps rather swans, one individual standing by synecdoche for the whole class), by the silver gulf, and probably also by the doves, so that the picture of Greece is flooded with white light. Moreover "le bleu Titarèse" introduces a note of blue (not in Homer) into the Greek landscape which is necessary if we are to see its full Mediterranean splendour. And each country has its characteristic colour: the green of Scotland, the brown of Italy, the whiteness of Greece. Where in Chénier we found unrelieved whiteness, we have here a chromatic range (green, brown, blue, silver, white) which is not really conceivable in poetry before the Romantic period. This is a feature which Gautier stresses in that amusing parody of the Romantic style, *Daniel Jovard* (1833, two years before the *Nuit de mai*): "il lui monta une palette flamboyante: noir, rouge, bleu, toutes les couleurs de l'arc-en-ciel, une véritable queue de paon".[2] In so far as a poet can be regarded as a painter in words, we see that this word-painting is evolving in a characteristically Romantic way. In fact the old argument between the partisans of colour and of draughtsmanship, which had already erupted in the seventeenth century between the supporters of Rubens and of Poussin (in other words between baroque and Classicism) re-emerged in the nineteenth with Delacroix and Ingres. On the one hand design, structure,

---

[1] *Le Vocabulaire de Racine* (Paris, 1946), p. 90.
[2] *Critique artistique et littéraire*, ed. Gohin and Tisserand (Paris, 1929), p. 119.

intellectual organization, on the other, colour, movement, and sensual effect: all this can be seen in our two lines when they are replaced in context.

We are left with the difference between Chénier's *et* and Musset's *à* (mistakenly quoted as *et* by Bloch). The effect of *et* is to place the two figures side by side in a single plane, one might say with the bas-relief technique often employed by neo-classical painters (Prud'hon again offers good examples). With *à*, on the other hand, a powerful reciprocal relation is set up:

> le golfe d'argent,
> Qui montre dans ses eaux, où le cygne se mire,
> La blanche Oloossone à la blanche Camyre.

Both towns are reflected in the water, or rather the reflection of one is visible from the other. This may be taken as a prefiguration of another painting in words, Elstir's 'Le Port de Carquethuit', where the reflections of town, harbour and ships repeat and re-echo the real structures until land and sea are intermingled and we are unable to distinguish between them. This ultimate refinement of impressionist technique far transcends anything that Musset or his contemporaries were capable of, but we can see in the earlier work the beginnings of movement within the landscape picture, even though the general effect remains static. An objection may be raised at this point. Are we not dealing with a mere accident? If we picked two other lines from Chénier and Musset, might we not find the positions reversed? Can we draw conclusions on this scale from such trifling details? The first answer is *context*, always vital in any question of style: obviously *à* could not carry the meaning suggested without the verb *montre* and all the accompanying circumstances. But secondly we have to start somewhere and we have to start with what is in front of us. It is possible that on reading other lines, by these two and other poets, we might have to modify the conclusions or even change them altogether, but we must have a position to modify, a working hypothesis.

If this is accepted, we can now see the differences between a neo-classical and a Romantic poet writing the same, or nearly the same, line, and incidentally in comparing Chénier with Racine we have seen at least something that separates neo-classicism from Classicism *tout court* (colour in Chénier even if it is only white, no colour in Racine). However, the similarities between Chénier and Musset remain very striking, especially the repeated *blanche* and its preposition, which throws the idea, or rather the sensation, of whiteness into stronger relief, the Greek names (in Racine too), and of course the sea. Clearly all three poets are working in the same tradition, however necessary we find it to attach them to different schools or movements. Neo-classicism is exactly contemporary with what is called pre-romanticism and is most difficult to disentangle from it. On the one hand it is the extreme point of the Renaissance, the ultimate expression of the Classicism of which Romanticism is the absolute antithesis. On the other, it leads straight to that very Romanticism: Greece and Rome are no longer regarded only as sources of a timeless perfection, but also as objects of historical and archaeological study (Herculaneum and Pompeii for example). What emerges is the Romantic notion of local colour. We know that in Racine there is little mention of material objects and virtually none of those which are historically characteristic of antiquity. But in Chénier, not so much in the Néère poem but in *La Jeune Tarentine* or better still in *Le Mendiant*:

> Sur ses mains, de l'*aiguière d'argent*,
> Par une jeune esclave une eau pure est versée.
> Une *table de cèdre* où l'*éponge* est passée,
> S'approche, et vient offrir à son avide main
> Et les fumantes chairs sur les *disques d'airain*,
> Et l'*amphore* vineuse et la *coupe aux deux anses*.[1]

the silver ewer, the cedar table, the sponge, the bronze disks, the amphora, the two-handled cup – all these might be objects in a museum if they were not fused by the poetry into a single living scene. And in contrast with the precision of these *mots propres* there is also a certain aura of wistfulness, a feeling for the irrevocable pastness of antiquity, which heralds the Romantic sense of the historical and the relative (again as in Prud'hon). Of course this is not so new: it comes through very strongly, for instance, in Du Bellay's *Antiquités de Rome*. But we could hardly find better examples than in the Néère epigram or *La Jeune Tarentine*, unless

[1] *Bucoliques*, ed. Dimoff (Paris, 1937), p. 207.

it is in the *Ode on a Grecian Urn* where archaeology becomes mystery:

> Who are these coming to the sacrifice?
> To what green altar, O mysterious priest,
> Lead'st thou that heifer lowing at the skies... ?

In Goethe and Hölderlin, in Blake and Keats, as well as in Chénier and here at least in Musset, we can see a fusion of neo-classicism and Romanticism which offers us one more example of how extremes meet.

But we still have not fully explained the curious words of Bloch. Who or what is Proust aiming at? Bloch admires these two lines in Musset and Racine, and no others, because each is rhythmical and utterly meaningless. The Musset line, as we have seen, is far from meaningless when replaced in its context, and in the case of Racine the demonstration would be even more conclusive, but no doubt if the two lines are taken in complete isolation, as Bloch takes them, it would be difficult to say that they mean anything, or to deny that they are none the less haunting. To understand the idea better, we shall have to turn to the abbé Bremond and his prolific, if rather diffuse, writings on poetry. In *La Poésie pure* he says: "On ne sait pas, un homme de goût ne cherche même pas à savoir ce que signifie telle chanson de Shakespeare, exquise pourtant."[1] Or, still more to the point: "Avec tous ceux qui lisent poétiquement les poètes j'avais remarqué que, pour sentir le charme d'un vers, d'un lambeau de vers, pas n'est besoin de connaître le poème où ce vers, ce lambeau se trouvent. *La fille de Minos et de Pasiphaé*"[2] and the line recurs like a *leitmotiv* throughout *La Poésie pure* and *Racine et Valéry*. Bremond, it is true, has now added another idea to that of meaninglessness (still very much in harmony with the attitudes of Bloch and Gautier), the independence and validity of single lines torn from their context. (Incidentally, Proust also makes, in *Le Côté de Guermantes*, a specific attack on this fashion.)[3] But the main point is that Bremond is acting as the spokesman and popularizer of one of the most powerful concepts in modern poetic theory, the notion of pure poetry which goes back through Valéry (and Croce) to

[1] *La Poésie pure* (Paris, 1926), p. 19.
[2] *ibid.*, p. 36.
[3] *A la recherche du temps perdu*, vol. II, p. 471 and variant.

Mallarmé, to Pater, to Flaubert's dream of *un livre sur rien*, to Poe, to Gautier and the art for art's sake movement, ultimately perhaps to the aesthetics of Kant and Hegel. The heart of the doctrine is that poetry is not narration, description, explanation, teaching, moralizing, in fact anything that we ordinarily understand by meaning in its intellectual sense, but a core of ineffable emotion ("il y a d'abord et surtout de l'ineffable", says Bremond[1]) operating like music on the deeper centres of consciousness.[2] A hurried summary like this runs the risk of caricaturing the doctrine almost as much as Proust does, but we must understand that behind Bloch and Bremond there stands a greater tradition which is under fire and which goes back to the Romantic revolt against the supremacy of reason in literature.

Romantic too is the other idea in Bloch, Gautier, and Bremond, the independent validity, indeed superior perfection, of single lines, the logical conclusion of Poe's contention that a short poem must be better than a long one.[3] Poe's argument, it is true, is based on the principle of concentration, whereas the cult of the single line springs rather from the principle of fragmentation, which takes many forms in Romantic art and literature: the cult of ruins, often preferred to an intact building, the elevation of the sketch or drawing above the easel picture or of the writer's notebooks and private diaries above his finished and published works. Of more direct concern here is the Romantic fashion of the epigraph, again taken off by Gautier in *Daniel Jovard*:

> Une chose qu'il faut soigner, ce sont les épigraphes. Vous en mettez en anglais, en allemand, en espagnol, en arabe; si vous pouvez vous en procurer une en chinois, cela fera un effet merveilleux, et, sans être Panurge, vous vous trouverez insensiblement possesseur d'une mignonne réputation d'érudit et de polyglotte...[4]

What the epigraph does, apart from impressing the reader with the erudition of the author as Gautier suggests, is to evoke echoes from earlier literature, to convey a sense of mystery springing from the

---

[1] *La Poésie pure*, p. 16.

[2] Pommier ('Musset et Proust', *art. cit.*, p. 62) points out the symbolist heritage in Bloch's cult of the meaningless.

[3] 'The Poetic Principle'.

[4] *Critique artistique et litteraire*, p. 114.

isolation of the quoted words from their context. In fact it is very close to the sort of single line we have been considering. The culmination of the cult of the fragment is to be found, no doubt, in the magnificent conclusion of *The Waste Land*:

> *Poi s'ascose nel foco che gli affina*
> *Quando fiam uti chelidon –* O swallow swallow
> *Le Prince d'Aquitaine à la tour abolie*
> These fragments I have shored against my ruins.

Here, while we find the same polyglot erudition as in Gautier's skit (and though there is no Chinese, Eliot manages to end with Sanskrit), the fragmentary takes on more sombre implications. These fragments of mysterious (and meaningless) beauty are all that is left of a civilization which is itself in ruins, and it may be that Romanticism could go no further.

It may now be objected that this proves nothing except that Bloch's remarks reveal an attitude to poetry derived from Romanticism, which is not really surprising. But what is a little surprising, perhaps, is that Bloch's diatribe is typical of an anti-Romantic reaction, an attempt to create a new neo-classicism of which Charles Maurras was the great champion in France[1] and Eliot (greatly influenced by Maurras) in England. And our earlier sources for Bloch, that is Leconte de Lisle and Gautier, are often seen in the same light. Parnassianism, with its Hellenism, its insistence on form, precision, and impersonality (a favourite concept with Eliot also) does at first sight look like a reaction against Romanticism. However, when we examine these various classicisms of the nineteenth and twentieth centuries – Parnassianism, Maurras and the *Action française*, Cézanne and Cubism (at least as interpreted by Roger Fry), Irving Babbitt and Eliot – we see that all of them derive from Romanticism by links like those I have tried to explore in the case of "la blanche Oloossone". Maurras and Eliot are probably the most interesting because of the association of their Classicism with a reactionary political position which is itself a creation of Romanticism (Joseph de Maistre or for that matter Balzac).

What conclusions can be drawn from these remarks as far as the

[1] Maurras also quotes "la blanche Oloossone" in his essay on Chénier (in *Tableau de la littérature française*, preface by André Gide (Paris, 1939), p. 470).

question of Romanticism and Classicism is concerned? Shall we agree with T. S. Eliot that "the difference seems to me rather the difference between the complete and the fragmentary [again!], the adult and the immature, the orderly and the chaotic"?[1] (In fairness to Eliot it must be said that the fragmentary structure of *The Waste Land* may well appear as a classical protest against a world in which romantic values have triumphed. Still, his poetry does, objectively considered, represent one extreme point in the history of Romanticism.) Or should we rather accept the words of Jean Moréas on his deathbed (which caused a good deal of embarrassment to his disciple Charles Maurras)? "Il n'y a pas de classiques et de romantiques; c'est des bêtises."[2] Neither, entirely. We have seen that there are real and important differences between Romanticism and Classicism, whether Racinian Classicism or the neo-classicism of Chénier. We have also seen that there is an unbroken continuity (in so far as three lines of verse can show such a thing – but I think they can). We need to be aware of historical change but we also need to see the elements of continuity which link the most disparate or even contradictory manifestations of literature.

If I have chosen to base these reflections on three lines of poetry it is not because of any close adherence to the views of the abbé Bremond or Bloch – on the contrary – but because there is so much that is contained in every great or even important work of literature. If one is to do the job thoroughly there is simply not time for more than a line or two. Of course, there is another side: if we concentrate to this extent on single words and lines, we shall hardly ever read a whole poem, let alone a novel. The answer must lie in change of focus: sometimes we must enlarge the scale so that a single line occupies the whole of our attention; sometimes we must look at whole works, groups of works, genres, movements and periods, where the minor detail dwindles and larger structures and patterns come into view. The problem then is how to link up the different focuses, the microscopic and macroscopic methods. It would be wrong to pretend that this is easy, but I hope I may have offered, here and there, some suggestions of how it might be done.

[1] *Selected Essays*, 2nd ed. (1934), p. 26.
[2] Charles Maurras and Raymond de la Tailhède, *Un Débat sur le romantisme* (Paris, 1928), pp. 6, 39.

Victor Hugo's first melodrama

RICHARD FARGHER

In the *Nouvelle Revue Française* of 1 March 1939, M. Jean Montargis, heir of Victor Hugo's literary executor Paul Meurice, published Hugo's first dramatic work, *Le Château du diable*, a three-act melodrama of approximately 2,500 words. The hero, Raoul, Comte de Salandry, is a poor but valiant knight whose beautiful young wife Adélaïde has been disinherited, because of her marriage, by her uncle and guardian, the Comte de Richaumont. At the inn where Raoul and Adélaïde are spending the night, a peasant tells Raoul of the demons terrorizing the countryside from the near-by ruined castle. Raoul at once goes to the castle with his bibulous servant Robert. After many horrifying and apparently magical apparitions and threats, which Raoul valiantly withstands, he is sentenced to death by precipitation from a high rock in an underground cavern. Adélaïde also hurls herself into the chasm. The hellish ordeals are then revealed as an elaborate make-believe engineered by the uncle, who, convinced now of Raoul's merit, accepts the couple as his heirs. The manuscript, M. Montargis informs us, is a copy made by Juliette Drouet, but bears a dedication to her in Hugo's own hand, dated 9 November 1834, stating that he wrote the play in 1812, when he was ten. M. Montargis suggests that the *Le Château du diable* expresses the infant Hugo's emotional excitement at the arrest, imprisonment, trial and execution, in 1812, of his godfather La Horie – that mysterious Breton general who conspired against Napoleon, was hidden from the police by Mme Hugo in the garden of Les Feuillantines, and who, under the name of M. de Courlande, gave Latin lessons to the Hugo children. Adélaïde, the heroine of the play, is, according to M. Montargis, inspired by Hugo's future wife Adèle, daughter of General Hugo's friend Pierre Foucher, an official at the Ministry of War. The Hôtel de Toulouse, where the Fouchers lived in 1812, was also the scene of La Horie's court-martial: thus, M. Montargis argues, the children's games in the Fouchers' garden mingled, in the little Victor's mind, with evocations of plots, trials, dungeons and death.[1]

According to Mme Victor Hugo, Hugo had seen seven performances of Pixérécourt's melodrama *Les Ruines de Babylone*, during a month spent at Bayonne in 1811 on the way to Spain:

> C'était très beau. Il y avait un bon Génie magnifiquement costumé en troubadour, dont les apparitions étaient espérées avec anxiété... La victime du tyran, pour éviter la mort, se réfugiait naturellement dans un souterrain; elle y serait morte de faim et d'ennui, si le bon génie n'était venu de temps en temps lui apporter à manger et causer un peu. Une fois qu'ils s'oubliaient dans les charmes d'une longue conversation, le Génie apercevait tout-à-coup le tyran qui venait à pas sourds vers la trappe soulevée; alors le troubadour, sautant rapidement sur la trappe, renfonçait son protégé d'un prodigieux coup sur la tête, et le tyran restait stupide devant l'escamotage de sa victime... Heureusement que le lendemain, on donnait la même pièce... Cette fois les trois frères ne perdirent pas un mot du dialogue, et revinrent sachant les cinq actes par cœur.[2]

From this, and a reading of Pixérécourt's play, M. Montargis concludes that *Le Château du diable* is a "reflet" of *Les Ruines de Babylone*, which, though devoid of Hugolian language and imagery, nevertheless supplies the framework and machinery of the Romantic drama, and that "à dix ans, Hugo dramatisant était déja lui-même".

'*Les Ruines de Babylone, ou Giafar et Zaïda*, Mélodrame historique en trois actes en prose et à grand spectacle par R. C. Guilbert Pixérécourt, représenté, pour la première fois, à Paris, sur le Théâtre de la Gaîté le 30 octobre, 1810', was published at Paris in 1810. The scene of the play is at Baghdad, in the year 796, and in the ruins of Babylon, a few miles away. The extremely complicated plot hinges on one simple issue: will the Caliph Haroun-al-Raschid

---

[1] Mme Victor Hugo plainly states, however, that Hugo did not know, in 1812, that M. de Courlande was the La Horie whose execution he had seen announced on a poster, and that consequently "Victor se remit à jouer et à rire pendant qu'on fusillait son parrain". (*Victor Hugo raconté par un témoin de sa vie* (Bruxelles et Leipzig, 1863), vol. I, p. 188.)

[2] *ibid.*, pp. 113-14.

be prevented from killing his chief vizier Giafar, who has broken the royal command by consummating his marriage with Zaïda, the Caliph's sister? Naïr, the infant son of Giafar and Zaïda, is guarded by a faithful old man in underground chambers that had been used by Zoroastrians: communication between the ruins and the outside world is maintained by a trap-door in a forest pavilion. Eventually, thanks to the resourcefulness of the Frenchman Raymond, who is organizer of Court entertainments, the play ends with general happiness and reconciliation. In spite of the absence of the Devil from *Les Ruines de Babylone*, and numerous other major differences between it and *Le Château du diable*, some things are common to both plays:

PIXÉRÉCOURT	HUGO
The Caliph disapproves of the marriage being consummated. Giafar's woes are caused by the Caliph's favourite wife Almaïde, whose love Giafar has spurned.	The uncle disapproves of Raoul's marriage to Adélaïde. Ralph's life will be spared if he renounces his wife and accepts the love of the Bandit Queen.
Act III is set in the ruins, which include "les murs d'un château fort". Giafar's wife wanders disconsolate through the ruins, longing for death.	Act II is set in the abandoned feudal castle; Act III in the vaults beneath. Raoul's wife seeks her husband in the vaults, and throws herself from a rock into the chasm.
In the last scene, the Caliph says: "Zaïda, Naïr, Hassan, Raymond, venez tous dans mes bras."	In the last scene, the uncle, seated on a throne in a throne-room, says: "Raoul, Adélaïde, venez dans mes bras, mes enfants."

In both plays there are slaves, disguises, and masked figures who pounce upon people from out of the darkness.

A fact which gives the similarities quite a different aspect, however, is the prior existence of a play by Loaisel de Tréogate (1752–1812), with the same title as Hugo's: '*Le Château du diable*, Comédie héroïque en quatre actes et en prose par J. M. Loaisel Tréogate. Représentée, pour la première fois, sur le théâtre de Molière, le 5 décembre 1792.' It was published in Paris in 1793, and again in An X (1802). There can be no doubt that Pixérécourt knew about Tréogate's play. They shared the same publisher (*Les Ruines de Babylone* and the An X edition of *Le Château du diable* both

appeared "chez Barba"), and, in 1804, had collaborated in writing
'*Le Grand Chasseur, ou l'Ile des Palmiers*, Mélodrame en trois
actes en prose et à grand spectacle par MM. Loaisel-Tréogate et ***'.
The resemblances between Hugo's *Château du diable* and Tréogate's
are so obvious and manifold that – whatever the adult Hugo may
have imagined the case to have been when, in 1834, he bestowed
upon his mistress this "première pensée de l'enfant" – it must be
assumed either that he saw or read Tréogate's play and remembered
it with remarkable accuracy, or else that he wrote his version of it
with Tréogate's text, or a summary of it, beside him. We are told in
Victor Hugo raconté par un témoin de sa vie that in 1812 he regularly
borrowed books for his mother from Jean-Louis Royol's lending
library, and was himself a voracious reader of these books. The
inventory of Royol's stock in 1821 included: "Théâtre", 221 items;
"drames et mélodrames", 133 items.[1] Loaisel de Tréogate and
Hugo's mother were both Bretons; according to M. L. Guimbaud,
Mme Hugo visited all the Bretons of note in Paris during her attempt
to save La Horie from execution.[2] The fact that Tréogate himself
died in 1812 is an additional reason why his book might have been in
the Hugo household during that year.

   Tréogate's *comédie héroïque* is a typical eighteenth-century hotch-
potch of ruins, horrors, torments, and apparently diabolical interventions which are rationalistically explained, so giving the thrills
of the supernatural and the satisfactions of Enlightenment. The
abbé Prévost, in *Cleveland* and elsewhere, had already shown his
contemporaries what pleasures were to be derived from the contemplation of fictional caverns, killings, burnings, woes, miseries,
and the more horrific forms of moral and physical anguish. In 1767
Diderot, finding the scenes of ruins depicted by Hubert Robert
inadequately dire, suggested additional themes of hellish violence,
witchcraft, frenzy, heroism, outlawry, mock-medievalism and moral
uplift, material enough for half a dozen Romantic dramas:

   *Intérieur d'un lieu souterrain, d'une caverne éclairée par une
   petite fenêtre grillée placée au fond du tableau, au centre de la
   composition qu'elle éclaire... J'aimerais bien mieux y voir la joie*

[1] *ibid.*, pp. 181–3, and J. Seebacher, 'Le Bonhomme Royol et son cabinet de
lecture', *R.H.L.F.*, LXII (1962), pp. 575–89.
[2] L. Guimbaud, *La Mère de Victor Hugo 1772–1821* (Paris, 1930), pp. 191–2.

infernale d'une troupe de bohémiens; le repaire de quelques voleurs; le spectacle de la misère d'une famille paysanne; les attributs et la personne d'une prétendue sorcière; quelque aventure de *Cleveland* ou de l'Ancien Testament; l'asile de quelque illustre malheureux persécuté; l'homme qui jette à sa femme et à ses enfants affamés le pain qu'il s'est procuré par un forfait; l'histoire de *La Bergère des Alpes;* des enfants qui viennent pleurer sur la cendre de leurs pères; un ermite en oraison; quelque scène de tendresse. Que sais-je?[1]

It has, however, been suggested by M. Max Milner that Tréogate's precise source was an incident in *Olivier* (1763), by Cazotte, author of the more famous *Diable amoureux*.[2] The most interesting thing about Tréogate's *Château du diable* – which is set in the fifteenth century, with "costume de Chevalerie du quinzième siècle" – is the fact that it was possible, in Paris, six weeks before Louis XVI's execution, for the *ci-devant* "gendarme de la garde du roi", M. de Tréogate, to find a stage for a drama eulogizing knight-errantry and the minor feudal aristocracy. By 1802, when the second edition was published, such themes were, of course, welcomed by the propagandists for counter-revolution and royalist restoration.

The following examples suffice to show that Hugo had a good knowledge of Tréogate's *Château du diable*:[3]

TRÉOGATE	HUGO
Act I, Sc. iii.	Act I, Sc. i.
L'Hôtesse: Je ne les ai jamais vus, mais il n'y a guères de jour que je n'entende parler d'eux à mon époux, qui a servi comme aide-de-cuisine chez le baron de Mongrigny... *Robert:* Vous êtes bien instruite!	*Martha:* ... mon père était concierge dans le Château du vieux comte, et voici comment la chose se passa... *Robert:* Comment êtes-vous si bien renseignée? [Variante du texte: si bien instruite.]
Sc. viii.	Sc. iv.
Raoul (comte de Salandrie), Robert, un paysan.	Raoul (comte de Salandry), Robert, un paysan.

[1] Diderot, *Salons III, 1767,* ed. J. Seznec et J. Adhémar (1963), pp. 243–4.

[2] Max Milner, *Le Diable dans la littérature française de Cazotte à Baudelaire* (Paris, 1960), vol. I, pp. 85–6, 191–2.

[3] I have used the An X *Nouvelle édition revue et corrigée,* a copy of which my wife bought for half-a-crown at the Oxford cattle market in 1961.

Le Paysan: Excusez; c'est ici dit-on qu'est venu descendre un chevalier de haute apparence que j'ons vu traverser le village sur un grand palefroi? N'est-ce-ti point vous, seigneur?
Raoul: Il est vrai que j'arrive, et que j'ai passé par le village.

Le Paysan: M'est avis qu'un Seigneur chevalier en grand équipage v'nons d'descendre à c't'auberge, mais n'est-ce pas vous, Seigneur?
Raoul: Il est vrai, je viens d'arriver à l'instant.

Sc. ix.

Le Paysan: Je venons, seigneur, vous demander un sarvice au nom de tous les habitants.
Raoul: A quoi puis-je vous être utile, mon ami, parlez?
Le Paysan: Y a ici, tout près de c't'aubarge, un vieux châtiau abandonné, qu'on appelle le châtiau du diable... des revenants... ces maudits lutins... Tout-à-l'heure encore, Gilles, notre ménestrier, vient d'être roué de coups par un esprit sous la grande tour de ce manoir maudit.

Le Paysan: Ah, Seigneur, j'attendons d'vous et d'vot bras un service essentiel.
Raoul: Parle... quel est-il?
Le Paysan: J'allons vous dégoiser ça, à ç't'heure même. Il y a auprès de c't'auberge un vieux château abandonné qu'on appelle le Château du Diable, parce que le malin esprit et tous ses lutins y'revenont! Lublin, l'ménétrier du village, a été l'autre jour roué de coups par ces diables de lutins là.

Sc. x.

Robert:... visiter un château ruiné, dont les revenants prétendus ne peuvent être que des hiboux ou des chouettes qui sûrement y font leur nid.

Act II, sc. i.

Raoul: Nous avons visité tous les recoins du château; nous n'avons vu que des débris et entendu que les cris des hiboux qui habitent les tours de ce sombre manoir, ou le vent sifflant dans les longues galeries, à travers les crevasses de la muraille.

Act II. Le théâtre représente la salle basse d'un vieux château... Des branches d'arbres percent à travers les fenêtres, qui n'ont plus ni volets ni vitrages; la toile du fond représente une porte gothique pratiquée dans un mur qui menace ruine.

Sc. i.

Raoul: Je ne crois pas aux revenants; mais je crois aux fripons....
Robert: Vous me laissez seul?
Raoul: Tu as peur? (Il sort).

Raoul: Je ne crois pas aux esprits, mais je crois aux fripons.
Robert: Vous me laissez seul?
Raoul: Oui, tu aurais peur?

Robert: Non, mais j'aime la compagnie.

Sc. ii.

Robert, seul: Comme on est crédule! comme on est imbécile dans ces petits villages! Croire à des sorciers, à des revenants! Si un revenant paraissait devant moi, je vous lui assènerais le meilleur coup de poing!

Sc. iv. ... Au milieu est un tombeau surmonté d'une urne cinéraire. Quatre guerriers couverts d'armes noires sont couchés aux quatre coins du tombeau... Ils doivent paraître immobiles... Deux statues également armées... tiennent à la main une lance fort longue ... Une inscription... TEMERAIRE, QUI OSES PORTER TES PAS DANS L'EMPIRE DE LA MORT, FUIS, SI TU VEUX REVOIR LA LUMIERE DES CIEUX.

Raoul: Voilà un spectre qui connaît les lois de la chevalerie.

Sc. vi.

Robert, seul: ... Mais si un esprit s'était mis dans ce vase à la place du vin,... j'avalerais peut-être un démon, et j'aurais le diable dans le corps.

Sc. vii.

Robert, prenant Adélaïde pour un revenant: Seigneur, monseigneur le revenant... Monseigneur l'esprit, ne me tuez pas! je vous en aurai obligation toute ma vie. De grâce, ne me tuez pas!

Act III. Le théâtre représente une caverne vaste et profonde, d'un aspect horrible... Dans le fond du théâtre est un rocher beaucoup plus gros et plus élevé que les autres.

Robert: Non, c'est que j'aime la compagnie. (Raoul sort).

Sc. ii.

Robert (seul): ... Ah! qu'ils sont higauds, ces paysans, de croire à des démons, a des esprits. Ah, s'il s'en présentait un devant moi, comme je vous l'arrangerais! Je prendrais mon bâton et je lui ferais sentir la force de mon bras;

Sc. iii. Changement de décor. Le théâtre représente une sombre caverne au milieu de laquelle est un tombeau sur lequel sont écrits ces mots: FUIS CES LIEUX OU CRAINS LA MORT. Autour du tombeau sont rangés quatre soldats noirs immobiles dont l'un a le sabre nu. Une lampe est suspendue à la voûte.

Sc. iv.

Raoul: ... Tiens, voilà un spectre qui connait les lois de la chevalerie.

Sc. v.

Robert (seul). ... Mais non, le Diable n'a qu'à s'être fourré dans la bouteille! Ah, mon Dieu, boire un esprit, j'aurais le diable au corps.

Sc. v.

Robert: ... (A ce moment Adélaïde entre par une coulisse). Ah, monsieur le fantôme, épargnez-moi, pardonnez-moi, je vous prie! (reculant à mesure qu'Adélaïde s'avance). Ah, ah, ah, mon Dieu!!

Act III. Le théâtre représente un sombre caveau. Au milieu est un bûcher, à gauche est un énorme roc auquel Raoul est attaché par une chaîne qui lui entoure le milieu du

Raoul est assis, la tête appuyée sur un quartier de roc auquel il est enchaîné. Une lampe suspendue éclaire tristement ce lieu lugubre.

corps, au-dessus de lui brûle une lampe sépulcrale; à gauche dans le fond, on aperçoit un rocher fort élevé et qui perce la voûte du caveau.

Sc. vi.

Raoul, un esclave.

L'esclave: ... nous ne serons prêts que demain; mais si votre trépas est différé de deux jours seulement, je vous promets de venir, la nuit suivante, vous ôter vos fers et vous tirer de ces lieux.

Sc. vi.

Raoul. Un esclave.

L'esclave: ... enfin nous avons trouvé une issue, mais nous ne pouvons profiter de cette circonstance que demain soir. Si vous ne pouvez retarder votre mort, vous êtes perdu à jamais.

Sc. ix.

L'Ecuyer: ... Nous savons que ce misérable nous trahit; nous savons qu'il est le chef d'un affreux complot tramé contre nous et la guerrière que nous honorons. Pour lui prouver ton dévouement, prends ce fer; immole ce traître qui conspire notre perte, et que ton premier hommage à la beauté soit la tête de son ennemi.

Sc. vii.

Le Brigand: Eh bien, donne-nous une preuve de ton dévouement... va chercher un fer... (On déchaîne Raoul. Il va chercher une épée et revient. Le brigand montre l'esclave). Tu vois ce traître, nous avons découvert le complot qu'il a fait avec d'autres de s'échapper de ce château, coupe-lui la tête.

Act IV, Sc. ii.

Adélaïde: Barbares! qu'avez-vous fair de mon époux!... Ombre de Raoul! je vole m'unir à toi pour jamais. (Elle court vers le bûcher).

Act III, Sc. viii.

Adélaïde: Où est mon époux, barbares, où est mon époux?... Raoul, je vais te suivre. (Elle court au rocher et se précipite).

Sc. iv.

Baron de Mongrigny: ... Tout ce que vous avez vu n'est autre chose qu'une comédie exécutée par mes hommes d'armes, par des femmes et autres gens de ma maison.
Raoul: Quel était votre dessein, seigneur?
Mongrigny: De vous éprouver... Cher Raoul, votre alliance ne peut qu'honorer ma famille: j'approuve votre hymen, et je vous rends toute mon amitié.

Sc. ix.

Comte de Richaumont: ... ce que j'ai fait n'était que pour vous éprouver; ce n'était qu'une cérémonie jouée par mes hommes d'armes et mes vassaux. Raoul, tu mérites ma nièce; Adélaïde, tu as un époux digne de toi. Mes enfants, je vous donne tous mes biens, vivez heureux et contents.

Hugo's play is cruder, as well as shorter, than Tréogate's. In order to compress four acts into three, he has eliminated the blazing pyre on which Adélaïde is condemned by the brigands to be burned, but keeps a purposeless stage direction: "au milieu est un bûcher". The bed of roses upon which Tréogate's Raoul and Adélaïde find themselves after falling from the flames into "un lieu bas" is, however, the probable source of the only metaphor which the child Hugo permits himself:

TRÉOGATE	HUGO
Act IV, Sc. i, p. 39: Ainsi donc aura péri d'une mort barbare ce jeune héros... tandis que d'inutiles fardeaux de la terre traînent jusqu'à l'extrême vieillesse... Sc. iii, p. 44: A la place du bûcher, paraît un lit de roses, surmonté de guirlandes. On y voit Adélaïde évanouie, et Raoul cherchant à rappeler ses esprits.	Act III, Sc. viii: C'en est fait! Tu es donc mort à la fleur de ton âge! jeune héros, de même que la rose, une main barbare t'a moissonné!

But the ten-year-old Hugo seems to have been chary of female characters. It may be significant of his future attitude to women that Raoul's apostrophes to Adélaïde occupy much more space than the four short speeches she herself is accorded. The brigand queen, who occupies two-and-a-half scenes in Tréogate, is reduced by Hugo to one short stage direction. The hostess at the inn (unnamed by Tréogate, and presumably a distant imitation of Mistress Quickly) is given the Biblical name Martha by Hugo, but her speeches are severely docked. In Act IV of Tréogate's play, the valet Robert achieves the heroic dignity proper to right-thinking retainers of aristocrats during the Revolutionary years: refusing to possess himself of his employers' property, he calls upon their executioners to take his life also:

J'irais m'enrichir du bien de mes malheureux maîtres... Ah! madame, me méprisez-vous assez pour me croire capable de vous quitter dans un moment et dans un lieu comme celui-ci?... Tuez-nous tous deux ensemble. Madame, souffrez que votre fidèle serviteur partage avec vous le sort de mon cher maître.

In Hugo, he is merely bibulous and a coward. Raoul himself keeps, in Hugo, his heroic qualities. His knightly ideals almost inspire Hugo to an alexandrine couplet:

TRÉOGATE	HUGO
Je suis chevalier; ce titre glorieux m'impose la loi de secourir les opprimés partout où je les trouve... enfin de purger le pays d'un rassemblement ténébreux.	... un brave chevalier doit punir l'oppression, défendre l'opprimé.

Whatever it may indicate about Hugo's memory or mendacity at the age of 32, his free précis of Tréogate reflects great credit on his abilities at the age of ten. In only one place has his abridgment involved him in an infantile lack of logic:

TRÉOGATE	HUGO
Raoul: Oui, tu me vois prêt d'abattre la tête, non à ce malheureux dont je respecte l'infortune, mais au premier de vous dont la bouche infâme... (Une nouvelle troupe armée se poste sur les rochers... qui... paraissent hérissés d'armes meurtrières... On saisit Raoul, on veut lui remettre des fers)... Scélérats! vous n'aurez pas le plaisir atroce de voir vos mains et vos chaînes se rougir de mon sang... (Il court, s'élance au sommet du rocher désigné pour le lieu de sa mort... lève les mains au ciel... se jette lui-même dans le précipice, d'où l'on voit sortir des flammes.)	*Raoul:* Bien loin de couper la tête à ce brave jeune homme c'est contre vous que mon épée va se diriger pour le défendre de vos coups, mais vous n'aurez pas la gloire de tremper vos mains dans mon sang. Je vais mourir d'une mort plus illustre. (Il va au roc, monte en haut et se précipite.)

By the time he came to write his *Odes et ballades*, Hugo was old enough to realize that what, since the 1790s, had been referred to by good Republicans as "the odious vestiges of feudality"[1] had more serious connotations for partisans of throne and altar than the merely aesthetic or emotional thrills which classical ruins or Gothick follies had provided for eighteenth-century sensibilities. The Devil, too,

---

[1] e.g. Cabanis at the Institut, 8 Sept. 1796 (*Œuvres philosophiques de Cabanis*, ed. C. Lehec et J. Cazeneuve (Paris, 1956), vol. I, pp. 313–14); cf. Claude Tillier, *Mon Oncle Benjamin*, ch. viii: "l'ombre sinistre de ce vieux débris de la féodalité attristait tous les environs" (published 1842; 1906 Paris-Lausanne ed., p. 103).

had become more than a literary condiment.[1] The satanic forces which, according to the seers of the counter-revolution, had been allowed by Providence to take possession of France in the days of the Jacobins continued, under the restored monarchy, to assail poets of the *littérature frénétique* school. Politically and personally, Hugo is now aware of Evil. He laments the overthrow of ancestral beliefs, and the victories of anti-clerical regicides:

> Nous égorgeons les prêtres,
> Et nous assassinons les rois.
>
> ....
>
> Des anciennes vertus le crime a pris la place;
> Il cache leurs sentiers, comme la ronce efface
> Le seuil d'un temple abandonné.[2]

He also abhors Buonaparte, the destroyer, the emissary of Heaven who appears to come from Hell, the "élu maudit de la fureur suprême"[3]. And he feels himself to be encompassed by darkness:

> Toujours d'un voile obscur ma vie enveloppée![4]

Since childhood, he has been beset by dread, and visions of death and the abyss:

> Faible enfant, du malheur j'ai su les lois cruelles.
> L'orage m'assaillit voguant dans mon berceau.
>
> ....
>
> Mais quand mon cœur brûlant poursuivait ces beaux
> songes,
> Hélas! je m'éveillai dans la nuit d'un cercueil.
>
> ....
>
> L'œil tourné vers le ciel, je marchais dans l'abîme.[5]

It would, of course, be ludicrous to attribute solely to his study of *Le Château du diable* his obsession with the ruins, manors, hauntings, owls, spectres, demons, precipices and the like, which were

---

[1] Milner, *op. cit.*, p. 205, considers that there was nothing profound about eighteenth-century French occultism: "Dans le domaine limité mais significatif où notre enquête s'est cantonnée, nous avons rencontré peu de chose qui permette de souscrire à l'image d'un XVIIIᵉ siècle tourné vers l'ombre et fasciné par les puissances du mal."

[2] II, 3; *La Bande Noire.*   [3] I, 11; *Buonaparte.*   [4] II, 4; *A mon père.*
[5] v, 14; *Actions de grâces.*

commonplaces in European literature of the period. It is none the less a fact that much of Hugo's *paysage intérieur* in the *Odes et ballades* coincides with imagery which he had encountered in Tréogate's play in 1812.[1]

In his preface to *Les Burgraves*, Hugo compares the horrors and conflicts of that play with the tragedies of Aeschylus:

> Au temps d'Eschyle, la Thessalie était un lieu sinistre. Il y avait eu là autrefois des géants; il y avait là maintenant des fantômes. Le voyageur qui se hasardait au delà de Delphes et qui franchissait les forêts vertigineuses du mont Cnémis croyait voir partout, la nuit venue, s'ouvrir et flamboyer l'œil des cyclopes ensevelis dans les marais du Sperchius.

His preface concludes with a profession of faith in Reason, Progress, and a world-civilization dominated by France:

[1] e.g., *ibid.*:

> Sors-tu de quelque tour qu'habite le Vertige? *La Chauve-souris*, v, 5.

> Puis soudain tout fuyait: sur d'informes décombres
> Tour à tour à mes yeux passaient de pâles ombres;
> D'un crêpe nébuleux le ciel était voilé;
> Et, de spectres en deuil peuplant ces déserts sombres,
> Un tombeau dominait le palais écroulé.   *A G......... y*, v, 10.

> Damoiselle, entends-moi! de peur que la Nuit sombre,
> Comme en un grand filet, ne me prenne en son ombre,
> Parmi les spectres blancs et les fantômes noirs,
> Les démons, dont l'enfer même ignore le nombre,
> Les hiboux du sépulcre et l'autour des manoirs. *Le Sylphe, Bal.* 2.

(Cf. Loaisel, *Le Château de diable, ed. cit.*, p. 22: "A la pyramide sont ajustés des cercles de bras de fer qui tout-à-coup se croisent et embrassent Raoul fortement. ... A la pyramide, on peut substituer une cage de fer qui sort de dessous le théâtre et enveloppe Raoul; ou, si l'on veut, une figure colossale qui embrasse le héros et s'enfonce avec lui".)

> L'ardent foyer jetait des clartés fantastiques;
> Les hiboux s'effrayaient au fond des vieux manoirs. *Les deux archers, Bal.* 8.

> La nuit! − Ne crains-tu pas d'entrevoir la stature
> Du brigand dont un sabre a chargé la ceinture,
> ....
> Ces murs maudits par Dieu, par Satan profanés,
> Ce magique château dont l'enfer sait l'histoire,
> Et qui, désert le jour, quand tombe la nuit noire,
> Enflamme ses vitraux dans l'ombre illuminés. *A un passant, Bal.* 10.

Un jour, espérons-le, le globe entier sera civilisé, tous les points de la demeure humaine seront éclairés, et alors sera accompli le magnifique rêve de l'intelligence: avoir pour patrie le monde et pour nation l'humanité.

But even in this grandiose play of his maturity, there are apparent reminiscences of *Le Château du diable:* the sombre manor inhabited by a phantom, with caves opening onto an abyss; men hurled from the castle rocks by night but miraculously preserved; slaves incarcerated in the vaults; the young lover, surrounded by imaginary spectres and demons in the 'Caveau Perdu', given the choice by a pseudo-witch of executing his benefactor or causing the death of his beloved who, "vêtue de blanc, apparaît au fond de la galerie à gauche, chancelante, soutenue par les deux hommes masqués et comme éblouie".

When, in 1859, he published the first series of *La Légende des siècles*, Hugo had come to associate diabolical evil not, as in the *Odes et ballades*, with the men of the Revolution, but with monarchs:

> Si l'enfer s'éteignait, dans l'ombre universelle,
> On le rallumerait, certe, avec l'étincelle
> Qu'on peut tirer d'un roi heurtant un empereur.[1]

Eviradnus, the fifteenth-century knight errant who wields the sword of God against the fraud and iniquity of princes, is a regicide and emperor-slayer. The sources of *Eviradnus*,[2] as of all Hugo's works except his first, are multiple, but still, in this poem, he makes use of the self-same motifs which he had encountered in Tréogate's play about a fifteenth-century knight. There is still the ruined castle which the peasants fear to enter:

> Aussi, le paysan rend grâce à sa roture
> Qui le dispense, lui, d'audace et d'aventure,
> Et lui permet de fuir ce bourg de la forêt
> Qu'un preux, par point d'honneur belliqueux, chercherait.

As in *Le Château du diable*, an armour-clad statue springs to life; a man pretends to be devil and spectre; Eviradnus, like Raoul,

---

[1] *La Légende des siècles*, ed. H. J. Hunt (1945), *Eviradnus*, lines 1159–61.
[2] *ibid.*, p. 215, where Professor Hunt states that Hugo vaguely fixes a date for the story in the early fifteenth century.

refuses to touch the wine, but Joss and Zeno drink, and, like Robert, grovel before the phantom and ask it for mercy; a beautiful young noblewoman is about to be precipitated into the abyss beneath a sepulchral cavern; bodies hurtle from a vertiginous rock.[1]

It is, then, to the Breton Loaisel de Tréogate that we must ascribe the dubious honour of starting Victor Hugo upon his career as a melodramatist. The Hugo who campaigned for freedom and progress is, patently, the heir of the Enlightenment. But it is to the eighteenth century also that he is indebted for his initiation into the imagery of horror which, throughout the various stages of his intellectual and political development, he used to express the darkness and dread which underlay his own personality.

[1] *La Legende des siècles*, lines 175–8, 948–60, 964–76, 620–4, 763–816, 1082–7, 916–41, 595–9, 1136–69.

Baudelaire et *Marion de Lorme*

L. CELLIER

"Le terme de source, qui a jeté tant de discrédit sur l'histoire littéraire, ne doit être employé qu'avec la plus grande prudence."[1] Ainsi s'exprime Robert Kopp dans la préface à sa récente édition critique des *Petits poèmes en prose*. Et certes le maniement des éditions critiques est pour l'usager une épreuve pénible, soit que la multitude même des sources proposées pour tel ou tel vers suggère la conclusion qu'une formule aussi banale pouvait venit spontanément à l'esprit du poète, et d'autant plus que celle-ci se retrouve sous la plume d'écrivains médiocres, soit que les rapprochements paraissent tout à fait arbitraires, soit encore (si l'usager est lui-même un praticien) que tel rapprochement évident ait échappé à l'attention du sourcier. Qui voudrait aujourd'hui défendre cette pratique absurde? Or, voici qu'après m'en avoir détourné, la recherche sur l'Imaginaire paradoxalement m'y ramène avec une ferveur accrue.

Pour qui s'adonne à l'étude de la création littéraire, la recherche des sources n'est que l'aspect rébarbatif du problème le plus captivant, celui des influences. Déceler des influences, c'est en effet quitter le terrain ingrat de la culture pour pénétrer dans la zone mystérieuse de la passion. Pour l'écrivain, la découverte d'une œuvre a souvent la violence d'un coup de foudre: dans la vie de Baudelaire la découverte de son double fraternel, Edgar Poe, est plus bouleversante que la rencontre de Marie. Plus cette révélation est précoce, plus la fascination exercée est profonde et durable. Il peut s'agir d'une lecture, mais, comme nous le fait dire l'enfant des *Vocations* que l'on a mené au théâtre, il peut s'agir d'un spectacle.

Robert Kopp nous propose de distinguer entre sources explicites et implicites, les premières étant signalées par l'auteur lui-même.[2] Mais combien plus significatif est le témoignage de l'auteur lorsqu'il confesse l'émoi produit par une de ces rencontres!

[1] *Petits poèmes en prose*, éd. critique par R. Kopp (Paris, 1969), p. ix.
[2] *ibid.*

Je m'étonnais naguère de retrouver dans le théâtre de Hugo et dans celui de Claudel la même prédilection pour la 'situation dramatique' que Hugo définissait en espagnol "tres para una". De même que Doña Sol est convoitée par Hernani, Don Carlos et Don Ruy Gomez, dans *Partage de midi* autour d'Ysé tournent trois hommes: Mesa, Amalric et De Ciz; dans *le Soulier de satin* autour de Prouhèze tournent trois hommes: Rodrigue, Don Camille et Don Pélage. Que signifiait cette coïncidence? Hugo avait-il influencé Claudel? Je posais alors la question sans fournir de réponse.[1] Mais la réponse était inscrite dans ces souvenirs que Claudel avait intitulés *le Cor d'Hernani*:[2] "Pourquoi les deux émotions théâtrales les plus fortes de ma vie sont-elles dues à des poètes pour qui mon admiration n'a cessé de décroître?... C'était pendant l'Exposition universelle de 1878, et mon père s'était procuré deux places pour lui et moi au poulailler du Théâtre-français...".

Dans la *Quinzaine littéraire* du 15 juin 1967, le romancier José Cabanis a publié une lettre inédite adressée par Baudelaire à Hugo le 25 février 1840, après qu'il eut assisté à une représentation de *Marion de Lorme*. "Il y a quelque temps, je vis représenter *Marion Delorme* [*sic*]; la beauté de ce drame m'a tellement enchanté et m'a rendu si heureux que je désire vivement connaître l'auteur et le remercier de près." Le jeu de l'adolescent est facile à percer: il escompte recevoir une invitation, ou, à défaut, une réponse autographe. Mais sa lettre n'en est pas moins une lettre d'amour. "Je vous aime comme on aime un héros, un livre, comme on aime purement et sans intérêt toute belle chose... Puisque vous avez été jeune, vous devez comprendre cet amour que nous donne un livre pour son auteur, et ce besoin qui nous prend de le remercier de vive voix et de lui baiser humblement les mains...". Plus intéressant que ces déclarations passionnées est l'effort que fait l'adolescent pour justifier son enthousiasme: "Je vous crois bon et généreux parce que vous avez entrepris plusieurs réhabilitations."

Quelques années plus tard, l'adolescent désireux de se faire une place dans le monde des lettres tente de se poser en s'opposant. Nous

---

[1] voir dans la *R.L.C.*, XXXVII, (1964), mon article 'Paradoxe sur le parallèle', p. 242. Dans *Marion de Lorme* également, Marion est convoitée par Didier, Saverny, Laffemas. D'où la variante: A ce qu'il me paraît, nous sommes ici trois...

[2] Claudel, *Œuvres en prose* (Paris, Bibliothèque de la Pléiade, 1965), pp. 479–80.

ne serons pas surpris de le voir choisir comme cible à ses sarcasmes précisément *Marion de Lorme*. Dans le *Salon de 1846*, un "tableau de sentiment" lui inspire ce commentaire féroce: "*L'Aumône d'une vierge folle*. Elle donne un sou gagné à la sueur de son front à l'éternel savoyard qui monte la garde à la porte de Félix. Au dedans, les riches du jour se gorgent de friandises. Celui-là nous vient évidemment de la littérature *Marion Delorme*, qui consiste à prêcher les vertus des assassins et des filles publiques."[1]

Le débutant brûle ce qu'il a adoré. Mais nous sommes toujours dans le même climat passionnel.

Plus tard, et comme il est normal encore, Baudelaire, initié aux secrets de la maturité, dépassera cette insolence facile et retrouvera l'enthousiasme de jadis. De même qu'il écrira *les Yeux des pauvres*, il saura dire que "le poète se montre toujours l'ami attendri de tout ce qui est faible, solitaire, contristé...". Or, ce poète n'est autre que Hugo. Car, précise-t-il, "dès les débuts de son éclatante vie littéraire, nous trouvons en lui cette préoccupation des faibles, des proscrits et des maudits. L'idée de justice s'est trahie, de bonne heure dans ses œuvres, par le goût de la réhabilitation." Ainsi le Baudelaire de 1862 reprend le mot qu'il avait employé dans la lettre de 1840: réhabilitation, et il l'illustre par ces exemples: "*Oh! n'insultez jamais une femme qui tombe, Un bal à l'Hôtel de Ville, Marion de Lorme, Ruy Blas, Le Roi s'amuse* sont des poèmes qui témoignent suffisamment de cette tendance déjà ancienne, nous dirions presque de cette obsession".[2]

Toutes ces considérations nous convient à une tâche passionnante: relire *Marion de Lorme* avec les yeux de Baudelaire. Didier, le héros maudit, aime Marie, cet ange apparu dans sa nuit. Il ignore que Marie n'est autre que la courtisane Marion de Lorme. Quand il découvre la vérité, lui qui disait à Marie:

> Sois ma fortune,
> Ma gloire, mon amour, mon bien et ma vertu!

il connaît la pire désillusion qu'un être puisse éprouver. Mais il

---

[1] Baudelaire, *Œuvres complètes* (Paris, Bibliothèque de la Pléiade, 1961), p. 933. Marion de Lorme figure déja dans le *Salon de 1845* à propos d'un tableau de Lécurieux, Salomon de Caus à Bicêtre. "Nous ne comprenons pas l'effroi de Marion Delorme à l'aspect de ces aimables fous" (p. 843).

[2] Baudelaire, *Œuvres complètes*, p. 708 (repris, p. 786) et p. 788.

finit par comprendre que la courtisane s'était réhabilitée en l'aimant, que si elle se prostitue pour le sauver, c'est là un comble d'amour, puisqu'elle sacrifie sa pureté recouvrée; alors, s'élevant au-dessus de lui-même, il pardonne.

En 1846–7 (les biographes hésitent sur la date),[1] Baudelaire écrivait à Marie un lettre fameuse, qui nous apparaît désormais comme une tirade de Didier. "J'étais mort, vous m'avez fait renaître. Oh! vous ne savez pas tout ce que je vous dois! J'ai puisé dans votre regard d'ange des joies ignorées; vos yeux m'ont initié au bonheur de l'âme, dans tout ce qu'il a de plus parfait, de plus délicat...".[2]

Et Didier:

> Oh! vous ne savez pas, je vous aime ardemment!
> Du jour où je vous vis, ma vie encor bien sombre
> Se dora, vos regards m'éclairèrent dans l'ombre.
> Dès lors, tout a changé. Vous brillez à mes yeux
> Comme un être inconnu, de l'espèce des cieux.
> Cette vie, où longtemps gémit mon cœur rebelle,
> Je la vois sous un jour qui la rend presque belle.

Votre beauté, lit-on dans la lettre, "contient deux grâces contra-dictoires et qui, chez vous, ne se contredisent pas, c'est la grâce de l'enfant et celle de la femme." Didier, regardant le portrait de Marion:

> Comme elle est belle – et quelle grâce étrange!
> Dirait-on une femme? Oh non, c'est un front d'ange...
> Cette bouche d'enfant, qu'entrouvre un doux caprice,
> Palpite d'innocence...

Baudelaire, célébrant Marie Daubrun:

> Je veux te peindre ta beauté
> Où l'enfance s'allie à la maturité...
> ....
> Ta tête se pavane avec d'étranges grâces...

---

[1] Sur ce problème, voir l'édition critique de *la Fanfarlo*, éd. Cl. Pichois (Paris, éditions du Rocher, 1957), pp. 10–11.

[2] *Correspondance générale*, vol. I, pp. 99–104.

La fin de la lettre à Marie évoque singulièrement la fin du drame: "Tenez, je me mets à vos pieds; un mot, dites un mot...". Didier "s'agenouille devant elle":

> Dis un mot, tes mains sur mon front, je t'en prie...

Que Marie était Marion, Baudelaire ne pouvait pas l'ignorer, et la remarque vaut plus encore pour la Présidente en l'honneur de qui il reprit en 1854 les mots qu'il avait adressés à Marie: "Soyez mon Ange gardien, ma Muse et ma Madone, et conduisez-moi dans la route du Beau." Alors, à quelle réhabilitation rêvait-il? "Dans la réhabilitation de la courtisane, se demandait H. Bonnier au sujet de Hugo, n'y aurait-il pas comme l'écho d'une autre réhabilitation, plus intime, plus déchirante?"[1] *Les Fleurs du Mal* sont pleines de rituels, de liturgies intimes, où l'amour et la magie se mêlent de façon étrange. Quel espoir nourrissait donc le poète, lorsqu'il *faisait dire* à son idole:

> Je suis l'Ange gardien, la Muse et la Madone!

Ces divagations trouvent leur justification dans la suite de notre enquête. *Le Chant d'Automne*, "poème dédié à Marie Daubrun, semble, au dire de J. Crépet et G. Blin, devoir beaucoup à V. Hugo".[2] A côté des vers

> L'échafaud qu'on bâtit n'a pas d'écho plus sourd.
> ....
> Il me semble ....
> Qu'on cloue en grande hâte un cercueil quelque part...

les commentateurs inscrivent ces vers de *Marion de Lorme*:

> Qu'est ce bruit?
> C'est l'échafaud qu'on dresse, ou nos cercueils qu'on cloue.

Celui qui parle dans *Chant d'Automne* est un condamné à mort: "la tombe attend, elle est avide" ("la mort est à la porte" dit Marion en écho). Le drame romantique nous mène droit au cœur du spleen baudelairien.

---

[1] V. Hugo, *Œuvres complètes*, édition chronologique publiée sous la direction de J. Massin, vol. III, p. 723: *Présentation de Marion de Lorme.*
[2] *Fleurs du Mal* (Paris, Corti, 1968), p. 394.

Le lecteur du "Tableau parisien" *Brumes et pluies* ("qui, selon J. Crépet et G. Blin, aurait pu aussi légitimement figurer dans *Spleen et idéal*") retrouve dans les quatrains du sonnet un vocabulaire, des rimes utilisés pour un passage de *Marion de Lorme*, lorsque Didier imagine le nœud qui serre sa gorge:

> Mais après tout, qu'importe! et, si tout est bien noir,
> Pourvu que sur la terre on ne puisse rien voir, –
> Qu'on soit sous un tombeau qui vous pèse et vous loue,
> Ou que le vent des nuits vous tourmente, et se joue
> A rouler des débris de vous, que les corbeaux
> Ont du gibet de pierre arrachés par lambeaux, –
> Qu'est-ce que cela fait?

Les vers ne sont pas des mieux venus, mais y figurent déjà les *nuits*, le *corbeau*, le *tombeau*, et surtout les deux rimes en vérité peu courantes: *vous loue* et *se joue*. Et à l'essor baudelairien:

> Mon âme
> Ouvrira largement ses ailes de corbeau

correspond dans le couplet de Didier l'envolée célèbre:

> L'âme lève du doigt le couvercle de pierre
> Et s'envole...

Il y a mieux. De la notice publiée en 1852 par la *Revue de Paris*, *Edgar Alan Poe, Sa vie et ses ouvrages*, le deuxième développement s'achève sur un paragraphe consacré à l'ivrognerie littéraire et à son évolution: "Au XVIIIᵉ siècle, la tradition continue, mais s'altère un peu. L'école de Rétif boit, mais c'est déjà une école de parias, un monde souterrain. Mercier très vieux, est rencontré rue du Coq-Honoré; Napoléon est monté sur le XVIIIᵉ siècle, Mercier est un peu ivre, et il dit *qu'il ne vit plus que par curiosité*." A quoi Baudelaire ajoute en note: "Victor Hugo connaissait-il ce mot?" Ainsi Baudelaire, sourcier à sa manière et comme pour faire plaisir à Mrs Temple-Patterson, suggère que Hugo a pu s'inspirer de Sébastien Mercier. Car sa question en note renvoie à la scène viii de l'acte IV de *Marion de Lorme*. Le roi Louis XIII demandant à son bouffon l'Angely: "Pourquoi vis-tu?" le bouffon répond: "Je vis par curiosité."

Louis XIII déclarait à la scène précédente: "Je m'ennuie." Tout naturellement nous pensons au vers du *Spleen* LXXVI:

L'ennui, fruit de la morne incuriosité...

Et, comme il s'agit d'une scène entre un roi et un bouffon, plus naturellement encore nous pensons au *Spleen* suivant:

Je suis comme le roi d'un pays pluvieux.

On lit dans l'ouvrage d'un sourcier patenté, *l'Originalité de Baudelaire*: "Baudelaire a représenté l'âme prise du spleen par l'allégorie d'un roi cruel ennuyé... Sans doute cette conception doit-elle plus d'un trait aux types de rois faibles et vicieux, Charles IX et Louis XIII, campés par les romans et les drames historiques de Dumas, Hugo, Vigny, etc. Des expressions comme 'bouffon favori' et 'son lit fleurdelisé' font notamment penser au *Roi s'amuse* de Hugo."[1] A la suite de quoi, J. Crépet et G. Blin notent dans leur commentaire du *Spleen* LXXVII: "Vivier a fait remarquer que par un certain nombre de détails (faucon, bouffon, lit fleurdelisé, etc.) cette pièce rappelait des drames historiques de l'époque romantique, notamment *le Roi s'amuse* de V. Hugo."[2] J'observerai avec ironie qui si dans *le Roi s'amuse* il y a un bouffon – et certes Triboulet est plus connu que l'Angely – il y a aussi un roi et que François Ier n'est pas trop bien choisi comme archétype du roi 'impuissant'. Louis XIII en revanche semble tout indiqué. Relisons donc le *Spleen* LXXVII en regard de *Marion de Lorme*:

Je suis comme le roi d'un pays pluvieux...

A la scène vii de l'acte IV, la plainte du roi précédemment citée: "Je m'ennuie" rime avec le vers:

Ah! je suis bien à plaindre! Et toujours de la pluie.

Dans cette même scène le marquis de Nangis déclare:

Et le peuple des rois évite le balcon

que le *Spleen* transpose sous une forme plus pathétique, en y joignant le souvenir de la Saint-Barthélemy:

[1] R. Vivier, *l'Originalité de Baudelaire* (Bruxelles, 1965), p. 215.
[2] *Fleurs du Mal*, p. 423.

> Ni son peuple mourant en face du balcon.
> Rien ne peut l'égayer, continue le poète...
> Du bouffon favori la grotesque ballade
> Ne distrait plus le front de ce cruel malade...

Louis XIII de son côte dit à son bouffon:

> Viens! j'ai le cœur malade et d'amertume empli
> Point de rire à la bouche, et dans mes yeux arides
> Point de pleurs. Toi qui seul quelquefois me dérides, Viens.

Et plus loin:

> Comment me consolerais-tu?

Ou encore:

> Oui, la vie est bien sombre et la tombe est sereine.
> Si je ne t'avais pas pour m'égayer un peu...

L'allusion que fait Baudelaire à l'impudique toilette des dames d'atour rappelle le jeu de scène de Marion cachant la lettre de grâce dans son corsage. "Au roi, avec hardiesse, en montrant sa gorge: 'Sire, venez la prendre'. Et le bouffon d'ajouter: 'Tenez ferme! le roi ne met pas ses mains là.' "

Dans le *Spleen*, le mot *balcon* rime avec *faucon*. Or, pour tenter de sauver les deux jeunes gens condamnés à mort, le bouffon les fait passer pour deux fauconniers. Et le roi approuve: Le fauconnier est dieu!

Les bains de sang qui ne peuvent réchauffer le cadavre sont annoncés par la sentence: Sire! le sang n'est pas une bonne rosée; et précédemment les deux vers:

> Le savant qui lui fait de l'or n'a jamais pu
> De son être extirper l'élément corrompu

ne sont pas sans rapport avec les propos métaphoriques de Laffemas:

> Il faudrait un creuset d'alchimiste endiablé
> Qui, rongeant cuivre et plomb, mit à nu la parcelle
> D'or pur que ce lingot d'alliage recèle.

Pour finir, voici qui est plus probant encore. Le poème baudelairien commence par les deux vers:

> Je suis comme le roi d'un pays pluvieux,
> Riche, mais impuissant, jeune et pourtant très vieux.

Le sourcier Vivier propose ce commentaire: "Hugo avait dit dans un mouvement analogue (*Voix intérieures*, *XIX*): '*Riche* et sans volupté, *jeune* et sans passion';" mais il ajoute, hélas: "Et Gautier donne dès 1844 l'antithèse baudelairienne: (*A Zurbaran*) 'Tout jeunes, et déjà plus glacés qu'un aïeul',[1]" oubliant qu'au début de *Marion de Lorme*, Didier, héros fatal, proclame:

> Seul, à vingt ans, la vie était amère et triste...
> Si bien que me voici, jeune encore et pourtant
> Vieux...

Didier n'est pas Louis XIII, dira-t-on. Mais la superposition des deux personnages est naturelle pour le poète, soit qu'il fasse du roi mélancolique une image du poète maudit, soit plus subtilement qu'il dise: "Il serait peut-être doux d'être alternativement victime et bourreau."[2]

Baudelaire en proie au spleen est non seulement Didier et le roi, mais il est aussi le bouffon, comme le démontre J. Starobinski dans son remarquable commentaire du poème en prose *Une mort héroïque*: "Le rapport du prince et du bouffon, dans ce récit, est de nature sadique, la cruauté appartenant, à un titre assurément inégal, à chacun des deux personnages. Le prince... n'est pas sans ressemblance avec le 'cruel malade' de *Spleen*. Mais Fancioulle, pour sa part, ne s'est pas contenté du rôle traditionnel qui limite la contradiction apportée par le bouffon dans les bornes tolérables d'un bavardage irrévérencieux? Il a conspiré."[3] Dans *Marion de Lorme*, on l'oublie aisément, Didier et Saverny ne sont pas seuls condamnés à mort. Le roi envisage de gaité de cœur la mort de son bouffon, car l'Angely protège les victimes du roi et de son ministre et feint d'être le complice des rebelles.

Le poème liminaire des *Fleurs du Mal* où est dénoncé le péché par excellence, l'Ennui, qui *rêve d'échafauds*, confirme ces intuitions.

[1] Vivier, *op. cit.*, p. 214.
[2] Baudelaire, *Œuvres complètes*, p. 1271: *Mon cœur mis à nu*, I.
[3] 'Sur quelques répondants allégoriques du poète' *R.H.L.F.*, n° spécial sur Baudelaire (juin 1967), pp. 406–7.

L'ignoble Laffemas inspire au bouffon cette image:

Un chat-tigre de plus dans la ménagerie.

Dans la ménagerie infâme de nos vices, ajouterons-nous avec Baudelaire. Le même bouffon dit au roi:

> Je ne suis qu'un pantin dont vous tenez le fil.
> Mais votre habit royal cache un fil plus subtil
> Que tient un bras plus fort; et moi j'aime mieux être
> Pantin aux mains d'un roi, Sire, qu'aux mains d'un prêtre.

— C'est le Diable qui tient les fils qui nous remuent, affirme Baudelaire. Entre Richelieu et le Diable, certes, il y a un pas, mais que le roi franchit aussitôt après:

> Satan pourrait-il pas s'être fait cardinal?

Cette démonstration semble assez convaincante pour qu'il soit conclu que la recherche des sources elle même est aussi captivante que fructueuse, dès que la passion s'y mêle.

Alfred de Musset and Don Juan

RONALD GRIMSLEY

ALFRED de Musset was impelled by personal as well as cultural influences to interest himself in the Don Juan legend. His multifarious love affairs, his restless and at times desperate search for happiness through relations with women, together with his admiration for Mozart, Byron and Hoffman (to mention only three Romantic writers who wrote works about Don Juan), made it natural for him to deal with this subject at some stage of his career. Indeed, in 1833 he published in *La France littéraire* the first scene of *La Matinée de Don Juan*,[1] but as this work was left unfinished, the extant fragment is unfortunately too brief to provide any adequate evidence of the author's ultimate conception of the character. Various references scattered throughout his work none the less testify to Musset's continuing interest in Don Juan; it was especially in his poem *Namouna*, published in *Un Spectacle dans un fauteuil* in 1833, that he produced his most elaborate view of the theme. However, the vivid portrayal of Don Juan in this poem and its subsequent acceptance as a typically Romantic interpretation of the character should not be allowed to obscure the complexity of an attitude which becomes very apparent when the Don Juan of *Namouna* is seen in the light of Musset's other early works.

All the heroes depicted in the *Premières poésies* are men who are prepared to sacrifice everything, including, at times, their own lives, for the sake of their overwhelming desire for intense experience. It will be enough to recall the "embrace" and the "frightful kiss" through which Don Paez destroys his rival before going on to kill his mistress and himself in a final paroxysm of passion.

Rafaël, in *Les Marrons du feu*, "uncertain and changeable as a woman", pursues fleeting erotic pleasure as the only possible goal

---

[1] Musset, *Théâtre complet*, pp. 919–28 and 1593–5. (All references are to Maurice Allem's three-volume edition of Musset's complete works in the Bibliothèque de la Pléiade: I. *Poésies complètes*; II. *Théâtre complet*; III. *Œuvres complètes en prose* (Paris, 1957–60). These volumes will be referred to simply as *Poésies*, *Théâtre* and *Prose*.)

of his inconstant, contradictory character, whilst Carmargo feels an
all-consuming need to put "a part of her soul" into their relationship, recognizing at the same time that a man's love,

> C'est l'ombre qui s'enfuit d'une fumée au vent.[1]

Rafaël's instability is largely due to his fear of boredom − another
frequent characteristic of Musset's early heroes. Appropriately,
Rafaël mentions Don Juan just before he is stabbed to death by the
jealous abbé who is also seeking Carmargo's favours. "C'est du Don
Juan, ceci", he says as he seeks to extricate himself from the consequences of the intrigue which, unknown to him, is to be his last.
Although Mardoche, in the poem of that name, does not suffer
Rafaël's violent fate, he is represented as *un esprit fort* whose efforts
to escape from boredom through the pursuit of women leads him to
violate all religious principles. Once again, there is a brief reference
to Don Juan, for when the watchful husband suspects his wife's
infidelity with Mardoche, the poet tells us:

> Que Mardoche et sa belle, au fond, ne pensaient guère
> A lui, quand il cria comme au festin de Pierre:
> "Ouvrez-moi".[2]

Yet these heroes of promiscuity often retain a longing for innocence, which is revealed not only by the persistence of a childlike
element in their character, but also by the poet's frequent use of
the image of the "clear sky" as a symbol of their aspiration to purity −
a point also stressed by Musset in his own name when, in *Les Vœux
stériles*, his eulogy of Greece as "the eternal homeland of his mad
desires" leads him to say:

> J'étais né pour ces temps où les fleurs de ton front
> Couronnaient dans les mers l'azur de l'Hellespont.[3]

Before killing himself after "three years of pleasure, frenzy and
intoxication", Jacques Rolla seeks final earthly solace in the arms of

---

[1] *Poésies*, p. 35.
[2] *ibid.*, p. 104. Musset adds the following note to these lines:

> "Cette fin est usée, et nous la donnons telle
> Par grand éloignement de la mode nouvelle".

[3] *ibid.*, p. 115. Cf. also the famous evocation of antiquity at the beginning of
Rolla (*Poésies*, pp. 273–4).

a girl-prostitute, whose soul has remained uncorrupted by her way
of life. After watching her asleep, he declares:

> Mais ton sommeil est pur – ton sommeil est à Dieu[1]

Rolla is ready to die with the experience of a last chaste kiss.

It is especially in the character of the tormented Frank of *La
Coupe et les lèvres* that the conflict between vice and innocence is
most clearly revealed. Already in his *Invocation* the poet recalls that
the background of the Tyrol is particularly suited to the description
of a heroic nation:

> Beau ciel, où le soleil a dédaigné la plaine,
> Ce paisible océan dont les monts sont les flots!
> Beau ciel tout sympathique, et tout peuplé d'échos![2]

Frank himself, however, is a solitary, anti-social man who abandons
his home and his past under the influence of his powerful pride and
ambition; repudiating all traditional moral values and attachments,
he symbolically expresses his contempt for social convention by
burning down his own house. Yet his energy lacks any clear direction, since it cannot be permanently satisfied by the objects it encounters. He makes sporadic attempts to escape from his dilemma by
a liaison with the passionate and sensual Belcolore, as well as by
gambling and war. Nevertheless, nothing he does is really commen-
surate with his feelings and he plunges into vice and excess without
believing in them. Even when he is with the infamous Belcolore,
he cannot forget his dream of perfect fulfilment. Through his
passionate relation with her, he is nothing but a "ghost" of his true
self,

> Une ombre de moi-même, un reste, un vain reflet,

for her long black hair has become his "shroud", her beautiful body
his "tomb". Yet he is unable to shut out the light of the outer world.
He tells her to remove the torches from the room and half-open
the window:

> Laisse entrer le soleil, c'est mon dernier peut-être.
> Laisse-le-moi chercher, laisse-moi dire adieu
> A ce beau ciel si pur qu'il a fait croire en Dieu.[3]

[1] *ibid.*, p. 291.   [2] *ibid.*, pp. 159–60.   [3] *ibid.*, p. 174.

Needless to say, Frank's glimpse of bliss soon gives way to a more sombre mood. From time to time he also betrays an uneasy awareness of his inadequacy and misery; but since the darkness and confusion of his inner being prevent him from knowing himself directly, he takes an ironical pleasure in trying to see himself through others' eyes. He stages his own funeral, so that he can carefully observe other people's reactions to the news of his death, only to find that nobody knows him or accepts him for what he really is. Like so many Romantic heroes, he cannot overcome a "devouring, unquenchable thirst" for the unknown. Moreover, in the midst of violence and excess, he still clings to the thought of innocence, which he associates not only with the occasional glimpse of a "cloudless sky", as we have seen, but also with the affection of the childlike and pure Déidamia, who reminds him of his yearning for purity. But, like the sky itself, this innocence is beyond the reach of a man who is caught between the search for earthly pleasure and the thought of his ultimate nothingness. Frank becomes increasingly obsessed with the bitter-sweet thought of the indissoluble connection between "two destroying angels",

> Doux et cruels tous deux, – la mort, – la volupté.

The idea of death remains inseparable from the memory of sensual pleasure. Although in his most pessimistic mood Frank may declare:

> Mais je crois au néant, comme je crois en moi[1]

he cannot abandon his longing for the ideal. Even when it seems to have no precise object, he is still tormented by his "raging thirst" for perfection. When at last he comes to feel the real force of Déidamia's pure love, he cannot refrain from crying:

> Ah! j'ai senti mon âme
> Qui redevenait vierge à ton doux souvenir.[2]

But this discovery has come too late to save him. Although Frank himself does not die, it is because of him that the guiltless Déidamia is murdered by the avenging Belcolore. The play ends with the

[1] *ibid.*, p. 194.   [2] *ibid.*, p. 204.

inevitable fatal kiss – the first kiss Frank gives his beloved leads
immediately to her death.

As soon as it is purified, passion can open up the possibility of
true happiness by transforming itself into love – love as a primordial
power which involves both man and nature. As Musset declared in
Le Saule, love has an infinite dimension:

> Amour! torrent divin de la source infinie!

The universal power of love was, of course, to become a frequent
theme of his later work, but already in his first poems he suggests
that genuine feeling has a profoundly creative effect which makes
love resemble "genius". The great artist and the idealistic lover may
thus bear a very close resemblance to each other. Yet because art
and love spring from the depths of man's being, they often involve
suffering as well as beauty. Indeed, poetic beauty may originate in
personal suffering. Of lovers and poets Musset asks:

> Que demandent-ils donc tous les deux en retour?
> Une larme, ô mon Dieu, voilà leur récompense;
> Voilà pour eux le ciel, la gloire et l'éloquence,
> Et par là le génie est semblable à l'amour.[1]

The ambiguity of an idealism that can lead either upwards to the
vision of heavenly glory or downwards to the nothingness of death
is also evident in Musset's specific references to the Don Juan theme.
Don Juan not only flits from one female conquest to the next in his
relentless search for amorous pleasure; he is also the man who is
dragged to his death by a supernatural statue. While it would obviously be wrong to take too seriously the light-hearted reference to
Don Juan in *A quoi rêvent les jeunes filles*, it is worth noting that
Laërte reminds Silvio of the fate that awaits a seducer when he
arouses a father's wrath:

> C'est alors que le père,
> Semblable au commandeur dans le *Festin de Pierre*,
> Dans sa robe de chambre apparaîtra soudain.[2]

---

[1] *Namouna*, 3rd canto, verse xiii (*Poésies*, p. 258). Maurice Allem also points out
that the same idea was to reappear in *Après une lecture*, verse ix (*Poésies*, p. 424),
where Musset insists that both love and genius involve beauty and harmony.
[2] *Poésies*, p. 220.

Y

The same theme recurs at the end of Musset's apostrophe to Voltaire in *Rolla*. After describing the destructive moral effect of Voltaire's irreligion, the poet asks the famous *philosophe* whether he can truly "look upon his work" and find, like God, that "it is good". He then reminds him of the implication of the story of Rolla:

> Au festin de mon hôte alors je te convie.
> Tu n'as qu'à te lever; – quelqu'un soupe ce soir
> Chez qui le Commandeur peut frapper et s'asseoir.[1]

The sinister implications of this aspect of the legend are brought out more clearly by a later mention of Don Juan's death in *La Confession d'un enfant du siècle* (1836),[2] as well as by Musset's constant association of the statue-image with the thought of death. The two themes of love and death thus remain inextricably associated in his mind,[3] and their connection is undoubtedly strengthened by certain abnormal psychological tendencies in his own temperament. It is well known that Musset occasionally suffered from hallucinations whilst he himself has written about his nightmares. For example, the nightmare of the corpse, described in one of his very first works, a translation of De Quincey's *Confessions of an English Opium Eater*, was drawn directly from his own experience as a medical student and is not to be found in the original English text.[4] The idea of the poet haunted by the ghost of his own self in *La Nuit de décembre* may have a psychological relationship with the famous Franchart episode related by George Sand in *Elle et lui*: Musset is said to have had the curious hallucination of seeing himself as a broken old man. In view of all this it is not surprising that he should have associated the subject of the Don Juan legend with some of the deepest emotions of his own contradictory personality.

It is in *Namouna*, a poem hastily written at the publisher's request, that the complexity of Musset's attitude towards Don Juan is most clearly illustrated. Although the Don Juan theme receives detailed treatment in only one section of the long poem, it occasionally emerges in other parts. *Namouna*, with its mingling of reflective and emotional elements and its frequently ironical spirit, also

[1] *ibid.*, p. 284.   [2] *Prose*, p. 82.
[3] For a good analysis of the themes in Musset's early works see Herbert S. Gochberg, *Stage of Dreams, the Dramatic Art of A. de Musset, 1828–54* (Geneva, 1967).
[4] *Prose*, pp. 61–2.

suggests the influence of Byron's *Don Juan*, a work for which Musset had a particular admiration. Moreover, if the improvisatory character of *Namouna* accounts for its formlessness, it also enables the poet to give free play to whimsical and ironical reflection; and it is in this general spirit and mood rather than in any purely formal structure that the ultimate artistic unity and interest of the poem are to be found.

The content of the poem seems deliberately to ignore the promise of its title, *Namouna, conte oriental*, for the narrative element is so restricted that Namouna herself appears only at the very end, and then almost as an afterthought. Much more important than the narrative is the poet's desire to establish a dialogue with his reader whose inhibitions and prejudices he seeks to disturb; at the same time Musset makes a number of observations (at times deceptively light-hearted) about the nature of the poem itself and the more general subject of poetic composition and its relation to reality. As the present study is concerned principally with the Don Juan theme, it will be able to consider the wider aesthetic issue only very briefly, even though it is of cardinal significance for the interpretation of the poem as a whole.

The very first theme – Hassan's nakedness – is an explicit reminder that the reality of the body cannot be permanently concealed by false modesty or social hypocrisy. It seems, moreover, as though Hassan's shameless addiction to sexual pleasure is in complete conformity with this general acceptance of bodily appetites, for he is described as a man who smokes opium, knows no remorse and "loves sleep". Refusing, like Don Juan, to accept the idea of eternal love, Hassan keeps each woman for only "eight days", treating any longer relationship as a sign of servitude. Superficially, therefore, Hassan is an irresponsible Don Juan, moving from one conquest to the next with heedless disregard for the consequences of his actions. Like the other early heroes, Hassan, as a creature of impulse, has a childlike side to his character. At the same time, he has a grown man's sophistication; so that his "constantly changing tastes" make him both childlike and *blasé*, indolent and obstinate – in short, "a being impossible to describe": *un original*. Like Frank and the other characters, he is without roots, having abandoned his name, country and religion for life as "Hassan" the oriental Mohammedan. In spite of his instability, he is capable of moments of deep feeling. If his greatest ecstasy is the sexual "paroxysm", he does not treat it as a merely physical experience, for it gives way to an expansive mood that enables him to bare his soul to the mistress of the moments. This "bizarre intoxication" is his most intense emotional experience.

Already, however, the apparent contradictions of Hassan's character lead to a specific mention of the Don Juan theme, for it is in connection with these that Musset refers to the serenade sung by Don Juan in Act III, Scene iii, of Mozart's *Don Giovanni*. In fact, this episode expresses a double contradiction, for Don Juan, as he sings to Donna Elvira's maid Zerlina, is disguised as his servant Leporello, while Leporello himself is pretending to Donna Elvira that he is Don Juan. Musset, however, lays particular stress upon the musical contrast, pointing out that the melancholy, pitiful tone of Don Juan's song is offset by the lively, joyful spirit of the orchestral accompaniment, which seems to make fun of the song itself – not inappropriately, when it is recalled that Don Juan's professed feelings do not express his real intention. Musset concludes that love and deceit are inseparable, and that Hassan's vacillations simply correspond to a fundamental aspect of human nature. Yet these changing moods cannot conceal the childlike element in his character – "C'était un bon enfant dans la force du terme" – like the child, he allows himself to be completely captivated by the desire of the moment.

The description of Hassan's character thus leads to the recognition of an idealistic impulse in the heart of this contradictory being. In short, he has a soul as well as a body, and both sides of his nature have their own characteristic, if sometimes conflicting, needs. The poet himself, speaking in his own name, makes a number of humorous remarks about the perplexing aspects of the soul–body relationship and its strange effect upon the human personality. Even an intensely sensual man like Hassan has to admit the power of idealistic aspirations. Yet the poet gives the impression of not wanting to be caught taking this idealism too seriously, for he keeps breaking off the narrative in order to make ironical reflections about his poem which he claims had no 'subject'. From a consideration of Hassan's strange personality Musset is led to reflect on the problem of poetic composition, with its disconcerting mixture of truth and fiction. In spite of his flippant and sometimes impertinent remarks to his reader, Musset affirms the essentially heart-felt nature of poetic inspiration and the ultimate connection between love and genius. The analysis of poetry thus suggests the same contradiction between the ideal and the real as is apparent in the expression of other strong human emotions.

Then Musset passes abruptly to the Don Juan theme. He insists that there are two traditional types of Don Juan. He describes, first of all, the cold, reflective, Narcissus-like seducer, with this heartless, studied approach to the conquest of women, a man who is completely withdrawn into himself and incapable of any spontaneity or generosity; obsessed with his own power over women, he is beyond either happiness or unhappiness. Then comes the second type of Don Juan, the 'ordinary' seducer portrayed by Molière – a hard-drinking, wealthy, cynical aristocrat who pursues his selfish pleasures regardless of their consequences for other people. Beyond these two traditional types Musset evokes a third figure, an as yet unrealized possibility which has already been hinted at by Mozart and Hoffmann. It will be recalled that E. T. A. Hoffmann's short story, *Don Juan*,[1] had a decisive effect upon the subsequent development of the legend. In the course of this story, the narrator attends, in strange circumstances, a performance of Mozart's *Don Giovanni*, the interpretation of which he subsequently discusses in a letter to a friend. His main interest is in the character of Don Juan, who is described as a young man with a handsome body, fine education, intelligent mind and highly developed sensibility; he is "nature's favourite child, endowed with all that brings him close to divinity". This exceptional natural endowment makes Don Juan superior to other men and fills him with aspirations which are incomprehensible to the rest of the world. He is ever conscious of an "eternal, ardent longing" for perfection, and if he passes rapidly from one woman to another, it is simply because of his yearning for an ideal love, which he hopes to experience with each woman he meets. Since he finds only disappointment in every love-affair, the frustration of his idealistic longing turns him into a rebel against a hostile world and makes him destroy the very women through whom he has sought "ultimate satisfaction". Only in Donna Anna, "a divine woman

---

[1] *Don Juan, Eine fabelhafte Begebenheit, die sich mit einem reisenden Enthusiasten zugetragen* (completed in 1812) was included in *Fantasiestücke in Callots Manier*.

over whose pure spirit the Devil has no power", does he find a
worthy counterpart to his own exceptional character. As soon as she
meets Don Juan, Donna Anna knows that her own remarkable
qualities will make it impossible for her to resist him. She is the
only woman who might have rescued him from "the despair of his
vain striving", but Don Juan has met her too late; he is already so
steeped in wickedness that he can do nothing but ruin her. Even so,
he has made an indelible impression upon her, and this explains her
frenzied desire for his destruction.

Musset's portrait of the ideal Don Juan clearly owes much to
Hoffmann, although the darker side of the picture is also influenced
by the memory of early heroes of 'fatality', like Byron's Manfred
and Goethe's Faust. (As we have already seen, the character of
Hassan as well as the ironic, irreverent spirit of the whole poem also
suggest the more diffused influence of Byron's *Don Juan*.) Although
most of the characteristic features of Hoffmann's Don Juan reappear
in Musset's creation, the French poet has obviously tried to give
greater definition and relief to his hero by presenting him in two
antithetic portraits – of Don Juan before and after his experience of
women. Musset also emphasizes Don Juan's exceptional, solitary
nature by excluding from his portrait any specific reference to
Donna Anna.[1] His hero is also detached from his musical background,
so that the reader's interest in the main character is not diminished
by any extraneous aesthetic considerations.

We are first of all given the portrait of Don Juan as he was before
he began his amorous career – a tender, pure young man, almost
Christ-like in his capacity for love and suffering, living in tune with
a physical nature that is "as beautiful as he", full of hope and joyous
expectancy, inspired, above all else, by the desire to love and be
loved. Suddenly, this noble character, to whom the fulfilment of no
earthly aspiration seems likely to be denied, is turned into an incor-
rigible rake, a degraded, broken man, who brutally kicks aside the
body of the father he has murdered. To what is this extraordinary
transformation due? Not to any feeling of having been wronged by
the world. Don Juan is no avenger of personal grievances; he cannot
even claim, like Byron's Lara, to have been ill-used by his fellow-
men. His personality is too "vast and powerful" to be concerned

---

[1] There is a possible allusion to her in verse xlvii (*Poésies*, p. 266).

with such petty thoughts. The truth is that, at heart, he is a frustrated idealist, misunderstood by others but loved by the poet himself, a *candide corrupteur*, who, devoured by an impossible love, is searching for the infinite. Like Musset himself in a later poem, he could indeed say:

> Malgré moi, l'infini me tourmente.[1]

He is also reminiscent of an earlier Romantic hero such as René, for, like his famous predecessor, he is depicted as crying out his impossible desires to nature:

> Demandant aux forêts, à la mer, à la plaine,
> Aux brises du matin, à toute heure, à tout lieu,
> La femme de ton âme et de ton premier vœu![2]

Again like René, he moves restlessly from place to place, unable to settle anywhere; he cannot accept the "hideous truth" of everyday life and the harshness of a reality "whose brazen breasts he has sucked in vain". As he hopefully follows "an infinite road", he is like a "desperate priest vainly seeking his God". When death and divine vengeance finally overtake him in the person of the Stone Commander, he unhesitatingly accepts the statue's invitation and goes forward to meet his doom in an attitude that almost seems to welcome death as a happy release from his intolerable situation. The *rêveur insensé* has finally recognized the futility of his dreams.

Although Don Juan's oppressive sense of fatality gives him a certain affinity with Frank, who was engaged in the same unhappy search for an obscure and impossible ideal, he remains a more poetic figure, perhaps because his portrait has a literary and musical source; Musset is conscious of evoking a character that is "greater, more beautiful and more poetic" than any that has hitherto been imagined. Admitting that only Shakespeare would have been capable of dealing with such a challenging subject, he professes some misgiving about his own poetic attempt to describe the true Don Juan:

> Insensé que je suis! que fais-je ici moi-même?
> Etait-ce donc mon tour de leur parler de toi,
> Grande ombre, et d'où viens-tu pour tomber jusqu'à moi?[3]

---

[1] *L'Espoir en Dieu (ibid.*, p. 341). [2] *Poésies*, p. 265. [3] *ibid.*, p. 264.

His only excuse for his rashness is that he truly "loves" a man whom others had treated with "horror, doubt and blasphemy". Consequently, Musset has produced an ideal being who is sustained by his creator's energy and enthusiasm. Unlike the earlier portrait of Frank, Don Juan is not presented primarily as a dramatic figure, but as a poetic possibility. Moreover, Don Juan's existence possesses greater unity and consistency than Frank's, because his idealism, though constantly thwarted, is inseparable from his relations with women; in spite of his interminable disappointments, he still continues to seek fulfilment in the same way, urged on by the same unforgettable dream:

> Plus vaste que le ciel et plus grand que la vie.[1]

Musset obviously finds considerable poetic satisfaction in giving a typically Romantic development to the Don Juan theme by rejecting the traditional attitude of moral condemnation in favour of an interpretation that no longer treats Don Juan as a wicked man justly punished for his flagrant disregard of moral and religious values, but extols him as an idealist who should be loved and admired for his persistent, if fruitless, efforts to bring beauty and perfection into his life; Don Juan is henceforth judged to be on the side of the gods, an upholder of the divine possibility of earthly existence, a figure whose tragic death should elicit our pity and sympathy. The poet, in particular, is likely to feel a close affinity with Don Juan, for the intimate bond existing between love and genius means that the artist must also suffer the conflicting effects of his earnest attempt to express some of the idealistic possibilities of human nature.

This lyrical portrait of Don Juan is not allowed to stand unchallenged, for at the very end of the canto Musset briefly reintroduces Hassan. There is, at first sight, a similarity between the two characters inasmuch as both devote their lives to the pursuit of women. Hassan, like Don Juan, is conscious of an idealistic impulse, as is clear from his ecstatic moments of expansive emotion –

> Ce que don Juan aimait, Hassan l'aimait peut-être –

but the "perhaps" is a significant qualification of his final attitude. Hassan's brief moments of idealism and indulgence in expansive

[1] *Poésies*, p. 267.

feelings are not strong enough to distract him from the enjoyment of the pleasures of the flesh. Whilst Don Juan seeks his own victims, ever hoping that the next will bring him the perfect fulfilment he so desperately desires, Hassan is content to buy his women in the market-place or elsewhere, realistically accepting immediate enjoyment as the only one that is within his grasp. Whereas Don Juan's continual disappointments do not prevent him from clinging obstinately to his ideal, Hassan has no illusions about the ephemeral nature of his idealistic moods:

> Ce que don Juan cherchait, Hassan n'y croyait pas.

Hassan's down-to-earth attitude allows him to avoid Don Juan's violent fate, for he lives on to enjoy his mundane pleasures in the belief that

> le bonheur sur terre
> Peut n'avoir qu'une nuit, comme la gloire un jour.

Musset sets yet another limit to the potential seriousness of his subject by his frequent ironical interventions. He does not hesitate to poke fun at a poem that seems to lack all coherence:

> Le poème et le plan, les héros et la fable
> Tout s'en va de travers...

If he belatedly tells the story of Hassan and Namouna, it is only because he has started off by stating that the "story existed", and that, consequently, he must not disappoint the conventional reader who is still expecting the poet to tell a tale!

The poetic aura with which Musset invests the idealistic Don Juan should not be allowed to conceal the deeper contradictions of his attitude as revealed by his description of Hassan's character and his own ironical detachment from the substance of his poem. Moreover, the actual presentation of the two facets of Don Juan's career as a noble and gifted young man who is suddenly transformed by his desire for perfection into a seemingly base and despicable character suggests that the frustration of his idealism is ultimately due to the finite limitations of the outer world. It is clear, however, that this simple antithesis does not take into account a point illustrated by other references to the Don Juan theme – that an intense and single-minded dedication to the enjoyment of perfect love is not free from its own internal contradictions. Don Juan's idealism is hampered not only by the presence of external obstacles, but also by an inability to reconcile his dazzling vision with the darker, more tormenting aspects of his inner self. Because love originates in the depths of the self, it eventually encounters the contradictions inherent in every profound human aspiration. In the end, Don Juan has to reckon with the influence of the statue as well as with that of his own ideal. Perhaps the destructive force embodied in the statue of the Commander no longer symbolizes divine justice, as in the old legend, but expresses an irresistible impulse springing from within the human being himself. Be that as it may, Musset's use of the Don Juan theme, when seen within the wider context of his outlook as a whole, shows that he could not identify himself permanently with any attitude which failed to acknowledge the multiple, conflicting possibilities of his own Protean personality.

Mallarmé and Gautier:
new light on *Toast funèbre*

L. J. AUSTIN

MALLARMÉ'S *Toast funèbre*, published in 1873 in *Le Tombeau de Théophile Gautier*, is one of his last relatively 'long' poems. It is also, in the opinion of many readers, one of the finest formulations of his central convictions concerning the duty and the destiny of the poet. It has been considered in detail by more than 25 critics.[1] Three reasons may perhaps excuse yet another discussion of the poem: first, a hitherto unpublished version, containing a number of significant variant readings, has recently come to light; second, Mallarmé, who was steeped in Gautier's poetry, wove into his poem many subtle echoes which have not previously been noted; and third, exegesis has sometimes left little scope for appreciation, and much remains to be said on the value of the poem as a poem. For the reader's convenience I quote first the definitive version.

---

[1] See the bibliography in Jean-Pierre Richard, *L'Univers imaginaire de Mallarmé* (Paris, 1961). This omits Franz Nobiling, 'Mallarmé's *Toast funèbre* auf Gautier', in *Neuphilologische Mitteilungen*, XXX (1929), 118–42 (translation and commentary), and Walter Naumann, *Der Sprachgebrauch Mallarmé's* (Marburg, 1936) – a number of remarks on individual words. Since 1961 the following have appeared: Charles Chadwick, *Mallarmé. Sa pensée dans sa poésie* (Paris, 1962), see pp. 61–9; A. R. Chisholm, 'A Study of Mallarmé's *Toast funèbre*, *AUMLA*, No. 17 (May 1962), pp. 53–61, and *Mallarmé's 'Grand Œuvre'* (1962), see pp. 58–61; P.-O. Walzer, *Essai sur Mallarmé* (Paris, 1963) (Poètes d'aujourd'hui 94), see pp. 177–81; J.-Cl. Chevalier, 'Quelques remarques sur le vocabulaire du *Toast funèbre* de Stéphane Mallarmé. Champs sémantiques et fonctions de langage', in *Cahiers de l'Association internationale des Études françaises*, No. 16 (1964), *Littérature et Stylistique*, pp. 9–19; J. R. Lawler, 'Mallarmé and the "Monstre d'or" ', in *R.R.*, LV (1964), 98–110, and in *The Language of French Symbolism* (Princeton, 1969), pp. 3–20; Robert Greer Cohn, *Toward the Poems of Mallarmé* (Berkeley and Los Angeles, 1965), see pp. 96–110; Bernard Weinberg, *The Limits of Symbolism* (Chicago and London, 1966), see pp. 187–224; E. Noulet, *Vingt poèmes de Stéphane Mallarmé. Exégèses* (Paris and Geneva, 1967), see pp. 1–35; Frederick Chase St Aubyn, *Stéphane Mallarmé* (New York, 1969) (T.W.A.S. 52), see pp. 85–9.

References to Mallarmé's works are to the Pléiade edition of his *Œuvres complètes*, ed. H. Mondor and J.-P. Richard (Paris, 1951).

Toast funèbre

O de notre bonheur, toi, le fatal emblème!

Salut de la démence et libation blême,
Ne crois pas qu'au magique espoir du corridor
J'offre ma coupe vide où souffre un monstre d'or!
5 Ton apparition ne va pas me suffire:
Car je t'ai mis, moi-même, en un lieu de porphyre.
Le rite est pour les mains d'éteindre le flambeau
Contre le fer épais des portes du tombeau:
Et l'on ignore mal, élu pour notre fête
10 Très simple de chanter l'absence du poëte,
Que ce beau monument l'enferme tout entier.
Si ce n'est que la gloire ardente du métier,
Jusqu'à l'heure commune et vile de la cendre,
Par le carreau qu'allume un soir fier d'y descendre,
15 Retourne vers les feux du pur soleil mortel!

Magnifique, total et solitaire, tel
Tremble de s'exhaler le faux orgueil des hommes.
Cette foule hagarde! elle annonce: Nous sommes
La triste opacité de nos spectres futurs.
20 Mais le blason des deuils épars sur de vains murs,
J'ai méprisé l'horreur lucide d'une larme,
Quand, sourd même à mon vers sacré qui ne l'alarme,
Quelqu'un de ces passants, fier, aveugle et muet,
Hôte de son linceul vague, se transmuait
25 En le vierge héros de l'attente posthume.
Vaste gouffre apporté dans l'amas de la brume
Par l'irascible vent des mots qu'il n'a pas dits,
Le néant à cet Homme aboli de jadis:
"Souvenirs d'horizons, qu'est-ce, ô toi, que la Terre?"
30 Hurle ce songe; et, voix dont la clarté s'altère,
L'espace a pour jouet le cri: "Je ne sais pas!"

Le Maître, par un œil profond, a, sur ses pas,
Apaisé de l'éden l'inquiète merveille
Dont le frisson final, dans sa voix seule, éveille

35   Pour la Rose et le Lys le mystère d'un nom.
     Est-il de ce destin rien qui demeure, non?
     O vous tous, oubliez une croyance sombre.
     Le splendide génie éternel n'a pas d'ombre.
     Moi, de votre désir soucieux, je veux voir,
40   A qui s'évanouit, hier, dans le devoir
     Idéal que nous font les jardins de cet astre,
     Survivre pour l'honneur du tranquille désastre
     Une agitation solennelle par l'air
     De paroles, pourpre ivre et grand calice clair,
45   Que, pluie et diamant, le regard diaphane
     Resté là sur ces fleurs dont nulle ne se fane,
     Isole parmi l'heure et le rayon du jour!

     C'est de nos vrais bosquets déjà tout le séjour,
     Où le poëte pur a pour geste humble et large
50   De l'interdire au rêve, ennemi de sa charge:
     Afin que le matin de son repos altier,
     Quand la mort ancienne est comme pour Gautier
     De n'ouvrir pas les yeux sacrés et de se taire,
     Surgisse, de l'allée ornement tributaire,
55   Le sépulcre solide où gît tout ce qui nuit,
     Et l'avare silence et la massive nuit.

———

THE newly-discovered version[1] contains some 48 variants, including, tantalizingly, 11 illegible readings, which can be faintly discerned, but not deciphered, beneath the words written over them. Of the legible variants, 16 concern punctuation, 6 spelling, and 15 are word-changes: these are the most interesting and important. Finally, Mallarmé inadvertently omitted line 14: a caret sign indicates this.

a. *Illegible readings*
These afford further evidence of the care with which Mallarmé weighed his words. The following are the lines concerned: the

---

[1] I am grateful to my friend M. Paul Morel, son-in-law of the late Henry Charpentier, one-time Secretary of the Académie Mallarmé, for giving me a photocopy of this version, now in a private collection.

words beneath which there exists an illegible variant are in italics:

2. *Salut* de la démence et libation blême,
10. *Très-simple* de chanter l'absence du poëte.
17. Tremble de s'exhaler *le faux orgueil* des hommes.
18. *Cette* foule hagarde! elle annonce: Nous sommes
21. J'ai *prolongé* l'horreur lucide d'une larme,
24. *Roideur* de son linceul vague, se transmuait
39. Moi, *de votre désir* soucieux, je veux voir,
40. A qui s'évanouit, *hier*, dans le devoir,
42. Survivre, pour l'honneur *et le parfait* désastre,
49. Où le poëte pur a pour geste *humble* et large
54. Surgisse, *de l'allée* ornement tributaire,

"Prolongé" in line 21, "Roideur" in line 24 and "et le parfait" in line 42 are also to be counted among the legible variants, as they were replaced in their turn by "méprisé", "Hôte" and "du tranquille" respectively in the definitive version.

b. *Punctuation*
The punctuation variants of this version seem of no particular significance. Three exclamation marks are replaced by full stops; one full stop is replaced by an exclamation mark; some commas and colons are inserted or deleted.[1] Mallarmé, who regarded punctuation as vital to prose writing, later abandoned it altogether in some of his poetry.

c. *Spelling*
These variants are more important. They include one plural effaced to make a singular, two small letters replacing capitals, and three capitals, replacing small letters. The words concerned are in italics.

---

[1] details: line 11, colon after "entier"; 19, exclamation mark after "futurs", effaced to make a full stop; 22, commas after "vers" and after "sacre"; 25, colon after "posthume"; 30, no punctuation after "songe"; 34, no commas after "final" and "seule"; 36, the comma after "demeure" seems to replace a deleted question-mark, and "non" was followed by an exclamation mark of which the upper part has been deleted to make a full stop; 40, comma after "devoir"; 42, commas after "survivre" and after "désastre"; 45, comma after "diaphane"; 46, hyphen in "Resté-là"; 47, full stop after "jour".

28. Le néant à *Cet homme* aboli de jadis:
29. "Spectacle et Paradis, qu'est-ce, ô toi, que la *terre?*"
33. Apaisé de *l'Eden* l'inquiète merveille
35. Pour la *Rose* et le *Lys* le mystère d'un nom.
44. De paroles, pourpre ivre et grand*s* calice*s* clair*s*,

The important variants in line 29 ("Spectacle et Paradis") will be discussed under the heading of word-changes: what is relevant here is the small letter for "terre", which in the final version became one of five words to be capitalized and thereby given special importance. In line 28, the *C* seems to be clearly a capital letter.[1] By dropping this and giving a capital to "Homme", Mallarmé emphasized the deliberate antithesis of this latter word with "Maître" in line 32 on which the poem is built. The capital for "Eden" in line 33 is interesting. The replacement by a small *e* in the definitive version suggests that, as it is a synonym for "Terre", one capital suffices for both, and consequently that "éden" is used metaphorically. But the Biblical overtones remain obvious.[2] In line 35, "Rose" and "Lys" are capitalized, with double underlinings. But clearly they were originally written with small letters. In the volume *Le Tombeau de Théophile Gautier*, they were printed with small letters. The capitals were restored in the definitive version: they stress the symbolic value of the flowers. In line 44, the *s*'s were effaced, but are still perceptible. As the rose was evoked by the singular "pourpre ivre", the lily too was better suggested by the singular "grand calice clair".

[1] Those familiar with Mallarmé's manuscripts will know that he sometimes wrote a very large *c* in contexts where a capital would seem quite inappropriate: this feature is found among other nineteenth-century writers.

[2] see Léon Cellier: *Mallarmé et la morte qui parle* (Paris, 1959), pp. 150–1 (the whole of this chapter is most pertinent and illuminating). M. Cellier comments: "Au Maître est attribué comme à Adam la charge de nommer les créatures." – Curiously enough, Anatole France uses this detail and others faintly recalling Mallarmé's poem in his contribution to the *Tombeau de Théophile Gautier* ('Au poète', p. 69 of the original volume):

Heureux qui comme Adam entre les quatre fleuves
Sut nommer par leur nom les choses qu'il sut voir...

Un frisson glorieux saisit nos cœurs où passe
Son âme dispersée en ses créations...

Son souffle sibyllin autour de nous fait naître
Un astre enchanté, plein de suaves couleurs...

d. *Legible word-changes*
These are the most significant, and call for more detailed discussion. Some clarify the sense of difficult passages; all enhance the poetic resonance of the poem.

> *Title:* simply Toast (with the initial letter doubly underlined).
> 20. Mais le blason *funèbre* épars sur de vains murs,
> 21. J'ai *prolongé* l'horreur lucide d'une larme,
> 24. *Roideur* de son linceul vague, se transmuait
> 29. "*Spectacle et Paradis*, qu'est-ce, ô toi, que la terre?"
> 37. O *vous* tous *bannissez* une croyance sombre.
> 40.   le devoir
> 41. *Ancien* que nous font les jardins de cet astre,
> 42. Survivre, pour l'honneur *et le parfait* désastre,
> 50. De l'interdire au *temps*, ennemi de sa charge:
> 52. Quand la mort *haïssable* est comme pour Gautier
> 55. Le (*durable* sépulcre) où gît tout ce qui nuit,

The first two of these variants go together: Mallarmé transferred the epithet "funèbre" from line 20 to the title, which at first was simply *Toast*. The epithet is far more effective in the title, where it clashes in a striking dissonance with the festive connotations of a toast, than it was in line 20. Here the replacement of "blason funèbre" by "blason des deuils" gives a sharper concreteness, and the plural a greater generality. In the following line, "J'ai prolongé" resolves the ambiguity of the final version. "J'ai méprisé" could imply either that Mallarmé had scorned to weep, or that he had wept but had scorned this weakness in himself. "J'ai prolongé" makes it clear that the second alternative is correct. It would be interesting to know what word was replaced by "prolongé" and what by "Roideur" in the next variant (line 24). Here the bold expression "Hôte de son linceul vague" replaces the noun evoking the texture of the shroud itself. In both versions, "vague" is stressed by its position, separated from "linceul" by the caesura. Perhaps Mallarmé felt that "Roideur" and "vague" were contradictory, the first suggesting hard, stiff outlines, the second, a shapeless, blurred object.

One of the most interesting of all these variants is that at the beginning of line 29, in the dialogue between "le néant" and "l'Homme aboli de jadis". Mallarmé had written "Spectacle et Paradis", suggesting that the earth is at once a reality and an ideal: capitals emphasized the significance of these words, while "terre" itself was written with a small letter. The definitive version gives "Terre" its capital letter, and replaces the words in apposition by "Souvenirs d'horizons", even more evocative. The phrase suggests that the Earth is essentially the sum of human memories; and these memories are designated by the most general term imaginable, "horizons" as the quintessence of the physical world, and the limit of man's field of vision. Elsewhere Mallarmé calls man the "lecteur d'horizons".[1]

In line 37, "bannissez une croyance sombre" is replaced by "oubliez". Oblivion of outworn beliefs is preferable to their violent exclusion. There is a further variant in that Mallarmé had written "nous" instead of "vous" and "bannissons" instead of "bannissez". This is logical, since Mallarmé goes on to distinguish between "Moi" and "vous", when he writes of "votre désir".

Line 41 offers another example of the transposition of a word from one place to another. Instead of "le devoir / Ideal...", Mallarmé had written "le devoir / Ancien...". This is in harmony with Mallarmé's sense of the great antiquity of the poet's art. But "le devoir / Idéal" brings us to the heart of Mallarmé's poetics, to his cult of the "Idée même et suave" symbolized by the flower "absente de tous bouquets". It foreshadows the "Gloire du long désir, Idées" evoked by the vision of the miraculous flowers in *Prose pour des Esseintes*. And the variant liberates the word "Ancien", which can then be applied to something more ancient still than art, namely death (in line 52).

Death is already evoked by one of Mallarmé's characteristically oblique allusions in line 42 as "le parfait désastre", implying at once that death is the ultimate catastrophe and at the same time the crown and completion of life, "parfait" being taken in its Latin etymological sense of *perfectus*. The definitive version replaces "parfait" by "tranquille", stressing the serenity of the poet's death. (As was noted above, "parfait" is written over an illegible word.)

One of the difficulties of the definitive version has always been

[1] *Œuvres complètes*, p. 402.

Z

the precise meaning of "rêve" in line 50. It is unusual for Mallarmé to use this word in a pejorative sense. Before and after *Toast funèbre* he uses it with a capital letter, and sees in "le Rêve" the realm of the creative imagination and the glory of the mind. Why then should the poet exclude "le rêve" from his domain? In the context of the poem, "le rêve" could be interpreted as referring to the dream of the absolute or of personal survival, which has been decisively rejected throughout. But the variant "temps" bring new clarification, and confirms that "rêve" is here synonymous with transience or contingency, as Gardner Davis had rightly shown.[1]

We saw above how "Ancien" was liberated in line 41 by the definitive reading "devoir / Idéal". It is now used, in line 52, to replace "haïssable", an emotive and somewhat obvious epithet for death (Pascal used it more vividly and paradoxically for "le moi"). With "ancienne", Mallarmé brings out that death is the immemorial destiny of man, a fact calmly recognized with the serenity that characterizes the close of the poem.

The final variant enhances the beauty of the poem in another way. Mallarmé had written, in line 55:

> Le durable sépulcre où gît tout ce qui nuit,

with a transposition sign indicating that the order of the adjective and noun should be changed to read "Le sépulcre durable". Finally, he replaced the already powerfully evocative "durable" by "solide". Apart from its consonance in sound and sense with "porphyre" and "fer épais", the word "solide" brings another *s* and another *i*, thereby reinforcing the dominant sound-patterning of the triumphant finale of the poem.

————

THIS 'jeu de substitutions' offers one valuable means of observing the poet in his 'exercices de style'. Another means is the tracing of

---

[1] see Gardner Davies: *Les 'Tombeaux' de Mallarmé* (Paris, 1950), pp. 73–4. Soon afterwards was revealed Mallarmé's letter of September 1867 to Villiers de l'Isle-Adam, confirming the equation of "rêve" with "hasard": "J'avais...compris la corrélation intime de la Poésie avec l'Univers, et, pour qu'elle fût pure, conçu le dessein de la sortir du Rêve et du Hasard et de la juxtaposer à la conception de l'Univers." – S. Mallarmé: *Correspondance* 1862–1871, ed. H. Mondor et J.-P. Richard (Paris, Gallimard, 1959), p. 259. See also Noulet, *op. cit.*, p. 26.

the discreet but unmistakable echoes of Gautier which run through
the poem.[1] Mallarmé had chosen to celebrate Gautier's genius for
visual evocation. Gautier himself used to say: "Je suis un homme
pour qui le monde extérieur existe." Mallarme said: "Je chanterai le
voyant, qui, placé dans ce monde, l'a regardé, ce qu'on ne fait pas."[2]
The poem brings out "une des qualités glorieuses de Gautier: le don
mystérieux de voir avec les yeux". Conversely, it attacks those who
do not look at this world and do not transpose it on to the level of
consciousness by means of poetry and art, but place instead their
hopes in personal survival. When they reach the point of death, they
are unable to answer the essential question: "Qu'est-ce que la
Terre?" The poet and Master can and does answer, and he confers
on fleeting phenomena the only possible immortality. Mallarmé
in this way brings out one of the central principles proclaimed by
Gautier himself in one of his best-known poems:

> Tout passe. – L'art robuste
> Seul a l'éternité...
>
> Les dieux eux-mêmes meurent.
> Mais les vers souverains
>   Demeurent
> Plus forts que les airains.

Mallarmé had already celebrated Gautier nine years before, in the
first part of his *Symphonie littéraire* of 1864. But it was not the
"voyant" that he extolled there. Following closely Baudelaire's
two articles on Gautier, and the beginning of the *Poème du haschisch*,
Mallarmé then saw in Gautier's works "la plus haute cime de

---

[1] A. R. Chisholm draws some significant parallels from *Bûchers et Tombeaux* and
from *L'Art* (*art. cit.*, pp. 54–5, 58–9). His interpretation is one of the most
sensitive and illuminating of all; it is, unfortunately, severely abridged in
Mallarmé's 'Grand Œuvre', pp. 58–62. B. Weinberg, while disclaiming any
"intention to engage in a frenzied hunt" for them, recognizes that "the poem
is full of sources and analogues and parallels to Gautier's poetry", and quotes a
number of examples, including some of those mentioned here (*op. cit.*, pp. 217–
221). Weinberg's study is also of value, and, while debatable on details, is
excellent on the fundamental structure of the poem.

[2] Léon Cellier rightly remarks: "Si importante que soit cette déclaration (puisqu'il
apparait que le voyant ne voit pas autre chose que ce monde), Mallarmé ne s'en
pas tenu à ce programme. Il l'a élargi, pour définir avec plus d'ampleur la
fonction du Maître. Le poète n'est pas seulement celui qui voit, mais aussi celui
qui dit." (*Op. cit.*, p. 150.)

sérénité où nous ravisse la beauté".[1] In *Toast funèbre*, although Baudelaire's influence is still subtly and much less obtrusively present, the dominant influence is, rightly and appropriately, that of Gautier himself. From beginning to end, the poem is full of reminiscences of Gautier's own poetry, perfectly integrated into the texture of this poem in his praise.[2]

The echoes begin with the very first line:

> O de notre bonheur, toi, le fatal emblème!

For, commenting on the symbols of death, in *Deux tableaux de Valdès Léal*, Gautier had exclaimed:

> Voilà donc votre sens, mystérieux emblèmes![3]

And in *Le Thermodon*, evoking a picture by Rubens:

> Cette planche.....................................
> ....
> De votre destinée est l'effrayant symbole.[4]

The "magique espoir du corridor", used to evoke the possible apparition of Gautier as a phantom, can be paralleled from Mallarmé's own fragments for *Les Noces d'Hérodiade*, where the Princess orders the Nurse to bring the Saint's head at the risk of having his ghost walk:

> Va pour sa peine...
> Dût son ombre marcher le long du corridor
> M'en apporter le chef tranché dans un plat d'or.[5]

But Gautier too had associated ghosts with corridors, notably in *Inès de la Sierras*:

---

[1] *Œuvres complètes*, p. 262.

[2] Gautier's poems are quoted from his *Poésies complètes*, ed. R. Jasinski (Paris, Didot, 1933, rev. edn., 1970, with same pagination for text), 3 vols. Mallarmé had purchased in 1859, at the age of 17, Gautier's poetical works in the Charpentier edition, but was much less influenced by Gautier in his schoolboy poems than by Hugo and Musset. See H. Mondor: *Mallarmé lycéen* (Paris, 1954) and L. J. Austin, 'Les années d'apprentissage de Stéphane Mallarmé.' *R.H.L.F.*, LVI (1956), 65–84, especially p. 72.

[3] *Poésies complètes*, vol. II, p. 308.

[4] *ibid.*, p. 201.

[5] S. Mallarmé: *Les Noces d'Hérodiade*, ed. Gardner Davies (Paris, Gallimard, 1959), p. 73. This would seem to lessen the likelihood of the interpretation given by some critics, who see in the "corridor" a metaphor for the passage between the world beyond and this world.

D'un long corridor en décombres
Débusque un fantôme charmant.[1]

For the famous line:

J'offre ma coupe vide où souffre un monstre d'or!

Mallarmé's starting-point was a passage, not in Gautier, but in
Théodore de Banville, who had written, in *Songe d'hiver*:

Et je voyais s'emplir et se vider les coupes
Qu'ornaient des monstres d'or.[2]

Mallarmé transforms the static image into a dynamic one by sub-
stituting "où souffre" for "qu'ornaient". The line is mysteriously
suggestive and calls to mind many similar images throughout
Mallarmé's work.[3]

Mallarmé evokes the pagan symbol which gives the strongest
physical expression to the quenching of the flame of life:

Le rite est pour les mains d'éteindre le flambeau
Contre le fer épais des portes du tombeau.

This allusion is all the more appropriate because Gautier himself
refers to this rite in *Bûchers et tombeaux* and elsewhere:

Tout au plus un petit génie
Du pied éteignait un flambeau.[4]

The image of the poet's fame rising towards the sun concludes the
first section of the poem:

Si ce n'est que la gloire ardente du métier,
Jusqu'à l'heure commune et vile de la cendre,
Par le carreau qu'allume un soir fier d'y descendre,
Retourne vers les feux du pur soleil mortel!

For this passage, Mallarmé seems to have derived from Gautier, not

[1] *Poésies complètes*, vol. III, p. 57.
[2] Théodore de Banville, *Poésies complètes* 1840–1857 (Paris, 1857), p. 102.
[3] see J. R. Lawler, *art. cit.*, for a wide-ranging study of these parallels, based on
the view that "the 'monstre d'or' may well be taken not merely as a plastic
image but, more especially, as a symbol of poetry itself".
[4] *Poésies complètes*, vol. III, p. 73.

merely certain descriptive elements, but even the essential metaphor itself:

> Et la gloire, la gloire, astre et soleil de l'âme,
> Dans un océan d'or, avec le globe en flamme,
> Majestueusement monter à l'horizon!

> Plus loin, un rayon rouge allumait les carreaux.

> ... une gloire mystique
> Faite avec les splendeurs du soir.

> Toi, forme immortelle, remonte
> Dans la flamme aux sources du beau...[1]

The striking evocation of "Cette foule hagarde!" echoes Gautier's
words "troupe hagarde" applied to the Muses.[2] When Mallarmé
writes:

> La triste opacité de nos spectres futurs,

he is perhaps recalling a line of Gautier:

> Spectre dont le cadavre est vivant; ombre morte...[3]

But there is little doubt that he is following Gautier in his portrayal
of the funereal draperies of black hangings with embroidery of
silver tears:

> Mais le blason des deuils épars sur de vains murs,
> J'ai méprisé l'horreur lucide d'une larme...

Gautier has this close parallel, which Mallarmé must have had in
mind:

> Vous n'aurez ni blasons, ni chants, ni vers, ni fleurs;
> On ne répandra pas les larmes argentées
> Sur le funèbre drap, noir manteau des douleurs.[4]

The blasonry of mourning, literal in Gautier's lines, becomes meta-
phorical in Mallarmé's; and whereas in Gautier tears are repre-

---

[1] *Poésies complétes*, vol. II, p. 215; vol. I, p. 77; vol. II, p. 148; vol. III, p. 76.
[2] *ibid.*, vol. III, p. 104.   [3] *ibid.*, vol. II, p. 128.   [4] *ibid.*, p. 56.

sented by silver embroidery, Mallarmé evokes the possibility of real tears.

In the last six lines of the second section of his poem, Mallarmé presents, in a strange vision, reminiscent of some of Hugo's most cosmic, visionary verse, the dialogue of the dead Man with nothing-ness.[1] This man should have contemplated the world and sung of it. He has not done so. He is swept into the dense mist of death; and there nothingness shrieks a question to him, asking him what the Earth is. His only answer is that he does not know:

> Vaste gouffre apporté dans l'amas de la brume
> Par l'irascible vent des mots qu'il n'a pas dits,
> Le néant à cet Homme aboli de jadis:
> "Souvenirs d'horizons, qu'est-ce, ô toi, que la Terre?"
> Hurle ce songe; et, voix dont la clarté s'altère,
> L'espace a pour jouet le cri: "Je ne sais pas!"

In this passage, as throughout the poem, Mallarmé's thought and expression is a direct extension and deepening of those of Gautier. When Gautier uses the word *gouffre*, he follows the traditional usage, as exemplified by Bossuet for example, who writes that men "vont tous se confondre dans ce gouffre infini du néant". Gautier imagines the day when:

> S'entrouvrira le gouffre où je dois disparaître,
> Pour descendre au séjour des épouvantements[2]

Mallarmé reverses the image, making the dead man himself, not death, a "vaste gouffre". Similarly, Gautier uses the wind in a vivid and powerful metaphor:

---

[1] Opinions are divided here. Some of the best commentators believe this "Homme aboli de jadis" to be Gautier himself (Kurt Wais in 1938, E. Noulet in 1940, 1945 and 1967, G. Davies in 1950). This would seem to me to make the second section of the poem repetitive and pointless. But others (notably P. Beausire in 1942, A. Adam in 1951, Léon Cellier in 1959 and B. Weinberg in 1966) more convincingly and satisfyingly see the poem as built up on the antithesis between the (non-poetic) Man and the Master. See especially L. Cellier, *op. cit.*, pp. 147–9. It may be added that in 1872, just a year before the *Toast funèbre*, Mallarmé had described the fate of the unpoetic man in these terms: "L'âme, tacite et qui ne se suspend pas aux paroles de l'élu familier, le poète, est, à moins qu'elle ne sacrifie à Dieu l'ensemble impuissant de ses aspirations, vouée irrémédiable-ment au Néant." (*Œuvres complètes*, p. 694.)

[2] *Poésies complètes*, vol. II, p. 284.

> Et je sentis mon cou, comme un roseau, fléchir
> Sous le vent que faisait l'aile de ma pensée...[1]

Again, Mallarmé's metaphor of the furious wind of unspoken words is his own, conferring a positive function on a negative quantity. The "Souvenirs d'horizons" of the *néant's* question also echo lines from Gautier:

> Qu'un souvenir presque effacé
> ....
> Le vaste horizon du passé[2]

The metaphysical implications of this whole passage of Mallarmé are in conformity with Gautier's own views. Gautier believed in the immortality of the mind through its works:

> L'esprit est immortel, on ne peut le nier...[3]

But he was convinced that death in itself is definitive, and that annihilation is the ultimate end. From his earliest poems, he is haunted by the thought of the finality of death:

> A présent jeune encor, mais certain que notre âme,
> Inexplicable essence, insaisissable flamme,
> Une fois exhalée, en nous tout est néant,
> Et que rien ne ressort de l'abîme béant
> Où vont, tristes jouets du temps, nos destinées...[4]

The word *néant* sounds like a knell throughout his poetry:

> Le néant! Voilà donc ce que l'on trouve au terme

> Le néant vous appelle et l'oubli vous réclame...[5]

He imagines his own death, in lines suggesting "l'amas de la brume":

> Ce qui fut moi s'envole, et passe lentement
> A travers un brouillard...[6]

A setting like that of the dialogue between "l'Homme aboli de jadis" and "le néant" is evoked by Gautier in these lines:

---

[1] *Poésies complètes*, vol. II, p. 155.   [2] *ibid.*, p. 125.   [3] *ibid.*, p. 310.
[4] *ibid.*, vol. I, p. 53.   [5] *ibid.*, vol. II, pp. 31 and 56.   [6] *ibid.*, vol. I, p. 19.

> Elle s'en est allée en un lieu d'où personne
>   Ne peut la faire revenir:
>
> Quelque part, loin, bien loin, par delà les étoiles,
> Dans un pays sans nom, ombreux et plein de voiles,
>   Sur le bord du néant jeté;
> Limbes de l'impalpable, invisible royaume
> Où va ce qui n'a pas de corps ni de fantôme,
>   Ce qui n'est rien ayant été...[1]

But the dialogue itself reveals Mallarmé's originality. In Gautier, the living seek to read the secret of the dead, for death may bring the key to the mystery of existence:

> Car sur le front des morts le rêveur cherche à lire
> Ce terrible secret qu'aucun d'eux n'a pu dire...[2]

Gautier formulates this hope more explicitly still in these lines:

> Dieu seul peut le savoir; c'est un profond mystère;
> Nous le saurons peut-être à la fin, car la terre
>   Que la pioche jette au cercueil
> Avec sa sombre voix explique bien des choses;
> Des effets, dans le tombe, on comprend mieux les causes,
>   L'éternité commence au seuil.[3]

But Mallarmé makes death ask man for the explanation of the Earth.

To seek and to find this explanation, "l'explication orphique de la Terre",[4] is for Mallarmé the essential duty of man, "le seul devoir du poète":[5]

>   le devoir
> Idéal que nous font les jardins de cet astre.

Gautier himself had expressed the poet's duty in direct, traditional terms:

---

[1] *ibid.*, vol. II, p. 124.   [2] *ibid.*, p. 265.   [3] *ibid.*, p. 128.
[4] see L. J. Austin, 'Mallarmé et le mythe d'Orphée', *Cahiers de l'Association internationale des Études françaises*, No. 22 (March 1970).
[5] *Œuvres complètes*, p. 663.

Rêveur harmonieux, tu fais bien de chanter:
C'est là le seul devoir que Dieu donne aux poètes...[1]

Throughout the poem, Mallarmé has given his own extension and
deepening of ideas dear to Gautier, using imagery of a kind to be
found in Gautier's own poetry. The third section, evoking Gautier's
power of adequate expression, which confers on fleeting phenomena
the only true eternity, uses the metaphor of the garden of flowers
that never fade. Mallarmé was no doubt recalling here the "jardin
de vraie beauté" evoked by Baudelaire at the end of *Le Poème du
haschisch*. But Gautier also extols:

Les plus charmantes fleurs du jardin de beauté...[2]

And other gardens, symbolic of death or of mysticism as well as of
beauty, are to be found in his work.[3] Allusions to flowers abound,
especially to the rose and the lily,[4] and the word *calice* is one of his
favourite expressions.[5] Gautier also uses the metaphor *diamant* for
the eye, and for tears.[6] *Diaphane*, sometimes rhyming with *fane*,[7]
is a frequent word in his work, although he never speaks of an *œil
diaphane* nor attributes to the eye the magical effects that Mallarmé
assigns to it.[8]

In the fourth and last section, which brings the poem to a triumphant conclusion, although there would seem to be just one specific
detail echoing a line by Gautier, the theme as a whole sums up the

[1] *Poésies complètes*, vol. II, p. 80.
[2] *ibid.*
[3] *ibid.*, pp. 46, 47, 69. Mallarmé himself frequently used again this metaphor of
the garden of poetry, notably in *Prose pour des Esseintes*, and, in 1887, in a letter
to Calixte Rachet: "...vous constatez mon manque d'hésitation à me jeter au
gouffre du rêve apparu, quand je pouvais rester aux jardins anciens, parmi des
fleurs ordinaires et certaines" (*Correspondance*, vol. III, 1886–9, ed. H. Mondor
and L. J. Austin (Paris, Gallimard, 1969), p. 114; cf. also *Vie de Mallarmé* by
H. Mondor (Paris, 1941), pp, 510–11, and S. Mallarmé, *Propos sur la poésie*, ed.
H. Mondor (Monaco, Editions du Rocher, 2nd ed., 1953), pp. 153–4.)
[4] Gautier, *Poésies complètes*, vol. I, p. 39; vol. II, pp. 3, 22, 39, 47, 48, 148.
[5] *ibid.*, vol. I, p. 41; vol. II, pp. 65, 69, 195, 261, 274; vol. III, p. 111, etc.
[6] *ibid.*, vol. II, pp. 34, 48. See also the charming picture of a child watering a
garden with artificial rain, vol. I, p. 24.
[7] *ibid.*, vol. II, pp. 28, 70, 130, 141, 148, 160, 295, 302; vol. III, pp. 89, 101, etc.
[8] cf. J.-Cl. Chevalier, *art. cit.*, for a comment on "le regard diaphane", which
may have been suggested to Mallarmé by a passage in *Dogme et rituel de haute
magie*, by l'abbé Constant, alias Eliphas Levi: "Je veux parler de l'imagination,
que les cabalistes appellent le diaphane ou le translucide. L'imagination,
en effet, est comme l'œil de l'âme."

essence of Gautier's thought. Gautier had brought out a fundamental aspect of death:

Et du doigt clos ses yeux qui ne veulent plus voir.[1]

Mallarmé defines death as:

De n'ouvrir pas les yeux sacrés et de se taire.

His conclusion is made up of one long sentence of nine lines: its structure has a breadth and sombre magnificence worthy of its theme. If the poet has banished transience and contingency from the world, then, when death closes his eyes and hushes his voice for ever, as it has done for Gautier, his very sepulchre will rise up as a new thing of beauty adorning the garden of the earth, and buried within it will lie the two threats to the poet: his own inner inarticulacy and the menace of the outer void. The tomb has enclosed these two forms of death-in-life (a notion central to Gautier). Outside stands, in everlasting glory, the Poet,

Tel qu'en Lui-même enfin l'éternité le change.

[1] *Poésies complètes*, vol. II, p. 66.

Courage – c'est du René Ghil

VERA J. DANIEL

On the surface at least, René Ghil (1862–1925) was one of the most prickly poets of the Symbolist era, filled with a dogged conviction of his own importance, punctiliously, even vehemently, correcting as misjudgments any criticism of his work, poetically out on a limb after his break with Mallarmé in April 1888,[1] yet inspiring respect among poets as diverse as Viélé-Griffin, Valéry and André Breton for his unshakeable faith in his literary ideal.

Forty-six years have elapsed since his death and it would therefore seem possible now to take a cool look at the claims of a writer whose name is not forgotten but whose image was obscured by the heady vapours of megalomania. Indeed, if one penetrates beyond the protective barrage of pomp and circumstance there is something even attractive about this monolothic figure. Ghil, it transpires, had some sense of humour: he would read with gusto Georges Fourest's funeral instructions in *La Négresse blonde* (1909):

> Etendez-moi rigide au fond de cette bière,
> placez entre mes mains nos livres décadents;
> Laforgue, Maldoror, Rimbaud, Tristan Corbière
> mais pas de René Ghil, ça me fout mal aux dents!

In personal relationships he could be charming.[2] Yet virtually nothing of his personal life penetrates his poetry; periods of doubt or self-questioning are absent; the occasional first person in his verse is almost deliberately universal.

As for his literary reputation, Ghil was fortunate in attracting a circle of devoted young writers, who after his death endeavoured to keep his memory alive: to them we owe a careful *Choix de poèmes*

---

[1] See R. Ghil, *Les Dates et les Œuvres* (Paris, Crès, 1923), p. 114. Professor L. J. Austin's third volume of Mallarmé's *Correspondance* (Paris, 1969) furnishes further evidence of Ghil's relationship with Mallarmé.

[2] e.g. the testimony of the Russian poet, Konstantin Balmont; see Numéro spécial de *Rythme et synthèse*, 'Hommage à René Ghil' (1926), p. 70.

(1928), *Quelques lettres de René Ghil* (1935) and the *Œuvres complètes* (1938). Ghil's manuscripts are now scattered; even were they collected much patience would be required to decipher the tortuosities of his ornate handwriting. It is likely therefore that his reputation will rest on what is already known.[1] What does this amount to? – a mere name in literary history? a poetic deterrent?

Ghil's rôle in the formation of Symbolism is indisputable. His *Traité du verbe* was granted the accolade of a preface by Mallarmé, a preface which contained some of the master's most significant pronouncements. *Le Traité du verbe* has been likened to a latter-day *Préface de Cromwell;*[2] together with the poems of Ghil's collection *Le Geste ingénu* it offers a compendium of early Symbolist tendencies. The former was praised by Huysmans, notably for its rectification of Rimbaud's synaesthetic theories;[3] the latter, combining the legendary and the indefinite, constitutes according to Ghil himself,

> l'évocation à peine située d'une sorte de paradis légendaire. Là,
> le poète crée un couple, d'âme pourtant moderne
>> Deux parmi leurs pareils, qui seraient l'Un et l'Une.[4]

It was a work of suggestion, of dream, of sleep, of mood – rich with vowel music, suffused with the freshness of streams and morning light. And when the yearning for purity, for water, mirrors, snow,

---

[1] Ghil's work may briefly be summarized thus: his first volume of poetry, *Légende d'âmes et de sangs* (1885) was followed by the various, frequently revised, volumes of his *Œuvre*.

  1re Partie *Dire du mieux*
    Livre I   Le Meilleur Devenir (1889)
    Livre II   Le Geste ingénu (1887)
    Livre III Le Vœu de vivre (1891, 1892, 1893)
    Livre IV   L'Ordre altruiste (1894, 1895, 1897)
  2e Partie *Dire des sangs*
    Livre I   Le Pas humain (1898)
    Livre II   Le Toit des hommes (1901)
    Livre III Les Images du monde (1912, 1920)
    Livre IV   Les Images de l'homme (1926)
  3e Partie *Dire de la loi* (uncompleted)
    Livre I   Le Dieu qui détruit
    Livre II   Les Lois et les rites

His theoretical writings include *Le Traité du verbe* (1886), *En méthode à l'œuvre* (1891), *De la poésie scientifique* (1909).

[2] Professor G. Michaud, *Le Message poétique du Symbolisme* (Paris, 1947), vol. I, p. 10.

[3] See letter dated 8 août 1886, *Rythme et synthèse*, Numéro spécial (1926), p. 59.

[4] R. Ghil, *Œuvres complètes* (Paris, Messein, 1938), vol. I, p. 67.

precious stones, which marked the 1880s, had receded, Ghil's verse matched the increasing social consciousness of the 1890s. He evokes for instance with deep compassion the human problems of workers thrust into an industrialized age and slightly before Verhaeren treats the depopulation of the countryside and the upheavals of mechanization. This is the aspect of his verse which is now most dated, its relevance limited, related to a period of industrialization which we have long since outstripped.

Similarities with Symbolist aspirations persist throughout Ghil's work. His aim was a synthesis, a vast epic of humanity in which all episodes are intimately interwoven with the whole. Symbolist too is his exploration of the possibilities of language and in particular of a poetic language distinct from that of everyday. Of the Symbolist Ghil had the total devotion to his art, the fervent religious ardour which replaced, for so many of his generation, belief in established religion. His work is rooted in the nineteenth century: his love of vast myths and the alliance of poetry with music – at times power-fully Wagnerian, at others conveying the simplicity of folk-song – belong to Symbolist aesthetics and not to the pictorially discon-tinuous of the early twentieth century, of a Max Jacob, a Blaise Cendrars or an Apollinaire. If in the later volumes of his work such as *Le Pas humain* and *Le Toit des hommes* Ghil evokes the life of primitive man, the figures of early lake-dwellers with their totemic cults and mimed dances, this can in retrospect be viewed as a facet of the vast Symbolist interest in primitivism, in the common con-sciousness of man and the primeval source of his beliefs and reactions. Ghil's expressed aim was: "une pensée qui continuement, du détail relié au total, associe l'Homme à l'Universel, et tout moment de l'univers à sa durée éternelle".[1] To this end he traces man's development:

> à travers les Magismes et les Rites primordiaux, où se décèle sa foisonnante conscience d'être, en directs contacts avec l'Universel: quand, en même temps, vidant les Symboles et scrutant les Mythes – nous recherchons les vérités d'instinct, d'intuition et de connaissance, ésotériquement encloses en eux.[2]

[1] R. Ghil, 'Sur *les Images du monde*', *F.Q.*, (March 1921), p. 15.
[2] *ibid.*, pp. 10–11.

From the beginning, however, Ghil also expressed an interest in science. This gave rise to his "poésie scientifique", an appellation to which he clung despite the well-intentioned objection of friends. Not that Ghil envisaged producing text-book science in verse or a facile elaboration of "the marvels of science". His concern was rather the wonder with which a human mind contemplates scientific knowledge, an attitude comparable to that of the later Verhaeren. By scientific verse Ghil sought liberation from what he called egotistical literature – yet his verse is fortunately not wholly devoid of emotion. His theories, influenced by his reading of Helmholtz, also came to have a scientific basis, since "Idée et Verbe sont véritablement participants des ondes rythmiques de la Matière."[1] Taking as his starting-point the vibrations which are the foundation of speech, Ghil sought to link in his verse the vibrations caused by emotions and their expression.[2] The poet, endowed with the gift of penetrating to the essence of things, translates his vision into the expressions the inanimate objects would use if they could speak: "nous tendons... à l'identité du verbe et de la chose, qui semble se vivre et s'exprimer elle-même aux sons et au dramatisme rythmique, de manière que le poète soit mû par une âme de sens universel et en quelque sorte multiforme.[3] So far so good: but when in *En méthode à l'œuvre* consonants are identified according to their vowel associations with flutes, clarinets, violins and other musical instruments[4] and with colours and impressions,[5] the reader feels that such may be a writer's personal manual, something in the nature of an elaborate rhyming dictionary, a guide and aid to composition, but that it has little bearing on poetic appreciation.

Perhaps even more than with aesthetics Ghil was concerned with metaphysics. For him, man is the co-ordinating point of the universe. The intuitive energy of his subconscious links the distant past with the present. Thus

suivant le processus de l'Être, nous sentons progressivement avec l'émotion de nous référer continuement à l'universel, la matière

[1] R. Ghil 'Le poète philosophe', *Les Écrits pour l'art* (15 mars 1905), p. 10.
[2] *De la poésie scientifique* (Paris, Gastein-Serge, 1909), p. 44.
[3] *F.Q., op. cit.*, p. 12.
[4] see *Œuvres complètes*, vol. III, p. 231.
[5] *ibid.*, p. 239.

à travers les pensées animales et la pensée humaine aller son effort illimité à se savoir et se contempler harmonieusement.[1]

It would seem that Ghil believed not only in an individual, but also in a universal conscious and subconscious[2] evolving endlessly in time and space. Through intuition which affords him an insight akin to that of the mystics, the poet attempts to evoke the mystery of the cosmos with a total, religious emotion – an attempt which although it can never achieve complete realization since its basis is the frailty of man confronted with the absolute, nevertheless constitutes the justification of man's presence on earth: "Nous sommes au monde pour tendre à notre unité pensante et morale."[3] The place of man in the universe and the purpose of human life are indicated thus:

> Et l'Homme n'a de valeur, qu'autant qu'il regarde
> la Vie éternisant ses Yeux! et qu'il la garde
> et qu'il la mène aux voluptés du Mieux!
>   Et, comme
> La Vie aspire à se savoir et posséder
> et n'espère qu'aux voûtes de ton front: ô Homme
> ta vertu,
>   ne se mesure qu'à ta Sapience...
> Et parmi l'Univers et ses Êtres, puissance
> qui ne dois aux détours des destins, hasarder!
> elle seule, selon les lois du tournant pacte
> qui meut les Mondes et leurs Modes,
>   de tes êtres
> doit mesurer, vastes d'autant que tu pénètres
> pesant en toi sa somme, l'univers – la place
> et le geste que peut ton Acte,
>   dans l'Espace.[4]

Ghil's work in its entirety may be indigestible, but when the asperity of his convictions is no longer an embarrassment, when the

---

[1] *De la poésie scientifique*, p. 40.
[2] see N. Bureau 'De l'intuition dans la poésie de René Ghil', *Rythme et synthèse*, Numéro spécial (1926), pp. 100–4.
[3] *De la poésie scientifique*, p. 53.
[4] *Œuvres complètes*, vol. I, pp. 485–6.

neologisms and archaisms which weigh down his very personal form
of expression are not forced, he wrote both in prose and in verse
pages which deserve to endure. Such are the direct, simple melodies
of folk-song: witness *Les Etelles*:

> En m'en venant au tard de nuit
> se sont éteintes les ételles:
> ah! que les roses ne sont-elles
> tard au rosier de mon ennui
> et mon Amante, que n'est-elle
> morte en m'aimant dans un minuit...

or the graceful, nostalgic pastoral *La Plainte à la bergère*, which
begins:

> Il n'est pas de sentier sur terre – où des Amants
> ne soient passés, ma Bien-aimée...
>   A lourds serments
> dans la poussière des étés, depuis longtemps
> leurs pas – passants-passés se sont lointains, éteints:
> de la rumeur de tes moutons qui passe, éteints
> des gouttes d'eau qu'un temps amasse, en la ramée.

Ghil must have been an essentially lonely man, enclosed in
the strait-jacket of his theories and ideas, a strait-jacket which
impeded both the development of personality and of human relationships. It is pleasing to think that on occasion he transcended this
barrier and beyond the individual discovered notably in nature a
rooted fastness, unknown to science, a spring-board from which he
could attain release in the cosmic; his ego – a passing entity – is then
transfused in time and space and the scientific certainties, behind
which he took refuge, yield to an essentially emotional response. In
such verse the beliefs he expounded as "poésie scientifique" and
"rythme évoluant" attain serene expression in lines essentially
musical, where pernickety instrumental concerns of flutes and
oboes are forgotten in the cosmic timelessness of human yearning.

Much of Ghil's best writing – poems, letters, articles – reflects
his profound joy in the countryside around Melle, his home in
Poitou. This is undoubtedly the source of the poem *Les Batteuses*[1] –

[1] See my article 'Poems of René Ghil', *Western Review*, (Autumn, 1953).

memorable for a visual awareness which here combines with the
characteristic musicality of his verse, a successful little poem by any
standards, whether one lingers over the poetically charged neolog-
ism "emmurmurer", the bold and successful use of the dental
plosive 't' or the suggestive "hâtes pattues" of the returning flocks
in the still autumn evening.

> Et, toutes! elles se sont tûes
> les Batteuses du grain des soirs
> qui loin emmurmuraient d'espoirs
> les grand'terres aux tours pointues.
>
> Les pailles ardemment têtues
> ont rendu d'ors leurs lourds avoirs:
> et, toutes! elles se sont tûes
> les Batteuses du grain des soirs.
>
> Les trèves d'Araires, tortues
> hantent à demain les terroirs:
> maintenant, rentrent en tas noirs
> Les troupeaux aux hâtes pattues —
>
> et, toutes! elles se sont tûes...

At Melle, far from literary frictions, Ghil could delight in "des
peupliers tout endeuillés de pies,"[1] in the picturesque charm of
Les Sables: "toujours aussi prenants son petit port et son village
de la chaume aux petites maisons coloriées au long du quai — et des
couleurs de voiles qui rentrent: un calme tendre et barbare, toute
une primitivité qui me va si directement à l'être."[2] Or he submits
to the fascination of those strange Poitevin marshes just above
Niort where a stir whispers through the damp silence and the way
of life seems a century behind the modern age.

Two of the most evocative themes in Ghil's verse are night and
the sea — in face of these natural phenomena man's atavistic feelings

---

[1] Œuvres complètes, vol. III, p. 80.
[2] letter dated 21 juillet 1923, Quelques lettres de René Ghil, (Paris, Messein, 1935),
p. 59.

are strongest. Night opens up the long vistas of evolution through which life has progressed:

>Terre et grands horizons où va l'antan perdu.[1]

His finest verse is a compound of elegiac, mystical, cosmic inspiration as in *Le Chant dans l'espace* – a moment of sublimation beyond time, when, in the immensity of a starry night, the individual is raised to a transcendental plane:

>La nuit des astres nus est un sanglot qui s'est
>brisé...
>   Cette nuit, il le sent et le sait, mon
>cœur, qui n'est plus en moi! qui surmonte mon nom
>et mon instant de vie où l'éternité passe –
>et, d'une aspiration qui meurt de pureté
>brisé!
>supplie de le prendre et le Temps et l'Espace!...

This poem contains the line which has been said to epitomize Ghil's verse:

>Ma pensée est le monde en émoi de soi-même.

As he meditates on the timelessness of perpetual flux and change the poet evokes the limitless plains where for centuries men have reaped the golden grain of harvest and the religious rites which throughout the ages have betokened man's gratitude for the fruits of earth. Even the voiceless plants share dimly in the universal rapture:

>Des ignorés lointains où les moissons d'été
>rendent lourd de leur grain le vent souple, où les hommes
>multiplièrent dans la lumière les sommes
>de leurs vieux gestes, – les vallées en allées
>reviennent, et, tout haut remontantes, soutiennent
>aux horizons, droits d'attitudes étoilées!
>le vertige des Végétants dont le sursaut
>crie et pleure sa nuit, qui ne parle pas!

[1] *Œuvres complètes*, vol. III, p. 70.

From the external world, the poet returns to the world within him, to man's boundless longing for union with the totality of life of which he is but a transitory manifestation.

> Oh!
> cette nuit d'intérieur élan, qui soupèse
> l'illimité de ma native nostalgie
> et de mon souvenir, – d'un amour élargie
> et de ramures et d'épaules où s'apaise
> le dieu mouvant des Devenirs, oh! que voudrait
> l'être de l'univers que sépare un regret
> éternel, d'un possessoire arrêt où s'amasse
> le sanglot qui aime au sanglot qui ait aimé!
> emplir d'un émoi seul et le Temps et l'Espace...

It is apparent here that the suggestive natural imagery of his early verse has found a more definite framework, an integration which may indeed owe something to his views on scientific poetry, but which is now the confident source of a conviction orchestrated in a major key. As he breathes in the scents of earth brought to him on the wind from extreme distance, his being is dilated with serenity:

> Je remplirai et le Temps et l'Espace
> de la sérénité de ma tendresse,...
> et sur mes lèvres entr'ouvertes qui respirent
> pour soulever toute la Vie – également –
> l'intermittente animation du vent extrême
> met l'odeur de la terre et les mots qui attirent
> entre les points ardents de la distance...

> Je remplirai et le Temps et l'Espace
> de l'unité de ma tendresse, – cette nuit
> sur mes lèvres en remuement d'anéanti
> Baiser! quand, transparentes du palpitement
> où ne persiste de douleur – passionnément –
> que pour éterniser un amour trop immense
> mes tempes
> battent les amplitudes du Silence...

To hear this poem read in Ghil's grave and rhythmic voice as registered on the gramophone record at the Archives de la Parole in Paris is to share the ecstasy which inspired it. Apollinaire was impressed by Ghil's rendering at that strange medley of 'Symbolist' poets in the summer of 1913:

> Comme je fais mes poèmes en les chantant sur des rythmes qu'a noté mon ami Max Jacob, j'aurais dû les chanter comme fit René Ghil, qui fut avec Verhaeren le véritable triomphateur de cette séance. Le chant vertigineux de Ghil on eût dit des harpes éoliennes vibrant dans un jardin d'Italie, ou encore que l'aurore touchait la statue de Memnon et surtout l'hymne télégraphique que les fils et les poteaux ne cessent d'entonner sur les grandes routes.[1]

Similar to *Le Chant dans l'espace* is *La Nuit aux terrasses*, where the poet communes with the universe as he stands with his beloved on a lofty terrace gazing at the night. Poised thus between earth and stars he feels throbbing through his mortal frame the mighty movements of life and death, linking him in a common motion with the heavens above and with the earth below and bringing him back irrevocably, but serenely, to his place in the human condition:

> Or, – or
> sur les terrasses, en nous tenant aux épaules
> longtemps, parmi la nuit d'étoiles qui se perd
> aux ramures qui sont toutes
>   comme de saules
> appesantis sur d'amples eaux odorant l'air
> de vivre et de mourir: sur les terrasses hautes
> promenons-nous! aux pas mêlés au sol, des hôtes
> de la Terre...

Mer montante of 1916 – a vast, yet compact evocation of the sea at sunset – opens, as does all Ghil's best verse, the windows of the absolute, reverting however ultimately to the human and the individual:

[1] G. Apollinaire, *Anecdotiques* (Paris, 1955), p. 183.

Bruit qui ne s'énumère, et sous l'atone nue
le rond soleil qui mut sa loi, qui transparaît
en point ardent d'où s'amassa la révolue
cendre du soir désert,
                la Mer qui ne saurait
d'éternel arrêter la respiration tûe
de tous les hommes morts en trophées! arrivait
de dessous l'horizon qui limite ma vue
et le soupir de ma poitrine, – et elle avait
immensément, le mouvement qui outre-passe
et la grève et les pas et les mots qu'en vain tasse
le poids multiplié de nos vivants trépas:

et elle était – qui vient de soi-même suivie –
de l'étendue que le temps ne tarit pas
et sur ma lèvre un goût de sel, mouillé de vie...

These poems exemplify Ghil's belief that the role of poetry is to express the universal; the poet transcending his own personality identifies himself with total consciousness. Underlying his verse is an epic imagination which enhances the importance of human action and sets it against the eternal, a perpetual suggestion of the life-force, in movement behind all creation, which is the hallmark of his work.

Et des morts aux vivants va l'Esprit de la Vie.
Il se traverse lui-même en devenant et
mouvant tout, et mêle l'une en l'autre et en soi
la danse de détruire et de produire. Il est
qui a des noms est qui n'a pas un non: l'émoi
vertigineux qui d'éternité monte au long
du pied pressé du peuple-végétant, est la
sonorité de son élan.[1]

In such verse the Symbolist and scientific poet is harmonized. The "rhythme évoluant", powerful as a sea-swell, gives it its particular resonance and volume, unlike that of any other French poet. At times Ghil evokes comparison with Claudel, minus the essential

---

[1] *Œuvres complètes*, vol. II, p. 310.

Catholicism of the latter: both are basically religious, both aspire to cosmic oneness, both enunciate views on prosody whilst in form the 'verset' of Claudel is not totally foreign to the rich rhythms of Ghil. This is however a purely literary association, there is no proof that they ever met or corresponded. In its entirety, including the strange Oriental poem *Le Pantoun des pantoun*, Ghil's work as that of any other poet, is unique. "J'ai dit des choses universellement reliées dans leur suite éternelle," he wrote.[1] To this extent he deserves to be remembered for himself: other aspects of his work belong to literary history.

[1] Letter to Charles Cousin, 9 avril 1915, *Quelques lettres de René Ghil*, p. 28.

1. *San Francesco che sposa tre sacre Vergini*, from Rosini's *Storia della pittura italiana*, pl. xxv. (*Bodleian Library*.)

2. Sassetta: Saint François et les trois Vertus. (*Chantilly*, *Musée Condé;*
photo Bulloz.)

3. Bastien-Lepage: Jeanne d'Arc écoutant ses voix. (*New York, The Metropolitan Museum of Art, gift of Erwin Davis, 1889.*)

4. Bastien-Lepage: Études pour Jeanne d'Arc. (*New Haven, Yale University Art Gallery, gift of J. Alden Weir.*)

Renan, Zola, et les visions
de Jeanne d'Arc

JEAN SEZNEC

Iʟ existe dans la correspondance de Renan[1] une lettre inachevée, et dont quelques mots sont indéchiffrables. Elle est adressée à un peintre, et datée de Paris, 16 août 1855.

Monsieur,

J'ai rêvé toute la nuit à votre Jeanne d'Arc, et quoique de toutes les idées qui me sont venues aucune ne soit, je crois, réalisable, j'ai voulu vous les écrire, afin de vous prouver l'amour que je ressens déjà pour votre œuvre, avant même qu'elle soit née.

Il me semble que, puisque la légende est complètement acceptée, il faut s'y plier et qu'il serait difficile d'arriver sans cela à quelque chose de clair et de pleinement intelligible pour le public. Une Jeanne d'Arc solitaire, trouvant son inspiration dans son propre cœur, plairait plus à quelques personnes, à Martin, à moi-même, mais ce ne serait pas la Jeanne d'Arc consacrée. Je crois donc qu'il faut montrer les *saintes* en véritables inspiratrices. Il serait possible, ce me semble, d'indiquer par un trait léger que ces saintes ne sont que sa pensée elle-même, dédoublée et *objectivée* devant ses yeux. Cela s'admettrait d'autant mieux que les saintes qui lui apparaissaient n'étaient autres que celles qu'elle avait coutume de voir à l'église, *ses sœurs du paradis*, comme elle les appelait.

Je me la représente donc au pied du hêtre des fées, demi-assise, demi-agenouillée, et devant elle, dans une atmosphère chaude et lumineuse, trois figures célestes, qui ne seraient qu'elle-même, idéalisée, son type céleste en quelque sorte. Ces trois

[1] *Œuvres complètes*, éd. déf., vol. x (Paris, 1961), pp. 168–70. La lettre, annoncée en note comme "en cours de classement", n'est toujours pas accessible.

personnages seraient Sainte Catherine, Sainte Marguerite et
Saint Michel, ses trois saints favoris. Je leur donnerais à tous trois
une certaine ressemblance entre eux et avec elle-même, quelque
chose de simple, de virginal. Je les rangerais sur une même
ligne, côte à côte, longuement profilés, sans craindre les invrai-
semblances, puisqu'il s'agit d'ombres plutôt que d'êtres réels.
La candeur, la simplicité, la chasteté rayonneraient de l'un à
l'autre dans cet entretien céleste et formeraient un petit monde
à part de bonté et de douceur où ces êtres choisis vivraient comme
dans leur milieu naturel. A la vue de ses frères d'en haut, Jeanne
n'éprouverait aucun embarras; au contraire, elle serait là comme
en pays de connaissance et doucement ravie. Pour déterminer la
signification militaire et patriotique de la scène, Sainte Catherine
pourrait lui présenter l'épée; cette épée serait justifiée soit par
l'habitude de mettre une arme entre les mains des martyrs, soit
par l'épée de Sainte Catherine de Fierbois, à laquelle Jeanne
tenait tant. Une épée tenue timidement d'une main de femme
serait d'ailleurs le symbole de toute la vie de Jeanne. Saint Michel
porterait le fameux étendard (Michelet, p. 28). Le sexe de Saint
Michel serait à peine indiqué, il y aurait là une nuance analogue
à celle que les peintres de l'ancienne école italienne ont si finement rendue dans les Annonciations: un homme-vierge, si bien
qu'il entrerait dans ce concert tout virginal sans que rien de
l'instinct sexuel se révélât de part ni d'autre.

Pour le[...], les [...] de tête et la suspension des trois personnages célestes, je n'imagine rien de mieux que le mode adopté
par un ancien maître florentin dans un tableau reproduit dans
la planche de l'ouvrage de Rosini sur la peinture italienne et
représentant l'entretien de Saint François avec trois vertus. Je
vous montrerai cette ancienne gravure, s'il vous plaît de passer à
la Bibliothèque avant la fin du mois. Ces trois vertus m'ont
toujours semblé le modèle des apparitions idéales.

Je placerais l'église près de là. L'église a joué un si grand rôle
dans la mission de Jeanne d'Arc qu'on ne peut l'omettre: c'est là
évidemment qu'elle a tout appris. J'indiquerais même sa passion
pour les cloches (voir Michelet, p. 15) par un détail qui pourrait
vous sembler puéril mais qui se retrouve souvent dans les maîtres
italiens.

Le peintre à qui était destinée cette lettre n'a pas été identifié mais on peut présumer que c'était l'un des frères Scheffer, soit Ary (dont Renan devait commenter la *Tentation du Christ*[1]); soit Henry dont il allait devenir le gendre l'année suivante. Ni l'un ni l'autre, cependant, n'a peint de *Jeanne d'Arc écoutant ses voix*. Une esquisse d'Ary, conservée à Dordrecht, et datée de 1847, représente l'*Entrée à Orléans*;[2] le même sujet a été traité par Henry, dont la toile est au Musée de Versailles.[3]

La lettre de Renan est curieuse d'abord par ce qu'elle reflète de ses vues sur l'art religieux. Rationaliste, il rejette l'interprétation légendaire; mais il admet que l'artiste la représente, et même il lui prescrit de respecter l'iconographie traditionelle; c'est le seul moyen de rendre ce genre de sujets consacrés intelligibles au public; la règle vaut pour Jeanne d'Arc comme pour les récits de l'Évangile. Sans doute, à "quelques personnes" – entendez: aux esprits plus éclairés – une Jeanne d'Arc "trouvant son inspiration dans son propre cœur", c'est-à-dire représentée seule, conviendrait mieux. Henri Martin, expressément nommé à côté de Renan lui-même parmi ces "quelques personnes", avait écrit, en effet, dans son *Histoire de France* (1844) à propos des apparitions: "Elle s'était prise d'une vive tendresse pour ces êtres fantastiques, *forme idéale de ses pensées.*" Suivait une très longue note où Martin exposait les points de vue opposés des physiologistes et des mystiques sur les phénomènes de l'extase. A son avis, "l'illusion de l'inspiré consiste à prendre pour une révélation apportée par des êtres extérieurs, anges, saints ou génies, les révélations intérieures de cette personnalité infinie qui est en nous".[4] A l'occasion de la publication des *Procès* par Quicherat, Sainte-Beuve écrit en 1856, presque dans les mêmes termes: "Son idée fixe se projetait hors d'elle…et lui revenait en écho: c'était la *voix* qui désormais lui parlait comme celle d'un être

---

[1] Lettre de 1856 à Ary Scheffer (*Œuvres complètes*, vol. x, pp. 194–6): "Quand votre Satan sera livré au public, je tiendrai beaucoup à en parler"; l'article promis: "La Tentation du Christ par M. Ary Scheffer" a été recueilli dans les *Études d'histoire religieuse* (1863), pp. 423–32.

[2] Catalogue du Musée Ary Scheffer (Dordrecht, 1934), no. 78.

[3] Le traitement du sujet est entièrement différent. Le tableau, signé d'un simple S, est daté de 1843.

[4] 4e édition, pp. 143–4. "Du reste", ajoutait-il prudemment, "nier l'action d' êtres extérieurs sur l'inspiré… ce n'est en aucune manière révoquer en doute l'intervention divine dans ces grands phénomènes et dans ces grandes existences."

distinct d'elle-même''. Mais Sainte-Beuve ose donner au phénomène son nom scientifique'':

> Sans aborder une question qui est tout entière du ressort de la physiologie et de la science, je dirai que le seul fait d'avoir entendu des voix..., de se figurer que les pensées nées du dedans, et qui reviennent sous cette forme sont des suggestions extérieures et supérieures, est un fait désormais bien constaté dans la science: c'est le fait de l'*hallucination* proprement dite.[1]

Telle est aussi l'attitude de Renan, – une attitude dont la *Vie de Jésus* offrira bien d'autres exemples. Mais puisque, d'autre part, il veut que l'artiste "extériorise" les visions de Jeanne, le compromis sera de les représenter d'un trait aussi léger que possible, comme des ombres virginales, afin de suggérer qu'elles ne sont que "sa pensée dédoublée et objectivée". Renan insiste sur la "chasteté" de ces figures. Saint Michel lui-même doit être un homme-vierge, mieux: un être asexué. Il est à propos de rappeler ici que les juges de la Pucelle s'étaient montrés avides de savoir sous quelle forme elle avait vu Saint Michel: "Portait-il une couronne? Avait-il des habits? N'était-il pas tout nu?", s'attirant ainsi la réponse sublime: "Pensez-vous donc que Dieu n'ait pas de quoi le vêtir?" Sainte-Beuve, qui rapporte ce dialogue, est frappé de la matérialité de ces théologiens, de leur grossièreté d'imagination.[2] C'est précisément l'écueil que, selon Renan, le peintre doit éviter à tout prix: le réalisme. La prescription ne vaut pas seulement pour ce sujet particulier: elle s'applique à l'art religieux tout entier. Le traitement 'naturaliste' d'un thème, par définition, idéal, est une profanation. Un tableau religieux est "une haute représentation morale" – il faut donc l'épurer de toute note sensuelle et de tout détail concret.

Cette vue conduit Renan à condamner la "révoltante crudité" de l'art espagnol; à proscrire des siècles entiers de peinture italienne, et particulièrement le baroque; et à dénoncer, dans son propre siècle, les tentatives de Vernet et de Delaroche pour introduire dans les épisodes de l'Evangile des éléments anecdotiques ou des

[1] *Causeries du lundi*, article du 19 août 1856 (3e éd., Paris, 1868), vol. II, pp. 405–7.
[2] *ibid.*, pp. 415–16.

précisions archéologiques, les ravalant ainsi au niveau de scènes de genre.[1]

En fait, Renan, par son hostilité au "réalisme dévot qui veut toucher ce qu'il faut se contenter de croire", incline vers un art éthéré, idéalisé jusqu'à l'anémie. A propos de l'ouvrage d'un protestant libéral, A. Coquerel: *Des beaux-arts en Italie du point de vue religieux* (1857), il écrit: "Le livre de M. Coquerel renferme la théorie la plus épurée, la seule possible pour nous, de l'art religieux." Et c'est bien cette spiritualité protestante qui lui plaît dans les toiles des frères Scheffer.[2]

————

REVENONS à sa lettre. La description de l'héroïne, telle qu'il la propose au peintre, emprunte ses éléments à deux sources. D'abord Michelet, qui avait fait paraître en 1853 la première édition séparée de sa *Jeanne d'Arc*, incorporée dans l'*Histoire de France* dès 1841. Renan le cite expressément, on l'a vu, pour certains détails: l'étendard de Jeanne porté par Saint Michel, sa passion pour les cloches...[3] D'autres détails encore viennent de Michelet, quoiqu'il ne soit pas cité: le hêtre des fées; l'épée de Sainte Catherine de Fierbois, etc. Mais à ces textes littéraires, Renan ajoute un exemple plastique: celui d' "un ancien maître florentin" qui, selon lui, a fourni le parfait modèle de la manière de figurer des apparitions idéales dans un tableau représentant l'*Entretien de Saint François avec trois vertus*; ce tableau, Renan en a trouvé une reproduction dans "l'ouvrage de Rosini sur la peinture italienne". En effet, dans l'atlas de la *Storia della pittura italiana*, parue à Pise en 1839, on voit à la planche XXV *San Francesco che sposa tre sacre Vergini*. L'auteur est donné pour inconnu.

[1] 'L'art religieux', dans: *Nouvelles Études d'histoire religieuse* (Paris, 1884), pp. 400–12. Cf. J. Pommier, 'Ernest Renan et l'art religieux de son temps', *Studi in onore di Italo Siciliano*, (1966) II, 1018–30.

[2] Il admet que la *Tentation du Christ* aurait pu "déployer une exécution plus vigoureuse, et un coloris plus brillant"; mais, ajoute-t-il aussitôt, "l'éclat matérialiste de la couleur aurait donné trop de corps aux êtres charmants issus de son pinceau" (*art. cit.*, p. 432). Dans la préface des *Tendres Stocks* de Paul Morand, Proust décèle malicieusement des traces d'Ary Scheffer dans la *Vie de Jésus*.

[3] *Jeanne d'Arc*, éd. G. Rudler (Paris, 1925), pp. 31, 21 et note: "Elle avait une sorte de passion pour les cloches: *Promiserat dare lanas... ut diligentiam haberet pulsandi*" (Procès de révision).

Il s'agit, en réalité, d'un panneau du polyptique commandé en
1437 à un Siénois, Stefano di Giovanni dit le Sassetta, pour le
maître autel de San Francesco, à Borgo San Sepolcro. L'œuvre,
acquise en 1879 par le duc d'Aumale, est aujourd'hui au Musée
Condé, à Chantilly.[1] Ce que Renan y admire, à travers la gravure,
ce sont, particulièrement, les vertus: la Chasteté, la Pauvreté,
l'Obéissance, deux fois représentées: sur la terre, au moment où
Saint François épouse la Pauvreté en lui passant au doigt l'anneau
nuptial; et dans le ciel, où elles s'envolent ensuite, et paraissent
flotter: c'est précisément ainsi, "en suspension" dans l'air, qu'il
faudrait montrer les trois visiteurs célestes de Jeanne d'Arc.

C'est donc essentiellement un *procédé* que relève Renan, et qu'il
recommande à son peintre. Mais l'œuvre, dans l'ensemble, devait
lui plaire par une simple gravité, le plus souvent absente, selon lui,
dans l'art italien, mondain et frivole. A cet égard, Sassetta appartient
à ces rares artistes du quattrocento – tel Fra Angelico – qu'il excepte
de sa condamnation:[2] ils sont "purs". Cette pureté, dans la gravure,
devient sécheresse: mais dans l'original elle est toute fraîcheur.
C'est, comme le dit Berenson, une page des *Fioretti*,[3] à la fois
familière et tendre. La Chasteté, la Pauvreté, l'Obéissance, vêtues
respectivement de blanc, de brun et de rose, sont trois demoiselles;
le paysage est la plaine qui s'étend entre Campiglia et San Quirico
d'Orcia; les vertus s'élèvent vers l'horizon bleu, au-dessus du Mont
Amiata. Le sentiment seul dématérialise cette réalité, et la trans-
figure en idylle.

La Pauvreté, reconnaissable à ses pieds nus, était la préférée du
saint; c'est à son doigt qu'il met l'anneau; elle-même, dans un
geste touchant, se retourne en remontant au ciel, pour le regarder
encore une fois. Renan, qui avait une prédilection pour François

[1] Le panneau central, Saint François dans sa gloire, est dans la collection Berenson,
à Settignano; les sept autres à la National Gallery de Londres. Voir J. Pope-
Hennessy, *Sassetta* (1939), pp. 96–110; et dans le catalogue de la National
Gallery, les nos. 4757 à 4763, avec le commentaire de Martin David, *The Early
Italian Schools* (2e éd., 1961), pp. 502–12.
[2] 'L'art religieux', *art. cit.*, p. 400; "Dans les œuvres que nous a léguées l'Italie du
Moyen Age règne une tendance beaucoup plus artiste que chrétienne... J'excep-
terai naturellement celles d'Angelico de Fiesole."
[3] Et une page *inédite*. Comme l'observe Berenson (*A Sienese painter of the Franciscan
Legend* (1910), pp. 37–9) les biographes de Saint François parlent simplement
de trois jeunes filles qui rencontrent le saint, lui disent: "Salut, Dame Pauvreté,"
et disparaissent. Ils ne parlent pas de mariage mystique en cette occasion.

d'Assise, lui a consacré un essai[1] où il rappelle, justement, ce mariage mystique, et où il cite les vers du *Paradiso* (XI, 58, 63–7): "Veuve de son premier époux, la Pauvreté, cette fiancée à qui, comme à la Mort, personne n'ouvre volontiers sa porte, était restée onze cents ans méprisée, oubliée, quand celui-ci, devant le Père éternel[2] et devant la cour céleste, la prit pour épouse, et chaque jour l'aima davantage."

La rencontre du saint avec les vertus est empreinte d'un grand naturel. Renan voudrait que sa Jeanne d'Arc abordât ses trois saints favoris avec la même simplicité. Il l'imagine "sans aucun embarras... devant ses frères d'en haut; au contraire, elle serait là comme en pays de connaissance."

———————

LE tableau "rêvé" par Renan n'a donc pas été exécuté par son correspondant; mais au Salon de 1880 fut exposée une toile qui, par un trait du moins, semble la réalisation tardive de ce rêve: la *Jeanne d'Arc* de Bastien-Lepage. Il est regrettable que nous n'ayons pas, sur cette toile, le commentaire de Renan; mais nous avons celui de Zola.[3]

Ce qui plaît à Zola, ce sont, bien entendu, les éléments réalistes de la composition: l'héroïne elle-même, et le décor:

En songeant à la figure historique de notre Jeanne d'Arc, M. Bastien-Lepage a pensé qu'aucun peintre n'avait encore eu l'idée de nous donner une Jeanne d'Arc réelle, une simple paysanne dans le cadre de son petit jardin lorrain. Il y avait là une tentative naturaliste tres intéressante, dont il a compris toute la portée... Il a cru devoir choisir le moment où Jeanne entend des voix, ce qui dramatise le tableau et rentre dans la donnée historique. La jeune fille était assise sous un pommier, travaillant, lorsqu'elle a entendu les voix; et elle s'est levée, les yeux fixes, en extase, et elle a fait quelques pas, le bras tendu, écoutant

———————

[1] *Nouvelles Études d'histoire religieuse* (Paris, 1884); cf. préface, p. iii: "J'ai toujours eu beaucoup de dévotion pour François d'Assise."
[2] Le *patre* du vers 66 désigne en réalité non "le Père éternel", mais celui de Saint François.
[3] *Salons*, éd. F. W. J. Hemmings et R. J. Niess (Genève et Paris, 1959), pp. 246–8. La toile est au Metropolitan Museum of Art, New York.

toujours. Ce mouvement est fort juste. On y sent l'hallucination. Jusque là, tout est acceptable, tout rentre dans la donnée naturaliste du cas physiologique de Jeanne.

En somme, cette "paysanne hystérique" mériterait une place parmi les Rougon-Macquart. Malheureusement, il y a les apparitions. Au fond du jardin, impalpables comme des ombres, d'un contour si léger qu'ils en sont presque imperceptibles – enfin tels que les voulait Renan – sont suspendus en l'air Saint Michel, Sainte Catherine et Sainte Marguerite. Additions déplorables, au jugement de Zola:

> ... Mais M. Bastien-Lepage, sans doute pour rendre son sujet plus intelligible, s'est imaginé d'aller peindre dans les branches d'un pommier la vision de la jeune fille, deux saintes et un saint cuirassé d'or. Pour moi, c'est là un soin fâcheux; l'attitude de Jeanne, son gest, son œil d'hallucinée, suffisaient pour nous conter tout le drame; et cette apparition enfantine qui flotte n'est qu'un pléonasme, un écriteau inutile et encombrant. Cela me déplaît d'autant plus que cela gâte la belle unité naturaliste du sujet. Jeanne seule devait voir les saintes, qui sont des imaginations pures, des effets morbides de son tempérament. Si le peintre nous le montre, c'est qu'il n'a pas compris son sujet, ou du moins qu'il n'a pas voulu nous le donner dans sa vérité strictement scientifique.

Il y a plusieurs points à relever dans cette tirade. D'abord Zola qui, comme Renan, aurait souhaité que Jeanne fût seule, conçoit, comme lui, que les apparitions rendent le sujet plus intelligible. Pourtant il les condamne au nom de la science, alors que Renan les excusait au nom de la tradition. L'attitude de la jeune fille, son œil fixe, son bras tendu, étaient du reste à son avis suffisamment évocateurs: "Ce mouvement fort juste", à lui seul, révélait l'hallucination. Les études au crayon, conservées à Yale, témoignent que le peintre a tâtonné avant de trouver ce geste, et cette expression.

Une singularité du tableau, c'est que Jeanne tourne le dos à ses visiteurs célestes. Elle les entend, et même elle les voit – mais sans les regarder. L'intention de l'artiste paraît avoir été de suggérer l'irréalité des apparitions – qui, directement perçues, auraient pris un caractère trop concret. Bastien-Lepage s'est conformé ici, sans le savoir, au conseil que Diderot, jadis, avait donné à Deshays. Au Salon de 1765, Deshays avait exposé un *Saint Jérôme écrivant sur la mort*, les yeux fixés sur l'ange du Jugement, qui passe dans l'air en sonnant de la trompette.

> Que signifie cet ange? s'écrie Diderot. Que veut dire ce saint qui le regarde et qui l'écoute? *C'est réaliser autour d'un homme le fantôme de son imagination...* Que l'ange sonnât et passât, j'y consentirais; mais au lieu de lui donner une existence réelle en attachant sur lui les regards du saint, il fallait me le montrer [le saint], du visage, des bras, de la position, du caractère, dans la terreur de celui à qui toutes les misères de la fin dernière de l'homme sont présentes, qui les voit, qui en est consterné...[1]

Par le parti en apparence paradoxal qu'il a choisi, Bastien-Lepage a cru conserver à l'extase de Jeanne d'Arc son caractère hallucinatoire: "les fantômes de son imagination" sont présents, mais seulement aux yeux du spectateur.

————

LES termes généraux du problème de l'art religieux, posés par Renan, se retrouvent chez Zola; mais il aboutit à la solution opposée. Pour Renan, l'intrusion du réalisme dans un domaine qui est proprement celui de l' "idéal" est un non-sens et une corruption. Pour Zola, le naturalisme intégral, dans un siècle où la science a supplanté la foi, s'impose même dans les sujets sacrés. L'erreur de Bastien-Lepage a été de chercher un compromis.

Je soupçonne M. Bastien-Lepage de s'être entêté à montrer les saintes par un système de naturalisme mystique qui a des adeptes. On se pique d'être primitif, on peint, avec une naïveté affectée, un modèle d'atelier, puis on lui ceint le front d'une auréole d'or; de même pour Jeanne d'Arc, on veut bien la paysanne lorraine dans son jardin, seulement on plante en l'air une trouée d'or qui est là pour la pose de la croyance. Rien n'est plus

---

[1] Diderot, *Salons*, éd J. J. Seznec et J. Adhémar, vol. II (Oxford, 1960), pp. 97–8.

2B

distingué comme d'être primitif, tandis qu'il est grossier et anti-
artistique d'être scientifique. M. Bastien-Lepage, par sa vision, a
sans doute voulu échapper à l'accusation de faire de la physiologie;
et c'est ce que je lui reproche...[1]

Ainsi Zola condamne le "naturalisme mystique", comme Renan
– pour des raisons contraires – condamnait le "réalisme dévot".
Pourtant, quelques années plus tard, il allait lui aussi tenter dans un
roman un compromis étrange qui devait déconcerter son public,
et provoquer l'ironie de ses détracteurs.

Le Rêve, paru en 1888, est l'histoire des visions d'une jeune
ouvrière, Angélique, visions qui finissent par prendre corps dans la
personne d'un fiancé; mais, aussitôt après la cérémonie nuptiale,
elle meurt dans sa pureté, telle une sainte martyre.

Sans doute, Zola prétend-il avoir traité le sujet "scientifiquement".
Angélique, enfant trouvée, élevée par un pieux ménage de chasu-
bliers est, explique-t-il, "un rejet sauvage des Rougon-Macquart
transplanté dans un milieu mystique, et soumis à une culture
spéciale qui la modifiera". *Le Rêve* est donc encore un "roman
expérimental"; d'autre part, c'est l'étude d'un cas de physiologie:
la sensualité naissante engendrant des chimères. Toutefois, il est
difficile de lire cette histoire sans évoquer Jeanne d'Arc, et même,
par moments, la *Jeanne d'Arc* de Bastien-Lepage.

Angélique, elle aussi, a "ses sœurs du Paradis": Agnès, Agathe,
Dorothée, les vierges sculptées au tympan de la cathédrale. Elle a
son saint-chevalier, le Saint Georges peint au vitrail. Comme Jeanne
avait son "hêtre des fées", elle a son lieu privilégié, "le Clos-Marie,
ancien verger planté de saules et de peupliers", où viennent la
hanter ses apparitions. Elle y crée, à son insu, "le milieu de l'invisible": il naît "de son imagination échauffée de fables, des désirs
inconscients de sa puberté".

La légende avait lâché dans le Clos-Marie son monde surnaturel de saints et de saintes... Le miracle était prêt à fleurir...
Elle entendait bruire des voix dans ce coin de mystère peuplé de
son imagination... Mais qui donc annonçaient ainsi les chuchote-
ments de l'invisible? Que voulaient faire d'elles les forces

---

[1] Zola, *Salons, ed. cit.*, p. 247.

ignorées soufflant de l'au-delà et flottant dans l'air?... Etait-ce le
Saint Georges du vitrail qui de ses pieds muets d'image peinte
foulait les hautes herbes pour monter vers elle?[1]

L'incarnation se produit: l'ombre devient un jeune homme,
Félicien.

> Le prodige s'achevait enfin, la lente création de l'invisible
> aboutissait à cette apparition vivante. [Elle le voyait] à deux pieds
> du sol... Il gardait pour escorte le peuple entier de la légende,
> les saints, les saintes, et le vol blanc des vierges...[2]

Ainsi Zola lui-même a risqué la fusion du naturalisme et du
mysticisme – avec quel résultat? Dand son article célèbre sur 'La
pureté de M. Zola',[3] Anatole France raille "cette touchante merveille
d'une âme longtemps vautrée dans le fumier qui soudain aspire à
planer dans l'azur"; et il ne manque pas de dénoncer "l'étrange
anachronisme" par lequel Zola "fait vivre son Angélique dans ce
petit monde poétique qui emplissait de joie et de fantaisie les têtes
des paysannes au temps de Jeanne d'Arc."

---

[1] *Le Rêve*, éd. Rencontre (Lausanne, s.d.), pp. 110–12.
[2] *ibid.*, p. 116.
[3] *La Vie littéraire*, 4 vols. (Paris, 1888–94), 2ᵉ série, pp. 285 et 289.

On translating Zola

LEONARD TANCOCK

TRANSLATING a work of literature, it seems to me, involves know-ledge, skill, experience, instinct and something creative, akin to art. Like driving a car, it is also a matter of forestalling trouble in situations never the same twice. The main preoccupations of the translator should, I think be these:

He must love his text, or at least find it interesting, for if he finds it trivial or boring this will assuredly show in his translation. He must keep as close to the original text as style and clear English allow, or he will produce a paraphrase, which is not a translation. He must therefore always aim at accuracy of meaning first, however elusive the meaning may be and however much field-work may be involved. He must aim at producing upon his modern English reader, as far as he can, a similar impression to the one he has reason to feel the original had upon its contemporary readers, and that means not only reproducing style, tone, mannerisms, personal use of words, but avoiding the anachronism *either way*: using words, metaphors, constructions too jarringly modern for the date and matter of the text, or on the other hand using anything self-consciously old-fashioned or 'period' in his English, for a translation must speak in the idiom of the people to whom it is addressed. The only kind of text the translator would be justified in rendering into 'period' English would be one written deliberately by the author in a quaint, archaic style, for then he would be aiming at an equivalent effect. An obvious example would be the *Contes drolatiques* of Balzac, for which some sort of mock-Tudor English would be suitable.

What follows is some impressions and adventures during work on four Zola novels, *Germinal, Thérèse Raquin, L'Assommoir*, and *La Débâcle*,[1] with a few examples from other novels. I make no apology for being autobiographical. How else could this be done?

Of course some troubles in rendering the simplest things come

[1] in order of publication: *Germinal* (1954); *Thérèse Raquin* (1962); *L'Assommoir* (1970); *La Débâcle* in final stages of preparation, Penguin Classics.

not from any peculiarity of Zola's but from what T. S. Eliot calls the mutual inadequacy of the two languages. One language has no simple way of expressing the sense of the other without ambiguity or silliness. In *Thérèse Raquin* I had to manœuvre continually to save Laurent from 'getting a pain in the neck' from the terrible wound caused when his victim had bitten him during his death-struggle. Much simpler even than that, there was *un vieux chapeau d'homme* that poor Gervaise found in the old trunk.[1] 'An old man's hat?' '*Her* old man's hat!' Something like 'an old hat of his' is the only way out. And what of one of the great resources of French denied to us, the sudden change from *vous* to *tu*? Here is the birth of a deep affection between two men of different ages, class and background who had disliked each other:

> "Dites donc, ça devient grave, vous allez rester sur le flanc...
> Faut soigner ça. Laissez-moi faire."
> Agenouillé, il lava lui-même la plaie, la pansa avec du linge propre qu'il prit dans son sac. Et il avait des gestes maternels...
> "Tu es un brave homme, toi... Merci, mon vieux."
> Et Jean, l'air très heureux, le tutoya aussi, avec son tranquille sourire: "Maintenant, mon petit, j'ai encore du tabac, veux-tu une cigarette?"[2]

But things like these, infinitely more difficult to translate than they look, could occur in any French text. The translator's real task begins when he has to establish the meaning of words at some moment in history and convey the exact picture to his contemporary English reader without embarrassing him by displays of pedantry or quaintness. This is peculiarly applicable to authors such as Balzac or Zola. Each is haunted by *things*, each describes in great technical detail man's physical environment, Balzac sometimes with the sheer gusto of a boy displaying his collection of stamps or butterflies, Zola often forgetting his 'scientific' concern with *le milieu* and going off into poems of mood, atmosphere and colour made up of elements each of which in isolation is technically precise and must be rendered so. This ever-present problem in Zola I found virtually absent from

[1] *L'Assommoir*, vol. II, p. 375. For the *Rougon-Macquart* novels page references are to the Pléiade edition, 5 vols. (Paris, 1960–7). For *Thérèse Raquin* page references are to the standard Charpentier-Fasquelle edition (Paris, 1954).
[2] *La Débâcle*, vol. V, p. 481.

work on La Rochefoucauld or Benjamin Constant, where of course the problem is to establish the exact meaning of certain key abstract words denoting human relationships. How to convey to the modern reader the components of the dingy, fly-blown haberdashery shop of Thérèse Raquin, the garments Gervaise and her assistants dealt with in her laundry, above all the processes of coalmining in *Germinal*, for the whole thing has changed radically in the intervening years? The time will soon come when nobody understands regulators, coupling-rods and valve gear in *La Bête humaine*, for a generation is rapidly growing up that has never seen a steam locomotive. Nor does field-work necessarily help. I once described an operation to a colleague who had spent three years at the coalface, and asked him what he called the man who performed it. He knew the man I meant, but said "we all called him Ted". In a very technical description of Madame Hennebeau's flamboyant drawing-room occurs *un devant d'autel pour le lambrequin de la cheminée*.[1] Now the thing itself, made of velvet or plush with tassels or bobbles, has surely disappeared from every home, even if the elderly can remember one in their childhood. What word to use? Pelmet, valance, lambrequin? My point is that to the average modern reader for whom a translation is done the first suggests windows, the second beds, whilst the third, in this sense, is an Americanism. At this stage I asked an expert on antiques and Victoriana, and the answer was that the only word was 'mantel-border', and that also, I felt sure, would be meaningless to the reader. The only way out between respect for the meaning of the text and intelligibility seemed to me to fall back on the translator's stock recipe: juggle with parts of speech, turn the offending noun into a verb and say "an altar-front *draping* the mantelshelf".

This example has taken some time to set down, but in dealing with texts as densely packed with material things as Zola's the process of selection and rejection must go on all the time, and it can be as complicated as the instantaneous processes going on in a tennis-player's mind. Don't do this or you will expose yourself to that.

Every author has his mannerisms and fingerprints, and Zola has certain tricks and personal uses of words which, like the wrinkles on one's face, grow more pronounced as he grows older. How many

[1] *Germinal*, vol. III, p. 1319.

times does he employ *justement* when there is no question of coincidence or timing, and how many *Ah*'s are interpolated to suggest some sort of emotional value? And his eternal *Ce jour-là* can be as much of a formality as *In illo tempore* before the Gospel reading in a Catholic church. Similarly he has a habit of referring to a character's trade, profession or position in life as a substitute for his name or a pronoun: *dit la vieille mercière, répondit la blanchisseuse, dit le zingueur, demanda le chaîniste, l'ancien commissaire de police, le mécanicien, la herscheuse,* etc. Unless the English is to be grotesque these must be rendered as Madame Raquin, Gervaise, Coupeau, etc., or more often still just as he or she. Not to do so would be as didactic and unconvincing as those moments in a Corneille exposition when a man explains his ancestry and political career to his own wife or brother.

Another curious quirk is to make people *murmurer, répéter, balbutier* or *bégayer* when that is the last way one would think they would utter those particular words at that time:

"Nom de Dieu! c'est trop fort," *murmura-t-il.* "Ah! le sale mufe..."[1]

"Oh! Oh!" *murmurait* le garçon Charles, émerveillé, les yeux agrandis...[2]

"Qu'est-ce donc?" demanda Gervaise, effrayée.

"Les rats, les rats," *murmura-t-il.*[3]

It might be possible in the first case that he is *muttering* in a rage, but in the third, even if he was exhausted by *delirium tremens*, he was still bashing at imaginary rats on the wall of a padded cell. I prefer to be cowardly and omit any verb of speech.

It would be tedious to list words that Zola uses in a highly personal way, but *débandade* is his great resource for anything, however static, that is the opposite of tidy and orderly.

It is arguable that Zola's real claim to greatness is his mastery of pictorial effects, colour and above all the tricks of light and shade associated with his friends the Impressionist painters, whose lifelong champion he was.[4] One has only to think of the visions of Paris

---

[1] *L'Assommoir*, vol. II, p. 590.   [2] *ibid.*, vol. II, p. 400.   [3] *ibid.*, vol. II, p. 698.
[4] For some interesting parallels see Joy Newton: 'Emile Zola impressionniste', *Cahiers naturalistes* XXXIII (1967), 39–52 and XXXIV (1967), 124–38.

in *Une Page d'amour*, the emotionally charged autumn evening on the Seine just before the murder of Camille Raquin, the debauch of colour, light and sensuality in *La Faute de l'abbé Mouret*, the hallucinatory arrays of fruit, vegetables, meat and fish in *Le Ventre de Paris*. But through all this seems to come the colour *jaune*, which Zola calls into play for emotional effects whenever he wants to convey a colour that is nondescript, mean, dirty, dingy, depressing, sinister, unpleasant, disgusting, whether yellow or not. The corpse of Camille "avait seulement pris une teinte *jaunâtre* et boueuse,"[1] and back in the shop "l'étalage, *jauni* par la poussière, semblait porter le deuil de la maison".[2] The walls of the tall buildings along the railway just outside the Gare du Nord are "salis de la même teinte *jaunâtre* par la suie des machines".[3] And if this can be mixed with the emotive word *fauve*, so dear to Zola's boyhood hero Victor Hugo,[4] so much the more sinister and unpleasant:

La nuit tombait, un grand nuage *fauve*, qui *jaunissait* le ciel, éclairant le mourant d'un reflet d'incendie.[5]

Bientôt le soleil, qui s'était levé limpide, en fut caché; et il ne resta que ce deuil, dans le ciel *fauve*.[6]

And examples could be multiplied of *livide* and *blafard*. These words can seldom, if ever, be rendered by anything obviously related to the standard dictionary meaning. The translator has to fall back upon impressions and emotions.

But this vague and very personal use of colour is not merely a device for working upon the reader's emotions. It is also tied up with Zola's Impressionist affiliations. To the Impressionist eye colours and outlines are never clearly defined, everything is continually changing with the ever-changing conditions of light, almost as though it were glimpsed in an aquarium through quivering water. And indeed one of the most striking of the views of Paris in *Une Page d'amour* is treated in terms of a submarine landscape.[7] That is why the

[1] *Thérèse Raquin*, p. 13.   [2] *ibid.*, p. 105.   [3] *L'Assommoir*, vol. II, p. 768
[4] "Pendant une année, Victor Hugo régna sur nous en monarque absolu... il nous ravissait par sa rhétorique puissante," etc. *Documents littéraires*, ed. Charpentier (Paris, 1881), p. 89.
[5] *La Terre*, vol. IV, p. 454.
[6] *La Débâcle*, vol. V, p. 900.
[7] Part I, chapter 5, Vol. II, pp. 845–53, *passim*.

translator is always confronted with colours in -*âtre* and -*issant*,
abstractions like *un bariolage, un flamboiement, un rayonnement,
un éparpillement,* colours modified or juxtaposed, and he must in a
sense forget the words and see the picture, then describe in his own
words what he sees:

> En face, se dressait le grand massif rougeâtre des îles. Les deux
> rives, d'un brun sombre taché de gris, étaient comme deux larges
> bandes qui allaient se rejoindre à l'horizon. L'eau et le ciel
> semblaient coupés dans la même étoffe blanchâtre... Les rayons
> pâlissent dans l'air frissonnant...[1]

> Before them rose the great russet mass of the islands. The two
> banks, dark brown flecked with grey, stretched away like two
> broad bands that joined on the horizon. Water and sky looked as
> though they had been cut out of the same whitish material. . . .
> The sun's rays shine palely in the chilly air.[2]

> ... des raies de soleil entraient à gauche, par les hautes fenêtres,
> allumant les vapeurs fumantes de nappes opalisées, d'un gris-rose
> et d'un gris-bleu très tendres...[3]

My own rendering, still tentative, is:

> ... the rays of light, striking in through the high windows to the
> left, turned the steamy vapour into opalescent streaks (or layers,
> or some other word) of the softest rosy-grey and grey-blue...

Typically, Zola is very addicted to the adjective *tendre* as a means of
avoiding hard and fast colours, and it is not always easy to translate.
And lest it be objected that in both these cases Zola is necessarily
indistinct because of his subject-matter, here is an open field in the
blazing summer of Provence:

> Des poussières dansantes mettaient aux pointes des gazons un
> flux de clartés, tandis qu'à certains souffles de vent, passant
> librement sur cette solitude nue, les herbes se moiraient d'un
> tressaillement de plantes caressées...[4]

which is just as imprecise – quivering with heat perhaps?

[1] *Thérèse Raquin*, pp. 84–5. [2] *Thérèse Raquin*, Penguin Classics, p. 93.
[3] *L'Assommoir*, vol. II, p. 391. [4] *La Faute de l'abbé Mouret*, vol. I, p. 1369.

Of course some of these abstractions may well be a trick of style taken over from the Goncourt *écriture artiste*, such as "avec des vols de grues qui s'envolaient"[1] or "le bleuissement des violettes".[2] but experience of translating shows that the Zola world is never fixed, but an ever-shifting kaleidoscope moved by the action of light. This quotation from *Une Page d'amour* shows him in action, using most of his familiar tricks:

A gauche, les hautes cheminées de la Manutention, droites et roses, lâchaient de gros tourbillons de fumée tendre, d'une teinte délicate de chair; tandis que, de l'autre côté de la rivière, les beaux ormes du Quai d'Orsay faissaient une masse sombre, trouée de coups de soleil. La Seine, entre ses berges que les rayons obliques enfilaient, roulait des flots dansants où le bleu, le jaune et le vert se brisaient en un éparpillement bariolé; mais, en remontant le fleuve, ce peinturlurage de mer orientale prenait un seul ton d'or de plus en plus éblouissant; et l'on eût dit un lingot sorti à l'horizon de quelque creuset invisible, s'élargissant avec un remuement de couleurs vives, à mesure qu'il se refroidissait. Sur cette coulée éclatante, les points échelonnés, amincissant leurs couches légères, jetaient des barres grises, qui se perdaient dans un entassement incendié de maisons, au sommet duquel les deux tours de Notre-Dame rougeoyaient comme des torches.[3]

More difficult to discuss, because impossible to illustrate adequately without long extracts, are characteristic tricks of style and favourite constructions, particularly when the point of them is to shock slightly or arrest attention by the unexpected, and an English rendering ought therefore to be slightly strange or unidiomatic to produce a comparable effect. But there is one Zolaism which any reader will recognize, and it can be peculiarly awkward to render convincingly. It is his characteristic juxtaposition or confusion of the general and particular in personal descriptions. In its simplest form it can be quite logical and the generalization obvious in its application: "… il avait son air sec de bel officier bien tenu",[4] though even then the generalization would stand without any reference to

---

[1] *Une Page d'amour*, vol. II, p. 836.   [2] *Le Ventre de Paris*, vol. I, p. 622.
[3] *Une Page d'amour*, vol. II, p. 908.   [4] *La Débâcle*, vol. V, p. 885.

the man's good looks. Fairly simple also: "... de toutes ses forces de belle blonde potelée."[1] But more often there is no connection at all: "... dans ce logement où elle avait trôné en belle patronne blonde".[2] Why blonde? It seems to me that this dissociation is too violent to turn into comparably brief English, and my tentative version is: "... this establishment where she had once reigned as mistress and been admired for her blonde good looks".

And what of: "... son ancien regard noir de petite fille résignée et songeuse".[3] Why should the look (or eyes) of a resigned and dreamy little girl be black (or dark)? I suggest that here one must turn the whole thing from the physical to the purely moral or emotional: "... but kept her eyes, those sombre, resigned and dreamy eyes". And even then I have not fully brought out the force, if any, of *ancien*, though the repetition of "eyes" and the word "those" are intended to suggest that this was a thing of long standing.

There are hundreds of examples of this construction in Zola, where logic breaks down, but the effect of them is often as appreciable and memorable as some equally "meaningless" lines of Symbolist poetry.

Neither is Zola without striking poetic and sound effects which must be reproduced, or else the translator betrays his author. There are the last wonderful lines of *Germinal*:

> Des hommes poussaient, une armée noire, vengeresse, qui germait lentement dans les sillons, grandissant pour les récoltes du siècle futur, et dont la germination allait faire bientôt éclater la terre.[4]

which, after much trial and error, I ventured to turn into:

> Men were springing up, a black avenging host was slowly germinating in the furrows, thrusting upwards for the harvest of future ages. And very soon their germination would crack the earth asunder.[5]

[1] *Nana*, vol. II, p. 1169.
[2] *L'Assommoir*, vol. II, p. 731.
[3] *ibid.*, vol. II, p. 760.
[4] *Germinal*, vol. III, p. 1591.
- *Germinal*, Penguin Classics, p. 499.

Or this from *La Débâcle*:

Devant Maurice, un chêne séculaire, le tronc broyé par un obus, s'abattit avec la majesté tragique d'un héros, écrasant tout à son entour.[1]

Or again this reminder of *Le Dormeur du Val*:

Sous les frondaisons, dans le délicieux demi-jour verdâtre, au fond des asiles mystérieux, tapissés de mousse, soufflait la mort brutale. Les sources solitaires étaient violées, des mourants râlaient jusque dans des coins perdus, où des amoureux seuls s'étaient égarés jusque-là.[2]

What has been said so far has left aside the really formidable challenge to any translator, the supreme test not merely of his knowledge of both languages concerned, but of his ear. Dialogue is always difficult, but it is peculiarly so in Zola not only because of the slang element but because in some cases, notably in *L'Assommoir*, the slang itself was culled by Zola from 'Bookish' sources, sociological studies or dictionaries of *argot*. The famous *style indirect libre* and slang dialogue, brilliantly successful though it may be in this novel on grounds of social truth, narrative technique and even poetic rightness, is really a literary device, a synthesis of Zola's own early life in Paris, his field-work and his research in libraries. I tested this on three French people, two men and a woman. The girl Nana, showing signs of things to come, stood about for hours with nothing on but a tiny vest: "... et, comme toute la maison pouvait la voir par la fenêtre, sa mère se fâchait, lui demandait si elle n'avait pas bientôt fini de se promener *en panais*".[3] The last two words, which I had already translated as "showing all she'd got", were quite unknown to my three French people in that sense, though two of them (the men!) knew even coarser and obviously male meanings. Zola had of course taken it from A. Delvau: *Dictionnaire de la langue verte*, in which the definition of *en panais* is given as: "En chemise, sans aucun pantalon."[4]

Now the translation of any slang, swearing or 'strong' dialogue is self-defeating in the sense that the better it is done in the idiom

[1] *La Débâcle*, vol. v, p. 690.   [2] *ibid.*, vol. v, p. 691–2.
[3] *L'Assommoir*, vol. ii, p. 710.   [4] see vol. ii, p. 1600.

of the translator's own period, the more certainly it will be incomprehensible tomorrow, for nothing is more ephemeral than 'with-it' talk. Yet any attempt to do 'period' style will strike the modern reader as grotesque. But again, in his anxiety to avoid the Charybdis of 'ye olde' the translator must not fall into the Scylla of anything sounding even remotely like Americanism or modern 'kitchen sink' language, because that would be violently anachronistic, especially in *L'Assommoir*, where the subject-matter is constantly reminding us that we are in a world of bonnets and shawls, top-hats and horse-buses. Yet the original effect of shock and violence demands something fairly strong, and the only way seemed to me to choose in English popular speech the most timeless and universal elements, and here the current atmosphere of permissiveness allowed me to use obscenities and four-letter words which would have exposed me to legal trouble when I did *Germinal* 15 years earlier. Which in itself shows what a slippery, elusive thing the 'right' translation is.

Let one more example suffice, but this is one that shows how Zola can use the slangy, childish burblings of a drunken old fool and make of them something as beautiful as "Fear no more the heat o' the sun": "Tu sais, écoute bien... c'est moi, Bibi-la-Gaieté, dit le consolateur des dames... Va, t'es heureuse. Fais dodo, ma belle!"[1] It would take an article in itself to show the various considerations of tone, overtone, atmosphere, sound which prompted me to reject other, and at first sight more attractive, possibilities for nearly every word. At the moment of writing, I suggest: "You know, dear, listen . . . it's me, Bibi-la-Gaieté, known as the ladies' comforter. . . . There, there, you're all right now. Night-night, my lovely!" In parenthesis, I think one should never attempt to translate proper names – that way madness lies and great classical authors might become Pete Crow, Johnny Root and Nick Drinkwater. But this raises problems about female names preceded by an article, such as la Levaque, la Maheude, la Mouquette (daughter of Mouque), etc.

Some years ago I had a friendly argument with a distinguished translator who had published versions of Spanish as well as French masterpieces. He maintained that the translator's duty is to produce a text that is a coherent unit, and that to this end he should right

[1] *L'Assommoir*, vol. II, p. 796.

little wrongs, smooth out little roughnesses, iron out little incon-
sistencies. Such blemishes, he said, should be tactfully put right.
Here I emphatically disagreed, for it seems to me that these 'flaws'
are the very stuff of which the individual style of the author and
the flavour of his book are made. I think the translator, as his name
implies, should *pass across* his text as intact as he can, warts and all.
He is a translator, not an editor. Of course there are sometimes
variants . . . but that is another story.

This is particularly applicable to Zola, strangely enough when it
is remembered how meticulous was his documentation and how
methodical he was as a writer. He can even make glaring misstate-
ments of fact and discrepancies. The distant view of the Paris
Opéra in *Une Page d'amour* at a time when it was not yet built is
too well known to stop over. But at the beginning of *Germinal* we are
told that old Bonnemort is 58. Later in the novel he is 50, which,
since his son Maheu is 42, suggests that he had started early. When
we meet Gervaise for the first time she is "grande, un peu mince,
avec des traits fins",[1] but some years and 360 pages later she and
Coupeau go to a dance-hall looking for Nana "et, comme ils étaient
petits l'un et l'autre, ils se haussaient sur les pieds pour voir quelque
chose".[2] But these examples are trivial. The real trouble for the
translator begins when an author is quite inconsistent in the vital
matter of dialogue, and it multiplies when the dialogue is implied
in Zola's famous *style indirect libre*. It is scarcely conceivable that
this most conscientious of writers simply forgot or did not know
what he was doing, and so one must conclude, and my acquaintance
with him as a translator backs this up, that when the ignorant,
illiterate speaker becomes the mouthpiece for important reflections
or philosophizing, Zola considers it more important to express these
things with all the eloquence at his command and lets consistency go.

La Maheude, in *Germinal*, had worked in the pit from earliest
childhood, then brought up a family in misery and toil. Hers is the
voice of the victims of industrialism, her language is elementary,
for her schooling had been nil. But she also symbolizes the proletariat
revolting against social injustice, and expresses the yearnings of the
poor for a golden age of socialist happiness. At such times she goes

[1] *ibid.*, vol. II, p. 381.
[2] *ibid.*, vol. II, p. 739.

off into passages of demagogic eloquence quite beyond the intellectual equipment of her fictional character. Similar instances can be found in *L'Assommoir* and in *La Débâcle*.

Rendering this kind of thing into English is a very delicate matter. Of course one must respect Zola's mannerisms. Fortunately he himself has given the vital clue. He is usually careful to make a transition out of the familiar into the literary style, but most important, the ignorant or slangy speech, whether direct or indirect, is as a rule more or less correct *grammatically*, and the popular flavour is largely a matter of vocabulary. The eloquent or 'uncharacteristic' passage does not therefore involve a violent change of tone, but emerges, so to speak, into standard French by shedding the coarse, vulgar words. With all this in mind I felt that the translator should make his English tone slangy or ignorant by using vulgar or obscene words rather than ungrammatical phrases or phonetic representations of ignorant talk in silly spelling. To invent an example, it is better to say "he did bugger all" than "'e never done nuffink".

When all else is more or less settled the translator may have to contend with the over-helpful or finicky sub-editor, particularly in this matter of dialogue, where usage is to some extent a matter of early environment. Recently, to the amusement of all concerned, a publisher's sub-editor telephoned me to find out what I meant by "There was one dress in particular that suited her to a t", for "Une robe surtout lui alla à la perfection...".[1] Of course I might have said "suited her down to the ground" had not the very next line explained that it was a short dress that showed her legs. The sub-editor had never heard of the phrase, which I had known since childhood, but with great presence of mind and my wife's help I was able to refer him to his own firm's dictionary, where the usage is listed as the first item under the letter T. Some years ago I had a long and acrimonious correspondence with another over some silly and dull English I had used, after a great deal of thought, for some of the deliberately silly and dull language of some ineffably boring people in *Thérèse Raquin*. The whole art of the novel was there, as it had been in the pomposities and platitudes of Flaubert's creations in *Madame Bovary*.

For real translation is an art, and not for nothing has the Tenth

[1] *L'Assommoir*, vol. II, p. 710.

Muse been called into being to preside over it. Some of its ingredients are an ear for sound, a sense of style, some historical sense and just plain common sense.[1] Above all one must write English which is real English and suitable for the text. The job is never finished, you are never satisfied, and no translator I have ever met did not feel he ought to scrap the lot and start again. And yet the late Arthur Waley, in a broadcast conversation about translation I once had with him and Mr Cecil Day Lewis, could dismiss some problem in Chinese with these words: "Oh well, of course that part is quite simple, like translating from French!" If only he had tried it.

Postscript

Since this paper was written, *L'Assommoir* has been published in Penguin Classics (1970) and the typescript of *La Débâcle* is now (1971) about to be sent to the printer, but the above text has deliberately been left unchanged. – L.W.T.

[1] I thought at one stage of an article on mistranslations or travesties of Zola, which would have been amusing and possibly instructive. Havelock Ellis's *Germinal* (1933) is written in pidgin English throughout. Arthur Symons's version of *L'Assommoir* (1958) has gross errors of meaning (*ramonait* = came up, *piler* = to take away), while *d'un air béat de coq en pâte* becomes *with the beatified expression of a man in clover* in V. Plarr's *Nana* (1957). The best examples are far too long to reproduce here.

2c

Balzac Concordance

THIS is not strictly a Concordance, only the material for one. All our references to *La Comédie humaine* have been to the Pléiade edition (Gallimard). To enable readers who do not have access to that edition to locate quotations in whatever edition they use themselves, we are giving the table of contents that appears in vol. XI of the Pléiade edition, slightly modified. All that is needed apart from this is a slide rule.

A.R.P.

Tome I

Tome II

2c*

Tome VIII

Tome IX

Tome X

Tome XI

List of subscribers

Professor Ian W. Alexander
Antoine Antonini
Colette Bach-Gruvel
Dr Robert Baldick
Professor W. H. Barber
J. D. Barron
Dr Edith C. Batho
Université de Berne, Séminaire de littérature française
The Library, Birkbeck College
Frank Paul Bowman
The Library, University of Bristol
British Institute in Paris
Sheila J. Browne
Edmond Brua
Professor J. H. Brumfitt
Professor C. Chadwick
Louis Charvet
Roland Chollet
John Christie
Professor Pierre Citron
Professor John G. Clark
Valeria H. Colonna
Mary Jane Culverhouse
Raffaele de Cesare
F. R. de Foville
Maurice Dernelle
Henri Dirkx
Professor C. R. Duckworth
University Library, Durham
Michael Edwards
Dr A. B. Emden
Dr Ryszard Engelking
Dr Liliane Fearn
Raymond Foltz

Lindy Foord
Dr K. H. Francis
University of London, Goldsmith's College Library
K. O. Gore
Charles and Margaret Gould
Professor Bernard Guyon
C. A. Hackett
D. R. Haggis
Dr H. Gaston Hall
Brynmor Jones Library, University of Hull
l'Institut de Littérature comparée, Nancy
Angela Ion
The Library, Jesus College, Oxford
Georges Joncker
Daphne C. C. Jones
Verina R. Jones
Professor B. Juden
A. A. Juillard
Kings College London Library
Professor R. C. Knight
Jean-Pierre Lacassagne
Library, Lady Margaret Hall, Oxford
Marie-Thérèse Francotte-Lamarche
Dr W. M. Landers
André Lang
Professor Pierre Laubriet
Jean Legueux
Dr A. E. Lequet
Bernard Leuillot
A. H. T. Levi
Ekkehard H. Löwenhaupt
U.E.R. d'Études Françaises (Université de Lyon II)
Charles Macris
Maison de Balzac, Paris
Margaret J. Majumdar, *née* Lifetree
Maurice Menard
Paul Metadier
Mrs Marjorie Miln

Dr Alan J. Mount
Jean Mouton
Breda Mulcahy
The University Library, Newcastle upon Tyne
M. C. Pakenham
Mary Pemberton
Professor R. Pouilliart
The Library, The Queen's College, Oxford
Renée Quinn
Dr A. W. Raitt
Professor Jean Richer
Dr Norma Rinsler
Romanistisches Institut, Saarbrücken
Professor Jacques Roos
Father J. Sablé
St Anne's College, Oxford
St Edmund Hall, Oxford
The Library of St Hilda's College, Oxford
The Library, St Peter's College, Oxford
F. W. Saunders
Professor N. E. Saxe
Robert Shackleton
Marjorie Shaw
Dr Judith A. Slater
Paul A. Smith
L. I. Stowe
Bibliothèque de l'U.E.R. lettres Modernes de Strasbourg
Dr J. Théodoridès
Jean-Louis Tritter
Professor R. V. Tymms
The Library, University College London
Professor Barbara Wright